MW00389704

"Where did America's evangelical [...] Should it be preserved or dismantle[...] pressing than in popular music—and that is where Mark Joseph confronts them head on. His portraits of famous and not-so-famous musicians are fascinating and often surprising, and his answer to the second question is bound to provoke debate both inside and outside the evangelical community."
—Martha Bayles, author, *Hole in Our Soul—The Loss of Beauty and Meaning in American Popular Music*

"I've known Mark Joseph as a modern Johnny Appleseed scattering precious gospel seed among the thorns of the entertainment business and the rocky soil of popular culture. His heart is right, and he knows what he is talking about!"
—Pat Boone, entertainer

"Christians need to understand culture before we can impact it. Mark Joseph's insightful, beautifully written book helps us to understand one of today's most powerful cultural influences—rock and roll. It is a must-read for any Christian who seriously wants to be the 'salt' Jesus admonishes his followers to be in a most impactful area."
—Bob Briner, author, *Roaring Lambs, The Leadership Lessons of Jesus*

"For almost half a century, teenagers have argued with their parents about the devil's music, rock and roll. In *The Rock and Roll Rebellion*, Mark Joseph finally wins the argument."
—Ann Coulter, columnist for *George* magazine and author of *High Crimes and Misdemeanors*

"Mark Joseph understands that these extraordinary times call for Christian artists to come out of the cultural ghettos in which they've grown secure and comfortable. They damage their artistic, moral, and spiritual development by cutting themselves off from the American mainstream, and they deprive a lost and drifting culture of the truth and light it desperately needs to hear. In the best sense, Joseph is preaching to the choir with this book, and though his words will discomfort many, they would be foolish to ignore his challenge."
—Rod Dreher, chief film critic, *The New York Post*

"Music to a great degree defines the world of teenagers today, yet many teens themselves view this music as having a destructive impact on people their age, encouraging violence and drug use and the degradation of music. Mark Joseph, in his fascinating and much-needed account, urges Christian musical performers and composers to fill the spiritual emptiness and feelings of hopelessness of teens with God's unconditional love."

—George Gallup Jr., chairman, the George H. Gallup International Institute

"A must for anyone captured by the power of music in ministry. A provocative approach to the vast and ever-changing philosophy behind Christian music."

—Dan Haseltine, lead singer, Jars of Clay

"Mark Joseph's richly detailed account is an amazingly fact-and-idea filled performance that brings to musicians a message that Christians in all walks of life need to hear: our calling is to speak and sing to the world, not to hide out in a marginalized subculture while the world turns to nihilism."

—Phillip E. Johnson, University of California-Berkeley law professor, and author of *Reason in the Balance* and *Darwin on Trial*

"Mark Joseph's book, *The Rock and Roll Rebellion*, gives the reader a striking account of how the fundamental world of Christianity has condemned artists of faith who sought to push the envelope to communicate the truth to this generation. *The Rock and Roll Rebellion* is a voice in the wilderness setting free the musician and the audience to move beyond do's and don'ts to a free, honest, and open relationship with God. I applaud him for his efforts. A 'must-read.'"

—Al Kasha, two-time Academy Award-winning composer and author of *If They Ask You, You Can Write a Song*

"At long last, someone has had the courage to say what Mark Joseph has so thoughtfully asserted in his new book. The issues—including the many debatable and controversial issues—are painstakingly examined with insight and personal conviction. *The Rock and Roll Rebellion* is a must-read for all those who have followed the various trends in contemporary Christian music."

—Dr. Patrick Kavanaugh, conductor and author of *Spiritual Lives of the Great Composers* and *Raising Musical Kids*

"Mark Joseph has written with great insight on the history of contemporary Christian music as we know it today. It is a much-needed volume to help us understand our past accomplishments as well as mistakes as we prepare to enter a new century. Anyone who wants an excellent overview of this vital subject ought to read it. I recommend it."

—Greg Laurie, pastor, Harvest Christian Fellowship

"Throughout history, music, in the intellectual and moral cosmos, constituted a secular substitute for religion. Therefore, it is no accident that certain concert halls were given temple-type facades, thus, exalting the moral status of the music. Joseph's fine work, *The Rock and Roll Rebellion*, visits an important subject of our time in a way that's both accessible and stirring."

—Michael Levine, author of *Guerrilla P.R.* and radio talk show host for KRLA-Los Angeles

"The contemporary Christian music debates are getting so hot that they are even beginning to show up in the 'secular' news media, as well as the magazines and newsletters that cover the Christian subculture. Anyone who wants to know what is going on in Christian music needs to wrestle with the thesis that Mark Joseph—a multimedia, free radical operating on the edge of this marketplace—has thrown into the mix. His bottom line: CCM is heretical, a system of self-imposed artistic and economic chains that keeps dragging down talented musicians and has helped keep music created by Christians out of the real world. Even those who passionately oppose Joseph's views are having to listen to what he has to say."

—Terry Mattingly, columnist, Scripps Howard News Service

"The story can now be told and has been told ably and fairly of recent developments in Christian music, its meaning and its future. This is the only narrative we have of these developments. Important for cultural history and for the theological study of the Christ and culture relationship in our time."

—Thomas Oden, Drew University professor and author of *After Modernity What?*

"In a time when popular music speaks loudly to youth and adults alike, Christians seem to have missed their chance at riding the wave of influencing, trend setting, and communicating. *The Rock and Roll Rebellion* is a look into time wasted, opportunities missed, and the surefire results in ministry if contemporary Christian music as a whole were to change the way they do 'business.'"

—Alex Parnell, VH-1

"A much needed call for rock musician Christians to be where it counts."

—Steve Turner, rock critic and author of *Conversations with Eric Clapton, Van Morrison—Too Late to Stop Now*, and *Trouble Man: The Life and Death of Marvin Gaye*

"I hope that leaders and teachers will give careful thought and discussion to what Mark Joseph says in *The Rock and Roll Rebellion*. His call is for Christian responsibility for the popular arts—for music in particular. God will be honored by Christians who are, simply, excellent musicians. And, by their presence, music as a life force in culture can be spared from domination by corruption, violence, and death, just because they know and live the world of God in its midst."

> —Dallas Willard, University of Southern California professor of philosophy and author of *The Divine Conspiracy*

"Popular American culture shifted on its axis on or about the time Elvis first swayed his hips. In that simple 1-2 step, the King inextricably entwined rock and roll with overt sexuality, passion, and the full range of indulgence. In his new book, *The Rock and Roll Rebellion*, Mark Joseph documents how Christian fundamentalists dug their heels in against Elvis's rock and roll and literally spooked future generations of Christian men and women out of participation in popular music (a.k.a. "the devil's music"). In doing so, Joseph details how Christians unwittingly censured their own voice, then brilliantly documents how future generations of Christian artists can push their spiritual conviction back into the mainstream of popular culture."

> —Armstrong Williams, author, talk show host, and *USA Today* columnist

"As a teenager in the mid-1970s, I used to listen to what was then called 'Jesus music' and lament that virtually no one from the mainstream rock music industry would ever even hear some of my favorite artists who plied their wares in this tiny niche. A quarter-century later, as everyone knows, Christian music has become big business . . . but it's still effectively a ghetto. Mark Joseph makes a persuasive argument in favor of talented Christian musicians speaking to the wider culture and not just preaching to the choir. In the process, he's also come up with the first real modern history of 'contemporary Christian music,' a field that's been crying out for this kind of comprehensive documentation. Fans of the CCM genre, and of what it might become, will want to hear Joseph out."

> —Chris Willman, senior writer, *Entertainment Weekly*

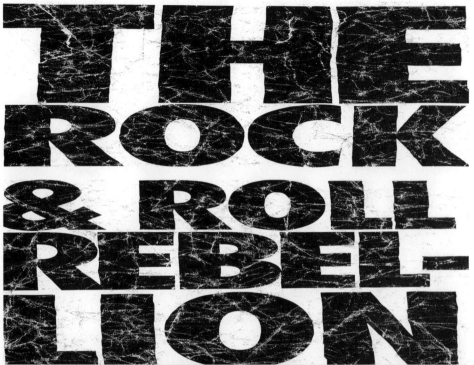

THE ROCK & ROLL REBELLION

Why people of faith abandoned rock music —
and why they're coming back

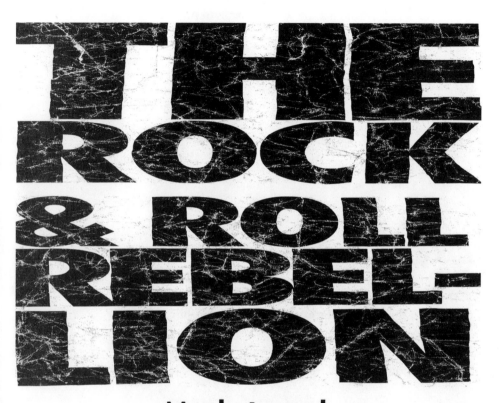

THE ROCK & ROLL REBELLION

Mark Joseph

B&H

BROADMAN
&HOLMAN
PUBLISHERS

Nashville, Tennessee

0–8054–2061–4

Published by Broadman & Holman Publishers, Nashville, Tennessee
Typesetting: SL Editorial Services, Nashville

Dewey Decimal Classification: 261
Subject Heading: MUSIC/CONTEMPORARY CULTURE
Library of Congress Card Catalog Number: 99-15106

Library of Congress Cataloging-in-Publication Data
Joseph, Mark. 1968–
     The rock & roll rebellion : why people of faith abandoned rock
music and why they're coming back / by Mark Joseph.
          p.   cm.
     Includes bibliographical references and index.
     ISBN 0–8054–2061–4
     1. Contemporary Christian music—Moral and ethical aspects.
     2. Rock music—Moral and ethical aspects. I. Title. II. Title: Rock and
roll rebellion.
ML3187.5.J67   1999
261.5'78—dc21
                                                                                        99–15106
                                                                                        CIP

     1 2 3 4 5 03 02 01 00 99

To Bob Briner:

A generous mentor and loving friend who finished well.

To my family:

Kenny, Lila, Kimbo, Bobb, and Jim—Thanks for pouring yourselves into me. And to the new additions: Georgia, Cindi, Kerrigan, Jacqueline, Reid, Christopher, Julia, Lydia, Daryl, Gail, Kirsta, Nathan, and Gumby. And to the newest addition: Kara—lover, companion, and best friend.

Contents

Foreword

Whenever people of faith speak out against some of the excesses of contemporary popular culture, they risk a contemptuous response from secular sophisticates. "If you don't like it, there's always the on/off switch!" is the most common refrain—or in the same vein, "If you don't like it, you can just turn it off!"

This declaration makes as much sense as telling worried environmentalists, "If you don't like the smog, then just stop breathing!"

Movies, television, and rock 'n roll music are part of the very air we breathe, comprising the cultural atmosphere for all Americans and playing a particularly significant role in the development of our young. You may attempt to deploy gas masks to mitigate the impact of some of the more poisonous components of this atmosphere, but this strategy can never wholly succeed.

Even those who make a personal decision not to partake of pop culture's products will find its influence inescapable. You can put your TV in the garage, avoid movies altogether, and use earplugs to spare your hearing from the sounds of hip hop or heavy metal, but these forms of entertainment will still change your life through their influence on everyone else in this society. Though you may struggle to protect your own kids from music that encourages violence or drugs or irresponsible sex, you can't possibly protect them from all the other kids in your community who have received full exposure.

No one remains entirely untouched by what goes on in the entertainment industry, and its attitudes penetrate even the most isolated enclaves on the continent. Amish kids in Pennsylvania, we recently learned, secretly listened to Marilyn Manson and smoked pot. Hasidic young people in Brooklyn may not buy Madonna's CDs but exposed as they are to newspapers, billboards, magazine covers, and the sights and sounds of the city, they most certainly know who she is. In elevators and shopping malls, in doctors' offices, airports, and even in school classrooms the noise and images of the pop culture assault our senses.

For many Americans, television and radio have become an essential accompaniment to a wide range of daily activities; they enjoy its offerings while they are jogging or cooking, cleaning the car, doing homework, eating dinner, or making love.

With the entertainment industry as ubiquitous as it is, we can hardly feel surprised that the old religious community tactic of ignore-it-and-it-will-go-away has proven so singularly ineffective. Countless studies, and our own real-world experience, make clear that the isolation strategy won't work and can't work. That doesn't mean that people of faith should give up all objections and criticism and even confrontation with rock 'n roll reality; but it does mean that engagement is a far more appropriate approach than isolation.

Mark Joseph's book provides valuable historical perspective on the inevitable tension between the religious sensibility and American popular music. He helps to provide thoughtful support for the notion that rock 'n roll will unavoidably influence religion, but religion can also influence rock 'n roll. People of faith cannot deny the world, but a sophisticated approach to the cultural challenges of our time makes it more difficult for the world to deny them. In confronting contemporary entertainment, denial is ineffective and defeatism is inappropriate. The creative engagement that Joseph describes may well represent the most constructive—and consecrated—path.

—Michael Medved
Author, radio talk-show host, and columnist

Preface

A book is like a lover. If one chases after it too hard, it will fly away. It must be pursued to be sure, but the pursuit must be unhurried. The seeds of this book were planted when I got my first job as a music critic at the age of thirteen for a small magazine on the outskirts of Tokyo, where I was raised. Six years later, I made my first attempt to write a form of this book and was mercifully turned down by a major publisher after a long courtship. The initial approach had been made to a publishing executive named Bill Watkins by my professor at the time, Gretchen Passantino. The times weren't ready, nor was I. Eleven years and hundreds of interviews and life experiences later, I received a phone call from a Bill Watkins, *that* Bill Watkins, telling me that he would be handling my book for Broadman & Holman.

I had long forgotten my earlier manuscript when I was challenged by my friend Michael Medved in 1993. When I asked him whether he might consider following up his best-selling book, *Hollywood vs. America*, with a similar book on popular music, he said, "No," but added, "Why don't you write it?" At the time, I chuckled and let the question linger in the air, but a seed of possibility had been planted.

A few years earlier, I had started MJM Entertainment Group, a company that had, over the course of a few years, signed and distributed thirty records by American artists in the Japanese music market—some of whom were associated with the contemporary Christian music (CCM) market in the United States. When these artists were introduced simply as musicians and not as "religious" recording artists, their music was accepted throughout the Japanese music culture.

When some of these artists asked me to help reposition their music in the American market, I agreed to try. Thus began several years of frustrating meetings with a dozen or so record labels in Los Angeles and New York, with producers who had no idea that the religious music ghetto existed, and who were dubious about any talent coming out of it. When they did spot potential, they still couldn't seem to grasp the idea that these artists wanted to step into the mainstream, keep their old fans, and bring in new ones. I quickly began to realize that until the basic story was told, nobody was going to get it.

Shortly thereafter, I collaborated with two friends—Kerry Livgren of the band Kansas and the classical music scholar and conductor Patrick Kavanaugh—on an essay for *CCM* and *World* magazines. Then one day I happened upon a website on the old Negro baseball leagues. I was surprised to discover the names of dozens of great players I'd never heard of. Suddenly it hit me that this was the same basic story I was trying to tell—the story of artists trapped, because of their faith, in the musical equivalent of the old Negro baseball leagues. This new insight led to pieces for *Regeneration Quarterly* and *Billboard* magazine. When a publisher expressed interest, I began writing this book. Later, more than halfway through, that publisher pulled out of the project, but I decided to keep going.

Although I have relied on a variety of publications for source material, I've also incorporated many interviews of my own into this work. Since 1985, I've interviewed hundreds of artists and scholars for the journals and television and radio networks where my work has appeared. While anchoring and/or reporting for CNN, Group W, NHK, FM Tokyo, FM Yokohama, the Chimes, the Matsukasa, and others, I interviewed people like the Bee Gees, Gary Cherone of Van Halen, Fleetwood Mac, Janet Jackson, Phillip Johnson, Pat Boone, Phillip Bailey, Nile Rogers, 2 Live Crew, Abe Laboriel, Amy Grant, George Gallup, Michael Medved, Steve Taylor, Bryan Duncan, Robert Sweet, and many others. I've combined these dozens of formal interviews and countless informal, unrecorded conversations with many others. In addition, the Renaissance Group has served as an important place to meet great ideas from people like James Davison Hunter, David Horowitz, Charles Colson, and Michael Levine.

—Mark Joseph

Acknowledgments

Dozens of people contributed to the successful completion of this work. Thanks to Mitsuharu Tanaka for giving a thirteen-year-old a shot; Gloria Tiede, Myrtle Kiker, Kaye Aoki, Kaye Lindskoog, Gretchen Passantino, and Roberta Ahmanson for not being afraid to use the red pen; Norma Farrand, Lyn Danner, Sue Surber, Betty Hollier, June Hook, Toni Russell, Jeanette Gustafson, Helen Ryttersgaard, Craig Eby, Steve Duhrkoop, Carl Long, Dave Bartlett, and anybody I missed at C. A. J.; Mom, for life, love, and faith; KK Nelson for *Love Not the World*; Kerry Livgren and Pat Kavanaugh for sharing the vision; Marilyn Gillen, John Styll, Marvin Olasky, and Drew Ladner for keeping the ideas in the air; Lela Gilbert, Mark Lusk, Bill Watkins, Len Goss, Lisa Parnell, Gary Terashita, Ken Stephens, Elizabeth Randle, Jennifer Willingham, Matt West, Betty Woodmancy, and Bucky Rosenbaum for making it happen; Margaret McCallister for getting the word out; and Jesus, William Turner, Lance Cook, and Michael Guido for guidance. Thanks for manuscript help to Steve Turner, Martha Bayles, Anda Foxwell, Lila Joseph, Ric Rodeheaver, and David Swaney. Thanks to Terry Mattingly for his generous spirit and commitment to seeing change and Stephen Prendergast, Ken Tamplin, and Shin Domen for friendship. YH'WH, whose silent hand guided the project. Two great lovers of the arts deserve acknowledgment: Howard and Roberta Ahmanson, who believe that ideas matter.

ONE

The Musical Negro Baseball League

From the moment Elvis first swayed his hips and Bill Haley rocked around the clock, rock and roll has been on a collision course with millions of Americans. Revival meetings complete with record burnings were not uncommon in America, and many attempts have been made to ban or label records that were deemed immoral, profane, obscene, or otherwise distasteful. The cast of characters changed over the years, but the problems remained and, in the eyes of some cultural critics, worsened. Opposition to a rock music culture that sometimes celebrated death, destruction, unrestrained sexuality, and rebellion served to unite strange bedfellows like William Bennett, Tipper Gore, Susan Baker, C. Dolores Tucker, Charlton Heston, Allan Bloom, David Noebel, and other cultural critics who argued that free speech should be balanced by good citizenship on the part of the artists.

Most of the criticism has come from conservative Christians who have long deplored not only the content of rock music but sometimes the very art form itself. Whether out of latent racism, because of rock's roots in rhythm and blues, or a genuine fear of "the beat" and its supposed evil effects, Christians—both fundamentalist and evangelical—often staked out a position against rock that with each passing year grew more irrelevant as the music became entrenched in the culture.

Today, as a new breed of artists turns out songs that can make even the hippest listener blush, it is difficult to imagine what early critics could have found objectionable about songs such as Chuck Berry's "Johnny B. Goode," the Beatles' "I Wanna Hold Your Hand," or Marvin Gaye's "I Heard It through the Grapevine."

The Culture of Opposition

Many arguments were used to advance the central thesis that—regardless of content—rock was inherently evil. Perhaps the most widely swapped story was the one told around countless dinner tables, at churches, during revival meetings, and wherever Christians congregated. It centered around the alleged experience of an American missionary who traveled with his family deep into the heart of the African jungle to work among the natives. As the story went, the family had just returned from a furlough in the United States and the kids had brought along their favorite rock records. When these albums were played, the native converts approached the missionary and asked him why his children were listening to the very beats that they had once used to conjure up evil spirits in their pagan dances. Horrified, the missionary trashed his kids' records and passed the word on to the church at home: rock and roll, whatever the lyrical content, was the devil's music and was to be avoided at all costs.

As stories like these began to take hold in a Christian subculture still reeling from cultural setbacks like the Scopes Trial of 1925, it is hardly surprising that young Christian men and women didn't make much of an impact on popular music. They were literally frightened out of participation in popular music.

A more serious challenge to the legitimacy of rock was waged by more learned men and women who sought to persuade young and old alike that it was inherently evil. Chief among these was a tall, bespectacled Coloradan named David Noebel, one of rock's chief critics, who launched blistering attacks on rock through books with fighting titles such as *Hypnotism and the Beatles*, *The Legacy of John Lennon*, *The Marxist Minstrels*, and *Rhythm, Riots & Revolution*.

It was the Beatles, Noebel said, who first caught his attention.

> Back in 1964, I was speaking to a group of young people. Afterwards, a lady came up to me, handed me a copy of the *Saturday Evening Post* dated August 8, and told me to read the article about the Beatles. . . . More than anything else, it was a statement by the Beatles' press officer, Derek Taylor, that shocked me. He was explaining the group's success, and he said, "It's incredible, absolutely incredible. Here are these four boys from Liverpool.

They're rude, they're profane, they're vulgar, and they've taken over the world. It's as if they had founded a new religion. They're completely anti-Christ. I mean, I am anti-Christ as well, but they're so anti-Christ they shock me—which isn't an easy thing to do." That's what got me started.[1]

Noebel's criticisms of rock were both specific to certain artists and general to the very form of music itself. It wasn't hard for him to find targets in the crazy world of rock and roll. "The Beatles were important," he said. "They wanted to subvert Western culture. They were pro-drugs, pro-evolution, and pro-promiscuous sex; anti-Christ and more. I wanted to look at the heart of the rock and roll subculture and these guys were the major voices of that subculture."[2]

Within the Beatles, Noebel aimed his fire straight at John Lennon. "I think Lennon was one of the most important figures in the twentieth century," he said. "I obviously needed a big rock figure who summarized my gripes about rock, drugs, sex, and revolution, and Lennon was better for that than anyone else, although Mick [Jagger] would have come close. But Lennon was the best candidate. Lennon is still important."[3]

Noebel believed that the music itself posed a fundamental dilemma. "Rock music is a negation of soul, spirit, and mind, and is destructive to the body," he argued. "The muscles are weakened, the heartbeat is affected, and the adrenal glands and sex hormones are upset by continued listening. . . . It's also been shown that rock music destroys house plants. If it destroys God's plants, what's it doing to young people?"[4]

Noebel wasn't about to confine his criticism to "secular" rock, however. "I'm not against contemporary Christian music. I'm against Christian rock. Good Christian music is good for the body, soul, spirit, and mind, and it has good melody, harmony, and rhythm. I think those seven parameters set out the difference. . . . Christian rock breaks down the barrier that should be raised in the church against the rock and roll subculture. It reinforces secular rock. The church should be the salt of the earth. We should have a new song and new music. Why would we want to baptize a form of music that is born, bred, and raised in sin? Why should we put our message in old wine sacks?"[5]

Noebel also was reported to have been the chief inspiration for the crusaders who founded and led a group known as the Parents Music Resource Center (PMRC), which waged cultural warfare on obscene rock in the mid-1980s. Formed by Washington power wives Pam Howard, Sally Nevius, Tipper Gore, and Susan Baker, the PMRC's goals were actually rather modest—the labeling of records based on content, much like movies and television shows are rated today. The proposed labels included an X for sexually explicit content, a V for violence, a D/A for references to drugs and alcohol, and an O for references to the occult. The PMRC had the support of some artists and media executives, like Mike Love of the Beach Boys, R&B crooner Smokey Robinson, the president of the Songwriter's Guild, and the vice president of the Camelot Music chain, who wrote, "Some popular performers have gone beyond the bounds of good taste and now are being held accountable."[6]

Yet, for a music culture not accustomed to outside scrutiny, the PMRC's focus on the underbelly of the nation's music was disconcerting and led in some quarters to hysteria.

"Fundamentalism is not a state religion," raged rock pioneer Frank Zappa during his testimony before a Senate committee investigating the effects of rock music. "The PMRC's request reads like a catalog of phenomena abhorrent to practitioners of that faith. How a person worships is a private matter and should not be inflicted upon or exploited by others. The PMRC proposal is an ill-conceived piece of nonsense, which fails to deliver any real benefits to children and infringes the civil liberties of people who are not children."[7]

"Where do you stop?" asked Harriet Wasserman, Sheena Easton's manager at the time. "Does 'Puppy Love' mean bestiality? Does 'On the Good Ship Lollipop' mean a psychedelic drug trip?"[8]

Record mogul David Geffen agreed. "I don't feel I'm in a position to evaluate the content of the records we put out," he said. "We record artists we believe in and they put out products they believe in."[9]

Others pointed out that many "Christian" songs themselves contained lyrics mentioning the various taboos.

"Christian artists wondered whether an 'O' label could be slapped on Michael and Stormie Omartian's 'Wachersign,' a satirical song about faith in astrology," wrote critic Steve Rabey. "Or would an 'S' label appear on Leslie Phillips's 'He's Gonna Hear You Crying,' because of its lyrics about teenage suicide? Would labels obscure the cover of the album containing Larry Norman's 'Why Don't You Look into Jesus,' a song with references to alcohol, cigarettes, drugs, illicit sex, sexual diseases, and despair?"[10]

Others feared that labeling would have the effect of muddying the waters even further by discouraging artists from making "clean" records, as had happened in the film industry where a "G" rating had come to mean "bad for business."

The Emergence of CCM

Amid these cultural skirmishes, and virtually unnoticed by the wider popular music culture, a new ghetto of American music, known as contemporary Christian music (CCM) emerged, populated with refugees from the rock world, as well as an entire generation of new artists who would be diverted from mainstream rock and pop music, thanks to the efforts of the many cultural critics of rock and roll, into the safe world of "Christian rock."

Beginning in the late 1960s and early 1970s, CCM began to distinguish itself from its roots in gospel music, whose own roots were set deeply in the rich soil of traditional American music. For most of the twentieth century, the gospel music market had been dominated by two large companies, the Texas-based Word Incorporated and the Benson Company of Nashville, Tennessee, but the emergence of CCM soon brought other players onto the field.

What made CCM remarkable and unprecedented was that an entire genre of music was created *solely* on the basis of lyrical content rather than musical style. In succeeding years, the difficulty of perpetuating such a concept was exposed by the prospect of fitting a wide range of styles from pop to rap to metal under the umbrella of CCM. When the CCM market became a virtual scrap yard of musical styles, united only by the "Christian content" of the lyrics, Christians who made music were effectively cut off from having any meaningful impact on the culture at large. The perplexing irony was that the censorship was largely *self-imposed*. In the great war of ideas and the battle for the hearts and minds of the culture, musical artists who were Christians exiled themselves from pop culture.

What began as an effort to bypass perceived censorship in the music industry resulted in the creation of a whole new "Christian music" industry. Though founded with the best of intentions, it seldom promoted the advancement of the message of the gospel into the wider culture. Believing that the "worldly" music system wouldn't allow them to express themselves spiritually, and intimidated by the power of the rock culture, CCM executives created their own musical universe, including "Christian" radio stations, record labels, music magazines, and a host of other support organizations, which catered exclusively to a small segment of the Christian community. While ordinary record outlets sometimes carried "Christian" products, too often these recordings were banished to the rarely visited "gospel" or "inspirational" sections in record stores. Mostly they were simply sold in Christian bookstores across the U.S.

Before long, nearly all orthodox Christian thought was pushed to the margins of American music, and records produced for the CCM market seemed increasingly artificial in their stubborn refusal to address the full range of human emotions. Too often these records seemed to deny two central components of a truly religious lifestyle—namely, relating spiritual beliefs to everyday life and making spiritual principles understandable to the wider culture.

Equally devastating was the effect that marginalization had on the popular music industry. A generation of musicians with genuine spiritual concerns were told, in effect, that their voices were welcome only in the CCM ghetto. As a result, the mainstream music community and the average listener heard very little serious Christian thought expressed in the music that defined much of the '70s, '80s, and '90s. For the most part, the non-Christians made music for the culture at large while the Christians made music only for themselves. Incredibly, successful artists who experienced life-changing conversions were encouraged to give up their loyal audiences, who may have been interested in hearing what their favorite artists had to say, and were relegated to the CCM ghetto and urged to make music for fellow believers. While CCM was clearly appreciated by some believers who were encouraged in their spiritual journeys, the reality remained that it was never any more effective at impacting the culture with the abilities of its members than the old Negro baseball leagues were in showcasing the talents of its players for mainstream America.

During the first half of the twentieth century, millions of baseball fans watched in awe as Babe Ruth, Ty Cobb, Lou Gehrig, Cy Young, Walter Johnson, and other legendary players dominated the major leagues. During those same years, few fans knew about players like Rube Foster, Martin Dihigo, Ray Dandridge, or Cool Papa Bell, even though they, too, were some of the greatest ever to play the game. Despite their immense talents, these men, and many others, were never allowed one pitch to the Sultan of Swat or a single swing at a Walter Johnson fastball, all because they were African American. Instead, these fine ballplayers played out their careers in the Negro leagues.

The Negro leagues were the result of collusion between separatists like baseball commissioner Judge Kenesaw Mountain Landis and the Negro league team owners, whose financial well-being was built on the perpetuation of the separate leagues. For those in power it was a most comfortable arrangement: Major League Baseball remained all-white, and the Negro league owners made lots of money. The losers were the fans and the

African-American players, who wanted to be known simply as baseball play-ers, not "Negro" baseball players.

As with baseball, strange bedfellows colluded to push musicians with orthodox Christian beliefs into the modern-day musical equivalent of the Negro baseball leagues—the CCM industry. This cooperation between naive or misguided Christians and militant secularists meant that most Americans never heard the music of brilliant artists like Larry Norman, Steve Taylor, Charlie Peacock, Paul Clark, Russ Taff, Phil Keaggy, Rex Carroll, Randy Stonehill, and hundreds of others.

The arrangement continued for the better part of three decades, and the formula was simple: Explicitly Christian lyrics garnered more airplay on Christian stations—and hence more money. Artists who happened to be Christians were signed to "Christian" record labels and encouraged to write God songs. Struggles with faith could be the subject of a song, but prefer-ably after a tidy conclusion had been reached.

Sanitizing the struggles of life eliminated such songs from considera-tion among non-Christians where people looked for more in a record than ten explicitly religious songs that lacked real world relevance. When such songs did emerge from time to time, making their way past CCM executives who were constantly searching for the next "God-single," these executives were in no position to bring such music to the pop market. For its part, the wider music community considered CCM songs to be programmed and arti-ficial, and the public troubles of "Christian" music megastars like Michael English and Sandi Patty proved painfully that there was a disconnection between the lives they were leading and the songs they were singing in the impossibly antiseptic world of CCM.

In Patty's case, though her fans were consistently treated to such stir-ring spiritual anthems as "Lift Up the Lord" and "Make His Praise Glorious," her decision to leave her husband and four children for a band member clearly showed that she had failed the basic test of artistic integrity by her unwillingness to level with her audience and share her struggles in her music. Patty's problems were in stark contrast to an equally popular per-former, Amy Grant, who courageously confronted the issue head-on with her 1988 track "Faithless Heart," and sang openly about her marital troubles on her 1997 album *Behind the Eyes*.

Those who preferred their music morality-free perpetuated the "Christian/Secular" split, and an entire generation of musicians, disc jockeys, music journalists, and record executives who happened to be Christians were effectively diverted out of the popular music scene and into the world of

CCM. Freed from the influence that would undoubtedly have been exerted by such people had they been in positions of influence in the "secular" music business, popular music came to represent their beliefs less and less.

The reality is of course that both the believers and unbelievers need each other in a big way. For far from damaging the creative impulse, the natural tension that will always exist between those who believe and those who don't helps it by moderating the natural excesses of each camp.

For the devout, there is often a tendency, especially after a glorious conversion experience, to be, in the words of CCM artist Chris Christian (his stage name), "too heavenly minded that we'll be no earthly good."[11]

The tremendous spiritual adrenaline rush that often follows a conversion experience can have the unfortunate tendency to produce music that the secular mind finds difficult to comprehend. In the rush to cast off their old lives and identify with the new, far too many artists use inside church language, themes, and ideas that they themselves wouldn't have understood before their own conversions. In their zeal to be acknowledged by fellow Christians, too often they tended to forget to sing of their newfound faith in the language of the nonbeliever.

Negro Spirituals

Rock and roll's roots extend far deeper than the Rolling Stones, Elvis, and the Beatles, back to the Negro spirituals. These heartfelt songs, from the lips and souls of slaves, blended the beats and rhythms from their native Africa with the principles of a new religion that seemed to encourage faithfulness in the midst of slavery, rather than immediate emancipation.

Unlike baseball, which was first played by whites and later adopted by blacks, rock evolved from a form of music originally developed in Africa, which white musicians adopted only after they saw it performed and popularized by blacks. It had its roots in the Negro spirituals, many of which grew out of the time of spiritual revival known as the Great Awakening.

"Fiery preachers drew huge crowds to open-air gatherings in the woods, termed camp meetings, where new hymns and camp songs were sung with abandon into the small hours," noted the *Rough Guide to World Music*. "At the fringes of these meetings, African slaves listened to the music and were enthralled, music being an integral part of the tribal religions banned by slave masters in the New World. Slaves who converted gave new life to the hymns and religious songs with a transfusion of West African rhythms and vocal stylings, producing an entirely new song form. The first true folk music of America, they came to be known as the 'Negro spiritual.'"[12]

Revival meetings served as more than a place for blacks to learn the Christian faith. They also were an important setting for the races to mix and showed many whites that faith could be something lively and exciting as well as cerebral.

> The Methodist and Baptist camp revivals of the South and Southwest provided the setting in which most American blacks found or confirmed their religious identities in the eighteenth and nineteenth centuries. With their hundreds and thousands of people, young and old, men and women mixing indiscriminately in states of high excitation and breaking out at will in shouts and songs, all gathered to hear an itinerant preacher, usually—but by no means always—white, the camp meetings operated on something like the model of extended kin and communal rituals familiar to Africans, and in part reproduced in the plantation milieu, and they presented a vivid contrast to the configurations of religious conversion known to whites in the Northeast.[13]

The Negro spirituals were often both worshipful and subversive, in the best sense of the word, full of double entendres that seemed to slip right past their masters, who may not have realized that when the slaves sang "Let My People Go," they were singing as much about their own plight as they were of the Israelite captivity in Egypt.

Gospel

Two centuries passed before the Negro spirituals gave rise to gospel through the pioneering work of a Chicago-based piano player and born salesman named Thomas Dorsey, who married Negro spirituals with blues and jazz rhythms and sold his work to churches around the country calling it "gospel music." Dorsey took young artists like Sally Martin and Mahalia Jackson on the road with him, popularizing his "gospel" sounds during the '20s and '30s.

Though he was the son of a minister, Dorsey got his start writing blues songs. But after hearing the work of a composer named Charles Tindley at a National Baptist Convention meeting, Dorsey began to write songs that kept the bluesy music but changed the racy lyrics, which didn't sit well with the religious hierarchy of his day.

"Naturally, the old guard conservatives considered this blending of the sacred (spirituals and hymns) and the secular (blues and jazz) as 'the devil's music,' and shunned it," observed writer Phil Petrie. "By its actions, the church declared Dorsey's brand of gospel music unworthy of a hearing within the sanctuaries of the day, a story quite similarly echoed by churches responding to the rock and roll Jesus Movement that swept the country in the early '70s. In both instances, the traditional church failed to see the positive influence contemporary music could have, blessing its listeners and encouraging them to draw near to God."[14]

Such opposition did nothing to stop the young Dorsey, who was determined to make church music relevant to his culture.

"When I realized how hard some folks were fighting the gospel idea, I was determined to carry the banner," he remembered. "I borrowed five dollars and sent out five hundred copies of my song, 'If You See My Savior,' to churches throughout the country. . . . It was three years before I got a single order. I felt like going back to the blues."[15]

Dorsey's music slowly began to be accepted by some churches; before long, gospel music had worked its way into the fabric of American life.

"The end of World War II ushered in an era generally acknowledged to be a golden age for gospel music," noted one critic. "Over the next twenty years, thousands of gospel artists packed churches and concert halls across America, often selling records in huge quantities. The first stars of the gospel boom were the quartets. Stylistically, quartet singing had taken a leap: the smooth harmonies of the jubilee groups were now being joined by one or two lead voices that were not afraid to make use of all the range and histrionic emotion at their disposal."[16]

Although some white churches accepted the new "gospel" sound, others—particularly in the South—objected to the African influence on church music, preferring what came to be called southern gospel. Others embraced it.

"The white churches of the rural South shared hymns, spirituals, and rhythms with their African-American counterparts," observed the *Rough Guide to World Music*. "They too knew about grinding poverty; they too longed for a better deal on the other side of Jordan, and expressed their longing in song. And, of course, many future luminaries of country music cut their teeth on gospel."[17]

The "Christian Music" Business

Benson

One of the oldest and largest purveyors of southern gospel, the Benson Company, was started in 1902 by John T. Benson, who began to print and publish church songbooks. As Benson's children became involved in the family business, one son, John T. Benson Jr., became heavily involved in the small music publishing division of the company. Soon Benson Jr. purchased the music division from his brothers and launched out on his own.

"He had an ear for great gospel songs," recalled Robert Benson of his grandfather. "He would travel around the country looking for songs. He even took the train to New York and bought 'Love Lifted Me' from a woman for thirty dollars."[18]

As the Benson Company's music publishing interests continued to grow, John Benson Jr. discovered that signing talent would increase his publishing business, and the company formed a record label. When Benson Jr. approached a traveling evangelist about singing the songs the entrepreneur had acquired, the evangelist said he'd agree if Benson would fund a record for him to sell on the road. It was a deal too good to pass up.

"My father didn't really know anything about marketing or production," said Bob Benson. "The Benson Company started out making and selling records to artists who sang them."[19]

Some of those early artists included southern gospel favorites like the Speer Family, the Soul Singing Rambos, J. D. Sumner and the Exciting Stamps Quartet, the Oak Ridge Boys, Doug Oldham, the Bill Gaither Trio, and Henry and Hazel Slaughter.

With the dawn of the 1970s, Benson began its foray into the Christian soft rock and adult contemporary market, with albums by Dallas Holm and other younger, nontraditional artists. By 1979, Benson, a $400,000 sheet music company only two decades earlier, had become a $15 million publishing and recording company with various divisions, including a talent agency and book division.

In the late '70s, Benson was purchased by the Zondervan Company, a publisher of religious books and Bibles, and was managed by a former Zondervan sales representative named Jerry Park who brought newer, more contemporary, talent into the Benson fold with the addition of artists like Debby Boone, DeGarmo and Key, Brown Bannister, and later, Sandi Patty.

One of Benson's more sensational moves was its alignment with Enigma Records to release the records of the heavy metal band Stryper into the CCM marketplace in the mid-1980s. After several successful records, Benson abruptly terminated the relationship with Enigma and Stryper in early 1990 because of dissatisfaction with the spiritual content of the group's final studio record *Against the Law*.

Shortly after the Stryper termination, Benson was purchased by a New York based music company, Music Entertainment Group, which subsequently sacked Park. Later, Benson was purchased by Zomba Music, which had experienced success with the band Jars of Clay through its CCM imprint, Brentwood.

Word

Benson's primary competitor in the world of CCM was Word Incorporated, for years the largest seller of religious oriented books and music in America. The Benson Company printed all of Word's books in the early years, and Word was Benson's largest account for many years. Its entry into the "Christian" rock music market was a rapid one. "In 1975, about 5 percent of the recorded product sold was contemporary," wrote CCM historian Paul Baker. "Only three years later, the amount had increased to 60 percent."[20]

By 1977, Word's major music label, Myrrh, had signed many of the top CCM artists of the day, including B. J. Thomas, Randy Matthews, Chris Christian, David Meece, Second Chapter of Acts, and Honeytree.

Founded a few years earlier in 1972 by a young executive at Word Records named Billy Ray Hearn, Myrrh was to become Word's most successful label.

"I had been at Word for four years when we started Myrrh," he remembered. "We started discovering a lot of young writers and artists, so by '72 they let me start a label just for contemporary music—and I named it Myrrh. Within a year or two, [Myrrh] was a major part of Word's sales."[21]

The choice of the name "Myrrh" spoke volumes about the direction the burgeoning CCM movement was taking, because it was a name that was unpronounceable to anyone who wasn't intimately familiar with the story of the three wise men. It was a symbol of the way Hearn and others would promote their music over the years—geared toward Christians exclusively. Hearn was never shy about his goal, which was nothing short of leading a fundamental retreat from the "secular" world.

"I wish the industry had not gotten enamored with the secular market," he would later say, referring to attempts to cross "Christian" pop into the mainstream market. "I never wanted to be a part of that world and I got out of it."[22]

Sparrow

Before long, Hearn left Word and returned to California in 1975, starting a new company with what he felt was a different vision. "I was given the opportunity to start a record label by a publishing company with a Christian book division, but a year and a half later, that company sold to ABC, which owned Word," said Hearn. "The offer was made available to me to purchase the company outright, so I borrowed the money."[23]

Eight artists comprised Hearn's initial roster at Sparrow, which later grew to include Phil Keaggy, Steve Taylor, BeBe and CeCe Winans, Margaret Becker, and Steve Camp. Of Sparrow's early days, Hearn recalled, "Our quality emphasis was not necessarily on the recording technique . . . [but] the quality of the artists and their ministry orientation, that established the basis for what kind of company we would be. . . . We were a very diverse label musically from the start. We even had a Nashville-based artist in our original roster and signed Danniebelle Hall as our first black artist a bit later."[24]

In the late '80s, Hearn's son Bill took over the company and helped to engineer the purchase of Sparrow by EMI, which seemed to share the elder Hearn's goal of enlarging the Christian consumer base in order to sell more records to more Christians.

Maranatha!

Whereas Word and Benson had roots in traditional gospel music and publishing, a new company, Maranatha! Music, rode the wave of the Jesus Movement, a movement of hippie converts to the Christian faith that was led and nurtured by a visionary, a Costa Mesa, California, based pastor named Chuck Smith. Maranatha! quickly became a radical force in the contemporizing of gospel music but did little to get the music into the mainstream of pop music culture, and the mass exodus of Christian artists out of popular music continued.

Maranatha! was founded in 1971 by Tom Coomes and Chuck Fromm with the encouragement of Smith. Coomes was a member of an early band called Love Song, and Fromm was a nephew of Smith's who eventually became CEO of the company.

Coomes remembered the simple origins of the company. "Six of us were living in a house together and four of us came to the Lord," he said. "One afternoon we went to see Pastor Chuck and said, 'We've been coming to church for about a month now and we've written some songs and were wondering if we could sing them in church.' Chuck said, 'Would you mind if I heard a couple of them first?' So we came in with a couple of acoustic guitars and sang 'Think about What Jesus Said,' and [Pastor Chuck] just began to weep. He said, 'I've been praying for something like this for a year.'"[25]

"As they started to sing, it touched a responsive chord in my heart," said Smith. "I began to weep. It was an expression of a fresh experience with Jesus Christ. Their music began a musical revolution and a whole new dimension of worship of the Lord."[26]

As several bands began to coalesce around the church, the record company was born in one of the church's Sunday school rooms, and they recorded their first album with a $2,500 loan from Smith. It was a heady time and the music was flowing.

"God was giving people songs and people were getting excited about reading the Bible for the first time in their lives," remembered Coomes. "Part of the beauty of it was that we were so naive. Most of us didn't grow up in church, so we didn't know what you were supposed to do in church and what you couldn't do in church. When some money would come in from one album, we would send another group in to record. When the money came back from that album, somebody else would go in."[27]

That first record, *The Everlastin' Living Jesus Music Concert*, was released in 1971, and went on to sell 160,000 copies, leading to the creation of tens of other Jesus Music bands like Love Song, Sweet Comfort Band, Hope of Glory, the Way, Children of the Day, Country Faith, Karen Lafferty, Mustard Seed Faith, and Blessed Hope.

As the '70s came to a close and CCM began to take on more of a corporate image with stiff competition from the likes of Sparrow, Word, and Benson, Maranatha! began to retreat and focus on its staples of church oriented worship music and children's records.

Ushering several of its artists to other labels, Maranatha! got back to basics. Although the company would later flirt with contemporary music with the Arcade label, it was clear that its days as a leading force in the world of Christian rock music were over. The Jesus Music hippies were now aging baby boomers who wanted comfortable, polite music for their church services and to train their kids in the faith. Speaking to the culture through the popular music of the moment no longer seemed to be a priority.

"We wanted our kids to have fun and have their minds filled up with the good things during their formative years,"[28] said Coomes of Maranatha!'s change in direction.

Maranatha! president Chuck Fromm confirmed this in 1991 when the label celebrated its twentieth anniversary. "Our vision at Maranatha! Music is to make every car, every home, every church, every heart a sanctuary. As providers of worship resources, it is up to us to continually focus on the power and purposes of God and not on the instruments of worship."[29]

Frontline

In many ways, Frontline Records picked up much of the slack from Maranatha! in the mid-1980s, providing a home for many artists who might have signed with Maranatha! had its vision continued. Frontline's founder, Jim Kempner, seemed to believe that the mantle had been passed to him.

"God showed me to start up my own record company after a conversation with Chuck Smith in September 1985," said Kempner, a former used car salesman whose business was called P.T.L. Motors. "I found myself complaining about a lot of what I saw in the Christian music industry, and I realized that if I was not going to do something constructive about the problem I had no right to complain. I decided to take my life savings and see if I could take my administrative talents and give a platform to some of the artists I believed in."[30]

Kempner had been meeting lots of artists in his position as director of Calvary Chapel's Ministry Resource Center, helping to record low-budget records for many of the musicians who came to the church. So when Frontline was launched, it instantly became the center of attention in the southern California CCM scene, luring in top talent willing to make records for paltry budgets of $15,000 or less. Within five years, the company had released 250 records, but there was constant grumbling from artists, many of whom signed away their publishing royalties to Frontline.

CCM, the Magazine

The glue that held Kempner, Hearn, and the rest of the CCM community together since the late 1970s was John Styll and his magazine, *CCM*, which he started in 1978 in Laguna Hills, California. Styll had gotten his start in Calvary Chapel's bookstore working in the cassette section and later hosted a radio broadcast, "Hour of Praise," on a local radio station. Each afternoon at three, Styll would play contemporary religious songs, later parlaying that success into what eventually became the industry bible.

"Though Jesus Music recordings had been in the marketplace since around the turn of the decade," remembered former CCM staffer Thom Granger, "the efforts to make it really grow as an effective business/ministry had been scattershot at best. *CCM* magazine was born in July of 1978 out of the need to provide the emerging Christian music industry with news, sales, and radio airplay charts; and well-written features, record reviews, and concert schedules for the fans."[31]

Although *CCM* magazine served as the official cheerleader of the burgeoning scene, to his credit, Styll often allowed it to be the vehicle for those who were not as enthralled with the CCM genre. Chief among these critics was John Fischer, whose columns graced the back of the magazine for fifteen years and often questioned the very existence of the CCM genre.

Styll himself seemed to be caught between two worlds—at once content with the status quo and vaguely disconcerted with the "industry" that had sprung up around him. From time to time he would write pragmatic essays that seemed to have elements both of cheerleading and deep criticism. These were often difficult to read because Styll seemed to be at war with himself, knowing in his heart that the creation of a category of music known as CCM was both artificial and ultimately destructive, yet realizing that as the publisher of a magazine called *CCM*, his success was tied to its advancement as a genre.

In a 1992 essay, Styll quoted numerous critics of Christian music who decried the separation of art into the artificial categories of "sacred" and "secular." Concluding that "contemporary Christian music can be defined as any music by a believing artist which testifies to the Truth as found in Scripture, knowing that the Scriptures address all aspects of life. Christian artists must address the issues of everyday life in addition to devotional subjects in order to avoid the trap of the unbiblical concept of sacred and secular."[32]

In an earlier essay, Styll had bravely asserted that "there's no such thing as Christian music. I can prove it too," only to conclude the article with the statement that "Christian music can have both ministry value and entertainment value."[33]

Styll sought to harmonize two distinctly different sets of worldviews: One sought to continue a divisive genre of music called CCM, and the other sought to abolish the genre and let the artists, beliefs intact, step over into the society at large, thereby influencing the wider culture. Though his heart was with the idea of crossing over, his head seemed to be with the perpetuation of the CCM subculture. When *CCM* magazine continued to grow and expand, Styll moved to Nashville and became the head of the Gospel Music Association, later expanding his CCM empire to include radio and television interests before selling the company to Salem Communications.

The Great Retreat

What caused a generation of gifted men and women to retreat to the safe world of CCM? The roots of the secessionist movement is traced by some to the aftermath of the Scopes Trial early in the century and the seemingly relentless pace of scientific and social progress that left Bible-believing Christians on the defensive.

"Within the span of one generation between the 1890s and the 1930s, this extraordinary influence of evangelicalism in the public sphere of American culture collapsed," wrote George Marsden, a noted expert on Christian fundamentalism. "Not only did the cultural opinion makers desert evangelicalism, even many leaders of major Protestant denominations attempted to tone down the offenses to modern sensibilities of a Bible filled with miracles and a gospel that proclaimed human salvation from eternal damnation only through Christ's atoning work on the cross. Fundamentalism was the response of traditionalist evangelicals who declared war on these modernizing trends."[34]

The "Monkey Trial" of 1925 proved to be a hollow victory for William Jennings Bryan, the great orator and one-time presidential candidate who argued the orthodox Christian cause in the case of a Tennessee schoolteacher accused of teaching Darwin's theory of evolution in the classroom. Bryan swayed the jury, but in the court of public opinion Christianity was the big loser, perceived as being clearly incapable of keeping up with scientific progress. Things only got worse from there.

"The controversies of the 1920s strengthened the hand of people who wanted to secularize the culture," observed Marsden. "They were able to argue that religion is divisive and they argued that to keep the peace is to restrict religion to the private domain. By the 1940s, hopes for political action to promote an evangelical America were far more dim than they had been in the 1920s. Prohibition, after all, had been a recently enacted manifestation of 'Christian civilization' in the earlier decade."[35]

America's triumph over imperialism in the east and fascism in Europe did little to change the growing contempt for orthodox Christian thought in American society.

"By 1947, fundamentalism seemed a cultural and intellectual wasteland," wrote Marsden. "American opinion makers typically portrayed Bible-believing evangelicalism as a stifling vestige of the small town past. . . . Fundamentalist leaders . . . felt keenly their lack of respect at the centers of culture. . . . Meaningful media access was equally difficult. In Hollywood's view of America in 1947, Bible-believing Protestantism almost did not exist. If it did, it was an aberration."[36]

Though not as hostile as it would later become, Hollywood took no notice of evangelical Christianity. "The radio, at least the radio that received press coverage, was much the same," wrote Marsden. "Jack (Benny) and Bing (Crosby) did not talk about religion. Nor was religion a serious topic on *One Man's Family* or *The Romance of Helen Trent*."[37]

Years of being rejected by the mainstream culture produced something of an inferiority complex among Bible-believing Christians, and the answer for many was to go underground—a process that had begun earlier in the twentieth century but was speeded up in the postwar years. These believers seemed to give up on transforming institutions that had in their eyes gone wayward and, instead, seemed intent on starting new ones to rival them.

Fuller Theological Seminary was their response to the wayward Yale School of Divinity. The Bible Institute of Los Angeles would take Harvard's place. Wheaton College would train up Christian intellectuals instead of Dartmouth. The media culture was no different. Charles E. Fuller's radio ministry flourished, as did Billy Graham's film studio, World Wide Pictures, and Moody's television, film, and radio interests. Popular journals like Graham's *Christianity Today* and others like *Christian Life, Campus Life,* and *His* catered to evangelical reading interests. The parallel universe and culture was underway.

Yet, in the midst of all of this activity, few seemed to take notice of the obvious fact that such a parallel culture by necessity would have the effect of causing the primary culture to be unresponsive to the interests of the departed and, over time, even grow increasingly hostile to them. Amazingly, the Christians didn't seem to care, and when they finally became concerned, instead of blaming themselves for their own decision to leave the culture, they pointed fingers at the output of those leaders who by default had taken the reins of the culture.

TWO

Out of the World

espite the ruckus caused by the introduction of rock and roll, the
1950s were a time when spiritual songs like "He's Got the Whole
World in His Hands," "Peace in the Valley," and "Gold Mine in the Sky"
were commonly heard on popular radio stations—but not for long. "In the
early 1960s . . . the musical tastes of America began to change," wrote music
critic Paul Baker. "The war babies had become high school teenagers and
would soon be in college. . . . The generation gap widened. Religious sentiments in pop songs faded. From 1961 until 1964, except for Christmas music
each December, there were no major pop hits of a religious nature."[1]

What explained this absence of Christian sentiments from popular
music? "Rock was becoming an alternative to all forms of traditional culture
including church," suggests noted British rock critic Steve Turner. "Chuck
Berry sang 'roll over Beethoven' and 'deliver me from the days of old.'
Church, politics, the army, business, suburbia, etc. were all part of the 'days
of old.'"[2]

By the mid-1960s the mood changed and pop songs again began to discuss spiritual themes. Elvis recorded "Crying in the Chapel," the
Impressions released "People Get Ready," and the Byrds' "Turn! Turn!
Turn!" and other songs like "Spirit in the Sky," "Oh Happy Day," "That's
the Way God Planned It," and "Put Your Hand in the Hand of the Man"
shot up the charts.

19

"Drugs were the trigger," says Turner, explaining the sudden openness to spiritual themes. "People suddenly had experiences which seemed to have explanations in esoteric literature. They felt 'spiritual.' John Lennon in 1966 was reading books about gnosticism. The first specific mentions of Jesus didn't come until 1968 ("Mrs. Robinson"), but these weren't songs of faith. Jesus became an okay sort of guy in the early 1970s because he could be seen as a prototypical hippie."[3]

That hospitable climate slowly began to change at just about the time Christians took their marbles and left the pop music culture. "Just as Jesus became an okay guy in pop, Christian musicians left to form their own little industry," notes Turner. "And that's why Christ has been absent from rock ever since."[4]

Rock music became increasingly hostile to the values of the faith community as the cultural retreat was completed in the late '70s and early '80s. The trend was unmistakable: the stronger and more pronounced the "Christian" music industry became, the less responsive the mainstream music industry was to issues dear to ordinary American believers.

"As Nasty As They Wanna Be," a record from a Miami-based rap group called 2 Live Crew, was the last straw for many cultural critics who were mortified at the group's lyrics, which were deemed obscene by a federal judge in Florida—a ruling eventually overturned.

Although Christian evangelists, record burners, the PMRC, and cultural critics like C. Dolores Tucker and William Bennett all decried how outrageous some rock, pop, and rap lyrics had become, it is important to note that if this was true, it was because people of faith had failed to make their own music heard by the wider culture, choosing instead to huddle together in the corner of the popular culture playing inspirational music for each other as they cursed the darkness.

Rock and Roll Gets Nasty

Disc jockey Alan Freed of WJW in Cleveland is said to have coined the term *rock and roll* in 1953. Freed called his late-night R&B show "Moondog's Rock and Roll Party," and it was no secret that it referred to intercourse. Perhaps, then, it is no surprise that rock spent an inordinate amount of time dealing with sex.

Sex sells, of course, and some artists simply used it to get rich. In a review of Prince's album *1999*, the *Rolling Stone Yearbook* concluded, "Prince parades his dirty talk and kinky propositions, but beneath it all resides a tantalizing utopian philosophy of humanism through hedonism which suggests that once you've broken all the rules, you'll find some real values."[5]

Prince was not alone. Many other artists explored the depths of unrestrained sexuality. Rock's excesses, both sexual and otherwise, pointed out the need for musicians and industry executives who were Christians to exert their influence in the mainstream market. Without that influence, popular music failed to reflect their ideals.

"By the 1980s, heavy metal had quit bothering with euphemism—or with intercourse for that matter," observed music critic Martha Bayles. "Good old promiscuity went the way of the dodo bird as speed metal and death metal groups beefed up their acts with bloody sadism. The mid-1980s were the heyday of rock videos depicting female victims chained, caged, beaten, and bound with barbed wire, all to whet the appetites of twelve- and thirteen-year-olds for onstage performances such as the [infamous] one in which the group W.A.S.P. . . . pretended to batter a woman's skull and rape her with a chain saw."[6]

Rock's flirtation with drugs began in the '60s, sharpened in the '70s, and despite the government's "Just Say No" campaign, thrived underground during the '80s. In the '90s, popular bands like the Black Crowes and Porno for Pyros were vocal in their support of the legalization of pot, and Irish pop singer Sinead O'Connor went out of her way to show her support, saying in 1993 that "selling marijuana is one of the most respectable things anyone can do."[7]

Of course, the popularity of marijuana didn't begin with Sinead O'Connor. Songs celebrating the joys of smoking pot filled the airwaves in the '70s in such songs as "Panama Red" by the New Riders, Neil Young's "Roll Another Number," "Champagne and Reefer" by Muddy Waters, and "Don't Bogart That Joint" from the film *Easy Rider*.

With a more relaxed drug culture in the '90s, perhaps encouraged by a president who told an MTV audience that he, too, had smoked the weed, groups like NORML (the National Organization for the Reform of Marijuana Laws) began to gain some traction among the general public and among various rock and rap groups, most notably the band Cypress Hill.

"Pot was so prevalent on their first album," observed industry watchdog *Media Update*, "that they were featured on the cover of *High Times* magazine and became the first music group endorsed by NORML. They openly smoke pot at their concerts. And this group is not obscure and they are not going away anytime soon."[8]

Popular music also evinced an obsession with God, in the form of "mock rock," as it was dubbed. Among a certain subset of the rock world, it became popular to choose provocative band names like Liquid Jesus, Jesus Lizard, Eyehategod, Godflesh, Deicide, and God's Girlfriend. A singer for the band Dayglow Abortions went by the name Jesus Bonehead.

Unorthodox notions of God flooded pop and rock music in a way that seemed out of sync with a nation where at least half the population claimed to attend a weekly religious service.

"God, sometimes you just don't come through," taunted rocker Tori Amos. "Do you need a woman to look after you?"[9]

Metallica's "The God That Failed" expresses similar sentiments: "Broken is the promise/Betrayal/The healing hand held back by the deepened nail/Follow the God that failed."[10]

"He sewed his eyes shut because he is afraid to see," sang Trent Reznor of Nine Inch Nails on the song "Heresy." "He dreamed a god up and called it Christianity. Your god is dead and no one cares; if there is a hell, I will see you there."[11]

The seeds of such public expressions had been planted years earlier when the faulty theology of separation took hold in American evangelical and fundamentalist circles. Many young artists of deep spiritual conviction decided for a variety of reasons to leave the culture and record for the insulated and separatist "Christian" music market.

Larry Norman

Larry Norman is widely regarded to be the founder of the "Christian" rock movement, but far from leading a retreat out of the culture, Norman's aim was to marry his Christian beliefs and his love of rock and roll and record for Capitol Records. A native of San Jose, Norman grew up in the church but never understood why the songs he heard there couldn't be sung in normal English.

"I had gone forward in church to accept Christ when I was five," he remembered. "I strained to reach the high notes when we sang the hymns and I struggled to understand the lyrics, which were filled with things like 'bulwarks never failing.' If the hymns seemed archaic to me, well that made sense. God was very ancient too. These hymns were probably written back when he first made the world."[12]

As he would do for many others both in and out of the music world, Elvis changed the way the young Norman looked at music in general and the church in particular. "When I was young, I heard Elvis Presley sing 'Hound Dog' on the radio, and I began to wonder why there couldn't be church music that sounded a little more modern," said Norman. "So I began to write songs in the fourth grade. A few years later, I sang 'Moses' and some other early songs at the church picnic, but I felt embarrassed and just a little angry when no one really understood what I was trying to do."[13]

Norman's songs were even less understood by his conservative parents. "My father, bless his heart, did not allow me to listen to the radio anymore, and tried to encourage me to give up music entirely," Norman said. "I was obedient on the first count, but couldn't bear to stop writing songs. And so for many years I felt alone in my enthusiasm for Jesus rock music. Periodically, I performed in public, and upon leaving school I signed with Capitol Records, but it was a long time before I met anyone who understood me."[14]

"Larry had been playing musical instruments since he was three," noted Paul Baker. "His first guitar had been slipped under the bed to hide it from his father. Being a musician was not exactly the most respectable or profitable job in the eyes of his dad, but to Larry it was just about everything."[15]

In 1968, Norman moved to Los Angeles hoping to bring his unique brand of rock to the music world, and his band, People, began to attract a local following that led to its signing with Capitol. Before long, the blond hippie and his band had a hit song, "I Love You," that climbed to number fourteen on the pop charts. Already a devout Christian at twenty-one, Norman wanted to call his record *We Need a Whole Lot More of Jesus and a Lot Less Rock and Roll* and arranged to have an artist's rendition of Jesus on the cover. Capitol would have none of it, however, choosing instead to call the record *I Love You*, using a picture of the band for the cover. Frustrated, Norman left the band, but was eventually invited back by Capitol to record as a solo artist.

"In 1969," he recalled, "after the release of my third album for Capitol, *Upon This Rock*, it seemed that people were ready for a modern approach to Christian music. Within two years, there were a dozen or so groups or solo performers just in California who were recognizably contemporary."[16]

"With his long, straight, blond hair, his incisive lyrics, and his gutsy rock tunes, Larry shocked just about every adult who came into his path," wrote Paul Baker. "Enigma though he was, he carried the Good News of Jesus via a medium which was readily understood by the young people."[17]

Widely acknowledged to be the first "Christian rock" album, it was vintage Norman, mixing apocalyptic Christianity with psychedelic rock and roll. The album also launched several modern Christian hymns like "I Wish We'd All Been Ready" and "Sweet Song of Salvation."

Though he started with revolutionary intentions, difficulties in Norman's personal and professional life, including severe physical problems and marital troubles, left him isolated from both the rock and CCM worlds—but within the subculture his records were widely distributed and heard.

Clearly it's difficult to pin the blame on Norman for the cultural isolation that would come to characterize CCM because he hadn't intended to start a new genre of music. He would have preferred mainstream acceptance for himself and other artists with orthodox Christian impulses. What he accomplished was to boldly lay down for future artists the proposition that rock and roll could be used to communicate an essentially conservative, orthodox, Christian message.

In his autobiographical song, "Why Should the Devil Have All the Good Music?" Norman made his case: "I ain't mocking the hymns. Just give me a song that has a beat. I ain't knocking the hymns, just give me a song that moves my feet. I don't like none of them funeral marches. I ain't dead yet."[18]

Rejecting the CCM movement's tendency to use "insider" lingo, Norman sought to write songs for the wider, "secular" culture. "What I wanted to do was learn how to explain God without using any of the language or ideas that I had been taught in the church," he once observed. "I felt everybody's been exposed to the church, so the minute you start saying to them something from their childhood, they're going to say, 'Oh yeah, I've been to church. I've had that experience. It didn't work out.' So I tried to use secular sounding words to express what happened to me spiritually."[19]

Norman even wrote the obligatory Vietnam War era protest song, but with a twist. "I was never trying to be a revolutionary," he maintained. "I was not so much against the things like the war in Vietnam just because war kills people, because given time everybody shall die. I was for Jesus. I wanted the soldiers in Vietnam to know about Christ, and I wanted the other side to know about Christ."[20]

His song "I Am the Six O'clock News" chronicled the media's indifference to suffering—an unusual protest in 1968. "I was not, in my mind, a traditional rebel," Norman remembered. "I was angry about injustice and deceit, but my songs weren't written to stir anybody up to any focus other than Jesus. Outside of Christ, my songs have no value."[21]

Andrae Crouch

If Larry Norman was the John Lennon of CCM, Andrae Crouch was Marvin Gaye, James Brown, and Michael Jackson rolled into one. To this day, he is widely considered a living legend in the gospel world. Crouch's father managed a family-owned dry cleaning business and a restaurant, and cared for the sick and needy in the evenings and on weekends, before becoming a pastor when young Andrae was nine years old. When the pastor needed accompaniment, he prayed that his son would be given the ability to play the piano.

"Within two weeks, you were picking out the melody of 'What a Friend We Have in Jesus,'" remembered Crouch's mother in a letter to her son. "Through the next years, Jesus did become your special friend. Your inborn love for music inspired you to practice every morning before going to school, and the day always ended with the ringing of the piano."[22]

Crouch formed his act, Andrae Crouch and the Disciples, in 1965 and began to perform at his father's Christ Memorial Church of God in Christ in California's San Fernando Valley. He soon got his first break on the CCM label Light, then headed by a talented conductor named Ralph Carmichael.

What Carmichael found was a twenty-something minister's son who had grown up singing and playing in his father's church and had maintained a passion for reaching his generation through music. "After the usual amenities, we began exchanging ideas about music—its trends, its potential and how it can be used to get to kids with the gospel of Christ," remembered Carmichael. "I soon discovered that under his mild manner and warm smile, Andrae was a guy with a very serious purpose that had reached 'do or die' proportions. . . . This unchurched generation of teenagers stop to listen to his music, and before they can move on, they have heard his testimony and it's for real."[23]

"When this whole thing started with me, Christian record companies would not even sign an artist unless they saw him minister," remembered Crouch in a 1988 interview. "Light Records was like that. The record company would have to hear the songs and testimony. If the artist wasn't visibly sincere in feelings and heart attitude, then he wasn't signed by the company. So in the late '60s in Christian music, we really wanted our music to say something. There was an evangelistic approach to reach people when we started out."[24]

One of CCM's brightest stars during the 1970s and into the early '80s, Crouch broke down the barrier that had traditionally separated blacks and whites musically, becoming the first "crossover" artist to bring black gospel into white CCM circles. "My father's grandfather was white and Jewish—so was my mother's father," explained Crouch. "There's a lot of white influence in our family, so I had a tremendous outlook on balance and had friends of all colors growing up. That gave me a sensitivity to reaching people of different races with my music."[25]

With that heritage, Crouch was uniquely gifted to bring black gospel to the CCM audience, which he began to do at the dawn of the 1970s. Crouch churned out hit song after hit song in the CCM world and left a legacy of songs that were destined to become hymns, such as "My Tribute," "Through It All," and "The Blood Will Never Lose Its Power."

Of course, endorsements from many of the CCM world's brightest white stars didn't hurt, either, and the fact that a legend like Carmichael was willing to produce Crouch went a long way in reassuring white CCM audiences that Crouch was spiritually "one of them." Endorsements from other white southern gospel stars like Audrey Mieir were displayed prominently on Crouch's records.

> This vibrant, exciting young man cannot be described in a few words. He possesses several rare qualities—all gifts of God used without reservation to witness to the lost. When Andrae sits at the piano, a light turns on from inside. Sometimes, the music is haunting—tugging at the heart. His handsome face glows with inner warmth. The music flows from skillful hands and the message penetrates to the hearts of the listeners. Sometimes the strange pulsating rhythms electrify the audience. One foot beats a hole in the carpet, fingers fly over the keyboard—head, back, face aglow, the mood reaches the listeners. Hands clap, feet must pat and amens must be said! Some songs are exquisite with pathos, others rich in strange harmonies, yet again the whole place "turns on" as the rhythm becomes ecstatic and wild![26]

By the early 1980s, Crouch had left Light and had begun to record for Warner Brothers. In 1982, he encountered his biggest trial yet—one that would leave him alienated from much of the CCM world and cause him to retreat from the gospel world for nearly a decade—when he was arrested on cocaine possession charges. Crouch insisted that the vial belonged to some friends who had been staying at his house, and that the white powder found on the floor of his car was a diet drink powder. The charges were later dropped, but the "Christian" music world had become wary.

> It was the end of a long road for me. I'd felt so rejected by the church for so long—so rejected by people who didn't understand what I was

trying to do with my music—that I'd separated myself from all of it. . . . Then the devil did his number and I thought, *I'm through*. I felt there was no way I'd ever be able to get close to any community of Christians again. . . . At this time, I figured God was just trying to show me something. He had to get me in a position where I was just flat on my back. I remember standing in front of the mirror and telling Him, "God, I've been through hard times with You before. But I cannot handle this one. I can't take this one."[27]

Although Crouch did receive support from much of the CCM community, to others his story was simply too difficult to believe. He spent most of the next ten years in unofficial exile, singing backup for artists like Michael Jackson, Madonna, Diana Ross, and others.

As the memories in the CCM market of Crouch's ordeal faded, he again returned to active recording, signing a seven-year record deal with Quincy Jones's Qwest label. Crouch finally had found a situation that would allow his records to be heard in both the CCM and mainstream markets, and he clearly relished recording for Jones, selecting from among the five hundred songs he had written during his hiatus.

"I just didn't know what songs to put on this record, that's one reason it took so long to put it out," said Crouch at the time. "I like them all, and then I started working on them, and God would give me other ideas. But I'm glad I have that problem."[28]

In 1996, Crouch received the greatest tribute of all from the mostly white CCM establishment—an indication of just how deeply his songs had affected Christian America—when *Tribute—The Songs of Andrae Crouch*, was released, featuring the vocal talents of Michael W. Smith, Bryan Duncan, Twila Paris, Clay Crosse, and others.

"Andrae opened a lot of doors for a lot of people, and he doesn't get enough credit for that," observed Crouch's producer and longtime friend, Bill Maxwell. "He's so respected by the normal music world. Artists like Michael Jackson, Stevie Wonder, and Diana Ross have all called on Andrae to arrange vocals on their records. And that's because they know he's better than they are. He's just extraordinarily gifted."[29]

Although Crouch's musical progeny, artists like BeBe Winans and Kirk Franklin, would succeed in taking their music into the center of pop culture, Crouch for most of his career was relegated to the gospel bin and kept out of wider circulation. Even his current recordings with Qwest are not marketed to the general market with the same push and vigor that a Franklin or Winans album is marketed. Crouch himself has contributed to sidelining his influence by primarily releasing spiritual songs and neglecting to write songs about the nonspiritual aspects of his life—his earthly passions, for example.

Yet, to his credit, Crouch had managed to hold on to his faith in the midst of life's trials and stayed true to the vision that his parents had for him. Mindful of the many pitfalls that had trapped and ultimately destroyed other church-reared young African-American singers like Marvin Gaye and Sam Cooke, his parents once wrote to him, "Son, God has given you many songs that thrill the hearts of people as they hear the message that Jesus loves them. Remember that we love you, but more than that we love the God who gave you to us. He has given you a very special gift, that of being able to communicate His love through music. We pray that you remember that blessings are given so that you may again give to others. Your giving in music will bring a song to many a sad heart, a smile to many a troubled face and hope to many who have lost their way."[30]

Crouch's life in music had answered at least half of that prayer, for although his music was rarely heard by the wider culture, he did manage to hold on to his faith, not an insignificant achievement in a musical world that seemed to delight in turning the faithful against their roots.

Phil Keaggy

To evangelical Christians who populate the subculture, Phil Keaggy is perhaps the greatest symbol of their exile, martyrdom, and continued cultural isolation. Keaggy's musical talents are widely admired in the CCM culture, where he has made his home since 1973, but outside the subculture he is known primarily among musicians who appreciate great guitar playing. Keaggy is regarded by many as among the best of all time, and rumor has it that guitar greats like Jimi Hendrix, Eddie Van Halen, and Ted Nugent have all been fans of his guitar work.

Ted Nugent reportedly wondered aloud what happened to Keaggy, the brilliant artist from Ohio who played with such emotion. Before abruptly "leaving the world," as Christians called their disengagement from the "secular" mainstream, Keaggy had attracted attention for his work with the band Glass Harp. Signed to Decca, Glass Harp, led by the then seventeen-year-old wunderkind Keaggy, toured with bands like the Kinks, Alice Cooper, Traffic, Yes, Iron Butterfly, Grand Funk, and others.

"My formative years were the '60s," recalled Keaggy. "I was very influenced by people like [Eric] Clapton [and] Michael Bloomfield. Joe Walsh was a real inspiration to me. With the kind of guitar things that go on these days, I'm kind of glad I do the old style. As a matter of fact, someone was talking to Steve Lukather [of Toto] and he said, 'Have you ever heard of Phil Keaggy?' He said, 'Yeah, I have. He's from the old school isn't he?'"[31]

Glass Harp was formed in 1970, with Keaggy, John Sferra, and bassist Dan Pecchio. Over the course of the next several years, they recorded three albums, *Glass Harp*, *Synergy*, and *It Makes Me Happy*. Keaggy experienced a conversion shortly after Glass Harp came together, and found his music increasingly turning to spiritual matters by the time *Synergy* was recorded. When his lyrics began to include lines like "the answer is Jesus, believe me he'll open the door," tension within the band began to mount. Keaggy recalled the troubles almost apologetically.

"We all knew there was a place for religion—being raised Catholic—but it was another thing to bring it to the stage. It was obvious we were headed in different directions."[32]

Keaggy soon succumbed to the pressure of other Christians around him and got out of rock, a decision that was made by many of the other early Jesus musicians, and which ultimately led to cultural isolation and separation. "There came a time, quite simply, when my Bible became more important to me than my guitar," recalled Keaggy. "I left because of some internal conviction. I wanted to do what I do completely, 100 percent for the Lord and there were a number of Christians who felt I needed to leave rock and roll."[33]

Deciding to record, instead, for the growing CCM market, Keaggy left the rock world behind. Did he miss his calling? Did he allow the voices of cultural separation to drown out the voice of his Maker? Keaggy recalled wistfully the efforts of one ardent Glass Harp fan named Turley Richards, who urged Keaggy not to abandon his growing position of influence in the rock culture.

"[He] came all the way to New York City . . . to try and talk me out of leaving the band, because of the influence I was having," remembered Keaggy. "But I had to go. I needed a sabbatical."[34]

His "sabbatical" lasted twenty years—or is still going on, depending on one's perspective. In 1993, Epic picked up Keaggy's *Crimson & Blue* CCM record and released it to the pop market with the new title *Blue*, but it was cursed from the start by being tagged as a gospel record and never had much of an impact. The album's lack of commercial success was not only due to its being marginalized as gospel; Keaggy himself seemed to value family time over success and fame and was the first to admit that he was unwilling to do the things necessary to make the record a hit.

"You have to be willing to tour if you want a company like Epic or RCA to really get behind you," he said. "They're not going to promote an album without seeing a lot of blood, sweat, and tears out there on the road. I'm not into spending half the year away from my family. A career and sales aren't that important if it means sacrificing time with my wife and kids. If it stayed this way, I'd be very grateful."[35]

Like many musicians who traveled down the road of ardent Christian faith, Keaggy regretted some of his actions during his early years as a believer, a time he later viewed as one of misguided zeal. Once, Keaggy recalled, after doing a show with Ted Nugent, Nugent had approached him and asked how to play a certain lick Keaggy had used in his set. Ever the dutiful evangelist, Keaggy replied, "I will [show you] if I can tell you about Jesus."[36]

"Today, I'd probably just teach him the lick without placing a condition on it," he said. "I was so full of zeal, so outgoing with my faith, that sometimes I would push it on people." Keaggy learned a deeply spiritual lesson from such episodes. "The Lord really wants us to be more giving of ourselves and let God take care of conversions. God wants us to be available to be there to listen and share what's going on in their lives and maybe something on the guitar—just befriend someone. That's what the Lord did and that's what we ought to do."[37]

Because Phil Keaggy left the ugly world of rock and roll for contemporary "Christian" music, few in the pop music culture have ever heard the pleasant sounds of this amazing guitar player and able vocalist, and never heard Keaggy's thoughtful commentary on abortion in his song "Little Ones," his emotional ode to a Dorothy Stratten figure in "Nobody's Playgirl Now," his loving remembrance of childhood in "A Child in Everyone's Heart," and his sorrowful acknowledgment of his own failings in a stunning cover of Van Morrison's mournful "When Will I Ever Learn to Live in God."

A great man of faith and art was lost to the world—to the detriment of an entire generation of music fans who could have benefited from his music and his faith.

Randy Stonehill

Randy Stonehill was a nice, Jewish-Portuguese kid from the San Francisco suburbs who grew up listening to music and along with Larry Norman practically invented Jesus Rock. "I started singing when I was four," remembered Stonehill. "My mom listened to a lot of folk music—the Weavers, the Kingston Trio, the Limelighters, and others—so I grew up listening to it. I started listening to the Top 40 radio by the time I was eight, and by the time I was ten I was convinced I wanted to play guitar."[38]

Soon Stonehill was listening to Jimi Hendrix, Janis Joplin, and other acts at the Fillmore West nearly every weekend. It was a chance encounter with Larry Norman, however, that set the course for Stonehill's life, both musically and philosophically. Norman recalls that meeting:

> In 1967, my sister told me about this boy who had seen me perform in concert with my band, People, and wanted to meet me. I didn't think much about it until one day I came home to find my sister on the couch and heard someone singing in the other room. I walked into the next room and saw this skinny little high school kid singing 'Bluebird' at the top of his lungs. I joined in on the harmony. That's how I met Randy Stonehill. Although it was a few years before he would become a Christian, he identified with Jesus rock from the time he first heard it. And so, quite suddenly, there seemed to be the two of us.[39]

In 1970, after knocking around in several garage bands, Stonehill moved to Los Angeles at Norman's invitation to realize his own dream of being a rock star. In Hollywood he bumped into more Christians. "I saw something different, something vital in their lives," he remembered, "and when I asked them what it was, they said, 'Jesus, and don't take it from us, you can go talk to Him about it. He's exactly what He claims to be, and He's not afraid to prove it.'"[40]

Like many early CCM artists, Stonehill grew up in a less-than-religious family. His parents, a disillusioned Catholic mother and an equally disillusioned Jewish father, told their son, "Look, we don't really believe in God, but when you feel like you're old enough and you want to go to explore Him or go to church, it's up to you, do what you like."[41]

Stonehill did as he was told and found a path radically different from that of his parents. "I had a pretty textbook case lightning bolt experience in the Holy Spirit," he recalled. "I asked Christ into my life and it was just such a stunning shock to me."[42]

"The Spirit really started to descend on the room and I felt naked in the most permeating way I had ever felt. I couldn't wipe the grin off my face. I heaved a big sigh and a great weight left me. It was a weight I didn't even know I had been carrying. It was a very physical feeling and I think God knew he had to do something really dramatic in my life. I was so used to tactile things—drugs and chasing girls—that God used the approach that if you hit the donkey over the head, you can get the donkey's attention and lead him wherever you want him to go."[43]

Like most artists who write from their life experiences, Stonehill began to write songs about his conversion. "I just naturally started writing about it with the tools I'd been given," he said. "I'd always expressed myself through my music, and now I had something life-changing that I was so excited about sharing."[44]

Norman and Stonehill began playing around Hollywood at coffee houses, church youth groups, and clubs. "Kids . . . were just flocking to our concerts," remembered Stonehill. "They were just hungry for God's life and his truth. But they were hearing it for the first time without all of the cultural baggage that came with walking through the church doors."[45]

Not everybody was flocking, however, and to their surprise the young rockers faced stiff opposition from other Christians. When *Time* and *Newsweek* took notice of the Jesus Music phenomenon, opposition from within Christendom continued to build. "The very people who we thought would support us in the church were really raising an eyebrow at us, saying, 'How dare you cheapen the gospel!' They had seen the damage that rock and roll had done and viewed it like it had a conscience of its own, which it doesn't. It's just a thing. You break it down and it's rhythm and melody and harmonies. God has created it so it can be either used or misused."[46]

In 1970, Stonehill and Norman, low on cash but high on spiritual passion, hit on a plan to finance their respective recordings. They would ask the devout crooner Pat Boone for a loan. They visited Boone's shiny Beverly Hills mansion, sat in the living room, and explained their Jesus Music to the '50s icon. The only thing the perfectly coiffed and outfitted Boone had in common with the hippies was faith, but with the four Boone girls sitting on a nearby sofa staring in stunned silence, their father agreed to give the young rockers several thousand dollars to finance their projects.

"It was so cute," remembered Stonehill of the perfect Boone family. "They would look at us, then they'd look at their dad; then they'd look back at us with our long hair and our patched jeans and they'd look at their dad as if to say, 'Is this what real hippies look like and may we keep them as pets?'"[47]

Stonehill's first sighting of Boone was memorable. "He came in from the backyard swimming pool with his perfect tan and his white swim trunks on and his perfect Pat Boone hair and I thought he was gonna break into 'Aprilllll Luuuuuve.'"[48]

Most importantly, Boone listened and took the hippies seriously. "We talked to him about our vision and the fact that these kids were flocking to our concerts and we wanted to have something that they could take home with them that they could hold up and share with their friends and say, 'See, this says what I'm about,'" remembered Stonehill. "Pat said, 'You know, you guys are reaching a part of the culture that would never listen to me, just like I'm reaching a part of the culture that would never listen to you.'"[49]

After receiving money from Boone, Stonehill and Norman set to work on their records. Stonehill recorded *Born Twice* on an eight-hundred-dollar budget, and Norman spent the rest on *Street Level*. Both began to tour nationally.

"Sporting a hideous black and white screened cover with a photo of Randy just in from the dead zone, Stonehill played covers of acceptable pop/gospel tunes like 'He's Got the Whole World,' along with a few originals," observed critic Thom Granger of Stonehill's first effort. "The songs were decent, the energy was rock and roll, and the total effect was underwhelming but still vital at the time."[50]

In 1973, Stonehill recorded *Get Me Out of Hollywood* released in England on the Phonogram label, but it was his 1976 recording, *Welcome to Paradise*, that is regarded today as one of the greatest records to emerge out of the subculture. "It represented the bohemian Christian artists' dream," noted critic Granger: creative freedom in the studio, a respectable budget, artistic control over the entire project, and national distribution and support from Word Records. It sounded like real rock and roll, with real guitars and drums mixed high enough to hear properly, and a batch of songs so good you would play 'em to your unsaved friends. I think I still would."[51]

Stonehill recorded a number of albums for Myrrh that would catapult him to the head of the CCM class, beginning with *Between the Glory and the Flame*, *Equator*, *Celebrate This Heartbeat*, and *Love Beyond Reason*, a 1985 record that featured a duet with white-hot Amy Grant. Feeling musically restless with the polite but sincere pop records that had taken him to the top of the genre, Stonehill emerged in 1987 with a gritty, streetwise rock record titled *The Wild Frontier*, which came hot on the heels of Word Record's distribution deal with A&M Records. *Frontier* proved to be Stonehill's one open shot at mainstream exposure and it was a solid effort. Much of the credit for the record went to its producer, a guitarist named Dave Perkins, who had paid his dues in the New York club circuit for years, touring with Carole King, Jerry Jeff Walker, and others.

When Stonehill told Perkins that he planned to call his record "The Wild Frontier," Perkins chuckled, "Great title. Now you're going to have to live up to it."[52] He promptly threw out all of Stonehill's songs and encouraged the musician to dig deeper for eight original tunes, which they recorded along with a cover of the Yardbirds' "Get Together."

Thanks to Perkins, Stonehill came to a profound conclusion too often ignored in the safe harbor where CCM was docked, far from the crashing waves that most people found themselves in. "If you want to win hearts," Stonehill said, "as a Christian, as an artist, you've got to have yours on the tape."[53]

Stonehill's heart was definitely on tape, but it was up to A&M to make sure the rock world heard about it. The Word/A&M distribution agreement had been set up primarily to allow Amy Grant to reach the general market-place, and thanks to her brilliant managers, Michael Blanton and Dan Harrell, the arrangement had worked. Grant's 1985 album, *Unguarded*, had landed on the pop charts and produced a smash single, "Find a Way." Whether other Word artists could follow Grant's lead was still a question mark, though several were primed and ready for crossover success.

The Word/A&M deal, like Word's subsequent deal with Epic and other such arrangements, was problematic from the start. CCM, as an explicit genre, was a tough sell to a population trained to distrust informa-tion from explicitly self-identified religious sources. Tagging a musician with the name "CCM artist," "Christian artist," or "gospel artist" usually ensured their irrelevance among a skeptical music establishment that was inbred with a disdain for Christianity.

There was also the tendency of higher-ups at "secular" record labels to make deals without realizing that their underlings were quietly sabotaging CCM records with their friends in the rock press and at radio stations. At A&M, for instance, it was not uncommon when asking about CCM artists to be told, "Oh, that's some gospel music deal we're stuck with. What's really hot this month is Janet Jackson and Sting." To this day, Michael Parkinson, who oversaw the Word/A&M deal as one of A&M's vice presidents, denies that such sabotage ever took place, but those in the trenches knew and the result was that non-Amy Grant CCM records like Stonehill's never had much of a shot.

Ever the realist, Randy Stonehill remembers the A&M experience with just a hint of bitterness. "They did come out, and they did applaud," he said of the A&M executives. "They came backstage and took my picture, but then they went back and got on the phone with Sting. I got polite applause, but when it really came to company muscle, that didn't happen. There was just not enough ground support."[54]

Nevertheless, in his heart, Stonehill carried the deep satisfaction of knowing he had made the record of his career. "I came away saying, 'Well, I made one rock and roll album that was a real return to that facet of what I do—real, passionate, passionate music about a God that I'm passionate about.'"[55]

As one of the fathers of Jesus Rock, Stonehill looked back on the CCM scene that he in part created, and was circumspect and surprisingly in agreement with much of the criticism. "I listen to a lot of Christian radio and much of it sounds like it was produced by the same guy—drum machines and a lot of synth/bell/synth patches," he said in the early 1990s. "In an effort to be accessible and confronting and direct, it's gotten to be this safe, synth, pop stuff."[56]

Although he was encouraged by some of the lyrics, Stonehill nonetheless was disappointed by the music. "There's a lot of stuff that I hear on the radio that I think, 'You know, this is sincere and it's biblically sound, but it just bores me. It doesn't have any edge to it, it doesn't take any chances, there's not enough humanity in it.' It's our responsibility, as we try our best to be artists, to find new and compelling ways to articulate the greatest news you could ever share with anybody, to articulate the wonder of God's love and the incredible rich fabric of the Gospel."[57]

What would Randy Stonehill circa 1971 have thought of the modern CCM scene?

"I would have been disappointed to see that after we have built each other up and established an inner-church network with how to deal with our music, we seem to be hesitant or unable to take these God-given tools and build strong bridges into the mainstream music industry."[58]

Keith Green

Although most Americans have never heard the name Keith Green, he is the closest thing modern American Christian pop culture has to a saint. Green debuted his brand of Jesus music in 1977 with his first CCM album, *For Him Who Has Ears to Hear*. Before he died in a plane crash in July 1982, Green recorded several records and performed hundreds of concerts urging fellow believers to leave behind compromise and sin and live a missions-oriented, holy life.

Although closely identified with CCM, Green was actually one of the first "defectors" who started in pop music before making his way across the cultural divide into CCM shortly after his conversion. He was not the first, but he was certainly among the brightest.

The son of a professional baseball player and a musically inclined mother, Green was reared in the San Fernando Valley suburb of Canoga Park. By the age of five, his musical abilities were already becoming noticeable to his family. By age eight, tougher critics began to take note of the budding young singer. Green's theater debut in Arthur Laurent's *The Time of the Cuckoo* was reviewed favorably by the *Los Angeles Times*, whose critic noted: "Roguish-looking, eight-year-old Keith Green gave a winning portrayal," adding that Green "stole the show."[59]

As the precocious preteen continued to shine on the stage, playing characters like Kurt Von Trapp in a production of *The Sound of Music*, he also began to play nightclubs and added rock and folk songs to his repertoire. He soon came to the attention of several record executives, who saw potential in the curly haired boy with the amazing talent. When Decca Records offered Green's father a five-year contract for Keith, the eleven-year-old wunderkind was on his way to certain superstardom in an era that had not yet heard of preteen sensations like Michael Jackson and Donny Osmond.

Green's signing caused a small stir, not only in kiddie fanzines like *Teen Scene* but in the serious press as well. The *Times* noted of Green: "Keith's first disc will be released in March and one of the many songs he'd written has been published. The name of the song is 'The Way I Used to Be,' which at Green's age doesn't leave much leeway. He's only eleven. Absolutely nothing else can be heard when, with amazing gusto, the husky blond boy starts slamming away at the piano and singing all out in an alto that promises to become a strong baritone."[60]

Green's first song, published by the American Society of Composers, Authors and Publishers (ASCAP), made him the youngest member of the society, and he was soon featured on the *Jack Benny Show*, the *Joey Bishop Show* and Steve Allen's program. *Time* magazine also took note of Green, observing, "Decca Records has a pre-pubescent dreamboat named Keith Green. . . . He has already written fifty rock 'n roll songs, which he croons in a voice trembling with conviction."[61]

So close to superstardom, Green's high hopes for a career as a national teen singing sensation failed to materialize and the mantle of boy wonder was passed to Donny Osmond, who soon burst onto the national stage.

If such setbacks fazed the young performer, he didn't let on, continuing to perform throughout his teens at clubs, bars, and coffee shops, and no doubt hoping for another shot at the big time. Green got a second chance in September 1971, when he signed a contract with Amos Records to record an album he called *Revelations*, but it, too, failed to catch fire.

Green soldiered on, eventually finding himself in the center of the hippie culture, smoking dope, traveling up and down the West Coast, playing music, and searching for spiritual truth. As he studied various religions and spiritual teachers, he became intrigued with the idea of Jesus Christ.

"Even though Keith was turned off by the idea of an organized group, there did seem to be one common thread running through all of the teachings Keith had studied," wrote Green's wife Melody. "That thread was the person of Jesus Christ. Everybody seemed to say that, at the very least, Jesus was a good guy. Some said that he was the Son of God, others that he was an ascended spiritual master—even Buddha thought Jesus was OK. Everyone said something different, but it was all positive. And to top it off, Jesus even said good things about himself. He said he was the only way to God."[62]

Although it would take several more years of spiritual searching and acid dropping before Green would fully come to terms with the decisions he was quietly and gradually making, he noted in his journal on December 16, 1972: "Jesus, you are hereby officially welcomed into me."[63]

As Green's Christian faith deepened, he began to meet like-minded artists like Randy Stonehill, Buck Herring, Kelly Willard, and Phil Keaggy.

Inspired by their bold musical declarations of faith, Green began to write songs for a possible record, but when he shared his desire to sing for non-Christians and not just the home crowd, he was discouraged by prominent Christians, including Herring, the producer of the up-and-coming CCM group Second Chapter of Acts.

"We tried it, brother," said Herring. "Our first contract was with MGM and the secular machinery didn't know what to do with an album full of Christian songs. . . . It won't matter how good your album sounds, a secular label still won't know what to do with it."[64] Green remained unmoved, responding, "I'm not into singing just for Christians."[65]

Green continued to shop his demos around Hollywood to various labels and achieved what he thought was his big breakthrough when Clive Davis, Arista Records' colorful president, asked him to fly to New York for a private audition. The morning of the audition, Davis kept Green waiting for two hours, and when he was finally ushered into Davis's office, the meeting went uneventfully. For Green, who had spent a lifetime chasing a record deal, being considered and turned down by the most powerful man in the music business was a sign from God. Perhaps others, later, would reach out to the culture and sing for nonbelievers, but Green turned his energy toward fulfilling what became his unique calling: challenging fellow believers to live as true Christians.

"Mostly he was wondering what God might want him to say to all these Christians," remembered Melody Green. "We'd seen some glaring inconsistencies. A lot of people were going to church and to Christian concerts, but not many of them seemed really excited about Jesus. Keith wondered how God felt about that."[66]

The lyrics of a song he had recently completed with Randy Stonehill seemed to confirm his decision. "Your Love Broke Through," turned out to be Green's signature song, propelling him and his debut record *For Him Who Has Ears to Hear* to the top of the CCM charts. It opened with the lines: "Like a foolish dreamer trying to build a highway to the sky, all my hopes would come crumbling down and I never knew just why, until today when you pulled away the clouds that hung like curtains on my eyes, I've been blind all these wasted years and I thought I was so wise, then you took me by surprise."[67]

For Him Who Has Ears to Hear arrived in Christian bookstores in the summer of 1977, and Green began to tour the country in support of it. Far from being a typical CCM record—deep on theology and light on humor or earthly love—*Ears* was actually a well-rounded record that could be whimsical at one moment, with songs like "The Devil's Boast"; inspirational at another, with "Your Love Broke Through"; and confessional and very down to earth, with "I Only Want to See You There," a song Green wrote to his parents in which he admitted to being "so full of pride."

Sparrow Records hungrily anticipated record number two, and Green set about finding his place in the CCM market. His role was to be a prophet sent to tell Christians that their God was not pleased. It was a role Green was well suited for temperamentally and carried out masterfully.

Calling the record *No Compromise*, Green set about to challenge his new Christian family with songs like "Asleep in the Light," and "To Obey Is Better Than Sacrifice." The new album was confrontational, almost accusatory in its attitude toward fellow believers, and Green's lyrics were fighting words for fans used to hearing soft and groovy affirmations of faith.

"Keith's idea was to shake Christians awake from the comfortable slumber we'd seen," recalled Melody Green of his second album. "Even the artwork was going to reflect the 'no compromise' theme—one man standing up in the midst of a crowd that was bowing to an earthly king who obviously wanted to be worshipped. One of the guards was angrily pointing at the lone man with a look that said, 'You've had it.' The picture reminded you of Daniel in Babylon."[68]

Though not as wildly popular as his first record, *No Compromise* quickly established Green as CCM's premiere artist and prophet.

Green was an unusual man of solid principle, who quickly began to question the "Christian" music system, specifically the way artists charged for concerts and records. First, he decided not to charge money for concerts, then to offer his records to the public for whatever the buyer could afford to pay. There was one small problem: Green was still signed to Sparrow Records, which was *not* in business to give away records.

"Keith was never one to beat around the bush," recounted Melody Green of the conversation that took place between her husband and the man who had signed him, Billy Ray Hearn, at Hearn's spacious home. "He said, 'I need to ask you to let me out of my contract. . . . I blew it. God just told me to start my own label and give my records away. I'm really sorry. I don't know what to do. I know I signed a contract and I'll honor it if I need to. But I'm asking you to release me from it. I'm not going to another company. I'm starting my own. I won't even be selling my records in the bookstores.'"[69]

"If God doesn't want you at Sparrow, and I try to keep you, then I'd be fighting against God," Melody Green remembered Hearn responding. "That means God will be standing against me and the whole company. Keith, if you want to be released from your contract, I will not hold you to it. I'll let you go."[70]

The Greens mortgaged their home to pay for the production of a record called *So You Wanna Go Back to Egypt*, released on their own label, Pretty Good Records. Incredibly, as promised, the albums were offered for whatever the buyer could afford.

On *Egypt*, Green took a slight step back from the condemning tone that had characterized *No Compromise*, but it too had its unsettling moments for the complacent believer, on such songs as "You Love the World (But You're Avoiding Me)." For Green, who often seemed to lack a basic element of the Christian faith called grace, *Egypt* became the record that balanced out some of the attack songs with a touch of human and divine compassion. Green even titled one track "Grace by Which I Stand" and surrounded it with other introspective songs like "I Want to Be More Like Jesus" and "Pledge My Head to Heaven," a song on which Green was joined by a recent friend, Bob Dylan, on harmonica.

Predictably, Green's new pricing policy was a hit with his fans but a disaster for the bottom line as unscrupulous concert goers made mad dashes for the back table, scooping up records by the armload. Green amended the policy, allowing one album per household, but still with the provision that buyers should pay according to what they could afford. The pricing episode was vintage Green, an idealist who sometimes didn't stop to think about the wisdom of decisions on which he was sure he had heard from God.

As he prepared for what would prove to be his final studio album, *Songs for the Shepherd*, Green seemed to sense that his time was short. Taking an inspirational song that Melody had written five years earlier, "There Is a Redeemer," Green added a new verse that his wife thought odd: "When I stand in glory, I will see his face. There, I'll serve my King forever, in that holy place."[71]

"I liked it," said Melody Green, "but the verse seemed slightly out of place with the rest of the song. It even seemed a little odd that Keith took the song in that direction, going from thanking God to meeting Him face-to-face."[72]

As he sang the song, Green was often brought to tears. Within months, he would be gone—lost in a tragic small plane accident that also took the lives of two of his young children.

What remained of Green's message after his untimely death was a powerful brand of Christianity that challenged believers to a deeper walk with their God, urging them not to compromise their principles and beliefs under any circumstances. Unlike most CCM stars, Green's decision to record in that market was difficult to question because of the clarity of his calling and the obvious reluctance with which he acceded to it. Like the prophets of old, Green would challenge God's people. Yet for far too many Christians, Green's decision to sing in the subculture became an excuse for them to hang out in the mess hall where life was comfortable and the food was good, forsaking the battlefield. It was a legacy Green would no doubt wish were different.

DeGarmo and Key

Among those who shared an "us v. them" mentality that pervaded the CCM world and ensured its continued irrelevance to the wider culture were Eddie DeGarmo and Dana Key, who formed one of CCM's first legitimate rock bands, DeGarmo and Key. While artists like Keith Green desperately wanted a mainstream deal, DeGarmo and Key seemed content with their refusal to sing to the unsaved on their turf.

Childhood buddies, who grew up in Memphis in the shadow of Elvis, DeGarmo and Key formed their first band, The Sound Corporation, in the sixth grade.

"Everybody in Memphis wanted to be a musician," remembered Key, a distant relative of another famous American songwriter, Francis Scott Key. "There was this huge mansion set in the midst of our little middle-class neighborhood. Elvis was obviously our most successful citizen. Music was to us what basketball might be to some inner-city kids: a way of becoming affluent and successful immediately. We'd see the pink Cadillacs and other signs of extravagance. Also, Elvis was more accessible then. You could go sit on his fence and he would ride his horse out and talk to you."[73]

They formed a band in high school called Globe, and signed a five-record deal with Hi Records, a subsidiary of London Records, home to the Rolling Stones and the Moody Blues.

One weekend in 1972, the band collapsed when Eddie DeGarmo was invited by his brother to watch a concert by the early CCM crooner Dallas Holm. Responding to an altar call, DeGarmo was converted. "Dana, you're not going to believe what happened to me. I found Jesus," said DeGarmo across the crowded hallway at school the next day. "I didn't know he was missing," replied Key before insisting that the discussion take place in a janitor's closet so that none of their friends would hear the religious nonsense.[74]

When Key followed DeGarmo into the Christian faith, they immediately decided they had to leave the band—not an easy decision for a couple of guys who had spent their formative years walking past Graceland and dreaming their own rock and roll dreams. But they were convinced that their newfound faith was incompatible with their less-than-spiritual songs, and the record business seemed scary. The words of one London Records executive frightened Dana Key.

"What he said was, 'You know, if we decide to manufacture a star, we can manufacture a star.' And he started giving me examples! I was very disappointed by that. I had believed people were successful because they were really good. Also, I was now close enough to the secular music industry to see that there were some real low-lifes in the business. That was disillusioning."[75]

Initially, at least, DeGarmo and Key didn't see themselves getting back into music. "When I became a Christian, I didn't see any future playing Christian music," remembered Key. "I did want to communicate my faith, so I went through the Youth for Christ internship program and got on staff full time. In fact, Youth for Christ gave Eddie and me both jobs so we had a little bit of income; we were with them for a little over four years."[76]

When a friend played Larry Norman's "Only Visiting This Planet" for the duo, Key began to change his mind about music. "This is great, Eddie," he remembered telling his partner. "This is what *we* need to do."[77]

Though they had walked away from what was a clear shot at stardom, the duo pursued and were turned down by every Christian label, including Larry Norman's Solid Rock. Norman, who had pioneered the concept of speaking the message of Christ to the culture without being preachy found DeGarmo and Key's style not to his liking. "Larry said our lyrics were too didactic," said Key. "We had to look *didactic* up in the dictionary."[78]

"Inclined to teach or moralize excessively" would correctly define DeGarmo and Key's work for years, and though Norman was not in the business of "excessively moralizing," the duo found a supporter in Pat Boone and his Lamb and Lion label.

Over the years, they became the premiere CCM rock ensemble, next to superstars Petra, releasing albums like *Straight On* and *This Ain't Hollywood* for Pat Boone before moving on to the Benson imprint, Power Disks, where they eventually enjoyed their fifteen minutes of fame when MTV refused to air their groundbreaking video for their single "666"—ironically enough, because of its violent content. When the burning Antichrist figure was edited out, MTV did briefly play the video.

What troubled some observers was DeGarmo and Key's penchant for citing persecution stories to justify their decisions to reject various offers from the mainstream music culture. "We were offered a major contract just a couple of years ago," said DeGarmo in a 1989 interview, "and a tour with one of the top bands in the world. There's no reason to say who that is, but they all have long beards, and the only string was, 'Guys, why do you have to talk about Jesus—is that necessary?'"[79]

"Their manager thought our band was wonderful," added Key, "and he wanted us to tour with them provided we not talk about Jesus and we not talk about sin. He didn't think his audiences wanted to hear about Jesus or sin, and he's absolutely right. Jesus made it real clear that if the world doesn't love him and we love him, then the world won't love us either. Singing about Christ and sin is going to hurt you commercially. We had to pass on that opportunity."[80]

Of course it's only natural that ZZ Top wouldn't want proselytizing at concerts, and it was a perfectly reasonable request to ask DeGarmo and Key to just do their music (since they were musicians, trained to communicate through their music) and not launch into protracted sermons at a rock concert. In fact, had the reverse been true—had ZZ Top been opening for DeGarmo and Key—it would have been equally reasonable for DeGarmo and Key to ask ZZ Top not to make statements they disagreed with to their audience. Such is the nature of give and take in the real world, where principled and strategic compromises are a part of daily life.

Key did not agree. "That wasn't my calling nor of D&K," he said. "We were called to ministry first and music secondarily. We used music as a vehicle to get in front of crowds."[81]

Unfortunately for millions of unbelieving fans who could have been affected by their music, DeGarmo and Key chose to perform primarily for fellow believers.

DeGarmo and Key also had problems cooperating with fellow CCM artists as well. "[We] never really built our career opening for other acts," said Key. "We did one tour with Petra and one tour with Servant, both of which helped establish us with a national audience. But we were so pigheaded; we wanted to do it our way. We wanted to give an invitation every night and you can't if you're the opening act."[82]

As invitation after invitation poured in, DeGarmo and Key continued to turn down offers to sing in the middle of the rock culture. "Another time I can remember is after the album *Straight On* came out," said DeGarmo. "Mercury Records offered us a recording contract to do a secular album. . . . It's always the same story. . . . They always come out and see the band and love what we do with the exception of Christ. And I can understand that. Jesus himself said, 'Hey guys, don't worry when this world doesn't like you 'cause they didn't like me either.'"[83]

DeGarmo and Key developed a clear view of what it meant for them to be uncompromising believers, and they remained skeptical and critical of those who sought to cross over into mainstream music.

"It irks me when people use the Christian music industry as a stepping stone to get into secular music,"[84] said Eddie DeGarmo, who must have been especially irked a few years later when dc Talk, one of the bands signed to his record label Forefront, moved on to Virgin Records after five albums in the CCM market.

"I wish that those who aspire to go on to the 'big leagues' would just go on," added Dana Key. "They're just embarrassing us all."[85]

What DeGarmo and Key had in mind was the advancement of a genre of music known as Christian contemporary music. "Our goal is not to be on a secular label," admitted Key. "We've had that opportunity. Last year, three companies approached us and it really caused us to evaluate what we were doing. We saw that we'd gotten where we were by slowly chipping away, by being consistent. . . . The way we're going to crack the secular market is not by playing their game, but by getting so big that they can't ignore us anymore. Let's face it, the world doesn't like Jesus, He tells us that over and over, and I'm finally starting to get it through my head."[86]

DeGarmo concurred. "We decided we liked being a Christian band," he said. "Last year more than three thousand people came to Christ at our concerts. We're growing by leaps and bounds. Christians are bringing their unsaved friends and that's really how we reach most people. The seeds are planted and we come in and harvest. That's what we're getting known for. When that happens, you don't mind making sacrifices."[87]

Although many within Christian circles have bemoaned the CCM sub-culture, DeGarmo and Key celebrated it. "It's much more organized. There's real radio, a concern about quality, and a sense that we're getting the message across," enthused Key. "There have always been people who want to hear what we're saying. It's just been a question of getting it to them."[88]

DeGarmo and Key's most fundamental misunderstanding was their notion that in order to evangelize the "lost" they must not compromise their methods in any way, and that they could somehow reach their target audi-ence by shouting loud enough from within the CCM subculture rather than bothering to go to the other side where their potential audience actually lives.

"It's all a matter of what you're called to do," maintained DeGarmo. "We've always felt we were called to win kids to Jesus Christ. That's our mis-sion. That's our goal. There are a lot of people out there who are called to make great music and entertain people, and I'm not arguing that. But evan-gelism is our original mission. And as long as we keep winning kids to Christ, I know we're in the Lord's will."[89]

Key compounded the misunderstanding when he produced a song in response to Eric Clapton's "Tears in Heaven," called "Dear Mr. Clapton," which he recorded on a solo album released in the CCM market. It was a stunningly beautiful song that began, "Dear Mr. Clapton, I have heard of your loss."[90]

The only problem was that, as much as he might have thought himself part of a larger dialogue, his song was never heard outside the subculture because it was released on Ardent, his CCM label, and distributed by DeGarmo's Forefront into the CCM market. Key's beautiful response to Clapton was fundamentally irrelevant, to the great loss of the culture and to Clapton himself.

For the hundreds, perhaps thousands, of unbelievers who somehow found out about a DeGarmo and Key concert, made their way across the cultural divide, entered the land of CCM, and heard the message of DeGarmo and Key, their concerts no doubt became a life-changing experi-ence. However, in choosing ideology over people, DeGarmo and Key

severely limited the impact they might have had on the culture had they continued with Globe and become a top-selling band.

As their time as DeGarmo and Key came to an end, Dana Key
remained blissfully unaware of the music culture around him.

> The only time I listen to secular music is when I'm doing research
> for my book, and I think it is important to see what the enemy is say-
> ing. People ask me when I say stuff like that, "Do you think all sec-
> ular music is wrong?" I don't think all of it is wrong, I just think 99
> percent of it is. You can go to the secular store and find a song here
> and a song there that is consistent with biblical principles, but you
> can't find many. I bought Spin Doctors and R.E.M., because I sur-
> veyed a couple of Southern Baptist churches in Memphis, including
> my own church, and found out what the Christian kids were pri-
> marily listening to, and I wanted to see if I could discern what their
> philosophy of life was. And I was disappointed.[91]

That disappointment led Key to become an author, penning *Don't Stop
the Music*, which he described as a book in which "I'll be analyzing R.E.M.
and Spin Doctors and whoever. You've got to be real careful when you get
to that section of the book, because by the time you get it published they'll
be saying, 'R.E.M. who?' There'll be some other disgusting group to take
their place, but the principles remain pretty much the same. There's certain
philosophies of life in secular music that are consistent. They are diametrically opposed to the teachings of Christ. Fundamental Satanism can be
summed up in two words: 'My will' or 'I will.' Fundamental Christianity can
be summed up in two words: 'Thy Will.'"[92]

Looking back on his long career in CCM, Key had few regrets. "I think
our main contribution through the years is that we've been consistent and
we have been faithful to our calling," he said. "When I go to bed at night, I
have a deep satisfaction that I've accomplished what God wants me to. I
think to be able to accomplish your ministry goals and still pay your bills is
great."[93]

As Key and DeGarmo made the transition from artists to record label
owners, they began to see their roles change, and Key in particular was less
dogmatic about some of his earlier pronouncements. "Look, this is not persecution," he laughed in a 1998 interview. "I have friends who are in Zaire
and they experience persecution. . . . If we were more like Jesus was when he
was talking to the woman at the well, we would be better received by this
culture."[94]

Still, Key remained convinced that artists who were Christians could
only go so far in pop music. "I think that Stryper was well accepted until they

convinced people they were serious about what they believed," he said. "Certain spiritual concepts can't cross over. Talk about God, talk about love—no problem. Talk about Jesus, his death, sin, . . . those concepts are very offensive. The cross is still a stumbling block. The mainstream rejects music that is straightforward Christian. . . . It's really a fear about the unknown, about Christ."[95]

Looking to the future, Key still hoped for a change. "I'd like to see this industry reformed," he said. "I agree with some of the writings of Franky Schaeffer and his father. I think the church should sponsor art and pay artists, because God's the ultimate artist."[96]

While maintaining many of the earlier views that kept DeGarmo and Key from penetrating popular music, Key had matured enough to know that the decisions he had made were not right for everybody. "I don't want anybody to follow in our footsteps," he said. "I wouldn't want to impose that on anyone else. We prayed about all of those [decisions]. All of our decisions are not to be applied to other artists. They shouldn't have to live with the restrictions we had."[97]

THREE

The Defectors

*H*ad the CCM market simply diverted emerging young artists from the popular music culture, the situation would have been bad enough. But the "Christian" labels added insult to injury by also dragging away from the primary culture the few successful artists who had become Christians. Soon after their conversions, many rock musicians were coaxed into the backwater of CCM by the pseudospiritual entreaty to "sing for the Lord."

B. J. Thomas, the '70s star who sang the hit "Raindrops Keep Falling on My Head," signed with Myrrh and released a pleasant record called *Home Where I Belong* to a giddy Christian market in search of musical legitimacy. Other albums produced for and marketed to the religious subculture emerged from such stars as Mark Farner of Grand Funk Railroad, Joe English of Paul McCartney's Wings, Barry McGuire of the New Christy Minstrels, Leon Patillo of Santana, Richie Furay of Poco and Buffalo Springfield, Dan Peek of America, Rick Cua of the Outlaws, Philip Bailey of Earth Wind and Fire, Dion, Al Green, and many others.

Unfortunately it quickly became apparent that these artists were proclaiming their faith exclusively to fellow believers. For the most part, non-Christians continued to make music for the culture at large while believers made music for the subculture.

As these artists and others left behind their "secular careers" and "secular fans," they were too often discouraged from singing about topics that were not directly related to their conversion experiences or subsequent spiritual triumphs. They were told to get out of rock and roll because it was a nasty place. They did, and in the eyes of many cultural critics, it really became a nasty place.

Pat Boone

Most such artists "defected" *after* their conversions, but a young crooner from Tennessee named Pat Boone was the exception; his religious commitment predating his superstardom. In the mid-1950s, he began serving up pop classics like "April Love" and "Loveletters in the Sand" to the delight of millions of fans around the world.

Once upon a time, Boone was Elvis's chief competitor for the hearts of fans across the country—and the competition was fierce but friendly. In 1956 *Collier's* picked up on the rivalry and ran a cover story with the headline "Rock and Roll Battle: Boone v. Presley."[1]

> I first met Elvis in Cleveland, Ohio. He was not known nationally at all—it was before "Heartbreak Hotel," before "Hound Dog"—but I'd seen his name on some jukeboxes in Texas and made note of the name. Now here comes Elvis, his collar's turned up—this was backstage— lots of hair hanging down in his face. We shook hands. I said, "Hello, Elvis, Bill Randall says you're going to be a big star." "Well, thank you very much," he just mumbled and looked up at me . . . stayed back against the wall, and I thought, *This guy is hopelessly shy. How can he possibly perform? This is going to be a disaster.* Thank God, I had two hit records then, and I was the star that night. Of course, I never followed Elvis again in any show, . . . because a person would have been a fool to go on after Elvis.[2]

Boone cherished the rivalry and acknowledged that it ultimately helped his career. "I had only a six- or eight-month head start on him," he recalled, "and we rode into the national limelight together. We were both from Tennessee; we were both from lower-middle-class economic backgrounds; we both grew up in church. But there the similarities stopped. I was salt and he was pepper. I was a conformist and he was a rebel. We seesawed up and down the record charts, bumping each other out of the number one spot time and again."[3]

It was a competition that eventually extended to films as well. "[We] launched our movie careers at just about the same time," Boone said, "and our fan clubs reached mammoth proportions simultaneously. As a result, every fan magazine in America ran contests: 'Who's your favorite? Elvis or

Pat?' The circulation of all the magazines soared. . . . Sometimes I'd win, but usually Elvis did. I have no doubt that my being in sharp contrast to Elvis actually helped my career."[4]

Born Charles Eugene Boone in Jacksonville, Florida, on June 1, 1934, he was the eldest child of Archie and Margaret Boone and a descendent of the American pioneer Daniel Boone. While still a baby, the family moved to Nashville, where his childhood became a storybook existence. By his senior year in high school, he had been elected class president, newspaper editor, and captain of the baseball team, and with his singing ability had won several talent contests. He capped off his meteoric teen years by eloping with Shirley Foley, the high school homecoming queen and daughter of country music legend Red Foley, and parlayed his talent show victories into bigger music wins on the nationally televised *Ted Mack Amateur Hour* and Arthur Godfrey's talent show. Boone eventually signed with Dot Records, recording his first hit song, "Two Hearts, Two Kisses," and later covering a Fats Domino tune, "Ain't That a Shame."

By the time he graduated magna cum laude from Columbia University, Boone was prominent enough to appear on the cover of *TV Guide* in cap and gown. Between 1955 and 1969, he compiled a string of fifty-eight tunes that hit the Hot 100, including five number ones.

Boone's carefully cultivated clean image endeared him to the conservative American culture that dominated the 1950s and led to the *Collier's* story comparing him with Elvis. According to Davin Seay and Mary Neely in their book *Stairway to Heaven*, two photos that accompanied the *Collier's* article aptly illustrated the images of both young singers. "The first captured Elvis reclining on a motel room bed, leering at a dew-eyed fan who'd won a date with the star. It was contrasted with a shot of Boone, exuding wholesomeness as he romped in his modest living room with his infant daughter, Debby, one of four button-cute Boonettes."[5]

Although Boone maintained the facade of a happy, Christian home, aspects of his life were far from wholesome and more like the image associated with Presley. "I have not batted 1000," said the former high school baseball star. "I don't know what my average is, because I've made mistakes and I've struck out sometimes. There was a time where I began to take [success] for granted and also felt my wife didn't appreciate me as much as she should, and so there were times when I made mistakes with the young ladies that were around. . . . Though we've lived past all of that and our marriage survived, I would avoid those mistakes, because they nearly cost me everything that was really important to me: my family, my children, my reputation. Those things are more important than any material things."[6]

By 1972, as a result of a hippie culture that would no longer tolerate a figure like Pat Boone, or perhaps because of the promise of further success held out by the CCM movement, Boone had retreated, forming his own label, Lamb and Lion Records, and later signing up artists like DeGarmo and Key and Gary Chapman.

Boone didn't fit the profile of the rest of the defectors—that of a wild and raucous rock star who converted and then disappeared into the subculture—because he had always been a believer and he didn't willingly disappear into CCM, but was exiled there by a culture that was no longer interested in his music or him.

"Pat was always looking to record in the mainstream market," maintained Boone's longtime assistant, Charlie Shaw. "He would have recorded with anybody, but nobody was interested. It was a general rejection of him and his work."[7]

Throughout the '70s and '80s, Boone continued to make records for his label, which was distributed by the Benson Company, but in the mid-'90s something snapped in the sixty-two-year-old crooner's mind. Whether he suddenly realized his own mortality or felt belated regrets for having vacated his position in the pop music world, a reinvigorated Boone decided to put his career—what was left of it—on the line with a project that shocked everybody, including his wife.

"My musicians, young guys, were saying, 'Pat, you've made so many records, let's go into a studio and make something together,'" said Boone. "And I said, 'Fellas, I've done country albums, I've done rock and roll, I've done movie themes, I've done gospel, I've done patriotic, folk—I mean, what else is there to do?' And one of them said, 'You never did any heavy metal.'"[8]

Intrigued, Boone began to research a genre that the Christian community—of which he was virtually the patron saint—had railed against for years, looking for songs he could cover. "I went through hundreds of heavy metal CDs until I was nearly deaf myself and my wife thought I was crazy, because she would see these pictures on the CDs of these demons, and KISS and Meatloaf coming up out of a grave, and all of these bizarre pictures and imagery," laughed Boone.[9]

After narrowing the list down, first to twenty and then thirteen tracks, Boone eventually settled on a selection of rock songs that in no way contradicted his beliefs but were known in rock and heavy metal circles as standards. Boone recorded songs like "Paradise City" by Guns 'n' Roses, Led Zeppelin's "Stairway to Heaven," and Metallica's "Enter Sandman," and brought in a cast of equally unlikely musicians to back him up.

"Ritchie Blackmore of Deep Purple played guitar on his song 'Smoke on the Water.' . . . So did Dweezil Zappa. . . . He came to our recording session, played a Jimi Hendrix guitar. Sheila E., of course, was with Prince for years, and she does bongos and percussion, along with Lenny Castro, on the Van Halen song 'Panama'; and on the Dio song, 'Holy Diver,' Ronnie James Dio himself sings with me."[10]

The record hit the charts and did respectable business, despite the initial catcalls from critics who never liked Boone to begin with. But when he playfully donned leather biker gear and presented an award at the American Music Awards, with fellow believer and shock rocker Alice Cooper, the backlash from the Christian community extended far and wide.

Boone's variety show, *Gospel Gold*, was dropped from the lineup on Paul and Jan Crouch's Trinity Broadcasting Network, and Cal Thomas, a former vice president of Jerry Falwell's Moral Majority, used his *Los Angeles Times* Syndicate column to denounce the move. "Which is the more offensive image," raged Thomas, "Pat Boone in a modified heavy metal outfit, or some overweight religious TV hosts who sit on overstuffed couches, with makeup so thick it resembles a death mask, and tacky sets that mimic the interior of Graceland? Boone demonstrated uncommon Christian charity in his response to the show's cancellation. He said he had judged the harder rockers without even listening to their music or trying to understand them as human beings with value."[11]

Of the cancellation, Thomas wrote, "It keeps the money flowing—from those who prefer their little corner of the world and its presumed safety to some TV evangelists who have entourages, ride in big limousines, live in fancy houses, and have little or no accountability. For them to ride on an ass would be redundant."[12]

For Boone, the judgment made by some Christians condemning him for his decision to wear outlandish costumes and record heavy metal songs only heightened his own need to offer mea culpas for the attitudes he himself had held as an influential member of the Christian subculture.

> Now the shoe, or the biker's boot, is on the other foot, and I've been identified in the minds of millions of people as another one of those metal scourges and scumbags, and I'm being judged in the same way that I judged. And I deserve it. Christians have got to deal with this judgmental, self-righteous, opinionated attitude that if somebody doesn't dress like we dress or doesn't like the same music, or maybe rides a Harley-Davidson, they must be heathens. [The] mind-set [that says], "We don't want to have anything to do with you or anything like you," is a turnoff to the very people we'd like to reach.

They see us as uptight, straitlaced, judgmental prudes and don't want anything we have to offer; and we're looking down our noses at them, thinking we sure don't want what they have to offer. Well, how in the world are people ever going to communicate when they judge each other that way?[13]

Dion

One of the biggest stars of the burgeoning rock scene of the 1950s, Dion Dimucci was propelled to stardom along with his band, the Belmonts, with hits like "The Wanderer," "Runaround Sue," "Teenager in Love," and "Donna."

A Bronx native, Dimucci embraced the Christian faith in the late '70s, whereupon he turned his back on his pop music career and signed with Word Records, with whom he released several albums, including the gospel Grammy-nominated "I Put Away My Idols."

Dion's parents were first generation Italian-Americans, and his father was a puppeteer who played "on the fringes of the old vaudeville scene, the Catskills, and the gilded movie palaces in Brooklyn and the Bronx."[14]

Two things stood out in Dimucci's memory of his early years—food and religion. One was important to all of his extended family members, and the other primarily to his grandparents. "The old folks, the ones who had come over on the boat, maybe they still knew what it was like to have religion, to pray and believe they were being heard," remembered the singer. "Their God was the one who brought the rain, the grape on the vine, and the harvest in its time. They had a faith that was tied to the earth and the seasons, but in the middle of that city, where only concrete and steel and brownstone brick broke the horizon, the old ways were passing slowly away. It was a new age in a new country where Frank and Maria and the other old timers held on to their traditions of drinking and the church, for dear life."[15]

It was a religion that Dion didn't quite understand. "I never found God in that high arched ceiling," he observed. "But maybe I wasn't really looking. God was a million miles away . . . somewhere up above those stained glass windows. The priests and nuns could give you the fear of God, all right, and the guilt that came from not following the rules, but they couldn't breathe life into the words and rituals."[16]

Radio quickly took the place of the church as the source of music in the youngster's life, and it introduced him to musicians like Hank Williams Jr.

It wasn't long before Dion's own career in music began. Hooking up with neighborhood buddies Carlo Mastrangelo, Fred Milano, and Angelo D'Aleo, Dion formed a neighborhood group known as the Belmonts and soon cut what would become his first major single, "I Wonder Why."

It was the beginning of a string of hits that would mesmerize fans and critics alike. "The first of these was 'I Wonder Why,' which matched the Belmonts' rousing group harmony support with Dimucci's soaring vocals, creating one of the decade's finest singles," gushed the *Rolling Stone Album Guide.* "It remains energizing to this day."[17]

Dion stayed with the Belmonts for three years and continued to churn out hits like "Why Must I Be a Teenager in Love?" released in 1959 on the group's debut full-length album, *Presenting Dion and the Belmonts.* The song defined the young singer and helped to launch an even brighter solo career. Success also brought money—and problems.

Dimucci had a drug problem and was unable to keep the secret to himself. When management learned of it, the twenty-one-year-old budding superstar was checked into a drug rehabilitation hospital called the Institute for Living, in Hartford, Connecticut.

It was a solution that proved to be temporary. "Weeks passed in a kind of haze before the guys in the white coats finally pronounced me cured," he remembered. "I walked out of the institute clean for the first time in years. Inside of a week, I was polluted again, making up for lost time and back into the whirlwind that was waiting for me. . . . Nothing had changed, except some part of me deep inside grew a little colder, a little more alone."[18]

Dimucci's solo career continued to progress in spite of his drug problems as he recorded the hits "Lonely Teenager" and "Runaround Sue," the biggest song of his career, which, according to one critic, "unleashed the persona that had only been suggested in his work with the Belmonts."[19]

"By 1964, I was using every day, mainlining smack and dabbling in amphetamines, doing lots of grass, lots of wine," remembered Dimucci. "I'd cycled in and out of heavy heroin use since I was a teenager, each year surrendering a little more of my will and self-esteem, each year finding reality a little harder to face. Then one day there just wasn't any more reality."[20]

Dimucci's slide into the depths of despair left him contemplating one way out. "I became convinced that there was nothing left for me and no way out but the grave," he said. "I decided to commit suicide." As he prepared to kill himself, he accompanied it with a desperate plea: "God help me."[21]

"Sodden with rage and misery, I walked out of the house, settled on killing myself by driving my car over the bridge—but the car was gone," he remembered. "Somebody had borrowed it; stolen it maybe. I had no idea what had happened, no memory of handing over the keys. I couldn't drive off the bridge, so I started walking down Route 92 toward town."[22]

As he walked, he felt his sanity return, and with it an overwhelming presence of peace enveloped his body, accompanied by a voice that spoke to the tortured singer's soul. "'Accept, receive, let go,' the Presence said. 'Let it happen.' And like the smell of a flower, like the smile on a kid, like a day when clouds as big as sailing ships skip across the skyline—a miracle—that's what I did. I let go. And when I did, the falling finally stopped. I landed, not crushed and broken, but safe in someone's arms."[23]

Though Dion's dramatic and narrow escape from self-destruction sounds much like a traditional conversion story, it wasn't—at least not the dramatic conversion story twentieth-century America has become accustomed to. "For me, healing, real healing was slow in coming," said Dion. "And when it did, it wasn't all at once, like some cosmic cure-all. It was one day at a time. . . . The warm glow of that night in Nyack would quickly fade, leaving all the dull aches behind. Nothing—no mystic moment under the stars, no voice in my head or pat on my back was going to soothe away a lifetime of sincere self-destruction. God wasn't waving any magic wands."[24]

As Dimucci descended again into a pit of drugs and despair that soon landed him back in treatment, this time at Mount Sinai Hospital, he began to see a ray of hope in the form of his father-in-law, Jack, himself a recovering alcoholic. When Jack's son died of alcoholic convulsions, Dion again received a warning that he was headed down a dangerous road. Traveling with his father-in-law to claim the body, the singer once again reached out to the unseen God.

"Something was consecrated that night in a Baltimore hotel room, April 1, 1968," he later remembered. "I bowed my head and bent my knee and begged for help. I said good-bye to drinking and drugs and all the devouring needs they fed—forever. A power much greater than I'd ever be— a power that had first been shown to me that night in Nyack—had just released me from the obsession for drinking and drugs. Such a joy welled up inside when I realized that I was finally free, when I knew this was something I wasn't fixing up on my own. . . . It was His mercy that released me from that stale captivity, not my frantic scheming."[25]

In 1968, Dion reactivated his stalled career with the release of the song "Abraham, Martin, and John," a folk music tribute to the slain leaders Abraham Lincoln, Martin Luther King Jr., and John F. Kennedy. In the late '60s and early '70s, he came back strong with several rock-tinged albums and a single about the dangers of drug abuse, called "Clean Up Your Own Backyard." Eventually he reunited with the Belmonts for a time, releasing *Reunion: Dion and the Belmonts*. Dimucci subsequently recorded two more solo albums, *Streetheart* (1976) and *Return of the Wanderer* (1978), but his audience was growing smaller and smaller.

"A single, 'I Used to Be a Brooklyn Dodger,' is one of Dion's most poignant vocals," observed one critic, "finding him looking back in fondness and in sorrow at his younger life and what he had lost over time."[26]

Off drugs and into exercise, by 1979 Dimucci had taken up jogging and was the father of three daughters and husband to a loving wife, who had stayed by his side through all the highs and lows. Still, he was vaguely dissatisfied. Perhaps a mid-life crisis, he thought. One morning, as he jogged near his home, Dimucci prayed for a closer walk with his God.

"Before the words were out of my mouth, a tremendous white light broke all around me, radiating out from my chest and streaming through every pore," he remembered. "I kept running, but it seemed like I was on air. It was a light so sudden, so brilliant, so profound that it just washed away everything that stood between me and it. I was bathing in the glow of a thousand candles, a million suns, a galaxy of stars."[27]

Then Dimucci came face to face with someone he had vaguely known.

> I saw a figure, a man in front of me, like he'd been waiting for me. His arms outstretched. And I heard him speak words of truth, not in my ear, but in my heart. "I love you," he said. "Don't you know that? I'm your friend. I laid down my life for you. I'm here for you now." . . . Maybe it was because my heart was willing and that the ten years I spent clean and sober had prepared me for that twinkling of an eye. He was a sly fox, old Jack. He must have known I'd never have accepted a God personal to just me as part of my recovery. Jesus for me was a plaster figure nailed high on the altar of a dusky church. So Jack could only tell me so much—just enough to get my attention. The rest of the story would have to come from Jesus. Jack could only take me so far. Christ had to carry me the rest of the way.[28]

Unfortunately for the pop music world, Dion saved some of his best music for the six records he recorded for the CCM market, beginning in 1980 with *Inside Job* and hitting his stride with the 1981 album *Only Jesus*, and the 1983 release, *I Put Away My Idols*, which were described by mainstream rock critics as "excellent" and "mesmerizing."[29] After several more CCM releases, Dion returned to the "secular" world in the late '80s, releasing several albums and penning his autobiography, *The Wanderer*.

Dimucci had fallen into the trap of making gospel music for the Christians and "secular" music for the rest of the world, but with his book, at least, he was able to tell the story of his long strange trip on the rock and roll road to faith in God to a mainstream audience, even though these fans would most likely never hear any of the records he had made for the CCM market.

Like many other fellow defectors, Dimucci realized too late that CCM limited his ability to communicate with his audience. "When I first decided to write gospel music, I started focusing on God's character and his nature, and I was just enthralled about the whole approach to music," he said. "I could talk about unconditional love from that perspective. Then, somewhere along the line, I realized he wants me to talk about myself too—my journey, my dreams, my growing, my humanity. I wanted to know who God was; now I want to know who I am."[30]

When Dimucci realized that these were themes he wouldn't be allowed to explore in CCM, he decided to return to the pop music scene, though he didn't leave without reflecting on the subculture. "There's an intolerance to any kind of individual expression," he said. "As I traveled around, I saw the beer-drinking friars and teetotaling Baptists, the high liturgy of Catholics and the Pentecostals. Then I went into the barrios and worshipped there and realized worship goes beyond anything we've seen."[31]

Ray Hildebrand

Recording under the name Paul and Paula, Ray Hildebrand hit the top of the pop charts in 1962 with the three-million-selling ballad "Hey Paula," reached number six the following year with "Young Lovers," and recorded three more hit singles in 1963.[32]

Hildebrand had written "Hey Paula" while in college and had recorded the vocals himself only when the scheduled singer, "Paul," failed to show up for the session. He then spent the next two years on the road, promoting the song and launching his music career.

Returning to Texas after a particularly grueling tour, Hildebrand found himself depressed. "I was tired of chasing around the world after something that I wasn't even sure I wanted," he said. "I had recorded a hit album, but the royalties were slipping off. I couldn't see devoting my life to dirty jokes and nightclubs. What for? That's when I started reading the Bible again. I had been raised in a Christian family, but I had never really asked the real questions about life or my faith. That's when I realized the Good Lord was trying to teach me something."[33]

What Hildebrand thought he was being taught was to leave pop music and record for the CCM market, which he dutifully did, recording *He's Everything to Me* for Myrrh in 1967. He went on to record several more records there, eventually moving to a Kansas City startup label, Tempo, and though he had recorded one of pop's classic ballads, he would never be heard again by a pop music culture that would have benefited from hearing of his spiritual journey.

Chuck Girard

Chuck Girard, a rising star on the West Coast surf music scene, managed to crack the Top 40 three times, twice with his band the Castells—with the song "Sacred" in 1961 and "So This Is Love" in 1962—before making his loudest splash in 1964, when he hit number nine with a peppy song called "Little Honda" that he recorded with his new band the Hondells.[34]

"He'd been singing and playing music for a long time," remembered Jay Truax, with whom Girard would later form the early CCM group Love Song. "I was just playing in nightclub situations. I had no direction to my music. I was just kinda earning money. We were both wanting a change—a fresh direction in our lives, some sort of goal."[35]

When a friend invited the pair to a Bible study, they began to immerse themselves in the Bible, combining its teachings with other philosophies they'd been studying. "I went to Kauai and lived in tents or anywhere else I could find," remembered Girard. "I became a sort of a holy man. I sat on a rock for five or six weeks, and gradually I began to feel a sense of doing nothing for anybody."[36]

Returning to the mainland, Girard was promptly arrested for drug possession and eventually landed at the spiritual mecca of southern California, Calvary Chapel. "When I came in that night," he said, "it was in the little sanctuary, before they had the big tent. It was a very cozy and warm atmosphere and the people were all singing praises to God. It was a real feeling of love. I was twenty-six or twenty-seven, but I could perceive emotions of a true nature. I was mentally and emotionally affected. . . . I really could feel a genuineness in those people. I felt they really did know God."[37]

When Chuck Smith, the pastor of Calvary Chapel, began to preach, Girard felt something different. "It wasn't like reading a portion from the Bible and then saying a bunch of words," he said. "It was like he was sharing someone he knew—Jesus Christ. He wasn't telling me about a God I'd someday find; he was telling me about his personal friend. He laid all the gospel down."[38]

Girard accepted Christ and not long after formed Love Song with a few friends. The band released its first album in 1972 on the fledgling Good News label.

Noel Paul Stookey and Peter, Paul, and Mary

"Carefully enunciating their lyrics while radiating an intelligent, unthreatening hipness, Peter Yarrow, Paul Stookey, and Mary Travers were folk popularizers, whose early gift was teasing a mainstream audience slightly leftward into music more rootsy than AM radio, and indirectly into politics of an earnest liberal stripe," wrote one critic in describing the '60s folk trio Peter, Paul, and Mary.[39]

Beginning with their eponymous debut record in 1962, the group released nearly two dozen albums over the next two decades and came to personify for many young Americans, the '60s ideals of peace, freedom, and progressive politics. Their biggest hit, "Puff the Magic Dragon," was believed by some to be a coded reference to smoking pot.

The group's leader, Noel Paul Stookey, was on a spiritual search of sorts and was sent to the Scriptures by a fellow artist. "His friend Bob Dylan had advised him to read the Bible," noted critic Paul Baker, "so Noel was somewhat ready when a young man came up to him at an Austin concert to talk to him about Jesus."[40]

"We got to rapping," remembered Stookey. "I had been reading the New Testament and looking for some kind of a moral way to live my life— something more fulfilling than what I had. I had no idea I was gonna get 'smote.' It was terrific. I went back to my hotel room and I asked Jesus to come into my life. I cried, and oh! what a fantastic time we had that night! It was just a very cleansing experience."[41]

In 1968, Stookey moved his family to Maine and formed a new band known as Star Song, whose members he eventually introduced to the Christian faith one by one.

By the mid '70s the band became known as Bodyworks, producing the first of several albums in the CCM market, called *Band and Bodyworks*. For Stookey, joining the subculture allowed him to moderate his dreams, focus on his own family, and still be a part of the recording process.

"We were in the process of a healing," said Stookey of his family, "and the whole notion of going back out and becoming a success was simply unthinkable. I began to understand things about myself; how I'd always been an anchor in the old days between Peter and Mary; how I was essentially content and centered and at peace with myself. That was what I wanted to bring to Bodyworks . . . a sense of perspective."[42]

Though he was a part of the scene for a time, Stookey professed not to fully embrace CCM. "We'll never be anything more than a facet of contemporary Christian music," he said. "We just haven't bought into that world. As to the degree that we've been thought of as a 'Christian band,' it's a label that's been forced on us. We're going for something different and really quite esoteric. Our calling is not only to worship God, but to present other aspects of his relationship to his children. God's truth is too big to put a label on. It speaks volumes by itself. I'm not going to call what we do 'Christian music,' because it's about the truth, and the truth in the larger sense blesses everyone, not just Christians."[43]

Barry McGuire

As leader of an up-and-coming group called the New Christy Minstrels, Barry McGuire quickly became a countercultural icon in 1965 with the release of his hit single, "Eve of Destruction," which seemed to foreshadow coming events in southeast Asia.

McGuire had begun playing music in 1960 at parties, bars, and clubs—anyplace that would have him—and soon formed the Minstrels. In time, they had several hits, including the 1962 cut "This Land Is Your Land," which went to number ninety-three on the charts, as well as bigger hits like "Green, Green," which rose to number fourteen, and "Today," which charted at number seventeen.[44]

All was not well with McGuire, however. "The happy minstrel became a soured cynic," observed Paul Baker. "He became disillusioned and started losing respect for the people around him, including his audiences. He began to peruse books on the sciences—biology, neurology and psychology—trying to find out why we think and how we think."[45]

Those studies carried him deeper into the mystical sciences, existential thought, and studies of the power of the mind. "Barry had always heard that the truth will set you free, and he continued to search for that truth," said Baker.[46]

By the time "Eve of Destruction" hit the charts in 1965, the Minstrels had broken up and McGuire's despair was palpable and evident in the song, which, because of its anti-war sentiment, was banned from many radio stations, fueling its rise to the top.

"I thought that 'Eve of Destruction' was the truth," said McGuire. "It was just a bunch of newspaper headlines set to music. It had to be sung. It was the first song I'd heard that laid it down just as it was. When the song was banned, it showed me that people don't want to know the truth. Isn't that incredible? People want to live in that make-believe dream world, or that Hollywood playboy fantasy. Happiness is a new home. Happiness is a Ferrari. Happiness is a black book full of phone numbers of pretty girls. And when you get down to the nitty-gritty, nobody wants to hear that the human race is about to blow itself from here to eternity."[47]

McGuire's disillusionment was not lessened by the success of his song, but it left him open to various spiritual influences, including what was to him the most unlikely at the time: the Christian faith.

> A guy came up to me [on Hollywood Boulevard], and told me that Jesus was coming back. I just shined him on, you know. In Hollywood, we called them Jesus Freaks. They were everywhere out there. I thought, *Come on man, don't hand me any of that Jesus jazz!* But then things started happening. Everywhere I went, I kept being confronted with the name of Jesus Christ. I was at a friend's house one day when I saw a copy of *Good News for Modern Man*. It was a modern translation of the New Testament, but I didn't know that until I had taken it home to read it. I was thirty-five years old, and I had never read a New Testament in my life. It blew me away! I discovered the truth I'd been looking for for so many years. It was Jesus![48]

Tired of running, McGuire prayed a simple prayer that was unlike the one typically prescribed in church. "I asked, 'Jesus are you really there?' 'Yes.' 'You mean all this time?' 'Yes.' 'You mean all these years?' 'Yes.' Then Christ opened up my memory and showed me all the things that my selfishness had done to other people. All the lives that I'd ruined—people that I'd turned on to drugs."[49]

McGuire believed and within three weeks had managed to get out of all his contracts. He soon retreated into the CCM world, signing a contract with Myrrh and recording three albums. Later, he followed Billy Ray Hearn to Sparrow Records, where he recorded several more albums for an increasingly smaller audience.

Still, the enormous success of "Eve of Destruction" had given McGuire some room to navigate with his newfound faith.

> Recently in England [1976] I was doing an AM radio interview for BBC. The DJ . . . said, "Well, McGuire, it looks to me like you've jumped on the Jesus bandwagon!" At first, it really turned me off to

hear him use the phrase "bandwagon" as a description of the life-cleansing, healing gift which is offered through the person of Jesus Christ. But before I could answer him back, the Lord spoke to me in my heart, and out of my mouth I heard myself saying, "That's right, man. I have jumped on the Jesus bandwagon, but let me tell you, his was the only wagon that was goin' anywhere. And I know that's true, because I've been on every wagon in the ballpark—and even a few outside the fence—and none of them ever went anywhere." I know the disc jockey was surprised by my reply. So was I. I went on to tell him a man would have to be a dummy to stand waving good-bye to the only wagon leavin' town, especially when he knows the exterminators are on their way to clean up whoever's left around. The person of Jesus is the only passage through which we can reach the ultimate high destiny for which mankind was created. I told the disc jockey I had decided to follow Jesus, and I extended an invitation to him . . . eternal healing, eternal understanding, perfect joy, and infinite relationship with our Creator God.[50]

Eventually, McGuire left CCM, but he continued to travel and sing, playing more than seventy dates a year. "What we are doing isn't so much ministry," he said. "We just want to bring some joy and laughter. There are lots of other good ministers out there. We want to bring wholesome entertainment. Not everything we sing is necessarily Christian. We will sing songs like 'Help,' 'Blowin' in the Wind,' and 'When the Ship Comes In.' We still do 'Eve of Destruction.' It continues to be more true each and every year. It's more true now than it was when I recorded it."[51]

McGuire also became a critic of the CCM industry, speaking out against what he saw as its redundancy. "I haven't made a record in almost seven years," he said in 1988, "because I am tired of making generic records. They all have the same words; it's all 'Hallelujah, praise the Lord,' which is wonderful in context. But there has got to be more. We have got to get out of just the Christian ear. See, when I first became a Christian, my whole emphasis was to reach the lost. But because the lost really don't appear to want to be reached, they don't come to Christian concerts and you end up preaching the gospel to a whole auditorium full of people who are already saved."[52]

Ultimately, McGuire believed, the question came down to a basic one: "Are you going to reach the lost or are you going to feed the saints? That is the question we have all been faced with. And most all of us opted out for feeding the saints, because trying to reach the lost is not an easy thing to do. It's easy singing at churches. . . . But the longing of my heart is to reach the people in the streets, at the airports, the schools, and the parking lots on Saturday nights."[53]

Though long forgotten by most fans of pop music, McGuire seemed content with his lot in life, continuing to play music for whoever would listen and continuing down the road of faith, even though that path had sidetracked what once was a promising career in popular music. "I don't know where God is taking me, but I know I am right where God wants me," he said. "I know that God is in control of my life . . . and I know I can trust Him. . . . It takes all the pressure out of my life."[54]

Johnny Rivers

Born Johnny Ramistella, singer Johnny Rivers came to the attention of the record-buying public in the 1960s with hits like "Memphis" and the campy "Secret Agent Man." In his pop career, Rivers recorded more than thirty singles before jumping ship in 1983 with the release of his first CCM album, *Not a Through Street*.

Rivers grew up around music in Baton Rouge, Louisiana, but it was a chance encounter with legendary rock DJ Alan Freed that set him on his career path and helped him forge a new identity. "He said if I'm going to put out a record, I ought to have a shorter name," said the singer. "Most people in the music business did it in those days, especially when they started out with long Italian names, before settling on something simpler like Bobby Darin or Dion."[55]

Like many artists before and after him, Rivers ended up in the CCM pond after a search for answers. "I was always very close to Christianity" he said. "The only thing I hadn't really done was make that serious commitment to live as a Christian and take the Bible literally. I always thought that the Bible was a book of symbols, that everything had some heavenly meaning you had to try to figure out through something like Eastern teachings. So I embarked on a journey to interpret what it meant. Later on, after studying, reading, and talking to various people, it started becoming obvious that it wasn't really a book of symbols. It was actually literal. . . . God didn't put His Word here as some maze you had to figure out. That realization also helped strengthen my faith in Christianity."[56]

Rivers's path was a slow and torturous one that included time spent in various Eastern religions. "I started becoming introspective and searching for God around '67 to '68," he recalled. "I had joined some yoga groups and was studying a lot of Eastern teachings. I was caught up in that whole movement and I guess it came out in my music. But my serious commitment came around 1980. I was just at a point in my life where I really needed a change."[57]

Rivers credited Dylan with helping to move him in the direction of living out his faith. "I suppose I was being influenced subconsciously by things around me," he said, "like Bob Dylan's conversion and his *Slow Train Coming* album. I also had friends who investigated Christianity and started going to church and rededicating themselves. I could see the change in them and of course that had an influence on me as well."[58]

Ultimately, Rivers moved toward God when he realized that success still left him wanting. "I had attained material success on just about every level and was at a point where I needed some new stimulation in my life," he remembered. "Something that was real this time. I think a lot of it has to do with one's age, after going through so many experiences and being disillusioned, you say it's time to figure out what really is truth . . . what can I use the rest of my life?"[59]

Rivers's music had been reflecting his spiritual journey since the late '60s, particularly two records, *Slim Slo Slider* and *Realization*, but this accelerated in 1980 with his last major effort for RSO Records, *Borrowed Time*.

Signing with the fledgling CBS-owned CCM label Priority, Rivers held out hope that his record would reach beyond the subculture. "It's not a gospel album in the traditional sense," he said. "I think it could probably be successful in the Christian market, but I also feel it could be successful with a secular audience. Hopefully, through that it would draw some people to Christianity, or at least give them something to think about."[60]

Rivers took the unfortunate approach of "Christianizing" his "secular" lyrics, a mistake Mark Farner of Grand Funk Railroad would repeat years later when he changed the lyrics to "Some Kind of Wonderful" for a CCM solo record. Substituting "Jesus" for "Baby," Rivers redid his classic "How Sweet It Is" with religious lyrics and changed the lyrics for "I'll Be There" to "He'll Be There."

The record didn't make much of a splash in the pop market because Priority was a CCM label and the lingo was for insiders, but it did embolden Christian audiences, who could add another major star to the long list of pop defectors.

B. J. Thomas

A country-tinged pop singer from Texas named B. J. Thomas became the most popular of those artists who left the pop world for the Christian music industry. Born August 7, 1942, in Hugo, Oklahoma, Billy Joe Thomas was the second son of an alcoholic air conditioning repairman.

"We had no discipline, no family unity, but mostly no love," Thomas remembered of his family. "And like all humans, I wanted to be loved. . . . I felt responsible for the fact that we always fought and yelled at each other. That's how we usually settled anything at home. We screamed, yelled, or punched each other—whatever it took—until someone won. Dad, being bigger and stronger, usually won, and Mom always gave in."[61]

Despite the chaos at home, Thomas's father gave his son a love for music that stayed with the budding singer. "Daddy sang mostly when he came home drunk," remembered the singer. "He especially liked the Hank Thompson song 'Hey Bartender Give Me One More,' and 'A Six-Pack for the Road.' I suppose that's the one thing my dad did for me—made me love music."[62]

As Thomas listened to artists like Hank Williams Jr. and Elvis, he never imagined that one day he, too, would become a singer. "Apparently, I had musical talent, and so did my dad," he remembered. "But people like us never thought about professional singing. I knew I could carry a tune, but I never thought there was anything unusual about me. Even if someone had told me I had a special musical gift, I probably wouldn't have believed it. I would more than likely have believed it if someone had said, 'Billy, you sing terrible.'"[63]

Jerry Thomas saw his brother's talent and recommended B. J. when some friends needed a singer for a high school band they were forming. B. J. quickly became the lead singer of the Triumphs, a group with which he would eventually record eleven albums. Thomas and the Triumphs' big break came in 1966 when they covered an old Hank Williams song, "I'm So Lonesome I Could Cry." It soon became the first of Thomas's million-selling records.

With the success of "Cry," the band was suddenly in demand. Offers poured in for shows and recordings. B. J. was excited, but the other members of the Triumphs were less than enthusiastic about the opportunities. "Too risky," one of the band members said about the offers. "Another had gone into a beer distributorship with his dad and felt he couldn't leave," Thomas recalled.[64] Instead, Thomas went solo, hiring a band of his own, and became known as B. J. Thomas.

By the mid-'70s, he was a superstar, selling in excess of twenty-five million records and scoring with massive hits like "Raindrops Keep Falling on My Head" and "Hey Won't You Play Another Somebody Done Somebody

Wrong Song." Thomas's inner world, however, was another matter, as he became addicted to drugs.

"In 1975, I began to realize that I was either going to die or I was going to make a decision to put the drugs down," he would later say. "I couldn't put them down, so I resigned myself to the fact that I was going to eventually kill myself. On many occasions, I would take over fifty pills at one time, and I would say, 'B, this is going to kill you.' And then I would say, 'Well, who cares?'"[65]

Separated from his wife, Gloria, whom he had married when he was twenty-six and she was seventeen, Thomas called her one day and noticed a change in her demeanor. "What's going on?" he asked. "Paige, [their daughter] and I, we have both become born-again Christians," Gloria said. "Oh," was all Thomas could muster—the same inwardly embarrassed, outwardly nonchalant response his own mother had uttered years earlier when the young Thomas had excitedly announced that he had been born again.

"During the sixth grade, I attended a Baptist church in Pasadena, Texas," Thomas recalled. "We lived next to the church, so it was the natural one to attend. I liked going there. It was my first refuge from a confusing home, and the people treated me well. One Sunday the pastor gave an invitation to accept Jesus Christ. I didn't understand it all, but I went forward. People prayed for me and told me that I had been born again."[66]

Though skeptical about Gloria's declaration of faith, Thomas, who had recently been near death after a drug overdose in Hawaii, agreed to come home to visit shortly after Christmas. After meeting her wayward husband at the airport, Gloria took him to see the couple who had facilitated her own conversion.

"Jesus Christ has already made a difference in Gloria's life," Gloria's friend Jim told B. J. "He can do the same for you. Why don't you just give Jesus Christ a chance?" The two men decided to continue their talk in the couple's den, and their wives soon heard the muffled sounds of the men praying. "Oh God, be merciful to me, a sinner," Thomas prayed after Jim.

As Gloria later recounted, "Just as B. J. raised his head, the grandfather clock struck midnight, January 28, 1976."[67]

"It was such a miraculous thing for me," he recalled. "When I received the Lord as my Savior, I just knew I was gonna go through some withdrawals. I knew I was gonna lose my mind. But I never had one shaky moment, one sleepless night. Nothing bad ever happened."[68]

After his born-again experience, Thomas continued to play shows and began to introduce some spiritual material. The change was palpable. At his first show in Atlanta, he declared from the stage, "You know, this is the first time I've ever seen the faces of the audience. For so many years I've come out on stages like this and I was always stoned. I was so caught up in my drugs, I never saw people. I was flying high. But one day God made a change in my life, and I'm different now."[69]

Later, at a show in Texas, he outlined his vision of fusing his "secular" pop and "gospel" songs into one complete package. "I'm a Christian who's an entertainer, but I'm not a Christian entertainer," he said. "I plan to keep singing the songs I've always sung, as well as new ones—both pop and gospel."[70]

Despite his stated intentions, Thomas soon signed with a CCM label. "During [an] engagement at Six Flags over Texas, a representative from Word Records came to the show," said Gloria. "He had heard about B. J.'s conversion experience and wanted to find out for himself. As a result of hearing B. J. that night, he got in touch with us and we signed a contract to record contemporary gospel music with Word."[71]

Thomas decided to make two separate records—one for the CCM market and one for the rest of the culture. The CCM record was full of direct songs about God and the walk of faith, while the record for the pop market was a collection of songs about love and life. Unfortunately, it was a move that would set the pattern for scores of other artists for years to come. His debut CCM record, *Home Where I Belong*, became one of CCM's biggest hits of all time, and his pop offering produced a Top 20 hit, "Don't Worry Baby." For Thomas, it was a way to please both worlds.

"I just wanted to cut Christian music," he would later say, "but I think that happens so many times with new Christians. If they have a certain career going, they think that God wants them to quit it and do only religious things. I talked to my pastor about it and he reminded me that a lot of people's ministry is not in a church. I began to realize that if I would just give my testimony at the end of my show, and just as God would have me say it, what a ministry that was."[72]

Although he had correctly diagnosed the problem of separation, his remedy further compartmentalized his music. To his credit, however, Thomas's mixing of pop and "Christian" songs in concert earned him darts from both sides.

Thomas went on to record a string of successful CCM records like *Happy Man*, *For the Best*, and *Love Shines*, but by 1982 his relations with the Christian world had begun to sour. Though his albums had sold well, he was criticized for never quite going along with the prevailing trend toward separation from the world—or in his case, separation from his past "secular" songs, even though they were not contrary to his beliefs. Thomas thought nothing of singing the songs that had made him a household name, like "Raindrops," right alongside songs like "Home Where I Belong," which had announced his conversion. "There's no such thing as gospel music or pop music," he said. "They're labels and cliches that we live under. There's just gospel *people*."[73]

Unfortunately, the powers that be and many fans didn't see it that way.

In 1982, Thomas and Andrae Crouch, two of the top draws in the CCM world at the time, teamed up for a nineteen-city tour that would take them across the United States. As it turned out, however, Thomas and Crouch were totally mismatched, philosophically, temperamentally, and musically. Crouch had been one of the earliest CCM stars and had always supported its separation from pop culture. Thomas saw things differently, and as the tour wound down, the chasm grew wider when Crouch, the opening act, seemed to be inciting the audience to reject Thomas's philosophy of mixing "Christian" hits with "secular" songs.

At a concert in Tulsa, Oklahoma, on August 4, Crouch assured the fans that his deal with Warner Brothers didn't mean he was going into the "other" music. He then went on to introduce members of his band as folks who were once involved with the "other" music. By the time Thomas began his performance, which included songs that Crouch had seemed to infer were "other" as well, the audience responded with catcalls. Crouch later insisted that the mix-up was unintentional, saying, "I always say that 'other' music when I mean 'secular,' so that I won't offend the audience. When I'm on stage, I forget who else I'm performing with. I certainly wasn't talking about B. J."[74]

When the tour moved across town to Norman the following night, Thomas responded to continued heckling by stalking off the stage, leaving behind whatever audience hadn't already left.

Subsequent dates brought more controversy despite Crouch's request that the audience not "hassle" B. J. about his performance; but in Denver, when the crowd began to chant "Jesus is Lord," Thomas erupted. "Are you trying to accuse me of something?" he shouted. "You know who our accuser is."[75]

By the late 1980s, except for an occasional Christmas record or hymns album, Thomas was finished with CCM. He continued to ply his trade quietly, playing at bars, casinos, and state fairs. Whatever the venue, Thomas continued to mix songs about love and heartbreak with songs of faith, sometimes telling hard-drinking audiences of his own conversion.

> Somebody had to take the beating and take the judgment and take the condemnation that I took in that time. Somebody had to come and do this thing in a real pop, secular way so it would open up the doors. Somebody had to show that it ain't a sin for somebody like Amy Grant to have huge pop records; that it's not something that doesn't glorify the heavenly Father; that it's not something you need to condemn. Our hearts were really broken over what happened, but I'm as proud of that as anything I've ever done. . . . We were one of the first artists who did music just like real music, instead of just singing Bible verses. I've never been an either/or kind of guy. I never saw any difference in music. All music is God's music.[76]

Although many in the CCM world were certain that Thomas had lost his faith, he really only lost *their* faith as he continued to play for people and in places where other CCM artists were simply unwilling to go. To B. J. Thomas's way of thinking, though, they were the kinds of places his Master surely would have gone.

Mylon Lefevre

The son of America's premiere traveling southern gospel group, the Lefevres, Mylon Lefevre learned all about music early on. "I've never known anything else but music," he said. "My career started when I grew tall enough to stand on the end of the piano bench to reach the mike."[77]

"I think if my parents would have been country singers, then that is what I would have been," he said. "I don't think I sang about Jesus because I loved Him. I think I did it because it was my heritage."[78]

At seventeen, he wrote a song, "Without Him," that would be recorded by hundreds of artists, including one named Elvis. It was a song that changed the teenager's life. "I was in the army, making eighty-four dollars a month, when Elvis did the tune," he remembered. "There I was, eighteen years old, and I received a royalty check for a small fortune. I had all this money and wondered, 'What am I going to do with all of this? Ninety days later, another big wad came. I had spent fifteen thousand dollars, but there was nothing else I wanted."[79]

When drugs and long sideburns got him kicked out of the family group, Mylon recorded a solo album that blended Christian beliefs and rock and roll aspirations. But to the aspiring rock star, the record was less about faith and more about going about the family business. "For me, it really didn't have anything to do with ministry," he said. "The reason I was out on the road wasn't to lead people to Christ; it was to make a living."[80]

Originally, Lefevre intended to record his debut album, *Mylon*, for Word, but when executives heard the record, which included a sitar solo, "They freaked out," he recalled. "You've got to remember, this was the Bible belt. They would hang you for anything 'eastern sounding' down here."[81]

Instead, Lefevre sold the record to the Cotillion label, which had released the Woodstock soundtrack.

Whatever his intentions, *Mylon* was heavy on faith, with songs like "Old Gospel Ship," "Sunday School Blues," and "Sweet Peace Within." In spite of pressures from management and his record label to tone down the religious fervor, Lefevre continued to record songs that reflected the family faith on successive records, *Mylon and Holy Smoke* and *Over the Influence*, which contained the campfire singalong song, "Waymaker."

While certainly not embraced by the church, Lefevre was equally disdained by many in rock music for his refusal to leave his faith at the studio door. Typical of such reaction was *Rolling Stone's* record reviewer Nick Tosches's scathing review of *Over the Influence*, in which he wrote that Lefevre was "a part of the whole Jesus creep movement. . . . Two-thirds of the songs on this album are totally devoid of any relation to the real world. No sex, no drugs, no booze, no cars, no worldly problems, no worldly happiness. Everything revolves around this ――― ghost Jesus. How can any human possibly comprehend 'Blue Suede Shoes,' and then turn around and warble stuff like 'Jesus is a waymaker/One day he made a way for me.'"[82]

Despite his lyrics, Lefevre remained galaxies away from the God he sang about. "We were a rock and roll band who believed that Jesus was the son of God," he recalled. "We didn't know the Word very well. We prayed before we went on stage, but we also smoked marijuana. Naturally, it was just a matter of time until the gospel was taken over by the rock 'n' roll. I got away from my family and I got away from my church."[83]

Amazingly, Lefevre began preaching from the stage, urging his audience to meet the God that he himself was mostly estranged from. "If . . . anybody had come backstage and talked to me, he would have decided that he didn't want any part of the life I was leading," Lefevre recalled. "But on stage, it was the Word of God, and the Word of God is still the Word of God, even if a donkey is telling it. It never comes back void."[84]

What Lefevre didn't get away from was the party lifestyle into which he plunged headlong, working and partying with the likes of Eric Clapton, Duane Allman, Billy Joel, George Harrison, and others. "I got as high as you can get and still live," he recalled. "One time when I was working with Stevie Winwood, Alvin Lee, Mick Fleetwood, Ronnie Wood, and George Harrison on one album, we were getting so coked up that we were staying up seven or eight days and getting in George's Lear jet and going to some strange places," he recalled. "When it's five in the morning and you got some blow that's got you so wired and you wonder what it's like in Mexico City, you can just go there! You can be there in a few hours. Why wonder? George would say, 'Hey, I'm gonna die before I can spend all this. You got an idea we haven't tried before? Let's do it!'"[85]

"The irony at that time," he remembered, "was the fact that after Bible studies, I'd get together with my friends to discuss the Bible and snort coke."[86]

Throughout the '70s, despite all the contradictions, Lefevre continued producing faith-filled rock albums, like *Weak at the Knees* in 1977, *Love Rustler* in 1978, and *Rock and Roll Resurrection* in 1979, which included songs from Kerry Livgren, and Jeff Pollard of Le Roux.

In 1976, Lefevre worked with Phil Keaggy, and it was the discovery of a whole new circle of friends that helped bring the artist back to his faith. "Before that, I hadn't had any real communication with Christians," he remembered. "They just put me down. . . . In the long run, when I figured it out, I knew I wanted to be more like those people who were dying to self, who were learning to be more and more like Jesus and less and less self-important. You could see what their lives stood for rather then who they were."[87]

One such person was Buck Herring, the producer of the popular CCM group Second Chapter of Acts. "He read me the Word every day," Lefevre recalled, "and just loved on me."[88]

Several other events contributed to the singer's eventual decision to return to the faith of his childhood, but there was one thing that had kept him away. "To tell you the honest truth," he said, "I had been making so much money, I couldn't figure out a way to make a living, and I was just scared."[89]

Lefevre's life continued to be an odd mix of Jesus and drugs, and the drugs almost won when he overdosed. "I went unconscious," he recalled. "After that, I realized that I really didn't know whether I would go to heaven or hell. That scared me."[90]

Lefevre had seen the effects of drugs on his friends, and his own brush with death was a wake-up call. "Do you know how many friends have been buried since I became a rock and roller?" he asked. "Duane Allman and Berry Oakley of the Allman Brothers, Jimi Hendrix, Elvis, Ronnie Van Zant of Lynyrd Skynyrd, Keith Moon of the Who, Al Wilson of Canned Heat, Keith Godchaux of the Grateful Dead. All of a sudden I took a look at my life. I had wanted to burn bright and then, when I was really high or something, just die. But I realized when I met death up close that I wasn't ready to meet God. I didn't want Him to judge me. I wanted time to look this thing over. Were all my sins forgiven? I wanted to know for sure."[91]

There was also the matter of his father's battle with cancer and the bond that developed in his final years between father and son. "My father had always been a harsh person," remembered Lefevre. "I loved him but I didn't like him. But then about three or four years before he died, he started getting to know the Lord better. He became a real kind, caring and gentle man. I asked him what was happening and he said, 'It's just Jesus.'"[92]

That answer caused Lefevre the rock star to pray his own prayer to a God from whom he had been far away. "I asked the Lord not to let me wait until I was dying to come to know Him. If Jesus could take one of the hardest men I ever knew and turn him into the kindest man I've ever known, I wanted to know that love too."[93]

It was in 1979 that Lefevre made the commitment from which he would never turn back, and before long he was feeling that he needed to completely sever himself from all of his business ties, a move that included signing away vast sums of money so he wouldn't be forced to work. "They just stripped me," he said of various agents and managers, "took my publishing, everything; it cleaned me out."[94]

In 1981, Lefevre was ordained as a minister, and soon released his first CCM record, *Brand New Start*, on MCA's start-up gospel label, Songbird. One song, "Stranger to Danger," became Lefevre's signature song. "I'm no stranger to danger," he sang, "but I'm brand new in love, and it's the last of the past that I'm finally free of. I was a child of the wild 'til your love set me free. I'm no stranger to danger, but I'm gonna be."[95]

After several successful CCM records, Lefevre called in some old favors in 1986 and made a rock record for CBS under the band moniker Look Up. Geared for the rock/pop market, Look Up was another of Mylon's attempts to integrate his faith and art, and he pulled it off brilliantly. Unfortunately, because the record was never released in CCM circles, it got little attention from the subculture or the rock world, which hadn't heard a Mylon record in ages.

"I went to write this album and I was going to write some secular-type tunes," he mused. "I'm not opposed to that. If you're a plumber, you plumb.

If you're a mechanic who gets born again, you still work on cars, not just on Christians' cars. I don't mind making music, I don't have any problems with that, but I just couldn't write 'em. I could not write a song that didn't include what I believe. I just didn't enjoy it. I could do it, but creating is fun when you're doing what means something to you. If not, you're prostituting your art."[96]

His own writer's block didn't preclude "normal" songs from appearing on the record, however. "A couple of songs don't have any message," he said. "There's one that Dana Key wrote about an old relationship. A girl walked out on him. He just dragged this sucker out of the closet and dusted it off and it was a good rock 'n' roll song. It ain't got nothing to do with Jesus. It's just a song and we recorded it."[97]

To those artists who dream of making it in the rock world with their faith in tow, Lefevre stands as a monument to the difficulties of such an endeavor. Still, he arrived at an outlook that balanced his spiritual responsibilities with the fact that making music was about art and having fun.

"It's a rock 'n' roll show that is a ministry," he said. "You can't separate the two. Rock and roll is what I do. I put on a good show. I entertain those people. I have a good time with them. It is very frustrating to some people who are not very free for other people to have a good time. We celebrate Christ, because that's the way I feel about what He's done for me. I'm not dying anymore."[98]

Although he was raised on the gospel music circuit and had recorded many albums for the subculture, Lefevre had no illusions about its ability to change lives. "I don't believe contemporary Christian music has ever changed anyone's life," he said. "The Word of God within Christian music might give a person the faith to make a decision for Christ, but music in and of itself will not do it."[99]

Analyzing his retreat from the rock world, Lefevre was surprisingly candid. "I could not live for Jesus and be around rock and roll. I didn't have the faith or guts to do it."[100]

Richie Furay

Recently inducted into the Rock and Roll Hall of Fame for his work with the pioneering rock bands Buffalo Springfield and Poco, Richie Furay today lives quietly in Colorado, where he has been pastoring a church for fifteen years. Furay was also among the early artists who left rock after their conversions and joined the world of CCM.

Before forming one of the best loved rock acts of the '60s, Furay and rocker Stephen Stills played in several bands. "When we first met," remembered Furay, "there was about an . . . eight-month period of time where we put together a group . . . called the Au Go-Go Singers, named after a club in New York City. That was after Steve auditioned for the Monkees. It was in between when he went out to California and when that project actually broke up."[101]

Fortunately for rock fans everywhere, Stills didn't get the Monkees gig and Buffalo Springfield was formed in the mid-'60s, with Furay, Stills, Neil Young, and Jim Messina. The band released its first, eponymously titled record in 1966. "Potentially nearly an American Beatles, the super group employed orchestral arrangements, four-part vocals, Wild West myth making, unrivaled instrumental prowess—and a fertile internal explosiveness along the lines of the Who," observed the *Rolling Stone Album Guide*. "Only two years after its dazzling start, the Springfield was just a memory. But a memory that lingers: rock and roll, this expert and melodic, would prove hard to find in the years to come."[102]

From the outset, Furay believed that Buffalo Springfield wouldn't last. "I think the record company was probably frustrated with us," he remembered. "The very first record we made went very smoothly. It was the most representative of who the band was. After that we just started falling apart because of various situations in people's lives. There were three Canadians in the group and Bruce [Palmer, the band's bassist] had some problems that kept getting him deported."[103]

After leaving the band, Furay and Messina began to play with a group that called themselves Pogo. It was a name that would be short-lived. "After playing in the Los Angeles area for about six months as Pogo, Walt Kelly who wrote the comic strip character, sent us a stack of papers about two inches thick that said, 'Get out of my tree,'" remembered Furay. "So after establishing the name and getting a following, we really didn't want to do anything too radical. . . . We liked to say we just took the little line off the *g* and called us Poco."[104]

Together with Messina, Randy Meisner, Rusty Young, Paul Cotton, George Grantham, and Timothy B. Schmidt, Poco created some songs that Furay believed influenced other artists. "We certainly didn't have the commercial success that the Eagles did, but I think we certainly opened up the doors for groups like the Eagles."[105]

Poco was the vehicle for Messina and Furay to pursue their country-influenced rock sound. The band debuted in 1969 with *Pickin' Up the Pieces* and went on to make more than a dozen records. Messina left after the group's third record, but Furay held out until the 1972 release, *A Good Feeling to Know*, before leaving in search of greener pastures.

"When I left Poco, I was really looking for success as far as the world's viewpoint of whatever that might be," he recalled. "Of course, Stephen and Neil had gone on to worldly success. Jimmy Messina, Randy Meisner, people I'd worked with [had found success], and I kept wondering why not me. I wanted to be a rock 'n' roll star just like everybody else."[106]

For Furay, greener pastures meant a new band, an experience that would take him in the opposite direction of the success he sought.

> David Geffen helped by putting me together with J. D. Souther and Chris Hillman, thinking that was all it was going to take. . . . When I left Poco, the Lord started to work in my life. I really didn't know He was involved at all. My life was not directed towards Jesus Christ at all. There was a guy in the Souther/Hillman/Furay band named Al Perkins. . . . I really didn't want to have anything to do with Perkins, because, to me, we were on our road to success and anything that had to do with Christianity or Jesus Christ was certainly going to get in the way. As it turned out, the Lord was really trying to get a hold of my life, and he used Al. It was after becoming a Christian I decided my real life calling was to pastor.[107]

Before pursuing the pastorate, however, Furay still had some more rock and roll left in him, and he recorded an album, *I've Got a Reason*, for Electra/Asylum that featured his conversion prominently in its songs. "We found so much resistance to what we were trying to do," he lamented. "Secular record companies just weren't sure what to do with someone like me. I still had hopes of being an artist, but I had to ask, 'Lord, what would you have me to do?'"[108]

Furay crossed over into the CCM market and signed with Word Records, where he recorded a stellar album, *Seasons of Change*, and later re-released *I've Got a Reason*. In the early 1980s, he began his work as pastor of Calvary Chapel of Boulder, Colorado. Furay briefly dabbled with his past in 1989, when he rejoined Poco for a reunion album and tour, but for the most part has focused on his pastoral responsibilities, occasionally allowing himself to record albums which were released in CCM circles only.

Dan Peek

Formed in 1970 in England by three sons of American servicemen stationed overseas, the '70s pop group America—Gerry Beckley, Dewey

Bunnell, and Dan Peek—met at London's Central High School and played in various incarnations of the band that would become their ticket to the big time.

After graduating from high school in 1969 and briefly going their separate ways, the three friends reunited and began to make music together. Their first record, released in 1971, contained the track "A Horse with No Name," which quickly became a pop standard. As their careers shot skyward, the band moved back to the U.S. and released a record in 1972 titled *Homecoming*. That same year, they won a Grammy award for best new artist.

Before they were through, America recorded nearly two dozen records, but somewhere in the middle of their great success, lead singer Dan Peek became a Christian and decided to leave his successful gig to jump into CCM. He said it was the final fulfillment of a promise he had made years earlier to God. "I remember praying to the Lord: 'If you will make me a success, I'll use that platform to spread the word about you.'"[109]

Unfortunately for Peek, money, fame, and drugs had kept him from fulfilling his promise earlier, and the singer had grown increasingly depressed. "I was completely overwhelmed. I began to wonder how I was going to live up to my part of the covenant. After seven years, I was miserable because I had wandered from the Lord, but I still had this tremendous kind of desire."[110]

Peek was sure that the answer was to leave America and release a CCM solo record, which he did in 1979 with *All Things Are Possible*. Because America was still a popular group in its prime, and Peek's signature vocal style was a big part of the group's success, his initial solo album spent some time on *Billboard's* adult contemporary charts.

Subsequent CCM releases never made an impact in the pop world, however. Though Peek experienced some success in the CCM market with albums like *Doer of the Word* and *Electro Voice*, by giving up his position in America, he lost the attention of most America fans and the record-buying public.

Al Green

Albert Greene, better known in the music world as Al Green, was the sixth of ten children born into a musical family. Led by Green's father, the family formed a group known as the Greene Brothers that toured the Midwest singing spirituals. "I started singing gospel because Sam Cooke sang gospel and I loved Sam's singing," Green remembered. "My brothers also sang gospel. When I branched out into R&B, I was looked down upon terribly. I became the black sheep of the family."[111]

Later, Green formed his own group, Al Green and the Creations, which gave the future soul superstar his first taste of success. The group's first hit, "Back Up Train," hit the R&B charts in 1967.

Green's early success brought him to the attention of Hi Records, where he began his solo career in 1970. At Hi he turned out hit single after hit single, eventually selling more than eight million copies of songs like "Let's Stay Together," "I'm Still in Love with You," and "Tired of Being Alone." His stats were impressive: five gold albums, six number one R&B hits, and fourteen albums in the Top 200.

Along the way, Green received what he later felt were warnings from the Almighty, including the night he received his "calling." "That happened one morning at 4:45 A.M., in Anaheim, California, in 1973," he remembered. "I wasn't given to sing just this or just that, I was just given the command 'Whatever it is, you honor me. You hold up the Light. You be a light.' . . . My commitment was: 'Whatever you do, wherever you go . . . to hold up the Light.'"[112]

Green apparently didn't follow that directive and soon experienced a life-changing moment that would send him back to the faith of his childhood. "In 1974, in what came terrifyingly close to a replay of [Sam] Cooke's sad end," wrote critic Steve Turner, "Green was trapped in a motel room with a spurned lover, who scalded him with hot food and then shot herself."[113]

Unlike Cooke, Green's life was spared and he decided he was through running away, telling Turner in 1976, "It's been coming for some time. But now it's here and I am . . . to be a minister of God for the people. I don't want to try and save the church folks. Go and save the sinners! Save the people definitely outside your field."[114]

True to his word, Green's next album, *Full of Fire*, though a deeply spiritual record, was aimed squarely at the pop/R&B market. "On the new album, you'll find three spiritual tunes," he said at the time of its release. "They're not gospel, but the love for a lady is translated into everlasting love."[115]

By the time of the release of the *Belle* album in 1977, Green had mastered the art of synthesizing his faith with his music in a way that compromised neither, singing to a woman on the title track, "It's you that I want, but it's Him that I need."[116] The album led one *Rolling Stone* critic to rave that it contained "a sense of liberation and purpose deep enough to make the sinner envy the saved."[117] Another reviewer wrote that the album's "gently funky heat can melt the coldest, most atheistic resolve."[118]

It was one of Green's finest moments when he drew from deep within to combine the best of his faith with the best of his music. He later told an interviewer, "It channeled both religion and rock and roll and it channeled them so well."[119]

Green began to pastor the Full Gospel Tabernacle Church in Memphis in 1976, and after making a record for Motown in 1978, he jumped into the CCM market and released the first of six records that effectively took him out of circulation. He recorded countless traditional hymns like "Amazing Grace," "Precious Lord," and "The Battle Hymn of the Republic," that, while engaging, were not a part of the fabric of the soul and pop music culture of the '80s.

Still, for whatever reason, Green felt it was the right thing to do. "I was offered some phenomenal deals by various record labels, who promised me this and that," he said in a 1980 interview. "I just selected the one which made the most sense. They didn't offer the most money, but they made the most sense. . . . I didn't expect any resistance from the gospel market, but I also didn't expect the overwhelming 'yes' I received from the Lord and his people. The material on the album was mostly selected by my wife, Shirley, who is a gospel fanatic."[120]

Although some Christians might have considered Green a wayward soul before he joined their world, Green was quick to point out that he had always been with them in spirit. "Even though I was recording secular albums," he said, "you'll find songs like 'Jesus Is Waiting,' 'God Is Standing By,' 'God Is Real,' all included on albums which were considered R&B or pop. So it really wasn't a big thing for us to say 'The Lord Will Make a Way' because we believed that before we made 'Tired of Being Alone.'"[121]

Though he sidetracked his music into the CCM subculture for most of the 1980s, Green still clearly understood the importance of preserving his voice in pop culture. "I think the Commodores did an excellent job with 'Jesus Is Love,'" he observed. "They did a good job. . . . They opened a lot of doors for gospel music and its artists to be accepted by the secular world. It may not mean so much for Al Green, but for my children it's gonna make it easier to bring the message."[122]

Green did not remain a hostage to the subculture for long, however, and by 1987 he had signed with A&M Records and released a record that sought to strike the same balance between sacred and spiritual that he had achieved with the *Belle* album. Although A&M clearly didn't understand how to market or promote Green, the artist himself showed occasional moments of his past brilliance on songs like "Everything's Gonna Be All Right," a song that opened with the lines, "Don't let this world mislead you, don't you ever go astray, trust in God's word and believe it, 'cause it'll never pass away,"[123] and eased into a funky, R&B groove.

By 1996, Green was back full force with a release on the BMG label that again mixed love songs with songs of faith. "Most people think performing comes naturally for me, but it doesn't," he said in an earlier interview. "I've come to notice, however, that when I have to do a work for the Lord, the charisma . . . that something extra that comes alive to the responsibility . . . I wish I could tell a thousand kids that life is for the living, and if they work things out by God's timetable, they will arrive at every place right on time. I know, because, after being called to serve the Lord, I ran for three years. But now here I am lifting him up and there is no greater feeling anywhere."[124]

Leon Patillo and Santana

Another of the early CCM artists to leave a popular group was Leon Patillo, a vocalist and keyboard player with the super group Santana.

The son of a taxi driver father and a homemaker mother, Patillo took to music at the age of five when a teacher urged his mother to start the youngster with piano lessons. While providing the foundation of Patillo's future success in music, the lessons also caused the youngster to miss out on childhood sports.

As he entered his teenage years, he began to sing at the small Methodist church his family attended. "I got an opportunity when I was twelve or thirteen to play for the choir at my dad's church," he recalled. "So that gave me an opportunity to play the organ, and I put together a choir."[125]

Though raised in the church, it wasn't until after Patillo joined Santana in 1973 that he began to think seriously about faith. "I had met this girl in San Francisco whose brother was a Christian. So every time I went to her house, here comes the brother! As I continued to go to this girl's house, finally I decided to go to a Bible study, and these people were on the money. They nailed me! . . . Later the brother asked me, 'How was the meeting?' and I said, 'It was pretty nice.' Then he said, 'How'd you like to be saved?' I said, 'No, man, I can't be saved. That would mess up the whole kingdom.' But I did pray with him right there in the car."[126]

Soon after, Patillo began to feel changed. "I began to experience a transition out of something old to something new. I could really feel that I had set myself up for a whole new lifestyle. Those first days were kind of rocky."[127]

Part of that new lifestyle involved Patillo's getting off of the drugs that flowed freely in the music scene, but it didn't happen immediately. "The cocaine dropped off right away. I never touched cocaine since that day." He said, "But marijuana I kind of fooled around with for another five or six months, and then finally the Lord took that desire away."[128]

Patillo jumped into CCM with both feet and was heartily embraced when he left his career with Santana behind. His departure might also have been out of necessity, however, because Patillo's beliefs seemed to get in the way of his relationship with Carlos Santana, the famed guitarist and bandleader.

"I was fired as soon as we got off the tour, because people were becoming Christian and nobody was becoming Buddhist," Patillo recalled with a laugh. "Carlos thought it was the best power play, since it was his ball and he could take it and go home. They said they were not satisfied with me as lead vocalist."[129]

According to Patillo, Santana later regretted his decision and asked him to come back and help with the recording of the *Festival* record. "I said, 'Well, I thought I couldn't sing,'" recalled Patillo. "'Oh, well, we've reconsidered.' At that point, I saw that it didn't have anything to do with my chops. It had to do with spiritual things."[130]

Patillo, however, never looked back because he had come to cherish his artistic freedom. "Santana didn't have any real spiritual overtones lyrically. So I was dying to put that aside and to be able to say something from my heart. A lot of times in these stadiums, I would be playing my piano and crying [thinking], 'Man, look at all these people. We could be telling them more than "*oye, como va*." I just pray that one of these days I'll be able to stand before thousands of people and be able to sing about the goodness of the Lord, his direction, and salvation.'"[131]

Patillo's move into the CCM world came as a result of his association with Calvary Chapel and its Maranatha! Music label, with whom he recorded the album *Dance Children Dance*. Before long, he moved on to Word, and after several successful records there, Patillo and Word decided to use the company's new relationship with A&M Records to make records that would appeal to the mainstream audience as well. Predictably, the strategy failed.

"We forgot we were still selling it to Christians as well," said Patillo. "We thought, 'OK, now we're gonna try to get some words into the secular mind and heart,' and it was a good effort. We made videos and all that kind of stuff . . . but it didn't explode like everybody had hoped."[132]

It wasn't just the lyrics that troubled many Christians, however. "I made a mistake in 1985, during the Love Around the World Tour. I was thinking of how to do something innovative. I came up with an idea for an all-girl band. Unfortunately, many people perceived it as presenting lust and not the Lord. It was a mistake and I guess I didn't think it through enough."[133]

By the early 1990s, Patillo was out of a record deal, but occasionally hosted and performed on the Christian-owned Trinity Broadcasting Network and later began a church in Long Beach, California.

Joe English and Wings

Founded by Ray Nenow, Refuge Records, a Pennsylvania-based independent CCM label, began signing Christians who were active in the rock and pop worlds in 1980. Refuge's first major release was a record by a drummer named Joe English, who had come to prominence as Paul McCartney's drummer, pounding the skins on Wings songs like "With a Little Luck" and "Silly Little Love Songs."

Born in Rochester, New York, on February 7, 1949, English began playing drums as a teenager, strongly influenced by the music of the '60s. "I remember sitting underneath this huge stage on the football field of Temple University stadium listening to Hendrix play 'Purple Haze,'" remembered English. "It was so loud that, when he started playing, the support beams shook. I stuck my head under my arms. It was like World War III."[134]

English joined the group Jam Factory in February 1968 and stayed for six years. The band had opened for artists such as Hendrix, Janis Joplin, and the Grateful Dead. As Jam Factory was winding down in late 1973, English began to experience personal problems.

"Two years ago, everything was working against me," he recalled in 1975. "My old lady and two kids left me. I had no gigs, no money. I was on the bottom." What English had going for him, however, was a loyal girlfriend, Dayle, who "stuck with me, kept my spirits up, and helped me get through the year,"[135] and a solid talent at drumming that allowed him to work various sessions around town for artists like the Allman Brothers and Bonnie Bramlett.

After leaving Jam Factory, English knocked around various gigs for two years before the biggest career opportunity of his life came knocking in the form of a friend, Tony Dorsey, who was McCartney's horn arranger. "Tony said, 'Paul might be firing his drummer,'" English recalled. "'If he does, are you interested in the job?' And I said, 'I'm not in the mood for any jokes.'"[136]

English realized it was no joke, however, when a ticket to Louisiana arrived shortly thereafter. "The next day, I got on a plane and went to New Orleans and started recording *Venus and Mars*," he remembered. "I didn't know any of the material, no audition, just came right in."[137]

After the session, McCartney was impressed enough to ask English to join the band.

> It was in L.A., on the way to Wally Heider's studio for mixing ses-sions, that Paul turned to Joe in the car and put the proposition to him. After all the difficulties he'd previously encountered finding a suitable drummer, Paul made his mind up fast about English. He was certainly impressed by his musical abilities, and perhaps swayed by a shared love of the rural life. Just as McCartney—the boy from the terraced streets of Liverpool—relished the role of gentleman farmer and part-time Scottish laird, so city boy Joe English found content-ment way down south in Georgia following rustic pursuits. "We have three dogs, twenty-five chickens, a goat, six horses, and a cat, Amos, who we brought back from near death after he'd been thrown out of a car," said English. "I like to run a Massey Ferguson 150 trac-tor, fish, and plow on the farm. It gets me away from the business."[138]

English spent three years with McCartney and Wings, touring, record-ing, and enjoying a close relationship with the former Beatle. But, before long, the Yankee was longing for home. "In the end days . . . with McCartney, they really wanted me to move over there," he remembered. "We'd ride around and they'd suggest different places to live. . . . Maybe it sort of let them down that I left. . . . I missed the good old U.S. of A."[139]

English also quickly came to miss the fast times and easy money that went along with being a part of the Wings organization. "I would pick up the phone and call the McCartney office and get some bucks—because, you know, 'money will make you happy.' I'd take drugs and still have a pocket full of money, so I had the best of both worlds. . . . I could have gotten all the money I wanted, and I wasn't happy. In fact, it made me worse. When I'd get depressed, I'd draw some money from the office and get on a plane in London or New York and fly to Los Angeles, rent a car, and drive out to the beach just so I could stick my toes in the Pacific Ocean."[140]

Returning to New York in 1977, English quickly joined a band called Sealevel and reunited with his girlfriend. His personal life was quickly over-come with turmoil, however, when she totaled her Porsche in an accident that left her in constant pain. Under heavy sedation, and with the help of a walker, she began attending a Bible study.

"They prayed for her, laid hands on her, and then she came back home—and when I came back from the restaurant, she was walking up and down from the basement to the first floor with no walker, banging on the side of her leg and laughing. I didn't know what to say. She explained it and . . . I'd always heard about things like that, but there it was."[141]

For English, who had read the Bible sporadically and was raised nominally Catholic, it was a clear message from the Almighty. "It was like a neon sign, and a hammer. . . . Some people get the little messages. I got this great big sign that said: 'It's TIME! Signed, God.' I said, 'OK, I don't have to have any of my loved ones killed . . . I don't have to have anything more to make me realize. . . . It was like a waking up thing."[142]

Although a baby in the Christian faith, English was already hearing messages from God telling him to leave Sealevel, with whom he was recording a third album, and work with a new friend, Ray Nenow, who was involved in the CCM world. "The Lord was really callin' on me," he remembered. "He said, 'Joe, leave and do this,' and I didn't listen. That was the worst month I've ever had in my life. You know how it is when the Holy Spirit calls on you and you don't listen? I mean, every day I went into the studio and said, 'Oh why did I tell these guys I'd do three [albums]?' 'Cause it was not fun."[143]

"He was a man of God who had something to say," said Nenow of English, "and Sealevel didn't give him a platform from which to speak. He was an incredible drummer who just sat in the background and made everyone look good."[144]

When English left the band after completing the record, he signed on with Refuge and recorded his debut album, *Lights in the World*. "Simple lyrics and fantastic production make this one of the year's more accessible and appealing releases," raved the editors of *CCM* magazine. "Play this one for someone who's never heard any contemporary Christian music; it's a good example of how far we've come."[145]

For his part, English claimed to have no intention of disappearing into the Christian world, at least initially. "I'm still working on getting the music out to non-Christians as well as Christians," he said in 1981. "Getting it into the street, getting it into the places where it doesn't get to and say, 'Hey listen, I *did* this and *had* that, and this means more to me—and it sure could work for you if it worked for me.' I don't know what the plan is, but I'll play anywhere. I'm not gonna restrict myself to Christian concerts, universities, and coffee houses. I'll go in as Joe English, and they can go by what I've done in the past, and if they like what I'm doing now, fine. If not, well . . . music is music is music. The message is what's different."[146]

Although the CCM community embraced English and his subsequent albums, Refuge's dream of being in the pop market never materialized, but English made some memorable albums, including *Held Accountable*, which shot to the top of the CCM charts in 1982.

English's contribution went beyond the records he made, however, for he educated a subculture that was suspicious of rock in general and drums in particular, showing that an instrument such as the drums could not be intrinsically evil, a widespread misunderstanding in the Christian world. "That's man's opinion, and opinions are like left legs—everyone's got one," said English of the controversy. "We've gone through thousands of years trying to come up with what man thinks; but it's not what man thinks, it's what God thinks. God has not told me, 'Joe, the drums are from the devil, the devil beats through the drums.' That's just an opinion. If a man's gonna give me a man's opinion, something that a guy thought up, took out of Scripture, out of context, put a word here and a word there, I don't want to hear it. I have one person I answer to."[147]

Rick Cua and the Outlaws

The second major signing for Refuge was Rick Cua, the bassist of the rock group the Outlaws. Cua, a native of Syracuse, New York, worked his way up to the Outlaws in 1980, paying his dues in various cover bands playing jazz, fusion, and then Top 40.

"When I joined the band, it was the prime time of their career," he remembered. "*Ghost Riders of the Sky* had gone gold for them faster than anything before."[148]

Being in the Outlaws gave Cua the visibility that was important to Refuge, and it would later be Cua's calling card in the CCM market. Though his conversion had preceded his joining the Outlaws, it had come at a time when he was surprisingly content with his lot in life.

"I got saved in 1977, and all my life I was striving and striving for a record deal," he remembered. "But finally God just made me realize, 'Hey, you've got a lovely family, you go to a great church, you're born again, you're a musician, and I've allowed you to make a living as a musician, even though it was just playing in a local place.' The fact was I was making good money and supporting my family. So I got that contentment, but about four months after, that's when the Lord really opened the floodgates and the Outlaws gig happened."[149]

Cua stayed with the band for three years and relished every moment of big-time stardom. He was also secure enough in his recently acquired faith to handle the pressures of being in a traveling rock band. "I stayed very strong in the Lord," he remembered, "and I believed that God wouldn't have made it available for me if I weren't grounded in the Word."[150]

What Cua didn't enjoy about being in the Outlaws was his inability to publicly declare his faith, especially to young fans, something he would have plenty of opportunities to do later in CCM. "I just really feel a burden for the kids in that age group," he said. "More than making an artistic statement that is so honed down to perfection, I want to reach people."[151]

Cua's 1982 CCM debut, *Koo-ah*, had the sound and feel—if not the lyrical content—of an Outlaws record, thanks to the superb playing of his Outlaws bandmates David Dix, Freddie Salem, Hughie Thomasson, and Billy Salem. It was a raging rock record that hit the CCM charts like a rocket, producing several Top 10 songs, including the energetic anthem "You Can Still Rock & Roll." Nevertheless, it wasn't quite the record Cua wanted to make, something he remedied on his second record.

For Cua, joining CCM was a bit of a culture shock when he realized that some of his newfound brothers and sisters objected to his playing "secular" gigs. "Growing up in New York [and] Italian Catholic, when we get born again up there—and if you're a musician—there wasn't the big feeling of, 'We can't play music unless it's for the Lord.' I mean, we were musicians, that's what we did, that was our career. So when I did the *Koo-ah* record, this was kinda like my coming out. By doing that record I was making a statement to the world that I am born again, I love Jesus, and there were some Christians then who would say, 'Wait a minute. How can you do this and play down at the Chinese restaurant on Erie Boulevard every Monday and Tuesday night where they serve liquor?'"[152]

It didn't take him long, however, to learn the CCM mind-set. "Very quickly I realized, 'Hey, I am now involved in Christian music. If I had to cross back over, first of all I'd be going *back*, but second of all I didn't have a base here to cross over from. People didn't really know who I was in Christian music, and I felt like, 'Why would God put me over here if it wasn't to get the church as well as evangelism?'"[153]

Cua was happy to play for CCM audiences, but it was doubtful that many fans of the Outlaws followed Cua to his new venues. "If something happens where we happen to write a song that the secular community wants to pick up on and release, then I would be thrilled to death. But it's not something that I'm counting on," he said.[154]

Those moves never happened, and Cua soon moved to Sparrow, and then on to the Reunion label, where with the help of producer Tom Hemby he further toned down his rock image in favor of a lighter pop sound designed to bring in female fans who had been missing from his earlier rock efforts. Cua's efforts never seemed to jell at Reunion, and in trying to please too many audiences, he ended up pleasing none. The teenage boys who had earlier bought up Cua's Outlaws-style brand of rock and roll eventually moved on to harder metal groups like Stryper and WhiteCross.

By the early '90s, Cua was finished as a force in the CCM market, though he continued to release records through his own label, UCA. Although Cua's music played a strong role in CCM circles, by giving up his role in a popular band and jumping to the CCM world, his voice was silenced in the general marketplace. Through it all, in spite of his decision to abandon mainstream rock for the CCM niche, he wasn't one who compartmentalized his faith or tried to separate it from his work.

"If you are saved you have a ministry," he said. "That's all there is to it. I don't care if it's a ministry at the grocery store where you work, being polite to your customers, or a music ministry, or if you work at the post office and you want to help the little old ladies so they don't slip on the sidewalk. If you're professing to be born again, then the word *ministry* is as sewn into our lives as life itself."[155]

Ultimately, like many other defectors, Cua grew content with strengthening the faith of young believers and singing for the rare non-Christian friend who might be dragged along to a concert. Stories about kids saved from the brink of death by listening to Christian music no doubt kept him plugging away. In particular, response was strong to a song Cua wrote about suicide, generally a forbidden topic in the CCM world. "One girl wrote us from a hospital bed in the Midwest and said, 'I've tried to kill myself three times'" remembered Cua. "'I heard your song and checked myself into the hospital.'"[156]

Cua's favorite story, however, was told by a Nebraska CCM station disc jockey who "heard a knock at the door of the station. When he got there, no one was there, but he found a song request tacked to the door. Some kid was going to kill himself at ten and he wanted to hear this song. He'd really planned this out and was planning to go on his own terms. The DJ got on the air and kept asking this kid to call in. He never did. So, at ten minutes 'til ten, he played 'Don't Say Suicide.' The kid called in and they prayed. I got a chance to meet the kid and the DJ."[157]

Philip Bailey and Earth, Wind, and Fire

Philip Bailey, the high profile lead singer of the super group Earth, Wind, and Fire, became a Christian in 1975 after being "witnessed to" by Leon Patillo of Santana, which was touring with EW&F. As Patillo talked about his faith and the importance of the Bible, several of the members of Earth, Wind, and Fire, including Bailey, became born-again Christians over a period of several weeks.

As word of Bailey's conversion spread in Christian circles, he was unprepared for the reaction from fellow believers. "Instead of people just saying, 'Praise God, a brother's saved! I hope everybody gets saved,'" said Bailey in 1985, the reaction was more like, "'How dare he stay in the band!' But Earth, Wind and Fire has never promoted any type of drugs, any kind of illicit sex. They've always been a very positive band."[158]

Perhaps partially acquiescing to such criticisms, Bailey decided on a middle course that would allow him to continue to record with the group: recording solo "secular" albums and solo CCM albums. Predictably, the move pleased no one completely and controversy raged in Christian circles when one of Bailey's "secular" records spawned a hit song, "Easy Lover," a duet with Phil Collins, which Collins had written.

"The first thing that I thought about when Phil brought the lyrics to me was Proverbs 7," recalled Bailey, "because I've read that so many times. What it means to Phil Collins and what it means to me may be two different things. I never sat down and talked about this with him, but to me it means what's good *to you* is not always good *for you*. It doesn't necessarily mean that it's a woman or whatever. We love a lot of things that are 'easy lovers.'"[159]

What made objections from the Christian community especially ludicrous was that, in the song, Bailey was urging the listener to stay away from the "easy lover." "The lyrics in no way condone that lover. In fact it says to leave it," he protested. "But people don't even stop to listen to the record and read the lyrics on the jacket. A lot of times people automatically associate a successful record with sin, and that's absurd."[160]

The misunderstanding was similar to one that had plagued another Christian, Cliff Richard, when he recorded a similarly themed track called "Devil Woman." The controversy stalled Bailey's career in the Christian world when, according to Bailey, some stations stopped playing his CCM record *The Wonders of His Love*.

Bailey continued to record marginally-successful records for that market, but he was often left perplexed and bewildered by the faulty theology that caused Christians in the pop world to feel under attack for remaining in their jobs. "Man, people are stupid," he said. "You ask people who become saved, 'Now, do you work for an all-Christian company? Do you only deal with Christian people?' 'Well, no.' Well, shut up. That's just as asinine as it is for them to think that somebody who becomes a Christian who's in the public eye should come off the television. What did the Lord save them for? To go hide under a bushel?"[161]

Part of the criticism of Bailey had to do with Earth, Wind, and Fire bandleader Maurice White's penchant for putting various mystical and religious symbols on the cover of the band's records, which Bailey had no control over and felt had nothing to do with the music. "It's different if somebody has to promote something that's not them. But we weren't promoting the signs and things that were on the record. That was just something that Maurice put on the cover."[162]

As Bailey turned out CCM records for Myrrh and pop records for CBS, his purpose became exceedingly unclear. Was he supposed to sing heathen music for CBS and religious music for Myrrh? Were the records supposed to be stylistically similar? In Japan, Epic's Japanese executives charged with promoting Bailey's CCM records seemed befuddled when a Word executive tried to explain to them what made Bailey's gospel records different from his "secular" records. It didn't make sense in Japan, because it didn't make sense in America.

Tom Willett, Myrrh's A&R director at the time, seemed disappointed with *The Wonders of His Love*, in comparison to Bailey's "secular" release, *Chinese Wall*.

"Everybody loved [*Chinese Wall*] over at Word," recalled Bailey. "I really liked it. And everybody that I talked to liked the record. Then, when *The Wonders of His Love* came out, everybody said, 'Well, it's not an "Easy Lover,"' which I really didn't expect from a Christian record company."[163]

While Willett denied any dissatisfaction with *Wonders*, he did allow that he hoped that Bailey's "next CBS album and his next Word album will sound about the same, and it's the lyrical content that will make ours different."[164]

Bailey's situation was a prime example of the basic CCM dilemma: He was effectively being asked to write two separate records with two separate sets of pressures from each side. As Willett and the religious music establishment leaned on the artist to write hot music with God lyrics, CBS was no doubt hoping that Bailey would write hot music without God lyrics. Both records would be marketed to their respective quarters (those who wanted to hear about God and those who didn't) and both companies would prosper.

The only problem with such an arrangement were those pesky words of Bailey's Savior in the New Testament about going *into* the world. Bailey clearly had qualms about singing about his faith exclusively to the converted. "The Lord does have people in particular areas," he said. "A lot of people don't understand that. They just perceive that if you're not doing it the way they think you're supposed to be doing it, then it's not happening."[165]

Bailey also saw the importance of artists identifying their calling and standing firm in the face of criticism. "It's important as a Christian artist that you identify who your particular ministry is to. . . . God gave me a gift to sing a song, and it's been good to me," he said. "That's the way I've supported my family, that's the way I've had the blessings of being able to do most of the things I've done in my lifetime. I love the Lord and I sing about it. But I'm not a preacher. That's not my calling. And if people are looking for me to be more than what I am, then that's their problem."[166]

Bailey finished his association with the CCM industry in the early 1990s with a "greatest hits" record, but continued to record with Earth, Wind, and Fire, and also released a solo record for the pop label Zoo in the mid-1990s. He had played an important role in bringing important issues to the fore of the CCM world and in his own way had clearly showed that the CCM establishment was sorely lacking when it came to having a consistent theology of cultural penetration.

Mark Farner and Grand Funk Railroad

Never a favorite of highbrow music critics, Grand Funk Railroad was led by singer/guitarist Mark Farner. Noted for songs like "We're an American Band," "I'm Your Captain," and "Some Kind of Wonderful," Grand Funk coasted through the '70s as every man's band, selling more than 25 million records along the way. In 1982, the band played its final concert at the famed Budokan in Tokyo to a throng of adoring fans. A year later, Farner's wife took their children and left him. It was the lowest point of Farner's life, but a moment that he would forever remember as a turning point.

Rock has sometimes been accused by its critics of harboring secularists, Satanists, and atheists, but Mark Farner was never one of those. Though raised in a home where, according to Farner, "the Lord's name was [frequently] used in vain," Farner came to a faith decision at a young age. "I watched a Billy Graham crusade on television and got on my knees in front of the television set," he remembered. The young Farner, whose father had just died, was looking for comfort. "The pain was eased and that was a phenomenon to me," he remembered.[167]

As is sometimes the case with conversions, however, once the pain was gone, Farner's vision of faith dimmed. "I asked Jesus into my heart, he came in, but I didn't act like it," he said. "I had no leadership, no discipleship, no indication of what to do, other than I believed Jesus came into my heart."[168]

Farner spent his teenage years playing football, only to be told by doctors, after several injuries, that he had to quit all sports. Seeing that her young son needed something to fill the void, Farner's mother arranged for guitar lessons for him. "I was picking up pretty good from him," recalled Farner of his guitar teacher. "I was quite sure that I could pick it up just by watching, so I did. I learned how to play just by watching."[169]

Farner studied the techniques of blues players like Johnny Winter, Eric Clapton, and Jimi Hendrix, as well as the vocal stylings of Howard Tate and Aretha Franklin. He began playing at parties, wedding receptions, and teen hops, and after high school played with bands like Terry Knight and the Pack, and the Bossmen.

Next, he teamed up with drummer Don Brewer and others, but trouble with some of the band members sent them looking for a new bass player. "A couple of the guys' wives threatened to divorce them 'cause we were on the road a lot," remembered Farner. "We got together and said, 'We'll get a bass player and make a three-piece out of it. It'll be a lot easier to take care of.'"[170]

Searching for the elusive third member, Farner and Brewer were meeting with a promoter when they heard music coming from a rehearsal room next door. "We couldn't see who it was, but we heard the bass coming through the wall, and we were going, 'This guy can play.' So we asked him if he wanted to join our band and he said yes."[171]

"He" turned out to be Mel Schacher, who had been playing with a band known as Question Mark and the Mysterians. Grand Funk Railroad made its national debut at the Atlanta Pop Festival in the summer of 1969.

Farner insisted that he was never entirely separated from God during Grand Funk's heyday, and he suggested that spiritual inspiration led to the creation of several songs. "I prayed for songs that would reach the hearts and the ears of people that [God] wanted reached," he said. "That's how 'I'm Your Captain,' 'So You Won't Have to Die,' and a couple of other tunes came along."[172]

In the Christian vernacular, Farner was in a state of "knowing but not serving" God. Instead, said Farner, he was serving *things*. "I bought so many

things. I spent millions of dollars in pursuit of happiness and I was avoiding
the thought of death. I was in spiritual bondage and didn't even know it. I've
spent lots of money. I know what money does. I had 1,600 acres, a farm; all
kinds of things. You can't buy things and be happy and have joy."[173]

After the breakup of Grand Funk, Farner recorded two highly
acclaimed albums for Atlantic. Meanwhile, his family was breaking up.
Abandoned by his wife, Lesia, and children, Farner was ripe for a lasting
conversion. "I went looking for God, very reminiscent of the time my dad
died,"[174] he said. He began attending several churches, eventually finding a
sixteen-person congregation in Onaway, Michigan, with an elderly pastor
who had probably never heard of Grand Funk Railroad.

"I felt the love of Christ, and they loved on me," recalled Farner. "The
pastor gave a message for Mark Farner that morning, like straight into my
heart." Farner was soon at the altar, on his knees, asking for one more
chance. "I asked forgiveness for all of the years that I was away from [God]
and that he would take me over and use me . . . all of the years of my life until
I drew my last breath." Farner also asked God to bring his wife back. As it
happened, fifty miles away that same morning in another church, Lesia
Farner was, in Farner's words, "accepting the Lord for the first time in her
life."[175]

Full of excitement and a desire to be used by God, Farner curiously
decided to abandon music. "I put my guitar down for a year," he said. "I
never played and never thought I'd even be involved with rock and roll
again."[176]

Instead, he spent time learning the basics of what it meant to be a
Christian. "Every time I had a question," he remembered, "I'd go to the pastor's house and he'd bring out all his versions of the Bible and say, 'Get to
where you're comfortable with your understanding on this.' We always
prayed that God would open the eyes of my understanding, and he did."[177]

In time, Farner regained the urge to make music, and the songs came
quickly. By 1984, he was writing and performing solo again.

As is often the case with new believers, Farner was somewhat of a
zealot at the outset of his Christian life. "I probably should have been locked
up the first year," he remembered with a laugh. "I had such a zeal to win people who were lost to the Lord. I probably came on a little too strong."[178]

After his conversion, Farner began to write songs, "backwards from the
way I had ever written before," he said. "I used to get the music first and then
go from the feeling to see what the words might say. Now, I was getting the

words and ideas that I wanted to express, and later I'd find the music to fit it."[179]

The first post-conversion tune Farner wrote was a barn burner titled "Come to Jesus," which opened with the Sunday school lines, "Jesus loves me this I know, for the Bible tells me so."

In 1988, after several years of playing churches, clubs, and prisons, Farner signed with Frontline, at the time, the hot southern California independent CCM label. His first album, *Just Another Injustice*, was released exclusively to that market. Like many records by formerly "secular" artists, *Just Another Injustice*, and its successors, *Wake Up* and *Some Kind of Wonderful*, went largely ignored by music critics and unheard by Farner's former fans.

Though signed to a CCM label, Farner continued to venture out. He made a point of tailoring his set to the crowd, much like B. J. Thomas, playing tracks from his CCM albums in front of Christian audiences, but mixing 70 percent Grand Funk tunes, with a few of his new songs sprinkled in for good measure, when he performed in clubs and bars. After the show, he would often spend time with his fans. "Not because they want an autograph," maintained Farner. "They want to talk about something serious. They've come to a point in their life where they're ready to deal with what's eating at their heart. I like to just let people know the reality of living for Christ."[180]

Amazingly, resistance to Farner's work came mostly from churches. "They discourage us from going in," said Farner, "but this mission came from God to go into the world and reach the lost. It's like the church has all these programs and guest speakers brought in to attract the lost to their building, but it doesn't look good to the lost. The church is so badly misrepresented [that] it's no wonder the lost, who have never heard the Gospel, stay away. It doesn't take a rocket scientist to see that what some churches are after is *dinero*. That's what the general public relates to the church."[181]

While Farner was making live music for all of his fans, his records were marketed only to those whom the CCM market machine was designed to reach: the converted. Frustrated, Farner eventually got out and focused on playing small venues across the United States.

"I feel compassion in my heart to go to the world," he said, "'cause I can identify with 'em. When I look at 'em, I see my former self. [The apostle] Paul would always remind us, 'Hey folks, don't forget that you yourself were one of these people.' We can't just get in a church, close ourselves in, and point a finger at 'em and go, 'Look at 'em. They're going to hell.' They see enough of that crap."[182]

Ultimately, the inbred nature of CCM, and what Farner perceived as the wrong motivations of many involved in the business, combined to send him back into the clubs. "I have a few misgivings, because people get their eyes on the things that I've already had," he said. "The Mercedes, Cadillacs, Lincolns, and all the toys. . . . I've already had that crap. That's what it is, crap. It's just poo-poo. It's useful while we're here, but it's of no value. The things that I value are the things that God is doing inside of me. I want my values established on the world to come, not the world we're in."[183]

Farner's post-CCM career took him into clubs, where he was billed as "Grand Funk's Mark Farner."

Eventually, the other members warmed up to the idea of touring again, and Farner re-formed Grand Funk to tour the nostalgia circuit, performing new versions of old hits, minus some of the randy lyrics. But for Farner, wherever the concert, whoever the audience, the message was always the same.

"The Word says, 'He who sinneth much loveth much,'" he said. "And I was a terrible sinner. I love Jesus so much, with all my heart, with all my soul, and with all my strength. I love the Lord my God and I'm not gonna do anything to compromise what he is doing with me. . . . I don't want to be part of a 'bless me' club. We have a long way to go as Christians before we achieve more of an outreach state of mind."[184]

FOUR

The Remnant

ot every artist who embraced the Christian faith defected to the religious music subculture. A remnant—including some of the more devout—refused to, upon their conversion experiences, leave their "secular" employment behind. Though some wrongly assumed that these artists hadn't been properly converted, the artists ignored the criticism and continued to toil quietly in the popular music market, often unnoticed by fans of CCM.

Johnny Cash

Johnny Cash was one such artist. Born into a poor farm family in Kingsland, Arkansas, in 1932, Cash came to faith early and hard. "The first preachers I heard at a Pentecostal church in Dyess, Arkansas, scared me," he remembered. "The talk about sin and death and eternal hell without redemption made a mark on me. At four, I'd peep out of the window of our farmhouse at night and if in the distance I saw a grass fire or forest fire, I knew hell was almost here."[1]

And hell was enough to scare the youngster into believing. "My father was the son of a Baptist preacher who died at a young age, when my father was twelve," remembered Cash, "so I already knew when I reached the age of twelve that, in my father's words, I had reached the age of moral and spiritual accountability. So while the congregation sang the invitational hymn,

'Just As I Am,' I walked down the aisle of the church and accepted Jesus Christ as my Lord and Savior."[2]

While the fear of hell kept the young Cash scared and glued to his seat in church, it was the music that gave him hope. "The music in the Pentecostal churches in the early years was wonderful. They were more liberal with the musical instruments used," he remembered. "I learned to sit through the scary sermons, just to hear the music; mandolins, fiddles, bass, banjo, and flattop guitars. Hell might be on the horizon, but the wonderful gospel-spiritual songs carried me above it."[3]

At an early age, Cash was drawn to the radio, where he listened to his favorite music: gospel. "When I was a kid, I was a fan of Ira and Charlie, the Louvin Brothers," he remembered. "They were on the Eddie Hill show from 12:00 to 1:00. The biggest thrill of my life was when, in 1947, I made the trip to Memphis, hitchhiking, and saw the show live. There they were on stage: Eddie Hill, the Louvin Brothers, Lightning Chance, bass player Paul Buskirk, Tony Inciola, the whole gang. I was thrilled beyond words. It was my first time to see a country show. I sent a request backstage to dedicate a song to my mother and they did it. On the show, Eddie Hill said, 'Here's a song for Carrie Cash of Dyess, Arkansas,' and the Louvin Brothers sang their new record, 'Kneeling Drunkard's Plea.'"[4]

For the young Cash, music was a soundtrack for life, and he spent his days working, sweating and singing the songs that fit his mood. "Reaching the age of twelve meant doing a full man's job in the cotton fields," he remembered, "which I did until I was eighteen years old and left home. Farming cotton, for me, meant working with the hoe and plow with mules in the spring and summer, and the cotton sack in the fall and winter. I never stopped singing in the fields. Morning to night, except for the hour off, from 12:00 to 1:00 to eat lunch and listen to the *High Noon Roundup* over WMPS, Memphis. I mixed them up, hillbilly, pop, blues, and my brothers and sisters sang along on the ones they knew. By mid-afternoon, when the day was beginning to really get hard, I started singing gospel songs."[5]

It was the kind of music that gave him hope when his fourteen-year-old sibling lay dying after an accident. "My brother Jack, two years older than me, was killed in my twelfth year. The last songs of the day were always the songs that were sung at his funeral. Don't misunderstand, it wasn't a sad thing. It brought us joy. In those songs was the hope eternal that we found in our religion. Songs like 'I'll Fly Away,' 'I Won't Have to Cross Jordan Alone,' 'I Am Bound for the Promised Land,' and others."[6]

"It was a beautiful death if there can be such a thing," said Cash of watching his brother pass on, "because he described heaven to us as he was dying. What Jack's death did to me musically is that those gospel songs that were sung at his funeral became a fountain of joy for me."[7]

Cash's love for gospel music, combined with his mother's sense of her son's destiny, gave the young singer a solid foundation. "My mother used to say, 'God has his hand on you. Never ignore the gift.' I never knew what she meant by the gift until I felt the gift leave me. When the gift comes back, it's so sweet."[8]

In Cash's case, "the gift" seemed to come and go many times as the singer repeatedly battled alcohol and drug addiction, culminating in his 1965 arrest for possession of narcotics. The following year, he was arrested and jailed again for disorderly conduct.

After spending time in the Air Force from 1950 to 1954, Cash moved to Memphis and worked several odd jobs. Together with two friends, Luther Perkins and Marshall Grant, he formed a band, Johnny Cash and Tennessee Two, that caught the attention of Sam Phillips and earned Cash a record contract from Sun Records, home to artists like Carl Perkins, Roy Orbison, Jerry Lee Lewis, and Elvis. Perhaps it would be more accurate to say that Cash *insisted* on getting the attention of Phillips.

"After numerous rebuffs by Phillips's staff, the young man tried the direct approach," noted writer Bill Miller. "He waited on the front stoop until Phillips arrived at work, and introduced himself and asked for an audition."[9]

Cash was signed by Sun, but he immediately encountered the problem that would plague artists of faith for decades to come. "Initially, according to Phillips, the group's material was all gospel," noted Miller. "He liked the songs, but told Cash that he couldn't merchandise him as a gospel artist. Phillips was impressed with the unique sound and encouraged Cash to return with some secular material."[10]

Cash complied and over the years turned out hits like "I Walk the Line," "Cry Cry! Cry!," "Hey Porter," and "Folsom Prison Blues."

The '60s were a blur for Cash as he developed an addiction to uppers and downers, enduring a seven-year struggle with drugs that he was finally able to beat with the help of God and a good woman, June Carter, who would later become his wife. Initially attracted by Carter's beauty and her voice, Cash discovered she was also tough as nails when they began to tour together.

"When June Carter came along, we decided to initiate her," Cash said, referring to his traveling companions Lewis and Perkins. "In some motel somewhere, we brought in one of those machines that suck up leaves and went to work on her room. [While she stood] in the middle of her bed, screaming, we opened her suitcase and she watched her clothes disappear, then the sheets she was standing on."[11]

Pranks were one thing, but when Cash grew increasingly violent, Carter put her foot down, as she would do later during Cash's battles with alcohol and drugs.

> Bottle breaking became a favorite steam valve until one night, backstage at a ballroom in Iowa. The opening band was on, we picked up the bottles to start. She picked one up [and] screamed, "I've had enough, I'm joining you!" But she threw the bottle at me. Then she turned over a clothes rack, then started throwing bottles at all of us, then against the wall. I yelled for her to stop, but she wouldn't, so I grabbed her and held her. "Okay," I said, "we won't do it anymore." "Promise me!" she said, with the meanest look a woman ever gave me. "I promise," I said. So beginning that night, she began the long, slow process of trying to tame me, and how sweet it was. But that streak was hard to get me off of.[12]

Cash dabbled in drugs and alcohol for years before hitting rock bottom. "By early October 1967, I'd had enough," he remembered. "I hadn't slept or eaten in days and there was nothing left of me. . . . I never wanted to see another dawn. I had wasted my life. I had drifted so far away from God and every stabilizing force in my life, there was no hope for me."[13]

Cash tried an unusual method of suicide, attempting to lose himself in Nickajack Cave on the Tennessee River near Chattanooga.

> I crawled and crawled and crawled until, after two or three hours, the batteries in my flashlight wore out and I lay down to die in total darkness. The absolute lack of light was appropriate, for at that moment I was as far from God as I have ever been. My separation from Him, the deepest and most ravaging of the various kinds of loneliness I'd felt over the years, seemed finally complete. It wasn't. I thought I'd left Him, but He hadn't left me. I felt something very powerful start to happen to me, a sensation of utter peace, clarity and sobriety. . . . The feeling persisted, though, and then my mind started focusing on God. He didn't speak to me, He never has, and I'll be very surprised if He ever does, but I do believe that at times He has put feelings in my heart and perhaps even ideas in my head. There in Nickajack Cave I became conscious of a very clear, simple idea: I was not in charge of my destiny. I was not in charge of my own death. I was going to die at God's time, not mine. I hadn't prayed over my decision to seek death in the cave, but that hadn't stopped God from intervening.[14]

Cash then wondered how he'd ever get out alive. "There I was . . . in total darkness, with no idea of which way was up, down, in or out of that incredible complexity of passages and chambers so deep inside the earth that no scent or light or sensation from the outside world could possibly reach me. How could I escape the death I'd willed? No answer came but an urging did: I had to move. So I did. I started crawling in whatever direction suggested itself, feeling ahead with my hands to guard against plunging over some precipice. . . . I began to see light, and finally I saw the opening of the cave."[15]

Cash recovered, but continued to struggle with drugs. "My liberation from drug addiction wasn't permanent," he wrote. "Though I never regressed to spending years at a time on amphetamines, I've used mood-altering drugs for periods of varying length at various times since 1967: amphetamines, sleeping pills, and prescription painkillers."[16]

Though by the dawn of the '80s he had begun to get his personal life together, the times were not kind to Cash the artist. "I went through a period of going through the motions," he remembered. "Nothing was happening. I was getting older—same old songs, same old me—not much excitement. But then something comes along to interject a shot. A shot of life, a shot of love in my direction."[17]

That shot was the attention of rock producer Rick Rubin, the founder of American Recordings, who signed Cash to his label and produced two records that breathed life into the aging superstar. Although Cash had been fairly vocal about his faith all along, even recording a record in 1973 called "Gospel Road," it wasn't until the American Recordings records that he was able to fully integrate his faith into his music. On the 1994 release and the subsequent 1996 record, *Unchained*, Cash did what he had always done brilliantly in his shows—mixed songs of faith with songs about real life.

"That album was songs coming out of nothing but me and my guitar, that's all, it's not coming out of a committee," remembered Cash of his first record with Rubin, titled *American Recordings*.[18]

For Cash's second outing, the brilliant *Unchained*, Rubin recruited the likes of Tom Petty and the Heartbreakers, Beck, and Chris Cornell of Soundgarden to help Cash create and perform songs that would reach out to a whole new audience. "This album is the same thing," he said, "except I got some support to bring it out of me. That's how I feel about my recording now with these great artists who came in and wanted to be a part of it."[19]

The record was never released in the CCM market, but it was a masterful statement of faith, particularly on an emotional ballad that combined faith and love, the ode to his wife he called "Meet Me in Heaven." "I always wanted to write a song called 'Meet Me in Heaven,' because those words are on my brother's and my father's tombstones," said Cash. "That song is one of those songs of peace that comes with my faith. The song was written to June, we've been together thirty-four years, and I think we're going to be together forever. I do believe in forever. That's what that song's about, people who are going down a trail together forever."[20]

"We've seen the secret things revealed by God and we heard what the angels had to say," Cash sang, "should you go first or if you follow me, will you meet me in heaven someday."[21] His lyrics seemed equally passionate in describing the God who saved him from sin as he was in remembering the woman who had saved him from himself.

It took him years to finally arrive at a place where his walk of life and walk of faith could be fully integrated into one cohesive worldview, and thus one record, but in his sixties Cash finally hit upon the formula that would allow his old fans, and many new fans, to understand what makes Johnny Cash tick.

"Because of his legendary status," wrote one critic, "Cash could be specific about the source of forgiveness without losing the attention of the audience. He had spent the best part of four decades trying to find salvation through wild excess. Now, at the age of sixty, he could afford to preach a little. 'The theme of the album is sin and redemption,' he declared at the 1994 Glastonbury Festival. 'Thank God for redemption. I wouldn't be here without it.'"[22]

Cliff Richard

"For young people in the British Isles, prior to the Bob Dylan of 'Slow Train Coming,' there was only one notable precedent for a Christian in pop or rock," wrote critic Steve Turner, "and that was Cliff Richard, who had announced his conversion in 1966 during a Billy Graham rally in London. . . . Although he was never frightened of expressing unpopular opinions and suffered personal ridicule for his faith, Cliff Richard was never combative in performances."[23]

In 1958, still known by his given name, Harry Webb, Richard made his first record with his group the Drifters, which included the songs "Move It" and "Schoolboy Crush." Throughout much of the '60s, Richard dominated the British charts with his music, but he attained his greatest notoriety when he stepped up to the microphone at Billy Graham's London crusade.

"I have never had the opportunity to speak to an audience as big as this before," Richard said to the crowd, "but it is a great privilege to be able to tell so many people that I am a Christian. I can only say to people who are not Christians that, until you have taken the step of asking Christ into your life, your life is not really worthwhile."[24]

All of England was abuzz with news of Richard's confession, and Brits wondered if he would immediately leave popular music. Richard himself wondered the same thing. "My first reaction was to pull out of show-biz and train to teach religious education," he said. "There were a number of reasons. For one thing, I was quickly aware of the pressures show-biz life puts on the Christian. It makes demands on your time that complicate your private life and cut you off from doing regular Christian work. It involves you in working alongside acts which you may feel are in bad taste or offensive. It puts you in a place where your beliefs are under pretty constant attack from people who entirely reject Christian standards."[25]

Yet as Richard spent time thinking through the issues of faith and culture, he ultimately began to question the philosophy of separation.

> Slowly, I came to feel that if I quit show-biz it would be like a rat leaving a sinking ship. I'd discovered, somewhat to my surprise, that there were active Christians in show business in far more difficult circumstances than I was. My modest little stand for Christ had obviously encouraged some of them a great deal—just as their stand has encouraged me since then. Should I pull out—with all my advantages as an established performer, able to be pretty choosy about his work—and leave them to get on with it? It was as much some of these active Christians in the entertainment world as anything else that swayed me to stay in and not quit. Surely, as a Christian living in a non-Christian world, I should expect pressure and learn to cope with it. This would be as true in a factory as on a film set. Running away from the world is no answer to its challenge . . . so I decided to stay put. Paul told the Christians at Corinth to stay in the position in life they were in when they were converted.[26]

One who supported Richard's decision not to forsake the rock and roll path was British pop star Elton John, who signed Richard to his Rocket label in 1976 and released "Devil Woman," a Top 10 hit in the U.S. Though wildly successful, the song was roundly criticized by traditionalists who thought it too racy, though it was actually a warning to beware the wiles of a dangerous woman. By then, however, Richard had come to a philosophical worldview that allowed him to stand vigorously for his faith without conceding an inch of territory in the pop music world.

"I'm a professional entertainer," he said. "That's my job. As I see it now, my responsibility is to do that job to the best of my ability and to the glory of God until He calls me to leave it and do something else. It does not seem to me any 'worldlier' then being a bank manager or shopkeeper. There is nothing especially immoral or sordid about the job itself, provided you don't allow yourself to be carried away by the glamour or the financial rewards. In fact, I find now that being in show biz is good for me, because it tests what I believe and so strengthens my own faith."[27]

While Richard's pop success in the U.S. was modest, he did manage to hit the charts hard in the late '70s with another pop smash, "We Don't Talk Anymore." Richard was becoming increasingly comfortable releasing records that addressed issues of life, love, and faith from a distinctly Christian perspective. "I am a Christian, so nothing I ever do now is secular," he said. "Even when I sing a pop song that doesn't mention Jesus, it's still a Christian song, because I am presenting it. If my record is played on a mainstream radio station, they are playing a Christian record whether they know it or not."[28]

It was a lesson his contemporaries across the Atlantic hadn't yet learned. Richard addressed the situation in a 1985 interview at a time when Amy Grant was beginning to be criticized for making moves toward the pop mainstream. "I'd like to say to Amy, 'You don't have to compromise anything and you don't even have to sing about Jesus all the time. Just do it your sweet way,'" said Richard. "If people like and respect you and if your walk with the Lord is good, then nothing you do will ever be secular, because you will have carefully thought out what you were going to do. You can sing about lost love and found love, and about love that's going to last forever. Then once people love you, you can slip them something that really explains what love is about."[29]

Although Richard served as a useful model of how an entertainer could stand in the middle of the public square, beliefs intact, he was not without his limitations. At times he seemed to miss the point of rock and roll, which was to struggle through and wrestle with the questions before offering conclusions. "Richard, who had virtually abandoned rock and roll in the late 1950s for a broader, safer style of pop, was not a songwriter, didn't see his music as a means of self-exploration, and was by nature a comfortable, 'nice' person," noted Steve Turner. "Whatever anger and frustrations he felt, they were not fuel for his music. There was nothing restless or urgent in the Cliff Richard experience. There were no abrasive edges."[30]

Richard could be feisty in defense of his faith, however, which Billy Graham discovered when he encountered the singer in the U.K.

> I will never forget a small dinner in London to which I had invited a dozen people. One of the guests that evening was a former prime minister, Sir Alec Douglas-Home. . . . Cliff Richard was also included as well as a prominent member of the royal family and her husband. Most of the conversation that evening revolved around Christianity—especially the deity of Jesus Christ. One of the guests could not accept this; he had been reared in a sect on the fringes of Christianity that denied the full divinity of Jesus Christ. Cliff exhibited an astonishing knowledge of the Bible and of theology that evening as they vigorously discussed what the Bible taught. I ended up saying very little, grateful for Cliff's willingness to take a stand for Christ.[31]

Bob Dylan

Bob Dylan shocked the music world with the release of his record *Slow Train Coming*, whose title song—a slow, foreboding track—had originated as a 1978 concert warm-up piece. *Slow Train* turned out to be the vehicle that delivered Dylan's musical born-again sermon. Recorded in Muscle Shoals, Alabama, and produced by the legendary Jerry Wexler and Barry Beckett, the album was a brooding theological treatise steeped in biblical phrasings that laid out for the listener a stark choice in the opening track, "Gotta Serve Somebody": "It may be the Devil or it may be the Lord, but you're gonna have to serve somebody."[32]

To fans unaccustomed to such fare from Dylan, it was, to say the least, a shock, compounded by Dylan's refusal at the outset to perform his earlier, much loved material. Fans weren't the only ones to be surprised by the turn of events. Catherine Kanner, the album's cover art designer was given specific instructions about what Dylan wanted. "The in-house art director at the label came up with a design and he rejected it," remembered Kanner, who was a freelancer at the time. "They were desperate to get something he'd approve, because he kept rejecting everything. He described the image he wanted: He wanted a train and a pick axe with a symbol of the cross. I was Jewish and he was, so it was a little weird, but how often do you get an opportunity like that?"[33] Typical of the reaction from outside the music industry were the words of one fan, who told biographer Robert Shelton, "I don't care what his religious beliefs are, but does he have to sing about it?"[34]

Of course, no one would have thought to say of Dylan in the '60s, "I don't care what his political beliefs are, but does he have to sing about them?" After being booed on a college campus, Dylan was particularly incensed. "The so-called intellectual students have shown their true monstrous selves," he fumed.[35] "When somebody says, 'I like the music, but the message I just can't get,'" he continued, "that's like saying, 'I like the eye, but the nose I just can't place. The ear's OK, but the neck just doesn't work.'"[36]

"I didn't mean to deliver a hammer blow," he said of his first batch of postconversion songs. "It might come out that way, but I'm not trying to kill anybody. You can't put down people who don't believe. Anybody can have the answer I have. I mean it's free."[37]

Some simply refused to believe that Dylan had become a Christian. "Even when . . . *Slow Train Coming* was released, Jan Wenner, the founder and editor of *Rolling Stone*, would trust none of his writers with the review but instead wrote it himself," noted Wheaton College professor Alan Jacobs in an essay posted on Bob Dylan's official website. "I smiled for weeks over Wenner's ingenious attempts to argue that the record didn't prove that Dylan was a Christian, his desperate protests that songs like 'I Believe In You' and 'When He Returns' didn't necessarily refer to Jesus. I smiled because Bob Dylan—Bob Dylan!—was on my side of the cultural street."[38]

In 1980, Dylan followed up *Slow Train Coming* with the more mellow and personal, but equally evangelical, *Saved*, with Beckett and Wexler again producing. As is often the case with spiritual conversions, the passing of time had given Dylan a sense of humility and left him a bit less self-righteous and accusatory. From "Saving Grace" to "What Can I Do for You?" *Saved* was full of gratitude and love for the "Lamb" who had saved him from "a pine box for all eternity."

By the time Dylan's third postconversion record, *Shot of Love* was released in 1981, he had successfully synthesized his faith into his life and was able to mix songs like "Property of Jesus" and "Every Grain of Sand" with love songs like the mesmerizing "Heart of Mine." He even mixed in a tribute song to the late comedian Lenny Bruce, and the result was an album less dogmatic, but no less Christian-oriented in its outlook.

While taking nothing away from *Slow Train Coming* and *Saved*, scholar Alan Jacobs believes that Dylan came into his own on *Shot of Love*. "I was so pleased when *Shot of Love* came out and I saw that there were some love songs and even a song about Lenny Bruce," noted Jacobs. "And the specifically Christian songs were more Dylanesque as in this . . . 'Positively Fourth Street'-like chorus: 'He's the Property of Jesus, resent him to the bone, you got something better, you got a heart of stone.' The way Dylan said 'stooooone,' with a contemptuous sneer—now that was the Man come back again."[39]

"They've evolved," said Dylan in an interview given between *Saved* and *Shot of Love*. "I've made my statement and I don't think I could make it any better than in some of those songs. Once I've said what I need to say in a song, that's it. I don't want to repeat myself. . . . But that doesn't mean that I won't keep singing these songs."[40]

Dylan's conversion was at once gradual and sudden, for as biographer Shelton observed, Dylan and Jesus had never really been strangers. "As early as 1962 in 'Long Ago, Far Away,' he'd talked about the crucifixion. As long ago . . . as the Basement Tapes, he'd written 'Sign on the Cross,' indicating how worrying the Christian question could be," Shelton wrote. "We've seen the slow buildup of born-again myth and the equally strong content of Judeo-Christian morality throughout his work. To believers, for a Jew to turn toward Christianity represents a form of 'completion.'"[41]

"Exile, redemption, salvation, righteousness, judgment, faith, and belief have all been constant concerns and themes in his work," observed another biographer, Jonathan Cott, "and he had always sung of Jesus—the greatest of Dylan's outlaw heroes—as one of the principled teachers and healers of the world, who was unjustly scorned, abused, and misunderstood."[42]

"I truly had a born-again experience," said Dylan in a postconversion interview given to Robert Hilburn of the *Los Angeles Times*. "I always knew there was a God or a Creator of the Universe, and a Creator of the mountains and the sea, . . . but I wasn't conscious of Jesus and what that had to do with the Supreme Creator."[43]

He had also long expressed a reverence for the Bible. "I had always read the Bible, but I only looked at it as literature."[44]

Dylan's transformation was also sudden because he believed in Christ after a "vision and a feeling" when, he maintained, the room had actually moved.

He had been influenced by his girlfriend at the time, the actress Mary Alice Artes, who had begun attending church services at a church called the Vineyard in Malibu, California, not far from Dylan's home. After Artes had rededicated her life to God, she asked several of the pastors to accompany her to visit her boyfriend. Pastors Larry Myers and Paul Edmond visited with Dylan, and their meeting resulted in the singer's subsequent public embracing of the Christian faith.

> We met a man who was very interested in learning what the Bible
> says about Jesus Christ [remembered Myers]. To the best of my abil-
> ity, I started at the beginning in Genesis and walked through the Old
> Testament and the New Testament and ended in Revelation. I tried
> to clearly express what is the historical, orthodox understanding of
> who Jesus is. It was a quite intelligent conversation with a man who
> was seriously intent on understanding the Bible. There was no
> attempt to convince, manipulate or pressure this man into anything.
> But in my view God spoke through His Word, the Bible, to a man
> who had been seeking for many years. Sometime in the next few
> days, privately and on his own, Bob accepted Christ and believed
> that Jesus Christ is indeed the Messiah. After yet more time and fur-
> ther serious deliberation, Bob was baptized.[45]

Dylan later claimed that, unlike many born-again experiences which
were birthed in turmoil, he had been doing fine and had "given up looking
and searching." He said, "Well, everybody has got their own truth. What
works for one man is fine as long as it works for him. If I was searching, it
was just to get down to the root reality of the way things really are, to pull
the mask off. My thing was always to pull the mask off of whatever was
going on."[46]

"Nobody ever told me Jesus could save me," said Dylan at a concert in
1980. "I never thought I needed to be saved. I thought I was doing just fine."[47]

"I was kind of skeptical, but I was also open," he said of the meeting. "I
certainly wasn't cynical. I asked lots of questions, questions like 'What's the
son of God? What's all that mean?' and 'What does it mean, dying for my
sins?'" Gradually, he came to the conclusion "that Jesus is real and I wanted
that. I knew that he wasn't going to come into my life and make it miserable,
so one thing led to another . . . until I had this feeling, this vision and feeling."[48] Dylan was baptized at the home of Vineyard pastor Bill Dwyer.

"I truly had a born-again experience, if you want to call it that," Dylan
told Hilburn. "It's an overused term, but it's something that people can relate
to. I just sat up in bed at seven in the morning and I was compelled to get
dressed and drive over to the Bible school. I couldn't believe I was there."[49]

"Jesus put his hand on me," he told another interviewer. "It was a physical thing. I felt it. I felt it all over me. I felt my whole body tremble. The
glory of God knocked me down and picked me up."[50]

"We had nothing to do with it compared with those people who prayed
for him for such a long period," said Kenn Gulliksen, senior pastor of the
Vineyard. "I just felt like he was being born and we kind of caught him as he
was coming out." Gulliksen added that Dylan subsequently spent five days a

week for nearly four months attending the church's school of discipleship, "learning the Word, growing in the Lord."[51]

"The students, numbering no more than twenty, included housewives, a fledgling film producer, an unemployed construction worker, a few lay ministers, and a man considered by millions to be the poet of our time," observed authors Davin Seay and Mary Neely. "Dylan fit tolerably well in the group, considering the shadow he cast; he spoke little, listened attentively, and practiced the guarded glances of the famous."[52]

For Dylan, attending the sessions was something he initially kept quiet. "I didn't want to reflect on the Lord at all, because if I told people and then I didn't keep going to the Vineyard, they'd say, 'Oh well, I guess it was just another one of those things that didn't work out.' I didn't know myself if I could go for three months. But I did begin telling a few people after a couple of months and a lot of them got angry with me. By that time, I was into it. When I believe in something, I don't care what anybody else thinks."[53]

"We strongly encouraged him that he had a platform that no one else had, and that he should continue in that position," recalled Kenn Gulliksen. "We told him to be open to God's leading if he felt he should do something else." Gulliksen also advised Dylan "not to get into the Christian circuit where so many celebrities go after they have come to know the Lord and are immediately put on a pedestal. They go through horrendous times of trial because they're expected to be mature in the faith when they're just brand-new babies."[54]

Though he never recorded for a CCM label, Dylan did associate with some in that scene, including perhaps the most honored member of the Christian music culture, Keith Green, who died in a plane crash in 1982. Green and Dylan enjoyed a close friendship, and Green's wife Melody's observations in *No Compromise*, her biography of her husband, are particularly poignant.

Green and Dylan met through the Vineyard, and before long, Dylan was at the Green's home for dinner and Green was visiting Dylan at his offices. Dylan, who was just then writing songs for his album, *Saved*, asked Green for input.

"Bob pulled out some lyric sheets and showed them to us," remembered Green's wife. "He wanted to know what we thought and we told him. The lyrics were great. Then Keith and I exchanged glances as if to say, 'Can you believe one of the world's greatest songwriters is asking our opinion?' Maybe it was his vulnerability that bonded our hearts to his in a special way."[55]

For Dylan, Green was more than just a musical sounding board; he was also a spiritual advisor of sorts. "Although [Dylan] was one of the most well-known musicians in the world, he was the same as anyone who wanted to know more about God," Melody remembered. "He was full of eager questions and fresh excitement about his spiritual discoveries. Keith loved him deeply and they talked a lot."[56]

Green, never one to be soft-spoken, once felt he had overstepped his bounds in making a point to Dylan a bit too aggressively. He wrote in his diary that night, "Tried to be the Holy Spirit to Bob Dylan today."[57]

But the most amazing thing that Green learned from Dylan was that one of the world's greatest singer/songwriters was literally evangelizing on the streets. "Bob would tell us that he loved to pick up hitchhikers in his beat-up old car and talk to them about the Lord—without letting them know who he was,"[58] remembered Melody. Dylan also revealed to the couple that he read several chapters in the Bible daily.

After Green moved to Texas, he and Dylan kept in touch by phone, and when Green traveled back to L.A. to record his third album, Dylan agreed to play a harmonica solo on the song "Pledge My Head to Heaven." Two years later, Green and two of his young children were dead and Dylan's haunting harmonica solo seemed almost prophetic in its profound sadness.

After a few years, Dylan became considerably less urgent in his once burning need to tell others about his faith. "It's in my system," he said. "I don't really have enough time to talk about it. If someone really wants to know, I can explain it to them, but there are other people who can do it just as well. I don't feel compelled to do it. I was doing a bit of that last year on stage. I was saying stuff I figured people needed to know. I thought I was giving people an idea of what was behind the songs. I don't think it's necessary anymore."[59]

"This is no Maharishi trip with me," Dylan had said, in response to a question from Hilburn who had wondered, "We've seen so many rock stars get involved with gurus and Maharishis and then move on."

"Jesus is definitely not that to me," Dylan added later. "When I walk around some of the towns we go to, however, I'm totally convinced people need Jesus. Look at the junkies and the winos and the troubled people. It's all sickness which can be healed in an instant. The powers that be won't let that happen. The powers that be say it has to be healed politically."[60]

"Whoever was supposed to pick it up [did]," Dylan said. "Maybe the time for me to say that has come and gone. It's time for me to do something else. Sometimes those things appear quickly and disappear. Jesus himself only preached for three years."[61]

After *Shot of Love,* Dylan withdrew most of his overt Christian material. There were several reasons for this, according to Al Kasha, an Academy award-winning composer, former Columbia Records executive, and spiritual mentor of sorts to Dylan. "I think what happened was he was concerned about Columbia after *Shot of Love,*" Kasha recalled. "The first album did well, but the second album didn't. He's still an artist and he still has to make a living. Columbia was concerned that he was just going to be a fanatic, which a lot of artists are. On top of that, what happened was that he would go out with these evangelists and he found a lot of them didn't live up to the standard that he thought they should live up to and he really wasn't discipled enough. That was the real problem—he didn't have a long enough discipleship before being sent out."[62]

According to biographer Robert Shelton, he began "spending considerable time at a Brooklyn center called Chabad Lubavitch, the Hasidic cult that puts music so centrally into its rituals and group life."[63]

Around this time, Dylan also traveled to Israel for his son's bar mitzvah and was photographed at the Western Wall. Later, a photo of the artist crouching on the Mount of Olives appeared on his next album, *Infidels.*

Partisans in both the Christian and Jewish communities claimed Dylan was in their camp. "Evidence of his Jewish involvement continues to mount," wrote Larry Yudelson in a moving, 1991 essay in *Washington Jewish Week.* "One friend of mine saw him at a Minneapolis bris. Another heard he davens at the UCLA Hillel. One writer tells the story of how Dylan attended synagogue in jeans, scruffy beard and a battered hat and was recognized by the rabbi and invited to open the ark. . . . More recently, Dylan wrote a cover blurb for Rabbi Manis Friedman's *Why Doesn't Anyone Blush Anymore*, in which the influential Minneapolis Lubavitch rabbi defends traditional Jewish rules of sexual modesty. . . . Dylan appeared on a 1988 Lubavitch telethon playing harmonica while his Sabbath-observing son-in-law played guitar and sang."[64]

Another, Bill Parr, who runs an Internet website devoted to proving Dylan's conversion to Christianity was not fleeting, countered that the strongest evidence was in the songs he continued to play live. "The most common claim is that Dylan has returned to Judaism and the theological position of the Lubavitchers," Parr said. "And the claim is made that he did this circa 1983. . . . [but] consider Dylan's persistent selection of 'In the

Garden,' for set lists, and citation of that song as being a song 'about my hero.'"[65]

Writer Steve Greenfield observed one such concert on July 17, 1988, in St. Louis. "Bob Dylan did perform one tune from his Christian albums," he wrote, "'In the Garden,' with Dylan singing with deep emotion as though the song was dear to him. He related the story of 'the Son of God' who 'healed the blind and crippled' and 'rose from the dead' to over 11,000 of his fans. They knew what he was talking about. As the song goes, 'Did they believe?' Someone in the crowd yelled, 'Jesus.'"[66]

While many Christians were troubled by Dylan's involvement with the Lubavitchers, Al Kasha, who had earlier followed a spiritual journey similar to Dylan's, found nothing inconsistent about it, admitting that he, too, though a believer in Christ, occasionally studied with the group. "Lubavitchers are like Hasidic Jews . . . [like] Jesuit priests," he said. "They're very much intellectuals . . . into the Kabbala. But they're spiritual, they're in constant search of the Scriptures. I go into a Hasidic synagogue sometimes to listen to the teachings since they're very good Rabbis and good teachers."[67]

In a booklet that accompanied his *Biograph* album, Dylan gave fans a taste of his theology. "I like to keep my values scripturally straight, though. I like to stay a part of that stuff that don't change," he said. "God is still the judge and the Devil still rules the world, so what's different? . . . Sound like a preacher, don't I?"[68]

According to Shelton, Dylan also disliked the labeling of that earlier period in his life as "the born again Christian period" and himself considered it "another label he couldn't tolerate."[69]

"The problem," noted Yudelson, "at least for one Washington area rabbi who had painfully excommunicated Dylan from his record collection when the singer converted, was that Dylan's return to Judaism, if it was that, was taking place without the publicity of his departure. Dylan would not leave his Christian stepping stones behind. Even as he recorded *Infidels*, he still professed belief in the Book of Revelation."[70] British music critic Steve Turner agreed with this assessment.

> Dylan did clearly retreat from the hot gospeling song introductions of 1981 in which he warned of the end of the world, and he avoided being labeled "born again" by interviewers. "Whatever label is put on you, the purpose is to limit your accessibility to people," he told *USA Today* in 1989. In the same interview, he denied that the trilogy was "religious," saying that the songs were "based on my experience in daily matters, what you run up against and how you respond to

things." At first glance, this seemed to be nonsense. How could he argue that songs about Jesus and the need to be saved, which sometimes quoted directly from the Bible, were not "religious"? Actually, however, Dylan appears to have been making the profound point that Jesus didn't come to start a religion but to enable people to know and glorify God in their everyday life. Dylan was writing observations not of religion but of his "experience in daily matters." It just so happened that Jesus had become a part of those matters. "Make something religious and people don't have to deal with it," he had observed in 1985. "They can say it's irrelevant."[71]

From time to time, his spirituality has oozed out, as it did in 1997 with the release of the much anticipated *Time Out of Mind*, which seemed to "reflect a peace with God," in the words of critic Dave Urbanski.

Dylan seemed to concur.

"A lot of the songs were written after the sun went down," he noted at the time. "And I like storms, I like to stay up during a storm. I get very meditative sometimes, and this one phrase was going through my head: 'Work while the day lasts, because the night of death cometh when no man can work.' I don't recall where I heard it. I like preaching; I hear a lot of preaching and I probably just heard it somewhere. Maybe it's in Psalms, it beats me. But it wouldn't let me go. I was, like, 'What does that phrase mean?' But it was at the forefront of my mind for a long period of time and I think a lot of that is instilled in the record."[72]

The passage was apparently from the New Testament writings of the apostle John who, in the fourth verse of the ninth chapter, quoted Jesus as saying, "I must work the works of him that sent me, while it is day: the night cometh when no man can work." (KJV)

"I know the mercy of God must be near," Dylan sang on "Standing in the Doorway."[73] "I feel like I'm coming to the end of my way, but I know God is my shield and he won't lead me astray,"[74] he continued on "Til I Fell in Love with You." On "Standing in the Doorway," Dylan sang, "I went to church on Sunday as she passed by."[75]

Were these simply throwaway lines from an inventive poet, or did they imply something deeper and more spiritually significant?

To T-Bone Burnett, who played with Dylan's Rolling Thunder Revue in the mid-1970s, Dylan's spiritual quest was always a steady trek. "Someone gave me a tape of a show he did—I think in 1971, when he was nineteen or twenty years old—at Carnegie Recital Hall," said Burnett. "One of the things he said on the tape was, 'I believe in the Ten Commandments. The first commandment, "I am the Lord thy God," is a great commandment. I believe that as long as it's not the wrong people saying it,' which I think, is the same thing he was saying during the time when there was the big uproar about him. In other words, I'd say the whole story of Bob Dylan is one man's search for God. The turns and steps he takes to find God are his business."[76]

Refusing to subscribe to any organized religious denomination, Dylan spoke about his faith at the time of the 1997 release of *Time Out of Mind*. "Here's the thing with me and the religious thing," he told David Gates of *Newsweek*. "This is the flat-out truth: I find the religiosity and philosophy in the music. I don't find it anywhere else. Songs like 'Let Me Rest on a Peaceful Mountain,' or 'I Saw the Light'—that's my religion. I don't adhere to rabbis, preachers, evangelists, all of that. I've learned more from the songs than I've ever learned from any of this kind of entity. The songs are my lexicon. I believe the songs."[77]

Dylan repeated those comments to Jon Parales of the *New York Times*. "Those old songs are my lexicon and prayer book," he said. "All my beliefs come out of those old songs, literally, anything from 'Let Me Rest on a Peaceful Mountain' to 'Keep on the Sunny Side.' You can find all my philosophy in those old songs. I believe in a God of time and space, but if people ask me about that, my impulse is to point them back toward those songs. I believe in Hank Williams singing 'I Saw the Light.' I've seen the light too."[78]

Both statements begged the question—which neither reporter attempted to answer—what was the theology in those songs? Williams's song in particular gave Dylan's Christian fans hope: "I wandered so aimless, life filled with sin, I wouldn't let my dear Savior in, Then Jesus came like a stranger in the night. I was a fool to wander and stray, Straight is the gate and narrow the way, But now I have traded the wrong for the right, Praise the Lord I saw the light."[79]

"Keep on the Sunny Side" was also fairly clear in its theology: "Let us greet with the song of hope each day, though the moment be cloudy or fair, let us trust in our Savior away, Who keepeth every one in His care."[80]

"Let Me Rest on a Peaceful Mountain," also known as "Hills of Home," was a song performed by bluegrass legend Ralph Stanley written to a departed friend that included the lines, "The Man who calls our number, somehow, you fit into His plans. I never questioned His decision, for I'm only a human, just another man . . . rest in peace . . . for one day this Earth I'll no longer roam . . . and once again we'll be together, side by side, in the hills of home."[81]

Such fans were also quick to swap stories of songs he performed in concert that backed up their belief, such as the hymn "Rock of Ages" he was reported to have performed at a February 2, 1999, concert in Pensacola,

Florida: "Rock of Ages cleft for me, Let me hide myself in thee; let the water and the blood, From thy wounded side which flowed, Be of sin the double cure, Save from wrath and make me pure. Could my tears forever flow, Could my zeal no languor know, these for sin could not atone—Thou must save and thou alone: In my hand no price I bring, Simply to Thy cross I cling. While I draw this final breath, When my eyes shall close in death, When I rise to worlds unknown, And behold Thee on Thy throne."[82]

Dylan's 1999 tour with Paul Simon found the singer opening his set with a bluegrass song, "Hallelujah I'm Ready to Go." "In the darkness of night not a star was in sight, on that highway that leads down below, then Jesus came in, and he saved my soul from sin . . . Oh sinners awake before it's too late, He's a wonderful saviour you know. I fell on my knees and he answered my pleas, Hallelujah I'm ready to go."[83]

Ultimately, the exact nature of Dylan's relationship with his God is unknowable and between him and his Creator, and those who were sure they had an exact handle on it would no doubt continue to be disappointed. Still, setlists like those kept his Christian fans coming back for more.

Yet, Dylan's greatest contribution to expressions of faith in popular culture remains his wise decision not to abandon his recording career and join the religious subculture as so many other musicians had done, choosing instead to fly his flag of faith for the popular music culture, and all the world, to see.

Alice Cooper

Perhaps the most stunning conversion of all was the quiet transformation of Alice Cooper, the ultimate shock rocker, who in 1994 released an album titled *The Last Temptation* that strongly hinted at a conversion experience: "What about Christ/what about peace/what about love, what about faith in God above," sang the rocker on "Cleansed by Fire."[84]

On "It's Me," Cooper seemed to embrace God: "Who's the man that'll take you in, when all your luck is gone, it's me, it's me, what are you searching for I know you can find my door, it's me, I know you've sinned every sin, but I'll still take you in, it's me."[85]

On "Nothing's Free," from the same record, Cooper sang, "When the trumpets sound and his light is all around and the saints all raise from the graves in the ground, we'll be going way downtown."[86]

Significantly, Cooper continued to record for his label, Epic, and shied away from public pronouncements, but his music was doing plenty of talking and people were noticing.

To those who hadn't heard the latest in the Cooper saga, it might have appeared to be a mystery when a TV newsmagazine show's hidden camera tracking down speeding cars in an Arizona suburb caught Cooper riding with country singer Glen Campbell. What could the chief shock rocker possibly have in common with the mild-mannered Campbell? The answer appeared to be faith.

Cooper was born Vincent Damon Furnier in Detroit, Michigan, on February 4, 1948, but his family eventually settled in Phoenix, Arizona. His father, Ether Moroni Furnier, became an ordained Baptist minister and a missionary to the Apache Indians. At Cortez High School in Phoenix, young Vincent and some high school buddies formed a rock band called the Earwigs and, later, the Spiders.

Moving to L. A., the band changed names again to Nazz before settling on Alice Cooper in 1968 and signing a record deal with Straight-Bizarre Records. In 1971, the band came to the attention of the music world with the release of its first hit album, *Love It to Death.*

For all his on-stage shenanigans, faith was never far from Cooper. His father wrote in the introduction to Cooper's 1976 autobiography, *Me Alice,* that his son had "drifted away from church attendance altogether," adding, "am I dreaming or suffering from wishful thinking that after all this decadence there will emerge from this dynamic personality a servant of God?"[87]

Ether Furnier's wish seemed to have been granted in the early '90s when Cooper reportedly began to attend a small Baptist church in his hometown, and his faith seemed to deepen with each passing year. Author Ken Myers, whose book *All God's Children and Blue Suede Shoes* dealt with rock music and pop culture, was shocked when Cooper approached him with a copy of the book in hand, requesting an autograph.

"Alice Cooper has had a real conversion experience," said Pat Boone. "He attends a Baptist church in Phoenix regularly—he and his wife and kids—and attends a Tuesday night Bible study there. In some of his stuff, I was astounded to find words that could be recorded by contemporary gospel groups."[88]

Cooper himself confirmed the story in an August 1997 interview with Knight Ridder, telling a reporter, "I'm not onstage preaching. I still do 'School's Out' and 'Eighteen.' I don't see why a Christian can't be a rock 'n' roller and have a really high energy show." He added that he had "had to get rid of the alcoholism that was really crushing me."[89]

Not unlike B. J. Thomas two decades before, Cooper refused to embrace the tag "Christian artist." "He's not a 'Christian rock artist,' and he's quick to make that distinction," noted writer Brian McCollum, "to separate himself from Petra or dc Talk, or others who have made spiritual music with a rock beat. But the forty-nine-year-old Detroit native will tell you, unabashedly, he is now a rock artist who's Christian."[90]

"This show is absolutely Alice Cooperesque all the way," he said. "Just know that Alice Cooper has never been a cult or satanic. We've always been a sideshow and we always had a certain amount of wholesomeness to it. People have always walked away saying, 'This was a great party!'"[91]

Cooper may have been downplaying, if the lyrics to songs on *The Last Temptation* were any indication, what appeared to have been a raging spiritual battle for his soul. "You lose and I win, you couldn't suck me in," sang Cooper on "Cleansed by Fire. "It's over, you have no power, you're lost and I'm found and I'm heaven bound. Go back where you belong, to where you fell, go to hell."[92]

On "Lullaby" Cooper sang, "All of my things that I play with in daylight you turn into monsters at night. . . . I don't want to follow you down to your place, I don't want to be a child of disgrace. You can take your whiskey soaked, foaming at the mouth, toilet talking pea soup spewing sweating demon breath out of my face. . . . Get down—back into hell, your black soul, you know you're black hearted I smell your sulfurous smell."[93]

As Cooper attempted to reconcile his outlandish public persona and reputation as a shock rocker with his newfound faith, he realized it was not an easy task. "Sure, it was tough," he said. "But at the same time, I don't think I'm doing anything offensive to the Christians. I don't find anything offensive about these songs. The theatrics that go on with our shows have always been RKO horror movies. When you can't be more shocking than CNN, it's time to not do it anymore. In the '70s, it was easier to shock people."[94]

Unlike many early CCM artists who were quick to shun their old songs and old audiences in favor of polite Christian crowds, Alice Cooper wanted to make sure his old fans would show up to hear his new message, and many of them did just that.

Michael Omartian

One of the most successful producer/artists in the pop music world was also one of the most devout and one of the best examples of an artist on the firewalk of faith. As a producer for artists like Rod Stewart, Christopher Cross, Loggins and Messina, Boz Scaggs, Al Jarreau, Dolly Parton, and many others, Michael Omartian established himself as one of the pop world's most respected producers.

Raised by a perfectionist mother who demanded success of her son, Omartian gravitated toward music early. "I started classical piano lessons at age four," he remembered, "took up drums at five, and studied jazz piano in junior high. It's the melding together of jazz, classical, and—in the later years—rock that made me whatever I am now musically."[95]

After moving to L. A. in the late '60s, Omartian got his first break in 1970. "Loggins and Messina got together to form a duo and Loggins got me involved," he remembered. "We recorded *Sittin' In* in 1971, and after the record did well they wanted to take this thing on the road for a tour. But by that time, through other associations and work, people were listening to what I was playing and they wanted me to play on their records. I was becoming very involved in session work."[96]

As a staff producer at ABC Records, Omartian oversaw several hit songs for the group Rhythm Heritage, including the theme from *S.W.A.T.*; "Keep Your Eye on the Sparrow," the theme from *Baretta*; and the theme song from *Rocky*, "Gonna Fly Now."

"This was back before *Miami Vice* and MTV," said Omartian. "At that time, people in the movie and television industry didn't know people in the music business. Somebody came up with a brilliant idea, that a show could go a little further with some exposure on Top 40 radio. We decided to do the theme from *S.W.A.T.* and got a number one record."[97]

A few years before Omartian achieved a degree of fame and fortune with the three hit songs, he had released an album of his own called *White Horse*. Originally recorded for ABC, *White Horse* was a pop record that also touched on topics like baptism, repentance, and faith, and ABC didn't know what to do with it.

"I went to the people at ABC and said I would really like to do a record," he said. "They were all gung-ho, so they said 'Go ahead and do it.' When they got the tapes, they were surprised. It was very progressive, even by the standards of secular music at the time, and they were all excited about the music end of it. But they couldn't figure out what the heck was going on lyrically and that kind of threw them."[98]

Though he had never intended to be in the CCM market, when Word Records heard of Omartian's project, they decided to release it into the Christian world, which didn't understand it either—but for different reasons. "Folks at ABC didn't grasp Stormie's lyrics, and gospel music buyers couldn't understand Michael's music," observed critic Steve Rabey, "but *White Horse* remains one of the best, most professionally produced Christian records around."[99]

Omartian recorded several more albums for various CCM labels, and though his production work kept him in the center of pop music culture, his own music was only heard by the subculture and the small coterie of musicians who knew him. "Some musicians I knew, like Jeff Porcaro of Toto and others, say they still pull that thing out and listen to it," said Omartian of his first record. "It was a musician's kind of album. *White Horse* got a tremendous reception, but it didn't sell anything. We didn't really worry about sales. We never looked at our Christian records as a money-making proposition, because we're doing fine on the other end."[100]

"The other end" referred to Omartian's astounding success as a producer, which eventually won him a Grammy award for his production work on a debut record by a soft-spoken Texan named Christopher Cross, which yielded several smash hits, including "Ride Like the Wind" and "Sailing." Though Omartian's faith was always solid and front-and-center, he faced head-on the many challenges of being a Christian in the middle of a pop music culture that was often in opposition to his own beliefs. Along the way, Omartian the producer made some decisions that Omartian the Christian later regretted, including production work on a racy single by Alan O'Day called "Undercover Angel."

"It was a giant mistake I should never make again," said Omartian of the song. "I was so into music at the time that the Lord had to teach me that I just couldn't focus on what I liked about the music. I had to step back and listen to what the person was saying. It was a matter of responsibility and listening to what was being said, and I'm glad that happened before I became a solo producer, because I really needed to understand that whole idea."[101]

Omartian's most public and embarrassing blunder was still to come. In 1983, he agreed to produce Rod Stewart's record *Camouflage*. Trouble soon brewed over a song that Stewart had begun writing after the project was underway. It was another sexy song, much like "Undercover Angel," which Stewart had titled "Bad for You."

"The song was still being put together," remembered Omartian. "There wasn't a title and there weren't lyrics, and this was five and a half months into the project. Well, he started singing these lyrics and I said, 'What in the world is this?' I couldn't believe it. I asked him if he was going to change it. He said no. I said, 'I'm going to have to do something about this. I need to put a disclaimer on there.'"[102]

Omartian did, and on the back of Stewart's record appeared, "Please note: The song 'Bad for You' does not represent the views of Michael Omartian, a born-again Christian."[103]

For Omartian, the period following the release of the album was a trying time when he wasn't sure if his career had been permanently jeopardized. "Something like the disclaimer can't help but cause ripples," he said. "You're dealing with an industry that is basically not godly and doesn't want to have anything to do with godliness. Consequently, I was sticking my neck out. I could have taken the advice of a lot of people who said to forget it—it would die or something. I just didn't feel right about it. I battled with it. I would go to bed at night thinking this would be the end of it for me."[104]

It was also a time when his priorities were clearly laid out and his loyalties were severely tested. "I realized I'm not serving these people," he said. "I'm serving God, so I have to do what He tells me to do. I believe that one of the reasons I'm in the music business is to stick my neck out—to represent the antithesis of all I see going on all the time. I'm not alone. There's other people out here doing the same thing. It's scary, but I feel I have a responsibility to God."[105]

"After that the album went very smoothly," remembered Omartian. "In fact there were two Christians in Rod's band, who drew strength from our conversations and our time together. I encouraged them toward getting back to church and reading their Bibles and praying. And Rod and I had many opportunities throughout the project to talk about the Lord. The first day in the studio, he was reading Pat Boone's testimony book, and later on he was reading books by Robert Schuller."[106]

For his part, Stewart didn't appear to be fazed by the dust-up. "There was one time [Omartian] wanted to change the lyrics in a song because he's a born-again Christian," he recalled. "But generally, speaking, I would love to work with him again, even though we did have a few punch-ups."[107]

Looking back, Omartian was unsure whether he had done God's will or not, but he was sure that he had been lax in seeking the opinions of those around him. "I usually seek God's guidance about whether I should do a particular project, but I had to debate this one harder because of all the ramifications of the thing. So my wife and I, and two other people, held a three-day fast about it, and after the time was over, I made my decision to produce the album before I asked the other people their feelings. That was wrong of me. It was not being obedient to God by not seeking counsel. That was my fault. I'm not saying that God would have said no to the project, but it was the wrong way for me to approach it."[108]

Walking the fine line between a paranoia that suspects that behind every disappointment in the entertainment business is anti-Christian bias and a blissful ignorance of the hostility for true believers that sometimes creeps into the rock world, Omartian realized that if your work was good, people would usually put up with your faith. "You know the same presidents of record companies who call me and tell me I shouldn't have put the disclaimer on the Stewart album call me up the next week and ask me to produce somebody for them," he said.[109]

Omartian arrived at a balanced theology of being in the middle of the music culture with his values intact, a position that allowed him to listen to the religious views of others while being articulate about his own faith. "At one point, they sat me down and started giving me their whole Baha'i faith trip," remembered Omartian of his work with the group Seals and Croft. "I listened to what they said and told them quite honestly that I didn't understand what they were talking about. Then I told them I believed in Jesus Christ and that He was my personal Savior, and they almost fell off their stools. . . . Or take what happened with Peter Cetera, the former lead singer for Chicago. He came to talk to me about me producing his solo album, and he wanted to know what this born-again Christian stuff was all about. I explained my faith to him and he said, 'I don't know if I believe all that, but at least I know I can trust you and work with you.'"[110]

As Michael Omartian, producer extraordinaire, learned the ropes in the strange world where pop music and faith intersected, he came to articulate a vision of faith in a fiery furnace that, to their shame, many believers stayed away from. It was easier, after all, to operate in the small Christian subculture they had neatly carved out for themselves, away from the dangers that inevitably lurked in the real world. For them, Omartian had a real life message: Stand tall, plant your feet, do the work, and refuse to compromise your beliefs.

"I don't see how a non-Christian can make it in this business," he mused. "The temporary euphoria you get out of having a Top 10 hit will never make it in the long run, because you're not going to have that forever. You're going to have to draw on something deeper."[111]

Donna Summer

Born LaDonna Andrea Gaines to a conservative, churchgoing family in Boston, Massachusetts, Donna Summer grew up singing in the church she attended with her parents, her brother, and five sisters.

"I came from a lower-middle-class black family," she recalled. "My mother and father worked real hard. He was a real dominating father but a very good father. He was a butcher during the war, so we always had meat. He was also an electrician and a janitor, and in his spare time he took care of buildings. There were times we didn't have anything, but my parents just never let us down."[112]

Summer credited her family, friends, and extended family for her desire to be successful. "Even as a child, I knew I was going to be something," she remembered. "I mean . . . I got credit in my neighborhood store just because everyone believed that one day I'd be successful. I could go down and take anything I wanted, and they'd write it down on a bill and say to me, 'You're going to be famous one day. You can pay it then.'"[113]

Despite such predictions of success, Summer quickly got tripped up by drugs. "When I was about sixteen, I went through a pretty heavy drug scene," she remembered. "That was the 'Janis Joplin' part of my life. I was in a rock 'n' roll group, the only female and the only black person in the group. I was the lead singer. It was the whole psychedelic period, when everyone was trying and testing new things, and I just went overboard. I finally went so far that, when I was eighteen, I said, 'Enough! God did not intend me to live my life this way.' And so I quit abruptly after two years, and I really haven't indulged in drugs since."[114]

Summer had given up church singing to play with the band and that work led her further down her chosen career path. "We wrote songs that were very hippy, kind of psychedelic lyrics," she remembered. "We were kind of in the Boston scene at that point. Then we went to New York, where I was discovered. I auditioned in New York for *Hair*, but I was accepted for the show in Germany."[115]

Germany was a place Summer felt comfortable traveling to because her father had once lived there. "He and my mother used to speak German around me and it used to make me mad, because I couldn't understand them. So I went, because I thought it was a good chance to learn how to speak another language."[116] It was in Europe that Summer met three men who would change her life. First, she married a member of the cast of the Vienna Folk Opera, Helmut Sommer, then collaborated with Giorgio Moroder and Pete Belotte, co-owners of the Oasis record label. Summer's first hit single was the raunchy "Love to Love You Baby," which Summer and Moroder produced together.

"I told Giorgio that I had an idea for a song," she remembered. "I sang the melody to him and he put down a track. I came into the studio the next day and he wanted me to put down my vocal, but I wasn't really prepared, so

I ad libbed and that was left on the song. I was goofing around. I was lying on the floor moaning and we were all hysterical. It was just too funny."[117]

One person who didn't think the song funny was Neil Bogart, owner of Casablanca Records who realized its potential and asked for a seventeen-minute version, which he subsequently encouraged radio stations to play after midnight because of its racy content. Within a matter of weeks, the record had sold half a million copies, and Summer was on her way to superstardom.

For the next five years, Summer reigned as the queen of disco, but in the midst of all the craziness she began to experience emotional and physical problems. It took paranoia, insomnia, and ulcers to drive her back to God and her faith commitment.

"The sudden, explosive fame almost precipitated a nervous breakdown," observed writer Elliot Mintz in a 1980 profile. "Traumatized by the frenzy and the new identity imposed on her, she went through periods of forgetting her name, developed a chronic ulcer, and occasionally checked into hospitals for a week at a time. To this day, she admits that her greatest fear is of losing control of herself, mentally and emotionally."[118]

By the time she recorded her first album for the Geffen label in 1980, it was clear that Donna Summer was a changed person. She had married her live-in boyfriend, Bruce Sudano, and set to work recording *The Wanderer*, a record that showcased a new Donna Summer who did not hesitate to sing about earthly love, but would not leave her faith behind. Facing the same pressures that caused other artist Christians in similar situations to either retreat to the religious music ghetto or fail to weave their faith to their art, she instead closed the record off with a hearty modern hymn, "I Believe in Jesus."

Rolling Stone's Dave Marsh, always a tough critic, wrote of the song, "'I Believe in Jesus' is the first convincing gospel-based vocal performance of Summer's career. Based on the militant fundamentalist hymn 'Onward Christian Soldiers' and the nursery rhyme 'Mary Had a Little Lamb,' the composition escapes being cloying only by the narrowest of margins—a chorus so perfectly sung that to deny it is practically inconceivable: 'I believe in Jesus you know I know him oh so well / And I'm going to heaven by and by 'cause I already been through hell.'"[119]

"*The Wanderer* was a big departure from Donna's earlier disco days," noted *Blues & Soul* magazine. "Based in traditional rock-soul-gospel, the title track became a million-selling single, much to the astonishment of everyone who expected her following to dwindle after she left Casablanca [Records].

Her music also began to reflect new beliefs, and 'I Believe in Jesus' won a Grammy for Best International Song."[120]

On her next outing, *State of Independence*, producer Quincy Jones surrounded Summer with the likes of Dionne Warwick, Lionel Richie, Michael Jackson, Stevie Wonder, James Ingram, and Brenda Russell.

Beginning in 1983, Summer teamed up with producer, and fellow believer, Michael Omartian on *Cats without Claws* and *She Works Hard for the Money*, both of which contained numerous, clear statements of faith. Summer also worked to bring CCM artists into the marketplace of ideas by singing a duet with Matthew Ward (of the group Second Chapter of Acts) on the track "Love Has a Mind of Its Own," and recording a ballad by writer/singers Dony McGuire and Reba Rambo called "Forgive Me," for which she won another Grammy.

Early on, Summer was not shy about telling her audience about her Christian beliefs. "Some of her born-again pronouncements alienated gay fans who had been among the first to buy her records in the '70's," noted critic David E. Keeps.[121]

"The media picked up the story and blew it totally out of proportion," observed *Blues & Soul*. "Her huge gay following turned away from her in droves. Her records were publicly burned. Demonstrations were held opposing the sale of the music and DJs refused to play her records. Donna Summer was persona non grata."[122]

The thought police had branded her politically incorrect, and though she never again experienced the commercial success she enjoyed during her reign as disco queen, Summer continued to release marginally successful pop records throughout the late '80s and '90s, before moving to Nashville to begin work on a musical based on her life.

Refusing to surrender to the pop music *zeitgeist*, Summer stood boldly on her principles and refused to concede her place in the musical marketplace of ideas. She almost certainly would have enjoyed a more lucrative pop music career had she continued to churn out variations of the degrading single that made her a star, or had she recorded strictly "secular" music that didn't reflect her faith, a phenomenon artist Steve Taylor sarcastically christened as "separation of church and mind." It's equally certain that she would have been hailed as a conquering hero in the Christian subculture had she decided to sing irrelevant "religious" music for fellow believers.

Through it all, Donna Summer survived with her faith, artistry, and integrity intact and remained a hero to the dance floor generation.

Kansas

Though its story contained elements both of the "defector" and the "remnant" because of the different paths taken by the different members of the group, the story of the rock group Kansas was ultimately about the challenges faced by those who sought to keep the faith and remain in the rock world. Known as the leaders of the art rock set, Kansas's searching ballads showcased a haunting spirituality, which, though far from articulating any orthodox faith, seemed nonetheless distantly respectful of all religions—until its leader embraced the Christian faith.

The band was led by chief lyricist guitar player, and keyboardist Kerry Livgren, and throughout the 1970s Livgren was on a spiritual search that took him through countless religions. At each stage of his spiritual journey, he wrote songs, resulting in Kansas albums that were an interesting assortment of various religious teachings and doctrines.

"Dust in the Wind," and "Carry On Wayward Son"—two deeply spiritual songs, though vague in their particular theology—were both recorded toward the end of Livgren's search. In the late '70s he found himself exhausted spiritually, having experienced every religion available, except one: the Christian beliefs of his parents. Though it was a faith he had marginally known and rejected as a child, something now gave him pause: Every religion he had studied, from Buddhism to Hinduism to the various gurus that were commonplace in the '70s, all held Jesus Christ in high regard. All regarded him as either a prophet of God or a good teacher.

Livgren was intrigued by this, and when a friend in a band that was opening for Kansas, named Jeff Pollard, told him about his own faith in Jesus, Livgren listened. "Jeff used a lot of material to build his argument for the historical reliability of the Bible," wrote Livgren in his autobiography. "At first, I was bewildered. I had no conception of why some things were so important to begin with. Jeff carefully explained to me the meaning and the significance of the biblical teaching about the person and the work of Jesus Christ."[123]

As Livgren continued to come to terms with what was happening within him, he suddenly became afraid of where it was all going to end. "Part of me kept saying, 'My God, you can't become a Christian. What would everybody think?' The last thing in the world I wanted to be was one of those fanatical born-again Christians. Because of my image of what Christianity meant, my concept of what Christians were like, and what it would mean socially, economically, and personally for me to become one, the thought absolutely terrified me."[124]

Livgren soon realized that his two worlds were on a collision course. "I began to get more agitated and emotionally upset than ever," he remembered. "It was as though a thousand pounds were weighing down on my shoulders. I knew I was heading toward a significant conclusion, but I didn't know what it would be. I was resisting a confrontation with the cross of Christ, but now I was forced to deal with it. I had to decide on the basis of a lot of evidence that I was hearing for the first time what that cross really meant and who Jesus Christ really was. His claims were so radical that, once understood, they could not be ignored. They had to be accepted or rejected."[125]

Livgren decided to accept those claims in a hotel room in Indianapolis at three o'clock one morning in the middle of Kansas's 1979 tour. "As I was sitting on my bed with open books lying all around me, I grew absolutely determined to get to the bottom of this thing once and for all," he recalled. "I reached over and picked up *Liberation of Planet Earth*. This book clearly described the separation between God and man and the steps God took to remove that barrier. I put down the book, tears welling up in my eyes, and I just said, 'Lord, if Jesus Christ is your son, then I want to know him. If he really is the living God, my Redeemer, and my Lord, then I want to serve him with all my heart.'"[126]

The experience was a dramatic one.

"I was overwhelmed," he recalled. "Laughing and crying at once, I felt that the huge weight on my shoulders was suddenly taken away, forever. I was so excited that I felt like running out into the hall and knocking on doors, waking everyone up and saying, 'Look what I've found! You've got to believe it—this is real. Jesus is your Savior. He died for you.' I couldn't contain myself, so I sat blubbering on the bed until the thought hit me, 'You've got to get a grip on yourself and get some sleep. You've got a concert to play tomorrow.'"[127]

Livgren's new life was confirmed for him the next morning when he stepped out of the elevator, heading for breakfast, and saw Christmas decorations and heard loudspeakers proclaiming, "Joy to the world, the Lord is come, let earth receive her King." It was the middle of July and Livgren was baffled.

"I thought I had lost my mind," he remembered. "As I walked out of the elevator, my eyes began to fill with tears as I heard the words to 'Joy to the World' and understood for the first time in my life what they really meant and what that joy was. I went into the restaurant unable to control my tears. The waitress asked me if I was all right. I answered, 'Yes, but please explain to me what's going on.' She replied, 'Well, it's an annual custom we have. It's called Christmas in July.'"[128]

Among Livgren's first postconversion work was a solo album titled *Seeds of Change*. Of Livgren's first eleven songs written in this period, seven were included on *Seeds of Change* and four on Kansas's next album, *Audio Visions*. Though a whiz on keyboards and guitar, Livgren was never much of a singer, so he gathered together vocalists Jeff Pollard of the Le Roux; bandmate Steve Walsh; Ambrosia's lead singer, David Pack; Ronnie James Dio of Black Sabbath; Mylon Lefevre; John Fristoe; Joey Jelf; and others, but it was his decision to include Dio that created controversy in Christian circles because of the singer's reputation as a devil worshiper.

"I chose Ronnie James strictly on the basis of his vocal abilities," remembered Livgren. "Even though he had begun to sing for Black Sabbath, Ronnie is no Satanist. . . . I saw him as the right singer for two of the songs. In addition, his work on my album gave him an opportunity to sing lyrics which are diametrically opposed to what he does in Black Sabbath. This provided a clear witness to him about Christ."[129]

Years later, Dio remembered his work with Livgren. "I didn't realize Kerry was a born-again Christian," he said. "I didn't realize that the song was a Christian song. I had no idea whatsoever, and he didn't tell me that until after I had completed my performance. So I sang the song as to how I saw it. It wasn't a God-like situation and it wasn't talking about King Lear, either," said Dio of the song "To Live for the King." "I think the music and the lyrics that he wrote and the way he wrote them, just led me to the way I performed it. He told me afterward that it was exactly the performance he wanted and that he wouldn't have done it any differently himself. So, perhaps unconsciously, I did realize what it was about and dealt with it that way. But I honestly didn't realize that it was a Christian song."[130]

Livgren also had Dio sing another track, titled, ironically for the lead singer of Black Sabbath, "Mask of the Great Deceiver."

> That one, I kind of got the message on that one [remembered Dio]. That wasn't so difficult. That was kind of where I was coming from anyway. I was in Black Sabbath at the time and "Mask of the Great Deceiver." I mean just the words themselves kind of conjure up images of some kind of cloven-hoofed, horned kind of a bad guy somewhere, so that wasn't a problem. But again, after he told me what the songs were about after I'd performed them, and told me how pleased he was and that was the way he wanted them done, I mean, I was just really gratified that I was able to please him. It wasn't something that really changed around in my Christian or religious attitude,

because I've always had the same one, which is "Be as good as you can" and "We're here to help each other and not to hinder each other." Maybe it's just my beliefs in the fact that there is good and evil and I'd rather be on the good part of it that unconsciously perhaps directed how it came out.[131]

After *Seeds of Change*, Livgren and Kansas began work on *Audio Visions*, which hinted at Livgren's newfound faith on songs like "Relentless." "It was obviously a sore point, but it was never addressed in the open," said Livgren. "The others were well aware of what I was saying, but their tactic was to accept it for what it was and hope it would eventually go away"[132]

The song chronicled Livgren's conversion: "A change has come upon me and I'm surely not the same . . . in a single timeless moment when the old was cast away, the new was born into a world of simple joy, and my life is still for living though it's seen through different eyes, and the truth's a burden easy to bear."[133]

For others, who spent less time with their heads buried in album lyrics, the change would be noticed most clearly on the subsequent album, *Vinyl Confessions*. Lead singer Steve Walsh was upset by the aggressive spiritual lyrics of Livgren's new songs, which were unveiled when the members of Kansas gathered for their first meeting in preparation for recording the album. The vague references to faith from *Audio Visions* had been replaced by stronger, clearer references to Livgren's beliefs. Although he avoided direct mention of the Almighty, the lyrics were unmistakable.

"Crossfire" painted a stark portrait of a world of black and white in which the listener was forced to choose between good and evil, with a closing nod to Christ: "Everybody faces it, now or later, you can't get around it 'cause it's human nature, and deep within the hardest heart there is something there that knows, there's a hunger life can never fill 'til you face the One who rose."[134]

"Borderline" contained similar sentiments: "It's gotta be your world or mine, so which way will you lean?" "Diamonds and Pearls" was a restatement of the message of "Dust in the Wind," with a bit more hope of eternal life. When Livgren presented these and other songs to the band, Walsh was adamant. He would have nothing to do with them.

"The main thing that ticked him off was the fact that I was writing songs about Jesus Christ," said Livgren. "And when we got to the rehearsal to do the *Vinyl Confessions* album, Steve refused to sing them. So it became rather obvious that this situation was not going to work."[135]

Livgren was genuinely confounded. What was the problem? Walsh had, after all, happily sung all the lyrics that had emerged out of Livgren's previous religious journeys. What was different about these? Walsh refused to relent and announced that he was leaving one of the most successful rock bands at the peak of its popularity. Why? Livgren wondered, and it became for him yet another confirmation that he had stumbled onto absolute truth.

"I think Steve found it particularly difficult because he had to say the words," Livgren remembered. "Anytime you're singing about something that embodies the Truth—when it's about a God with whom you are not reconciled and you're being forced to sing and give praise and glory to Him—that's a very uncomfortable situation."[136]

Livgren was unmoved by Walsh's departure, and his resolve was further strengthened when bass player Dave Hope announced that he, too, had become a Christian. With the Christian/non-Christian ratio now at 2:3, the band set out to find a new lead vocalist. Though Livgren hoped to find a singer who shared his beliefs, he also knew that any overt efforts on his part to bring this about would deepen the split that was quickly forming within the band. As word of the vacant vocalist position spread, demo tapes began to pour in from around the country from promising young singers eager to join one of the top rock bands in the world.

The most promising were quickly narrowed down to a handful, and among these was a singer from California named John Elefante, a twenty-two-year-old with dreams of becoming a big-time rock star.

Elefante had gotten his start drumming in Top 40 cover bands at the age of ten and was encouraged by his family to pursue his craft. In 1980, in the midst of chasing the dream and negotiating with labels like Capitol, his world was turned upside down when he became a Christian. Immediately, he began to question how his newfound faith would affect his craft.

"I began to think that I had to get out of music," he said. "How could I serve God playing nightclubs? I was totally confused, wondering what God was doing. I remember praying, 'Lord, is there a way I can play music and still serve you at the same time?'"[137]

Elefante turned to other Christians for advice. "I asked my friends to pray for me," he said. "I went to a Bible study; everybody there was praying for me. We were close to signing with Capitol and I was just freakin' out. What do we do? Do we call the guy and tell him to forget the whole deal? It was total chaos."[138]

The most useful advice came from his pastor's wife, who told the young singer, "John, take it one day at a time. Don't make any huge decisions right now. Just stay in prayer and see what God does."[139]

Not long after Elefante received that advice, a fellow musician named Chuck King heard on an L. A. radio station that Kansas was looking for a new lead singer. "I was doing a demo at John's little backyard studio," remembered King. "On the way over to his house, I heard on KLOS just one little advertisement in between songs that Kansas had lost their lead singer and 'if you knew anybody who's got the pipes to take the job, give them a call and look up Kansas.' I was kind of joking around and I said, 'Hey John, Kansas is looking for a lead singer.' Lo and behold, he looked up Kansas, got some of their songs—just him with a piano singing it in his little studio, and sent it over to them."[140]

Livgren and the rest of the band were intrigued by Elefante's powerful voice. Knowing nothing of Elefante's faith, Livgren called to tell him of their interest. To his amazement, Elefante said. "You know, Kansas is the only band I would want to join, because of the Christian influence in your group," he said.[141]

Livgren was astonished and overjoyed. "My heart nearly leapt out of my chest and I asked, 'You mean you're a Christian?' I nearly passed out from the shock."[142]

Livgren had vowed to focus on the best voice and not pick a vocalist just because of his faith, but he scored a twofer with Elefante, who soon became the band's new lead singer.

"He had the voice and he had the songs," remembered Livgren, "and the odds against this being coincidence is rather astronomical. Imagine finding someone who could fill Steve Walsh's shoes both vocally and as a writer, and then learning that he was also a Christian. It was just incredible and it became obvious to me and Dave Hope that our prayer had been answered in a very specific and dramatic way."[143]

For Elefante, being thrust into the limelight was difficult for obvious reasons. "They were some of the best years of my life, and some of the worst," he said of his time with Kansas. "First of all, I knew nothing about the business of rock and roll. . . . When I joined Kansas, I walked into a huge corporation. There was so much information for me to absorb and I went into it very, very naive[ly]."[144]

That would have been difficult for any twenty-two-year-old, but Elefante also found himself in the middle of an organization that was suffering the effects of Livgren's newfound faith. "His conversion just turned things upside down," remembered Elefante. "He went to the management and to the record company and said, 'Look my heart has changed and I want to write about different things.' Everybody was freaking out, certain this was going to spell the end for Kansas."[145]

Elefante's own faith added to the tension. "When they found that I was also a believer, they were scared about what I might say in interviews. I was urged to talk about what it was like being the new singer, chosen from among three hundred people. That was the angle. They did not want me to discuss my faith."[146]

Now the Christian/non-Christian ratio was 3:3; or 4:3 counting Dino, John's omnipresent brother and writing partner. The Elefantes didn't shy away from using John's new position to push their own songs on the band. Fortunately, for Kansas, they were very good ones. "Right Away" was a hard-charging, love song brought to life by Elefante's urgent vocals, and the rest of the songs, including one which John co-wrote with Livgren, were full of the Christian message.

On "Chasing Shadows," Elefante wondered aloud, "Are we running from the light? And our legs are growing weaker, chasing shadows in the night."[147] On "Face It," he continued the theme that Livgren had set with his own songs on the record: "And the point is either right or wrong, for when I'm weak then I am strong, and the truth will find us all some day and the price is more than you can pay."[148]

While searching for material for the record, Livgren, Hope, and Elefante's newfound faith was severely tested when they came across a song titled "Stay with Me Tonight" that had the signature Kansas feel to it. "Now, that runs 180 degrees against everything I believe," said Livgren, "but I did kind of like the music. So we got ahold of the writers and said we were interested in doing the song and would they mind if we redid the lyrics. They said OK, so I rewrote the song about concerts and music and bands being objects of great admiration in the eyes of a fan, and it's sort of looking at it from a bandstand point of this being a very hollow, empty, meaningless thing."[149]

"Stay with Me Tonight" became "Play the Game Tonight," and quickly hit the charts, becoming one of MTV's earliest video hits.

What emerged was a tight, two-fisted "message" rock record that found Kansas offering up conclusions and ultimate truth, and not all of the fans or others associated with the band were happy with the change. "The more outspoken we become as Christians the more flak we're going to get from the business end of it," observed Livgren at the time, "because, from their perspective, if it doesn't sell records or make us a more commercial entity—or 'product,' as they like to call us, then it's not something that should be in the forefront. So while I don't feel that it's being actively suppressed, it's not being met with a great deal of enthusiasm either; but rather it's being tolerated."[150]

By this time, tensions within the band were escalating as well. James Long, a journalist who traveled with Kansas during the fall of 1982 while working on a story, remembered the scene. "Faith had so polarized the group, it was even reflected in where each person sat," he observed. "There at the Republic Airlines gate, Kerry, Dave, [sax player] Warren [Ham], and I sat together. At the opposite end of the gate sat drummer Phil Ehart, violinist Robby Steinhardt and guitarist Rich Williams. Oddly, in the middle, as if not quite fitting in with either faction, stood John Elefante."[151]

Kansas's days were clearly numbered. "I don't look on that particular period as a real good one, because it wasn't working very well," remembered Livgren. "Scripture says 'a divided house cannot stand,' and we had a group of people with altogether different goals and different motives pulling at each other. . . . Living with that kind of tension wasn't real good."[152]

After one more record, 1983's *Drastic Measures*, Kansas's explicitly "Christian period," much like Bob Dylan's, was over. The references to Livgren, Hope, and Elefante's faith were obscure though not absent from *Measures*, surfacing in lines like, "Life only comes from the One who made it," but according to Livgren, the withdrawal was not his choice.

"On *Drastic Measures*, people were saying that Kerry Livgren was pulling out, wasn't doing that much, but that was not by choice. That was imposed. At that point, things in the group were becoming very political. . . . I took the material that they refused to do and decided, 'Well, I'm gonna go home and take my toys and do my own record.'"[153]

The band reemerged several years later without Livgren, Hope, and Elefante, but the momentum was clearly gone along with the passionate spiritual journey that had always been central to the band's music. "They listen in great numbers and great intensity when the message is 'I'm searching,'" lamented Livgren. "But when the message becomes 'I'm found,' then they tend to treat you with dissension."[154]

For Elefante, the parting was bittersweet. "I knew if I stayed when Kerry and Dave left, I would tend to go the way of the unbeliever," he said. "Besides, Kerry's faith was one of the main reasons I joined the band. With that influence gone, why stay?"[155]

Instead, Elefante began shopping demos around Hollywood in search of a solo recording deal. "I had the voice, I had the songs. I had all the elements, but the door was shut tight," he remembered. "Looking back, I'm so glad, I praise God for not giving me success after I left Kansas. Who knows what would have happened? I might have gone off the deep end. I might have gotten into drugs. I was a Christian, but I was also a twenty-three-year old kid who had been thrust into the limelight—making good money and being exalted by the fans, riding around in Lear jets, facing unique temptations. I mean, it was a big deal and it went to my head."[156]

Elefante believed that God withheld solo success to teach him a lesson. "I think God gave me my five minutes of fame so I would know just how empty it can be. . . . God had to rebuild me from the ground up. It's not that I had fallen away from God, but I had been walkin' the fence. So God completely broke me down and humbled me through that experience of not being able to score a deal. Then he started making me what he wanted me to become. He had to break me down so he could build me back up."[157]

Unfortunately for the pop music culture, Elefante dropped out of sight, plunging headfirst into CCM, producing acts like Petra and Guardian and releasing two albums with his band Mastedon. Elefante appeared to have no ambitions for the wider general market, but seemed content to release records for the Christian ghetto.

"I made a choice to serve the Lord, not to use the Christian marketplace to jump over to the other side," he said, leaving an unspoken implication that those artists who were Christians but remained in pop music or aspired to be there weren't properly serving their God. "I already know I'm good enough to play in the secular market. God has already proved that to me. If it's so cool over there, why have artists like Rick Cua, Mark Farner, Kerry Livgren, Mylon LeFevre, and Jeff Fenholdt come to the Christian market?"[158]

The answer, of course, was that it was generally easier and more financially rewarding to be a big fish in a small pond, making music for those who agreed with you, but it was a position that Elefante seemed happy with. Although some of his fans may have held out hope that an older and wiser John Elefante might strengthen his faith to a point where he could return to the rock world and survive spiritually, it is also possible that Elefante simply knew what he could and couldn't handle.

"I'm not about breaking down doors," he mused. "So many people set their goals to hit the big time, but for me it's just not worth it. That whole world is too chaotic for me. I know very few celebrities who have their lives together. The love of money can ruin lives and so many people just can't handle it."[159]

Elefante revived his solo career in the mid-1990s, releasing two solid pop records in the CCM market, *Windows of Heaven* and *Corridors*. Had the stunning ballad "Where Does Our Love Go?," from *Corridors*, been released in the pop market, it would have undoubtedly gone straight to the top of the charts.

Caught between two worlds, Elefante believed the single was too "secular" for Christian radio and the rest of the record too "Christian" for "secular" radio.

After leaving Kansas, Kerry Livgren and Dave Hope formed a new band, called A. D. After Kansas, Livgren found himself contractually "bound and gagged," forbidden from recording apart from Kansas. Realizing his only way out was to be granted a waiver to record for the "religious" marketplace, Livgren took it, despite his natural reservations. "A starving man will eat anything you put in front of him," he would later say of his decision.[160]

A couple of years of recording and playing almost exclusively for Christian audiences was enough for Livgren. Unlike Elefante, he saw very clearly the limitations of CCM. "More people have been led to Christ with 'Dust in the Wind' than with everything else I've ever written," he said. "Not only did that song not mention Jesus, but I was not a Christian at the time. It just happened to be a truth that the song emphasized. . . . What good is music if nobody hears it?"[161]

After several records with A. D., Livgren formed his own labels—first Kerygma, then Numavox—and continued to release records which were distributed in both markets.

Livgren left behind a powerful legacy, not only for Kansas fans, but for his fans in the subculture who recognized him as a man of integrity who consistently questioned whether CCM was reaching the ears of non-Christians; indeed, whether it was ever even designed to reach non-believers.

U2

Far from the American music scene, four young Irishmen were quietly working at their craft, writing and recording songs in a band called U2. Originally called Feedback, the group had met at school as teenagers in their hometown of Dublin and taken to playing music together.

"With the help of a sympathetic teacher, Donald Moxham, Feedback had acquired a rehearsal room in the school," wrote U2 biographer Eamon Dunphy. "The non-denominational rock band agreed to practice three times a week."[162]

They were among several bands that would simultaneously make a strong stand for their faith and against lifeless cultural Christianity. But as success catapulted them to the top of the pop music universe, even the casual observer could note that the band's early eagerness to communicate its faith and be understood was being slowly overtaken by the trappings of power, success, and money. Despite their best attempts not to be affected by those things, they were viewed by some as a band that had sold out for fame, fortune, and respectability.

In 1985, *Rolling Stone* declared them "the band of the '80s," a heady accolade but one that proved accurate. Yet, long before they made their biggest splash in American pop music with the 1987 release *The Joshua Tree*, U2 had been known as a band of Christians who made no effort to hide their faith. Songs like "Gloria," "With a Shout," "40," "Tomorrow," and "Rejoice" contained strong and clear references to a transcendent Christian faith, and in their early days, the band members seemed more than willing to talk about that faith.

In 1981, singer Paul Hewson, aka Bono, laid out the group's spiritual agenda, which he hoped would marry the anger of punk rock with the idealism of the hippie culture. "I'd like to think that U2 is aggressive, loud, and emotional," he said. "I think that's good. I think that the people who I see parallels with are people like John the Baptist or Jeremiah. They were very loud, quite aggressive, yet joyful, and I believe they had an answer and a hope. In that sense, I think we have a love and an emotion without the flowers in our hair, and we have an aggression without the safety pins in our noses."[163]

"I really believe Christ is like a sword that divides the world," the band's guitarist, who adopted the stage name the Edge, told journalist Terry Mattingly in 1982, "and it's time we get into line and let people know where we stand. You know, to much of the world, even the mention of the name Jesus Christ is like someone scratching their nails across a chalkboard."[164]

Though Bono would refuse the moniker "Christian artist," he was scornful of secularism. "I've spent most of my life avoiding labels. I don't intend to adopt one now," he said, adding, "I can't accept a belief that I just came out of gas, you know? That we as a race just exploded into existence—I can't believe that and I don't think others can, really. Maybe they can accept it on a sort of 'thin' level, but not really deep down. Deep down, everybody is aware."[165]

Three of the members of U2 were devout Christians who attended a prayer and Bible study group called the Shalom Group. "The group met twice a week, each meeting lasted two or three hours," observed biographer

Dunphy. "They began with songs, beautiful gospel songs, then people would discuss the values expressed in the Bible. . . . There was a spirit of humility, a sense of God in the form of goodness being present. His Word came to the meeting through the Bible and sometimes in the form of speaking in tongues, a stream-of-consciousness outpouring of the human spirit—most deeply felt angst and desires."[166]

What united the three believers in U2 was the simultaneous rejection of organized religion and the embrace of God and the Bible—and the Shalom Group met both of those seemingly incongruous needs. "The challenge for Christians in the Shalom Group: don't be ashamed, proclaim your values and your faith, read your Bible if you want to, whenever, wherever," wrote Dunphy.[167]

When on the road, the three Christian members of U2 made their own Shalom Group, reading the Bible and holding prayer meetings in their hotel rooms. "There was a responsibility to infuse your working life with Christian values," wrote Dunphy. "It wasn't for you to evangelize or proclaim too loudly, but neither was your faith to be denied, hidden away from those with whom you came into contact."[168]

Before long, however, time, money, fame, pride, and ego all stirred together began to affect the various members of the band—especially Bono, who became increasingly belligerent in his remarks about fellow Christians.

In his younger, more earnest days, Bono had been influenced by the writings of a Chinese prisoner of conscience named Watchman (To-Sheng) Nee, who spent the last twenty years of his life in Chinese prison cells for his Christian faith. In his books *The Spiritual Man*; *Table in the Wilderness*; *Sit, Walk, Stand*; and *Love Not the World*, Nee articulated a muscular yet humble vision of Christianity that, while encouraging his reader to be a part of the world physically, argued for spiritual separation from the unseen forces of spiritual evil that controlled the world system.

"Watchman Nee's idea was 'unless a seed shall die and be crushed in the earth, it cannot bear fruit,'" said Bono, "whereas rock 'n' roll had the idea, 'Look at me!' 'Outta my way,' 'Look out for number one!' 'I can't get no satisfaction!' Watchman Nee's attitude to that would be, 'So what? What's so important about you anyway?'"[169]

Yet, as Bono made increasingly disparaging statements about many modern expressions of Christianity, it was often left to the Edge to tone down the singer's statements. "It's wrong lashing out," said the guitarist. "You can't take responsibility for everybody's actions who call themselves Christians. I think it's much more important what you do rather than what you say. That's the kind of philosophy that we've had through our music, to try and explain where we are."[170]

For the Edge, the religious scandals that plagued America in the 1980s made life difficult for all believers, including the members of U2. "They're dark times aren't they," he said in 1988. "Especially for Christians. Aside from the TV evangelism scandals of the last few years, it's very hard to figure it out and sort out where you stand. You see so many things which you disagree with and you abhor going on in the name of Christianity and Christ. We still haven't figured it all out and I'm sure I never will."[171]

U2's spiritual slide became a cautionary tale for younger bands who wanted to maintain their spiritual integrity. They had gone off into the world of rock and roll to slay Satanic dragons without realizing that an artist of faith cut off from the source of that faith and fellow believers simply could not withstand the pressures of life in rock's fast lane. A friend of the band, Steve Turner observed,

> Since leaving the Shalom Group in the early 1980s they have been without a spiritual base and have therefore been deprived of systematic Bible teaching, discipline, fellowship, communication, and worship. This has led to a do-it-yourself theology that has gone unchallenged. It has also meant that they no longer see themselves as part of the whole community of Christians, young and old, black and white, fashionable and unfashionable, rich and poor, but as part of an elite who no longer need to follow the New Testament pattern of church life. Bono has claimed that "living by the Spirit" means "this is my life and it's between me and God and no one else"—an outlook that ignores the corporate dimension and leads to what has been called "Lone Ranger Christianity."[172]

The band's break with that teaching offered by the Shalom Group came about when the group's meetings "began to focus more and more on members' modes of living, less and less on the Scriptures," observed Eamon Dunphy. "In particular, the Shalom Group began to question rock 'n' roll and its relationship to God. . . . Most of those at the meetings lived ordinary lives. Their days were dull, some particularly sad and lonely. Life was not as exciting as it was for U2."[173]

At the time their record *Boy* came to the attention of the masses, the three Christian members had begun to work out their faith in a strangely un-Watchman Nee-like manner, acting as though faith should only be expressed in the way they lived their lives and not, at least overtly, in the music and public statements they made. It was a vigorous departure from Nee's idea of integrating faith with life.

"It's very important that we don't want to be the band that talks about God," concluded Bono. "I do not want to talk about it in terms of music. Anything that has to be said on that personal level is in the music or on stage and I don't want to go through the media. I don't want to talk to the world about it, because we will face a situation where people will see us with a banner over our heads. That's not the way U2 is going to work. If there is anything in what we have to say, it will be seen in our lives, in our music, in our performance."[174]

In spite of a reluctance to use the press to discuss their spiritual beliefs, U2's music did plenty of talking over the years on albums like *The Unforgettable Fire*, *The Joshua Tree*, and most notably and recently, *Pop*.

One of their biggest singles in the U.S. market, the 1987 cut "I Still Haven't Found What I'm Looking For," was viewed in some quarters as an affirmation of faith, in others as a rejection of it, for after singing "I believe in the Kingdom Come. . . . You broke the bonds, you loosed the chains, you carried the cross and my shame, you know I believe it," Bono added, "but I still haven't found what I'm looking for."[175]

Other songs like "Where the Streets Have No Name," a song about heaven, were less vague, and U2 was celebrated by some Christian fans for its strong presence in the mainstream of pop music culture.

The group's 1997 album, *Pop*, met with disappointing sales but contained several references to faith, though not the robust and confident faith that had characterized U2's music in the early days. "Jesus, I'm waiting here boss," sang Bono on "Wake Up Dead Man." "I know you're looking out for us, but maybe your hands aren't free. Your Father He made the world in seven, will you put a word in for me."[176]

A senior writer for *Entertainment Weekly*, Chris Willman said,

> I still occasionally hear some conservative evangelical Christians speculate that Bono is "one of us," on some kind of undercover mission, and I think that's foolish—just as much as it's wrong-headed of other evangelicals to think nobody in U2 is even a Christian anymore. Clearly those three guys are on a journey, and right now it's in a direction diametrically away from the born-again thing they were involved with in the early '80s. Whether the pendulum ever swings back that way for them or not, I think they still stand as the foremost example of people of this generation grappling with sincere faith in God in public. It's definitely a liberal kind of Christianity, but Christianity still. There are some dark or even disturbing elements to how they describe their spiritual paths in "Pop" and other recent albums, but it's in the darkest moments when Bono lets on just how "God-haunted" they really are. And just to have people that smart

and that artful—not to mention that prominent—dealing with how to approach Jesus in a blatant, thoughtful, emotional way . . . I find it kind of thrilling.[177]

T-Bone Burnett

Born in 1945 in Fort Worth, John Henry Burnett, known as T-Bone, was the grandson of the secretary of the Southern Baptist Convention, J. Henry Burnett. T-Bone got his start in his hometown playing in blues bands and later opened a small studio where he recorded other blues artists. In 1975, he met Bob Neuwirth, an associate of Bob Dylan, and was invited to play guitar in Dylan's Rolling Thunder Revue. It was a tour that would lead many of its participants to the Christian faith.

"I have no idea what happened on that tour," remembered Burnett, "but it is interesting that many people either became Christians or went back to church by the time it ended."[178]

A lanky six-foot-six cowboy, Burnett is known primarily for his production work for artists like his wife Sam Phillips, the Bodeans, Roy Orbison, Los Lobos, Bruce Cockburn, and others; but he has also been a noteworthy artist and songwriter in his own right, forming the Alpha Band in 1977 with Steve Soles and David Mansfield, with whom he recorded two records.

"He didn't see himself as an evangelist, but as an artist given the responsibility primarily to write well-crafted songs drawn from his observations of human behavior," wrote Steve Turner. "He drew inspiration not from Jesus rock or even gospel music, but from Catholic novelist Flannery O'Connor, Anglican poet T. S. Eliot, and Catholic writer G. K. Chesterton."[179]

Burnett's approach to creating music was markedly different from many Christians in music. "If Jesus is the Light of the world, there are two kinds of songs you can write," he told *L. A. Weekly* in 1980. "You can write songs about the Light, or you can write songs about what you can see from the Light. That's what I try to do. I'm still looking." He later told *Rolling Stone*, "A bricklayer's job is to build a good wall that will stand against the rain and wind. Writing Jesus on it isn't going to help it withstand the storms."[180]

In 1980, Burnett released his debut solo album, *Truth Decay*, and he continued to release records sporadically over the next dozen years, including *Trap Door*, *Proof through the Night*, and *Criminal under My Hat*.

The Call

Another band that quietly turned out deeply spiritual albums was the Call, led by singer Michael Been and produced by Burnett. On albums like *Red Moon* and *Let the Day Begin*, The Call showed themselves to be a band that took spiritual issues seriously and framed them from a Judeo-Christian perspective. Yet Been was often as critical of modern Christianity as he was of his godless generation.

"A lot of times Christianity and other religions are out to sell happiness, and I don't think happiness amounts to a lot," said Been. "It's fleeting, it comes and goes. Joy, the way I'm using the word, is something that would never come and go. It's much deeper. It's a state of being. Happiness is much more a mood. I think what Christians should do is go and enter into someone else's story. And then maybe on the other side of that, that joy, that real sense of peace comes out of it."[181]

At the same time, Been was keenly aware of the culture that dominated the pop music business. "I think I'm working against the current power structure, the ones who right now are making the rules and creating the values and the ethics of the country," he said. "I agree it is tragic what's happening, the voices that are being heard right now as the voices of influence. At best, they're spewing this kind of childish fantasy and denial; and at worst, very dangerous life-threatening ways of thinking—violent, materialistic."[182]

After a brief hiatus, in 1998 the Call signed a distribution agreement with the Nashville-based CCM label Cadence, allowing their latest record to be distributed to the Christian marketplace in addition to the general market distribution which its records had always seen.

Mr. Mister

Mainstays of mid-1980s American pop, Mr. Mister dominated the charts for a couple of years with hits like "Broken Wings" and "Kyrie," before quickly fading from the scene. The band's strongest influence was lead singer and co-lyricist Richard Page, raised in the church by his choir director father and church organist mother. While both of the hit singles were strongly spiritual, even evangelical in nature, Page consistently guided his band away from CCM.

"I really didn't want to be tagged as a religious band or as a contemporary Christian band," he said. "I felt like that was limiting our ability to communicate to all people. We just don't want to have Christian fans. We want to have all listeners and it's important that we reach everybody. But we can't help but find those little ties that draw people into our music. 'Kyrie' obviously has a Christian text."[183]

By the time of their follow-up album *Go On*, however, Page seemed to have shed all such inhibitions as the group recorded blatantly evangelical and spiritual songs with titles like "Man of a Thousand Dances," which ended with a chorus of "hallelujahs," and the moving "Healing Waters."

"Songs like 'Healing Waters,' I don't even know where that came from," said Page, "except that I grew up in church and sang in the choir . . . and I probably sang those words somewhere along the line in a high school choir somewhere, so these things are just sort of following me around. . . . I guess I'm following them around too."[184]

To Page, "Man of a Thousand Dances" was a deeply spiritual song that affected him on different levels. "Though I went into that song wanting all the choruses to be 'hallelujah,' I realized there was more to be said than just that exultation," said Page. "There's actually much more to be said about what's really happening with me and probably with a lot of other people than just 'praise God,' because it isn't always just 'praise God.' A lot of the time it's, 'Hey man, I don't know what's going on exactly and I feel isolated; I feel like my spirit isn't free; I feel like I'm standing in the shadows sometimes. I'm looking for the light but I don't always see it, and that's the reality of the situation."[185]

For Page, who never joined CCM, the dangers of the subculture were manifested not only in the people it excluded but in its effect on the creation of art, and the inability to be honest. "The problem I have with a lot of music that is strictly Christian-oriented is that it's all about praise, and that's okay when you feel like that, but we don't always feel like that," said Page. "I know so many of my friends, who are strong, deeply religious people, say the same thing: 'I don't always feel like I'm in the light,' and I think there's something to like, what U2 says, 'I still haven't found what I'm looking for.' It's not just candy coating, the thing about we're all happy and we're all in love with God. We are, but we're not *always* like that."[186]

Even in the midst of success that gave him and his band back-to-back Top 10 singles, Page's relationship with the God of his childhood was never far from his mind. "He just keeps following me. I can't really shake it, even though I don't really understand my own connection with God. I mean, I don't always. I know when I'm right there with Him."[187]

Stryper

In the quiet town of La Mirada, California, on the outskirts of Los Angeles, two teenage brothers were beginning to live out their rock and roll fantasies through their band Roxx Regime. Robert Sweet and his younger brother, Michael, were two normal kids in suburbia, thirty miles outside the capital of the burgeoning heavy metal scene that would propel bands like Mötley Crüe, Ratt, and Guns 'n' Roses onto the national stage.

"By the time I was nine, ten years old, I was really into the *Grand Funk Live* record," said Sweet. "I listened to everything from country music to heavy stuff, to Led Zeppelin . . . Elvis, Kiss, Aerosmith, whatever there was that I could find and I thought was cool."[188]

The furthest thing from the minds of the young Sweet brothers was religion until Robert became interested in a certain TV preacher. "Robert was really getting into Jimmy Swaggart," remembered Michael. "He was watching him all the time. Anytime he was on, he was watching him. Bob kind of got me, my mom and dad, and the whole family into watching it. One night, in front of the TV, we all accepted Christ."[189]

While many conversions produce instantly changed lives, the Sweets' conversion aftermath was less dramatic. "We backslid heavily," remembered Michael. "We were doing things and still thinking that we were Christians, yet we were complete heathens. We were out on the Hollywood strip, playing the clubs, scamming on women, drinking alcohol, not really heavily into drugs, but we were just complete heathens. We were living a lie."[190]

Playing local parties and high school gigs, the brothers soon met up with a guitar player named Richard Martinez, whose lifelong obsession with Black Sabbath's Ozzie Osborne had caused him to rename himself Oz Fox, and bass player Tim Gaines, who joined the band in 1983. Though the band that would become Stryper had formed, the lyrics were far from spiritual.

"Mike was writing a lot of tunes about being in love with some girl, or you know the dream of being stranded on some island with the most beautiful girl that you've always wanted to be with, and she could never get away," recalled Robert.[191]

Their first big show came on July 20, 1979, at the famed night spot Gazarri's. For the youngsters from La Mirada, opening for the white-hot heavy metal band Ratt was heady stuff. "This was my first taste of seeing all these people who would later become very famous people . . . the guys from Mötley Crüe and Poison," remembered Robert.[192]

God, however, was never far away. "I'm a firm believer in the fact that when you accept Christ you can never get away from him," said Michael. "Even though many times your flesh wants to and you wanna go and do things that aren't godly, his Spirit never leaves. He's always there, tugging at your heart. That's what the deal was with us—he never left."[193]

"Sometime in 1983, . . . Mike and I rededicated our lives back to the Lord. And shortly after, Oz did also," said Robert. "After we did, then I just kinda felt like we had to do the Stryper thing and we had to do the Christian lyrics."[194]

The change was reinforced when an acquaintance of the band dropped by one day bearing a message from God. "We were rehearsing, and Ken Metcalf came in and said, 'If you change your group around and glorify Jesus you'll go straight to the top,'" remembered Robert. "We rededicated our lives to the Lord and we said, 'We don't care if none of the record companies wants to sign us or if none of the clubs wants to mess with a Christian band, this is what we're going to do.'"[195]

Something clicked for the members of Roxx Regime, and they soon changed their name to Stryper, taking the name from Isaiah 55:3, a verse that Christians believe to be a prophetic reference to Jesus, that "by his stripes we are healed."

Stryper got its big break in 1983 when a friend at a nearby recording studio tipped the elder Sweet off about an important record executive who would be stopping by. "A good friend of mine at Casbah said, 'Hey I think you ought to meet this guy, Wes Hein. He's going to be pretty happening; he's signing a few bands and working with a few people,'" remembered Robert. "That was when I delivered the first tape to Enigma Records and that would have probably been around November 1983."[196]

It wasn't long before Stryper had a record deal, but not without a little sleight of hand by Robert, who presented Hein a tape of Stryper tunes without the Christian-oriented lyrics that had come to be the Stryper message. Once the contracts were signed, Sweet promptly substituted the original lyrics and Stryper had its record deal with an up and coming heavy metal label that would shortly align itself with Capitol Records.

"I was down at a studio working with a band," recalled Hein, "and a couple of guys with long hair came in and said, 'Oh wow, you're from Enigma. We want to give you a tape.' The three of them came up and played me a tape that just knocked my socks off. I thought it was great— what I considered to be different. The songs were great. The three people were Robert Sweet, Michael Sweet, and Oz Fox. I was so impressed with the tonal quality, the background vocals and what the songs sounded like. I really didn't pick up that they were a Christian band and they didn't necessarily volunteer this information."[197]

Later, when Hein discovered that the band was made up of strong Christians, it really wasn't much of an issue to him because the band hadn't made it much of an issue to begin with. "I thought about it and decided, 'Who cares?'" remembered Hein. "'That's not a big deal. They're a great rock band.' Then of course it seemed like everybody else thought it was a bigger deal than I did . . . [but] this is the music business and the music should come first."[198]

Stryper never signed a recording agreement with a Christian label and were never a CCM band. Following the original vision that Robert Sweet had conceived, they were in the world, recording for a rock label and touring with other heavy metal bands. It was only much later that Enigma struck a deal with the CCM label Benson to allow for Christian-market distribution of Stryper recordings.

"We didn't want notoriety simply with Christian audiences just so we could sign with a Christian record label," said Robert. "I believe the whole point of Christianity is to reach people who don't know Christ. By no means are we putting down anyone who is signed to a Christian label or who plays strictly to Christian audiences. But we know that it is our calling to get out there and try to sing to the people who need Jesus. It's the sick who need the physicians."[199]

The vision was equally shared by Tim Gaines, the quietest member of Stryper. "We don't really see too many places where the Christian labels are getting into the secular record stores," he said. "If they are, they're stuck in a section in the corner where nobody would even bother looking for an album or a tape. We want to reach people in mass quantities rather than just a small audience."[200]

Stryper's debut record, *The Yellow and Black Attack*, was as noteworthy for its cover art as it was for the music. Four missiles preparing for launch, directed toward Earth by the hand of God, gave the music-buying public the idea that this was not just another rock band—Stryper was on a mission from God.

The Yellow and Black Attack may have been light on Christian imagery, but the heavy metal world did not miss the message—especially when the band listed "#1 Jesus Christ (the Boss Man)" at the top of the album's credits.

The songs themselves were noteworthy for what they weren't about— no drugs, sex, partying, or any of the other themes that dominated metal music of the era. "Are you feeling lonely? Are you feeling blue? Does your life seem empty? You know what to do," went one.

It wasn't until the second album, *Soldiers under Command*, that Stryper began to reveal the full extent of their zeal. In the meantime, ever in search of the ultimate gimmick, yet by no means insincere, the band began the practice of throwing out Bibles, complete with the Stryper logo on the cover, to clamoring fans. Whatever the motive, it was an effective way for Robert Sweet to distinguish Stryper from the stampede emerging from the L. A. metal scene.

Many critics within evangelical Christianity found fault with Stryper for the Bible tossing and, ironically, the strongest attacks came from Jimmy Swaggart. In the October 1986 edition of *Evangelist* magazine, Swaggart described the purported scene at a Stryper concert in Baton Rouge, Louisiana, that he had presumably attended.

"The two warm-up rock groups were Journey and Ratt," he wrote. "After the strobe lights had beat their rhythmic pattern across the stage and the smoke bombs had gone off, after the prancing and display of the flesh had finally concluded, then Bibles were 'thrown out' to the crowd. Sad to say, most of them were not even picked up. They were just walked on. I could ask this question: 'Is the Word of God to be treated with such disdain that it is pitched as a morning newspaper to individuals who have absolutely no regard or respect for it?'"[201]

For Robert, in particular, the comments were difficult to handle. "First of all, I would like to state that I'm behind Jimmy Swaggart. He's the reason that I became a Christian. Through watching him on television I came to know the Lord," he said, also noting that Ratt and Journey had never opened for Stryper. Nevertheless, he refused to return fire.

"Our methods are not really that different from Reverend Swaggart's. He gets up and he plays his music and then goes out to speak. We get up and play our music and then go out to speak. Yeah, our clothing is a little different, our hair is a little different, but John the Baptist's clothing and hair were a little different too. He was accused of being a devil, but the Bible says there was no greater man than he, ever born."[202]

The Yellow and Black Attack was propelled by the group's success in Japan, which was largely due to an endorsement of the band by famed rock critic Masa Itoh, the man who ruled the Japanese hard rock/heavy metal scene, who many fans looked to for his evaluation of bands. Itoh had heard of Stryper, gotten in touch with their manager, Daryn Hinton, and liked what he heard. When he gave the band a positive review in Japan's heavy metal bible, *Burrn!* magazine, and played the album on his radio show, Stryper suddenly found themselves at the top of the metal heap in Japan with a record that was outselling Mötley Crüe, Bon Jovi, and every other metal band. Itoh was profoundly influenced by the band, even good-naturedly nicknaming himself "Messiah" in the liner notes he wrote for the album's Japanese pressing, and Stryper clearly owed a great debt to him. The band was on its way, and though its lyrics were often scathingly reviewed by critics for its light theology and heavy emotionalism, they nonetheless blazed an important trail that would make the way for future bands to be unabashed in their proclamations of faith.

Stryper also made another important contribution: they had no inhibitions about mixing songs about human love and divine love—often a no-no in early CCM circles, where the standard love song was one that could be taken to mean either God or one's girlfriend or boyfriend was the intended recipient. Stryper had its share of those songs as well, but by the time their final record, *Against the Law*, was released, they had begun to write spiritual songs like "Rock the Hell out of You," and simple love songs like "Lady" and "Two Bodies, One Mind, One Soul."

Unfortunately for Stryper, just as *Against the Law* was hitting the streets, heavy metal was falling out of favor and grunge was beginning to take over. The band's decision to drop the original Stryper logo, complete with the Bible verse, along with statements to the mainstream rock press that seemed less than evangelical concerning church attendance and drinking and smoking, caused Benson to stop distributing Stryper to the CCM marketplace, a move that sent a strong signal to the subculture that Stryper was foundering spiritually.

"In the group's recently completed album, *Against the Law*, the band has taken a different approach with lyrical content, one that does not contain overtly Christian lyrics," said Benson's CEO, Jerry Park, in a press release. "This indicates a new direction that does not conform to the mission of the Benson Company. We wish the members of Stryper well in its future endeavors."[203]

It was clearly not just the lyrics that troubled Park, but the public statements as well, especially a *Rolling Stone* article that described the band as "tired of having fans check their drinks for alcohol," having begun to "openly drink and smoke," and planning not to mention God on their forthcoming album.[204]

To Robert Sweet, the article was a hit piece designed to destroy the group's credibility with its loyal fan base. "They do have a few writers who don't care for Stryper and the stand we take," he said. "You feel so helpless as a rock musician if you take a stand. With Christian press, they won't drastically lie or misquote you, but with a secular magazine, where some of the writers are so atheistic in view, they sometimes have fun with it."[205]

Sweet admitted to being burned out by all the negative publicity the band had endured. "If they see Robert Sweet take a couple of girls in the bus, they might think the worst thing, but it might be my cousins," he said. "If they see me with guys, they figure I'm queer. As a band we say, 'If you love Stryper, thank you.' We hope we can put out music that people love, but we can't live up to people's standards. Nobody can. Everybody needs to keep their own act together with God."[206]

Years of being attacked in the rock press for its Christian-themed lyrics and Bible throwing had made the band weary of being critiqued not for the music, which was surprisingly good, but for their spirituality. By the time they released *Against the Law*, they longed to be treated not as televangelists but as musicians. "A lot of people feel we're either angels from heaven or demons from hell," said Robert. "We're neither. We're people. We're rock musicians who have had the courage to stand up for Christ and we've taken a lot of heat for it. We've taken verbal abuse and been made fun of, but we've done it."[207]

Against the Law made it clear that, far from renouncing their faith, they were simply reorganizing, trying to get away from the in-your-face religious imagery. "We're still Stryper, but it is a little different," said Robert. "It's a more aggressive sound, a little heavier, more of a fun sounding record. . . . You won't pick up this record and hear anything that says God or Christ. That was intentionally done. . . . Every single Stryper's ever had out has never mentioned the word God or Christ in it. Even big songs like 'Honestly,' which has been played at thousands of people's weddings, never mentioned God. We've had songs like 'You Won't Be Lonely Anymore,' which was purposely written in a double way which could talk about God or could talk about a relationship between a man and a woman. But people are hearing we're the heathens who have denied God and all that garbage and it's just not the truth."[208]

"We're the thundering sons, we're the undying ones, with the power of good, evil has never won," they sang on "Rock the Hell out of You." On "Not That Kind of Guy" they painted a picture they'd become all too familiar with—a band member dealing with a groupie. Still, in the music business, image is everything, and thanks to unfortunate timing, bad press, and a general breakdown in communication, Stryper was perceived to have given up its faith, and its days at the top of the heavy metal heap were over—at least for the moment.

Singer Michael Sweet, while insisting that he wanted a pop music career, settled for the same label that had dropped him—Benson Records, where he recorded two pop records before being dropped from the label. In 1999, Sweet signed a deal with Restless Records, a unit of Regency Pictures that had distribution into the CCM market as well. He looked back on the Stryper experience with fondness. "[God] could've used anyone out there and he chose us. The rest is history. When I think about that it just blows my mind. It is really something that should never have happened and it did. It was awesome."[209]

Tim Gaines and Oz Fox later formed a new band, Sin Dizzy, that remained unsigned, and Robert Sweet continued to work with his band, Blank, and on various side projects.

A reunion was hampered by Michael's lack of enthusiasm about playing with his old bandmates after his move to the East Coast with his wife and two children.

"I feel that Stryper was never over with," admitted Robert. "To this day, I still don't quite know why Stryper ended. . . . Stryper never got to do its seventh record. I feel it wasn't over. I feel it's not over. Hopefully, real soon, something will happen."[210]

The Stryper phenomenon ended, at least for the moment, but for nearly eight years they had shaken up a rock music establishment that had forgotten that addressing spiritual issues was once what music was all about, taking a jackhammer to the wall that had separated rock music culture from serious and orthodox spirituality. They had also proved quite convincingly that the notion that kids wouldn't buy a record with lyrics about God was a lie.

"We were as bold as it gets, yet we were a crossover success," remembered Michael. "Two-thirds of all the record buyers who bought Stryper records were not Christian, but there was something about the music that they liked. I'm a firm believer that there is a way to reach the secular side and not sell out or do away with the boldness. It's been proven it can be done. I think the key is it's gotta come naturally. You can't just sit down and plan it and say, 'We're gonna do this and that.' It's gotta come naturally."[211]

Stryper's contribution was their plowing of the ground, making it more receptive to bands with orthodox Christian beliefs, like King's X, who would come later.

"Stryper is four guys who don't deserve anything that God has given us," Robert Sweet was fond of saying. "We're no better than anybody else.

We're not great musicians. Without Christ, we're just four losers. We just want to tell people about Christ, because when they find Christ, their whole life will begin to change."[212]

Run-DMC

"Run-DMC invented rap as we know it," enthused a critic writing in the *Rolling Stone Album Guide*. As the '80s wound down and the group hit the top of the charts with a cover of Aerosmith's "Walk This Way," it was difficult to argue with those words of high praise.

The group's 1984 self-titled release signaled the beginning of a subgenre of rap music known as "New School," but for the members of Run-DMC, Joseph Simmons and Darryl McDaniel, it proved to be the beginning of the old story of popular success leading to personal turmoil.

The duo soon became the first rap act to have gold, platinum, then double platinum records, as well as the first such act to be played on MTV, and with each subsequent release the buzz only got bigger. After years of raising hell, rumors of a conversion began to surface.

"I have always been close to God and talked to him," said Simmons. "Both DMC and I went to Catholic school and D was even an altar boy. Though being Catholic is different than being born again, we were still always spiritually in contact with God. In fact, I have always felt that I was called by God to be a pastor or preacher. I cannot say exactly what brought about my conversion, because the process of becoming fully committed and born again came gradually, but it has happened."[213]

At the peak of their success the two began to pursue their faith in earnest. DMC said,

> Run and I always prayed on the road, because we knew God gave us the blessings and was in control of our lives. God made Run-DMC. We have always lived by the principle of love your neighbor, do good and good will come to you, give and you will receive. However, real change occurred in my life when I ended up in the hospital because I was over-drinking. Being hospitalized slowed my road enough for me to really take notice of my life. We were doing certain things that were prior to the Word of God, and even though we were following the basic principles of doing right, being in the hospital was God's way of saying, 'Boom. Stop drinking!' While I was there, my mother came to see me and gave me a New Testament with Matthew, Mark, Luke, John, and Revelation. I read the book over and over again, and I really felt God.[214]

Like the ancient ruler Nebuchadnezzar, who was dethroned and made to eat grass until he recognized a *higher* sovereign, Simmons and McDaniel attributed their downfall to their rebellious lifestyle. "God appoints the king and as long as the king gives God his props, God will carry him through life. During our eight years as Run-DMC, we forgot to give God his props. We had forgotten to recognize and honor God as the one who gave us everything we had. Time had come for God to remind us, 'Boom! Hold up. I gave you these blessings.' The Bible says that the high will be brought low, the last will be first and the first will be last. God needed to get our attention, so he let hard times come our way."[215]

According to McDaniel, it was one of their bodyguards who helped get them back on the straight and narrow.

> Bobby Walker . . . was always calling Run and telling him to come to his church called Zoe Ministries. Run always agreed, but he never went. However, one day, Run finally went and when he did, whatever happened that day, whatever God did to him, Run was brought to the point he is at now. Run was like, "Oh yeah! This is it! I found the truth." Run then approached me as Bobby had approached him and said, "You gotta come, D. My church is dope!" So I went and "Boom!" God came and got a hold of me. We started reading the Word and realized what we were really doing and not doing. Then as the change came, people said we actually started looking brighter and happier.[216]

While many high profile conversions gave birth to unrealistic expectations of instant spiritual enlightenment, Simmons and McDaniel seemed to clearly understand their level of maturity from the outset. "When a person is born again, his total transformation does not happen overnight," said McDaniel. "He becomes saved and born again and God comes into his life to be with him. Right now, Run and I are still young Christians. We are like children. We are learning to be obedient to God."[217]

It was at Zoe that the two rappers continued to grow in their faith, and, fortunately, it was a church group that did not encourage a CCM mentality that might have induced McDaniel and Simmons to leave popular music, according to Simmons.

> I have a pastor that pastors the flock. I listen to my elders and they tell me what to do. If my leaders tell me something, I will be obedient to them and the Word. I do not worry about what anyone else is thinking. I know there are some churches that would not let us rap for them, but not Zoe Ministries. We came out rapping "Down with the King" right in the church service. The church is totally behind

us, they prophesy over us, they pray with us and they watch the changes God has been making in our lives. The Bible says to praise God with the harp, the song, and the dance. We go to church and we get busy. We believe rap is the prime movement of God right now and we believe that we are the best in rap. God came and took Run-DMC away from the trash to show everyone what he can do.[218]

McDaniel, though sensing the risks inherent in making bold statements that would alienate old fans, while simultaneously refusing to jump into the CCM market and make new ones, was eager to fulfill what he saw as the group's calling.

Run and I are just making our statement. It takes boldness to stand up and say, "I am down with Jesus." A person can't be killed for saying that, because people do not want to hear it. However we are saying it and God is proving that he is with us. We can make the statement that Run-DMC is down with God and lose all our fans, and all the fame, and all the hip-hop essence of the street, but that is not going to happen. Though we are still learning, Run and I are staring life really hard in the face. We want everyone to know that we are rolling with the True Strength and the True Power. . . . Like our pastor says, we are going to go places and not even know why we are there, but God will tell us. . . . God will open doors again. There is no telling where Run-DMC will go.[219]

Take 6

The powerful influence of Stevie Wonder was felt by an up-and-coming group named Take 6, whose career was launched when Wonder reportedly ordered dozens of copies of the group's CD and gave them away as Christmas presents one year.

"He took us to his dressing room at Radio City Music Hall and told us that our music had changed his life," remembered group member Alvin Chea. "That has always stuck with me. You never think that people who are such music icons are affected by anything. You think they just . . . set the tempo for the world. But they have souls too and their souls are just as valid and just as hungry as a recovering drug addict who's homeless."[220]

Formed in 1980 by four freshmen at Oakwood College in Alabama, Take 6 launched its career in 1988 with the release of an eponymous debut album, which quickly garnered them three Grammy awards and four CCM Dove Awards.

"Stevie Wonder wanted to meet them, Quincy Jones took them under his wing, and invitations began to pour in from artists who wanted the group to collaborate on various projects," observed writer Deborah Akins. "The music industry greeted Take 6 with open arms."[221]

"We expected the hard work would pay off," remembered Chea, "but anybody can become an overnight success—that's easy to do. It's not something that's in your control, anyway. All of a sudden you're hailed as the next best thing to peanut butter, which is wonderful. But the hard part and where the prayers have to come in, is when a couple of years later, you do the same thing you were hailed for before, and all of a sudden it's not so great anymore. Not as many people care. That's challenging and it can do a really big thing with your head."[222]

Initially signed to Reprise, the group's records were distributed in the Christian world by Reunion and later by Warner Bros.'s CCM imprint Warner/Alliance, but musically and spiritually, Take 6 was always about breaking down walls and going where none had gone before.

"Our music is so eclectic it breaks down most barriers associated with ethnic music," said the group's leader, Mark Kibble. "We feel that jazz—which is an indigenous American art form—is like a prophet without honor in his own country, and we believe it was just the Lord's plan for us to bring elements of these classic styles together to reach a wider audience with gospel content."[223]

In spite of the album's high Christian content, many pop critics had nothing but effusive praise for the group. "Take 6 has revolutionized the pop vocal group tradition by using it as a vehicle for communicating its deep and abiding faith," wrote one critic. "But no matter how dazzling the medium, it never supersedes the message, which gains momentum with each song. . . . Powerful stuff, but it goes down easy and leaves you thinking."[224]

Despite the acclaim, for the members of Take 6, there was a constant feeling of being caught in the middle of two markets and not being understood by either. "To the gospel or contemporary Christian listening audience, Take 6 has always kind of been viewed as a mainstream group," said Claude McKnight. "And to the mainstream market, we've always been viewed as a gospel or contemporary Christian group. We always land somewhere in the middle, depending upon which camp you're talking to, and it's been somewhat difficult as far as perception goes."[225]

"We've never had a lot of radio success," added Chea. "Our thing has basically always been a word of mouth thing, but that has served to remind us that God is the one who's running our career. I sometimes feel like if we knew how to get a hit, or if we knew how to get on radio, we might become a little more self-sufficient and not turn to Him immediately. We praise God for the ministry of Kirk Franklin, the Sounds of Blackness, BeBe and CeCe, and on and on. There are lots of different success stories. It has eluded us to a point, but God did not call us to be . . . Elvis. How He's going to use us is how He's going to use us."[226]

By the mid-1990s their star had faded somewhat, but the members of Take 6 continued to produce pop/R&B albums and managed to garner seven Grammy awards. Some critics contended that in their zeal to avoid the pitfalls of Sam Cooke and others, Take 6 sometimes preached the gospel at the expense of artistry, altering the lyrics, for instance, to the classic Ambrosia tune "Biggest Part of Me," aiming the song at the Savior instead of a woman, then wondering why radio didn't embrace it.

"Radio is a little nervous when it comes to playing songs that either overtly mention God or are about spiritual things," complained Claude McKnight. "There are some songs by some artists who have been able to cleverly get past that, but for the most part it is still a challenge with radio programmers."[227]

Yet, regardless of the limitations imposed by a lack of success in the pop music world, McKnight believed that true success was measured by a different standard. "It is our responsibility to be true and to be consistent lyrically, more than anything," he said. "People are always wanting to see you fail, they always want to see you do something out of character. I think even Christians want to see that sometimes, which is unfortunate. . . . I think that a ministry, no matter what it is—as long as it's put before God daily and is meeting needs in lives—is a valid ministry. Our responsibility is not to be successful or to be platinum-selling artists. He just calls us to be faithful."[228]

Unlike other artists who jumped back into CCM for comfort and dependable record sales when they failed to meet with great success in the pop market, Take 6 continued to hold to its vision of being a force in pop music.

"One of the things we wanted to do over the years was to sing with and to the people within the industry who needed to hear it," said McKnight. "We've never been the kind of guys who necessarily have pulled people aside and witnessed to them and all of that. It's always been very important when we're doing something with somebody just to live the way we know how to live. We've been able to forge really great friendships with a lot of these people. I think that can be a catalyst, that can be a seed planted in somebody."[229]

King's X

Around the time Take 6 was hitting the charts, another band was busy shopping its demo around to various record labels. Originally known as the Edge, King's X was comprised of Doug Pinnick, Jerry Gaskill, and Ty Tabor. At Evangel College, in Springfield, Missouri, the threesome joined forces. All three had experience playing with CCM bands like Petra, Servant, Phil Keaggy, and Morgan Cryar.

"Doug and Jerry were great bandmates," remembered Keaggy, for whom the two played drums and bass. "Doug sang with such passion. You could tell he was going to go on to something deeper and more aggressive."[230]

Pinnick and Tabor had written several hit songs for Cryar's 1986 album, including an in-your-face response to the 1963 Supreme Court decision outlawing prayer in public schools called "Pray in the USA." "Til they steal your heart away, you can still pray in the USA," an impassioned Pinnick had written. Cryar's voice, though a mere shadow of Pinnick's own throaty vocals, carried the tune well, and in 1986 it had the Christian world defiantly rocking.

"We all had dealings in it one way or another," said Ty Tabor of CCM. "We all had played in Christian bands, but we wanted to do something different. I didn't have anything against the Christian industry. I just didn't feel it was what I was supposed to do. I felt like God wanted me to do something different. We wanted to be real artists—not confined by any industry. We didn't care if our stuff was sold in the Christian industry, but we didn't want it to be limited to that. We wanted it to be heard by anybody, not just on a Christian station."[231]

The band moved to Texas in response to an offer of financial backing that was later withdrawn, but there they met Sam Taylor, who was then involved with ZZ Top. Taylor agreed to produce the young band and renamed them King's X after a band he had heard in high school.

"The main thing he brought was discipline," remembered Tabor of Taylor. "Up until then, we didn't have a clue what real professionalism was. We didn't work real hard. I think Sam was the one who saw potential in us that we weren't willing to work and find out. And he helped to get us more disciplined at working and taking it seriously and being more of a professional band. And that was a big thing he did for us, which carries into now. We look at everything differently because of that now."[232]

Taylor's suggestion of the name King's X had deep meaning for Pinnick because it exemplified what he hoped to do: play music that reflected his Christian beliefs without being thrown out of the party.

"In Texas, there's a meaning for King's X when you're playing tag," said Pinnick. "If you cross your fingers, you're exempt from being 'it.' There's a legend that, in medieval times, when a king would send a message to another king, he'd use a messenger. If the king didn't like the message, he would kill the messenger. But if he had the mark of the king [who sent] him, which would be the king's x, then he would be exempt from punishment. So it's kind of an exemption thing when you get the king's x."[233]

One label interested in the band was the Irvine, California-based Frontline. Started in the mid-'80s by Jim Kempner, a well-known face in southern California "Christian" music circles, Frontline was the only game in town for many CCM bands. The deals offered to the artists were generally much worse than their "secular" counterparts received, because Frontline regularly gobbled up all or most of the publishing royalties that most other labels shared with the artists, and the royalty rates were substantially lower than those offered to general market artists.

Producer/singer Ken Tamplin received a call from Michael MacLane, Frontline's A&R director, wondering if Tamplin would consider producing a new band they were considering signing. "I met with them after a Knott's Berry Farm show," remembered MacLane, "and they gave us a demo tape. They were among a few bands that I talked with Kenny about producing."[234]

Tamplin, whose own band, Shout, had recently signed with Frontline and released a stellar album, was too busy producing a Canadian band called Angelica and begged off the project. With Tamplin unwilling to participate, MacLane decided against signing King's X.

It was a fateful decision that would haunt MacLane and Frontline, but one that benefited King's X and the rock music culture, for if Frontline had signed the band, the rock world would have been deprived of the music of one of the great rock bands of all time. Not long after the Frontline rejection, Megaforce Records president Johnny Z came calling, and with Taylor at the production helm, the promising new band that managed to bring Beatles harmonies and pop sensibilities to a dying heavy metal sound was off and running.

It's not altogether clear whether Megaforce realized that they had just signed three devout Christians, whose members had at one time played with well-known CCM artists.

"I did have an encounter with Jesus when I was around three," said Pinnick. "The way they told me is I had died. I know that Jesus came to my bed and he took me off to go with him and I got way far from the earth; far enough that I wanted to go back and I kept trying to let go of his hand. I pulled and tugged and tugged out of his hand and I remember him letting go of my hand and I came back, I remember, in my mom's lap."[235]

That incident cemented Pinnick's belief in a higher power. "I always knew he was there, and I always believed in him, and I always felt the presence of Jesus, the Holy Spirit, all my life. I don't know what it's like to be in darkness. But when I was twenty-one, I decided I needed to make a commitment."[236]

When Pinnick heard an evangelist speak of his need of salvation, rather than going forward, Pinnick headed for the back. "I went to the bathroom and I said, 'OK Jesus, hey, forgive me of my sins and let's move on.' I guess that's when our relationship really started. I really started to get to know him."[237]

Preparing for the release of its debut album, King's X began to gear up for obvious questions about their lyrics that would inevitably come from the rock press. *Out of the Silent Planet*, which featured a New Age-style cover that gave the buyer a glimpse of heaven, threw the rock critics off balance. King's X decided to play coy with the cultural gatekeepers who would decide their fate—and how much exposure they would receive in the market.

"We never set out to win the Christian audience," said Pinnick. "We just set out to play rock 'n' roll. Being a Christian band puts so many stigmas on you, so with the first album we kind of avoided the issue. We didn't talk about being Christians, and if anybody asked us about the lyrics, we just said they were spiritual, psychedelic, you know?"[238]

When the inevitable questions of faith came up, King's X simply responded truthfully, if evasively, that they were fans of the British poet C. S. Lewis and had named the album after one of his books as a way of honoring him. As Lewis himself had done in his own writings, King's X hid their spiritual fervor behind nonchalance and the careful turning of a phrase.

"All along we had said, 'Let's not talk to the press about our beliefs,'" said Tabor. "They're too dear. Every interview that we did got misrepresented to some extent. So many times people have misquoted us or totally misunderstood things and written articles about it. So we always—all along—said, 'Let's leave that out of the press, because it's too dear of a thing.' When we can talk to someone night after night, one on one, we can be clear; but the press is not the place for it."[239]

"We feel the music speaks for itself, we don't have to make some kind of stand or statement," said Pinnick in 1989. "If people expect more from us than rock 'n' roll, they're going to be disappointed. I don't want Christians to start using us as this banner: 'We've got another one, listen to this band, read the lyrics, it'll change your life.' Forget that. Just let us go on and do what we know how to do. Whatever's happening is happening, we're not oblivious, we get the fan mail, we know it's having an effect."[240]

With the song "King," for instance, by leaving out the word "the" and going with the refrain "King is coming," they managed to convey the essence of the message communicated by hundreds of gospel singers before them that God would one day return to punish evildoers and rescue his own, without sounding like they were delivering a musical version of Jonathan Edwards's famous sermon, "Sinners in the Hands of an Angry God." They also left room for another interpretation with the careful crafting of their video, which portrayed a young Pinnick, the only African American in the band, integrating his elementary school in the '60s in the South. Were they referring to Martin Luther King? Apparently some critics thought so, because the objections that might otherwise have engulfed such an obviously Christian-themed song were muted.

"I didn't want to say 'the king,'" said Pinnick. "I didn't want to say 'Jesus.' I wanted it to be sort of a blanket statement, like the big brother, somebody's coming to take care of this person who's always on my case all of the time."[241]

"King's X has always been a secular band of Christians," said Pinnick. "We want to remain that way so we can go on with our lives and do what we do without having the pressure of the Christian community upon us. . . . All we are is musicians who believe a certain way and it reflects through our music. We play our music and people who understand what we're saying get something out of it. People who don't get it like our music."[242]

Like medieval messengers who bore the mark of the King, King's X was not punished for the message it delivered, at least not to the extent that other messengers had been punished.

Like Donna Summer, Kansas, Stryper, and Dylan before them, King's X had learned that songs of human love and devotion belonged on a record devoted to God. On *Out of the Silent Planet* they included a delicious number, "Goldilox," about a young man who struggled to keep love from turning into lust. "I stand behind you and I watch you from a mile away, wishing I could be the one, but not here in this way. I've got to know your name. Yes, I must know who you are,"[243] sang Pinnick.

Britain's premiere hard rock magazine, *Kerrang!*, observed of the band's debut: "*Out of the Silent Planet* has had superlatives hurled at it from every angle, had writers groping for the words to describe its power and vision, the breadth of its invention and its stunning execution."[244]

King's X's second and third albums enlarged its audience and sealed its fate as a noncommercial but critically acclaimed band. By the time its second record, *Gretchen Goes to Nebraska,* was released, perhaps emboldened by their critical success, King's X told interviewers that they were followers of Jesus Christ. The songs seemed a bit bolder as well. "Over My Head" became a favorite on rock radio and was the most deeply spiritual song of the bunch, with the pounding chorus, "Music, music, I hear music . . . music, oh, oh, oh Lord, music over my head,"[245] culminating in the final bridge where Pinnick passionately sang, "Grandma used to sing, every night while she was praying, over my head." It was an electrifying moment not lost on CCM fans, who quickly rallied around King's X, though they were not officially a part of the CCM market.

Throwing caution to the wind, the band called its third record *Faith, Hope and Love by King's X,* and included the words to 1 Corinthians 13 inside the CD booklet. Recalling a conversation with then-manager Sam Taylor, Pinnick said,

> When we named the album, Sam said to us, "Well, what do you guys think right now? What's the biggest thing on your mind? What's happening in your life?" Ty said, "Well, faith." I said, "Hope," and Jerry said, "Love." Sam goes, "'Faith, Hope, Love' sounds like a title to me." The other albums, it was a subtle way that we spoke our faith. It was a way that I think people could hear it and not feel like I was being some kind of evangelist or something. . . . On this album, I wanted to get a little more drastic. I wrote a couple of songs that don't have anything to do with the Lord at all, and on the other hand, we wrote "Faith Hope Love," which basically says, "I believe the Word," and "He is alive." I just felt like I got bold there.[246]

Faith, Hope and Love's cover portrayed the history of the world through small paintings in the band's logo and included the act of Creation, Christ's first journey to earth, and his triumphant return. "The cover art's pretty up front," commented Pinnick, "but yet it isn't at the same time. I've always believed that if you take the gift God's given you and be artistic with it, God can shine through it so easily, rather than having to struggle through something that's bad art and putting Jesus on it."[247]

Though King's X rarely got around to naming Jesus in their music, like Kansas before them, in many ways their lyrics were more direct than simple praise songs. Perhaps taking a cue from Kerry Livgren's memorable line, "There's a hunger life can never fill 'til you face the One who rose," King's X sang in "Everywhere I Go," "I read the story—said You died, I turned the page—You were alive. With hope and love and mostly faith, one day I'll see You face to face."[248]

Then, in a move panned by the music reviewer at *Rolling Stone*, the three transplanted Texans had the audacity to include a politically incorrect, antiabortion track, "Legal Kill": "I know your side so very well, it makes no sense that I can tell, the smell of hell is what I smell and you hand it out with handshakes every day. . . . I can see the chance to live and walk free from a legal kill,"[249] sang Tabor.

It was Randall Terry cloaked in C. S. Lewis, and it put the rock culture on notice: King's X would not be going the way of U2. Their third album would not be *The Joshua Tree*, an attempt to make nice with the rock music culture by toning down clear messages and embracing establishment-approved causes.

"I had to really talk to the guys about what my goal was with the song before we decided to put it on, because it was an issue with a lot of people," remembered Tabor of "Legal Kill." "The fact that I put the lyrics in there that say, 'Look I have problems with the people with signs, but I feel the need to make my own,' was where I disassociated myself from organized anything and just said this is my personal stance and feelings."[250]

If such moves disappointed the rock culture, their statements probably disappointed the Christian subculture as well. Tabor remembers:

> We met people night after night who were so unopen to the idea of Jesus, just because of what Christians had represented Christianity as in the modern world. Nine out of ten people we met were so closed to anything Christian, because of their experience with the church, and it was all based on the fact that they didn't really know who Jesus was, they knew who the church was. A lot of them were people who went to church for years, they knew all the Christian lingo, Bible verses, or whatever, but still had not grasped who Jesus was. We all have gone through periods in the past where we have been very angry with the church—very angry with the Christian industry. The whole selling of Jesus like a cheap commercial just made me absolutely furious. Cheap salesman ministry and the worship of almighty ministries make me sick. People worship ministry for the sake of ministry above truth and serving God.[251]

"Far from embracing Christianity as a handy system of answers," observed the *Illinois Entertainer* in a feature on the band, "King's X sees it more as a better way of framing the questions."[252]

Part of that framing was a willingness to publicly embrace pain and doubt. "All this pain and suffering goes on and isn't cured," said Pinnick.

"The church sort of sticks its nose up or else it says, 'I'm going to go out and get those lonely people and turn them on to exactly what I believe, cut their hair, clean up their act, tell them, "Don't smoke, don't drink, don't cuss."' What's that got to do with Christianity? It's crazy."[253]

In 1991, Pinnick had been clear about King's X's mission. "This approach isn't for everyone," he noted. "We feel it's our calling. We are convinced that this is God's will for our lives. . . . We've all been Christians for a long time. I've been a believer for twenty years and I'm forty years old. We have worked very, very hard to be where we feel we're supposed to be in Christ, as people and as a band. We just want people to trust us and accept the fact that we're doing something that maybe other Christians are not doing."[254]

The success of King's X's first three albums helped them acquire new fans and opened new doors for touring, sometimes with bands that King's X had little in common with spiritually. "AC/DC asked us to be on the tour with them and needed us for Europe and America," said Pinnick. "I've been told that they're King's X fans and they all know our music and have our CDs and play them. They really respect us as musicians and they wanted us on tour. There were many bands who tried for the slot and they turned everyone down but us. So it was flattering to us and we said, 'We'll do it.' They were very, very good to us. They treated us like it was our show; not like an opening band at all."[255]

As the band prepared to release its fifth record, *Dogman*, Pinnick was going through a particularly difficult spell. But consistent with the band's policy of full artistic disclosure, his struggles were reflected on the record.

Though the 1996 release *Ear Candy* hinted at the possibility of a band breakup, by 1998 they had resurfaced on Metal Blade Records with a new album, *Tapehead*, as well as solo albums from both Pinnick and Tabor.

Tapehead was another King's X masterpiece that harkened back to earlier albums, but longtime fans could be forgiven for being disturbed by Pinnick's solo album, recorded under the band moniker Poundhound, and his subsequent public statements. On the song "Darker" Pinnick expressed doubts about his faith.

Pinnick's change of heart, it turned out, had less to do with theology and more with the practical workings of it. He finally admitted that he had been struggling with homosexual feelings for most of his life. Pinnick's admission was a setback to those who believed that men and women of faith could keep that faith alive in the world of rock and roll.

"They can say that if you're in a secular band, you're going to fall away," he said. "Well, let them say it, there's nothing I can do, because mainly we probably do. After you go out into the world and see it as it is and what it is, you get a whole different reality of what this whole thing is. After seeing the world, and seeing different cultures, and seeing different people with different religions and how they live, and how happy they are, and how their lives are full, then you go back and go, 'God, what's this? I'm seeing that people seem to be doing better than I'm doing and I'm going nowhere, I'm miserable.'"[256]

Ty Tabor was hard pressed to explain why some keep the faith and others fall away as a result of life in the public fishbowl. "I guess . . . the grace of God. I know a lot of people start out that way, with the intention, and things happen that just kinda get your eyes off of it. And after awhile, you change, and I know it can happen. I've seen it."[257]

However the final chapter of King's X would be written, it wouldn't diminish the fact that, for nearly a decade, a group of devout Christians had been universally respected by their peers. Some bands confessed that they waited to hear new King's X records before they began work on their own, and others, like the Scorpions, Pearl Jam, and AC/DC, asked King's X to be their opening acts on the road.

Still, despite the many accolades, Ty Tabor believed that their strong stand of faith had not come without a heavy price.

> I think we're very much hated by a lot of the world that is in opposition to what we think. That's the way it will always be. Just because somebody gets popular—so they sell 8 million albums or 8 million people love 'em and love what they're saying, or maybe even don't love what they're saying but just like the music, and maybe a small portion of them love what's being said—a lot of people hate King's X and will always hate King's X for the things we stand for and a lot of the things lyrically we say. We will always have enemies. It doesn't matter if some people are favorable with us—I think the world in general, the popular press and the popular political correctness of the U.S. will probably find offense in King's X.[258]

Gary Cherone of Extreme and Van Halen

Contemporaries of King's X, the Boston-based rock band Extreme followed a similar path. They had no ties with the CCM industry, and they were led by a devout Christian named Gary Cherone, who seemed to shy away from publicly discussing his faith, except on rare occasions, preferring to let his music do the talking.

Though raised by a Catholic mother, Cherone eventually left the church. "I consider myself a Christian," he said. "My mother's a Catholic.

She's kinda bummed out that I'm not a Catholic, but she's a Christian too. I was brought up as a Catholic and never doubted the story. I'm glad I always felt like I believed in [God]. I never doubted it. . . . I never had a doubt in my mind and I still don't."[259]

Of Christ, Cherone noted, "I would never deny him three times or one. He's the Son of God to me, period."[260]

Cherone credited radio pastor Chuck Swindoll with reawakening him to spiritual issues. "I was swearing, working at a car rental place, and at five o'clock one night . . . it was dark, winter, I was . . . miserable and I wanted to get home. Nothing was on the radio and Chuck was screaming at me. He just destroyed me. It was . . . in '85 when God spoke through Chuck to me."[261]

Cherone was careful not to label the other members of the band spiritually. "The rest of the band knows there is a God. Everyone knows there's a God, but like every other human being, we kind of turn away from him when we decide to do our own thing."[262]

Cherone and Extreme articulated a streetwise, in-your-face morality, an ends-justify-the-means vision of songwriting that sometimes used swear lyrics to arrive at a moral conclusion. Cherone admitted to having mixed feelings.

> What's my take on swear words? For people who do, and people who practice it, it's just a lack of vocabulary, which I can be guilty of. . . . But in defense of it, sometimes I don't think there's any other word for it. I don't think that any other word could be stronger. . . . It's an emotion that's a part of me. I'm honest. I get emotional when I sing, and sometimes that happens. I think it would be a little bit of a lie if I wasn't honest with myself, and then I'd be deceiving everybody. . . . In my life, there are probably more important things than that, which I would consider a compromise for my faith. . . . Who knows? Maybe it'll change. I know it won't get worse.[263]

Unlike the more cautious King's X, Extreme came out of the gate with an antiabortion track on its first album, a kamikaze move that the band survived, probably because few people heard of them until their second album, which contained two songs, "Hole Hearted" and "More Than Words," that received significant radio airplay.

Written by Cherone and Nuno Bettencourt, "Rock a Bye Bye" lamented the loss of unborn life over a powerful, weeping guitar solo by Bettencourt. "Watching, Waiting," another song off the first record, was a fairly straightforward depiction of the Crucifixion.

"'Watching, Waiting' is probably one of the most powerful stories in history," said Cherone. "Whether you believe that the man was God or that he wasn't, the story of the Crucifixion is so compelling that we wanted to tell it like a historian and kind of hide it. We do hide it . . . there are a couple of lines that hint to it. There are people who just like the song and they go, 'I'm staring at the Son,' and they look at the lyrics and go, 'That's not how you spell *sun*.' I believe in the story. If it can bring some people into the story, they're gonna have to have that battle like I did."[264]

Extreme's second album, *Pornograffitti*, decried the effects of pornography on a young mind and wrestled with issues related to temptation and sex. For Cherone, it was a deeply personal record that chronicled his life. "*Pornograffitti* deals with the morality of the last ten years of my life," he said at the time of its release. "Obviously, we hide it in a character named Francis. The names were changed to protect the innocent, but it's basically some of the things I had to go through."[265]

Cherone used the album to question society's permissive attitude. "'Pornograffitti' is another name for the 'decadence dance' of the world. How can I, or how can this young kid, go through life without being tainted by it and being scarred by 'pornograffitti' that surrounds him? He ends up pushing away women and losing out on love, and hating, because of the sexual temptation."[266]

For Extreme, "More Than Words" made the band a household name, and the follow-up song, "Hole Hearted," cemented their popularity. For Cherone, it was "Hole Hearted" that brought all of the songs on the record into a point of focus—a conclusion that reflected his own faith journey.

"I wanted it to be separate from the album, kind of like an editorial," he said. "It kind of talks about the whole record. How his life's ambition has occupied his time, that kind of stuff. He still hasn't found the peace in his heart to make him happy, but he's still looking for it. It could be a girl, it could be God. I don't want to tell you what it is, because I want people to put their own piece there. That's why we keep it general. To me, I'm looking for God."[267]

The big guns, however, were saved for the next record, the ambitious, Queen-influenced *Three Sides to Every Story*. The title alone was a shocker, because Cherone was laying down the gauntlet in the midst of a culture in which not all quarters accepted his premise that truth is absolute. Cherone's truth included the obligatory 'my side,' 'your side,' as well a third side—the Truth. "When I think of 'Three Sides,' I think of the third side. . . . I plagiarized the Bible with some of those lyrics," he laughed, "which I think is the only way you can't go wrong."[268]

The album's first single, "Rest in Peace," made a small splash on MTV but lacked the punch of previous singles. Nevertheless, the record proved to be Extreme's strongest work: comprehensive, visionary in its outlook, and aggressive both musically and lyrically. With songs ranging from "Rise & Shine," which quoted the prophet Daniel and Jesus, to the anthemic "God Isn't Dead," the album was also Cherone's most aggressive spiritual statement with Extreme. After one more record, *Waiting for the Punchline*, Extreme disbanded. Nuno Bettencourt started a new band, and Gary Cherone became the lead singer for Van Halen.

Cherone didn't leave Extreme without taking one last shot at unbelief, on *Punchline*, with his mocking "There Is No God," which set to music the biblical admonition, "The fool hath said in his heart, there is no God."

"I tried to pick apart the lyrics," he said, "and I've pitted religion versus science, and the parallels that they have, and the leap of faith that you have to take with both. I'm glad I have to take this leap of faith of believing in God. I don't think God would have it any other way. . . . The creation of God is the evidence of God. If you can't see that, then you're blind, and you're letting your intellect be your God, and that's pretty vain. That title— I don't know where it came from. It probably came from the phrase from *Time* magazine's headline, 'God is Dead.'"[269]

In many ways, Cherone's work with Extreme made him a point man in the counter-counter culture. "The spirit of rock and roll has always been against the establishment, against the norm," he said in a 1993 interview. "If what's against the norm becomes the norm, it ends up being rebelled against. What is rebellion? Is it a Jack Daniels bottle or is it a thought?"[270]

Cherone's greatest triumphs as an artist, musician, writer, and a man of faith were yet to come, however. Soon after his final Extreme record, Cherone was asked to join the legendary Van Halen, where he quickly assumed a strong role in the songwriting process and ended up writing most of the lyrics for his debut with the band, titled *III*.

For those familiar with Cherone's work with Extreme, there were few surprises. He again fearlessly integrated his faith into his songs about everyday life, and risked offending longtime fans of the party band by including thanks to the theologian R. C. Sproul in the album's credits. Sproul had also provided spiritual inspiration for another rocker, Alice Cooper.

Cherone wasted little time in moving Van Halen's focus away from the sexual innuendo of some of the band's previous material with a playful, but ultimately innocent, acknowledgement of his own nature on "Dirty Water Dog": "When heavy is the weight of the world and the river runs a little too deep/like a hound dog chasing a bird sometimes a certain Tom got a peep/I'm a peek a boy looking at girls and I think, I think I like what I see . . . /I'm just a hound-toothed heterosexual."[271]

On "Once," however, he demonstrated his grasp of theology, capably articulating the Christian doctrine of eternal security: "Once born can never not be conceived/Once embraced can't ever be let go. Once revealed can't ever be not shown/Once believed can't ever lose faith. Once shared can't ever be separate. Like the dawn of a brand new day/with the power of Deity, I can feel it inside of me. Can you feel it?"[272]

On "Fire in the Hole," Cherone was again up to his favorite old trick of lifting Bible verses—in this case from the Book of James—to drive home the ultimate depravity of the human heart and tongue. "We can make a large horse turn around and go wherever we want by means of a small bit in his mouth," wrote the apostle James in the third verse of the third chapter, "and a tiny rudder makes a huge ship turn wherever the pilot wants it to go, even though the winds are strong. So also the tongue is a small thing, but what enormous damage it can do. A great forest can be set on fire by one tiny spark. And the tongue is a flame of fire."[273]

"Rudder of ship which sets the course/does not the bit bridle the horse?" wrote Cherone. "Great is the forest set by a small flame, like a tongue on fire no one can tame."[274]

Cherone also used a website operated by two fans, Cherone.com, to help fans who occasionally wrote the singer with questions. One fan, Tracey Ecker, wrote, "Lately I have been reading a lot about you and your faith in God. My question is how do you keep that faith in God when there are so many terrible things happening to good people and in our world in general?"[275]

"Faith is only as good as the object in which it is placed" responded the singer. "Whenever I am asked 'Why do bad things happen to good people?' I immediately think of Proverbs 30:4 and know that God is sovereign over all creation and that the perpetrator of 'terrible things' is man, which leads me to my favorite argument for the existence of God: ultimate justice."[276]

To another fan, Cherone gave a sneak peek into the songwriting for his second record with Van Halen. "I hear you are currently working on the next VH album," she wrote. "Has anything inspired your lyrics?" Cherone's reply: "Relativism."[277]

For serious believers who paid attention to such matters, it was a moment of triumph and a signal to the rest of the culture that they had successfully infiltrated the rock music culture with one of their own, who was setting the agenda for one of rock's top bands. Gary Cherone was an accomplished musician, and a Christian, who was in the world but not of it.

Lenny Kravitz

If Cherone's occasional use of four-letter words to drive home a point made some believers uncomfortable, retro rocker Lenny Kravitz would push the envelope even further. Kravitz, half-Jewish, half-Bahamian, was the son of NBC producer Sy Kravitz and actress Roxie Roker, best known for her role as Helen Willis on the '70s sitcom *The Jefferson's*. He was also briefly married to another sitcom favorite, Lisa Bonet, Bill Cosby's daughter on the *Cosby* show.

When his mother's acting career began to take off, young Kravitz moved with her to California and settled in at Beverly Hills High School, where he joined the prestigious California Boys Choir, performing classical music.

He was also a convert to evangelical Christianity at a young age. "Lenny first met God when he was thirteen, a couple of years after he smoked his first joint," noted writer William Shaw. "A friend, the son of a pastor, converted Lenny after they got into a deep conversation about religion. Lenny is convinced that he felt God enter the room as they were talking. He teared up and started trembling. 'It was an overpowering feeling. I was just losing it.'"[278]

Despite a public image as something of a ladies' man, in his music Kravitz toed the line of adherence to the basic doctrines of the Christian faith. Most Christians would fail to embrace Kravitz, however, because of his public image that included outlandish photos on his album *Circus*, featuring such oddities as a mostly naked Kravitz with a tail protruding from his backside.

Ironically, *Circus* was probably one of the most direct Christian-themed records to emerge from inside or outside the CCM market. Kravitz seemed to share none of the hesitations that many believers in rock had about being forthright with their faith. He not only made clear references to God and Jesus, but he plainly pointed out the way of salvation and urged listeners to follow.

In the song "Believe" from the *Are You Gonna Go My Way?* record, Kravitz laid out his faith: "The Son of God is in our face, offering us eternal grace. . . . We'll one day leave this all behind, just put your faith in God and one day you'll see."[279]

"Lenny Kravitz's heart belongs to Jesus Christ and *Circus* is a heartfelt record," observed Shaw. "In its darker and more passionate moments, it's the clearest declaration yet of Kravitz's homegrown Christian morality. It veers from the hallucinatory 'Beyond the Seventh Sky'—Kravitz's own personal chapter from the Book of Revelation—to rock 'n' hymns like 'In My Life Today' and 'God Is Love,' both proud, unfashionable declarations of religious devotion. . . . They all share a clear sense of moral purpose. 'It is dark,' Lenny says, 'but dark in a spiritual way . . . very spiritual and surreal.'"[280]

Though selling modestly, *Circus* proved to be Kravitz's spiritual tour de force, an album he described as a criticism of the music industry and a quest to find God. On "Rock and Roll Is Dead," Kravitz, no fan of the Seattle grunge sound, pinned the blame for rock's demise on a bankrupted spirituality, while simultaneously urging his Seattle colleagues to practice their craft more. "You can't even sing or play an instrument, so you just scream instead," he sang. "You're living for an image, so you've got five hundred women in your bed. But it's hard to be yourself when you're living with those demons in your head."[281]

On "Beyond the Seventh Sky," he sang of heaven to a pulsating beat: "Beyond the seventh sky, there's a room where we are with God. . . . Where the angels will be our guard, where the weather doesn't change. Every day is summer . . . the place where life was formed . . . the place where Jesus Christ was born."[282]

With "God Is Love," Kravitz was equally direct: "God loves everyone, that's why he gave his Son. God is love, He'll get you through your pain and sorrow, God is love, He's coming back, maybe tomorrow. . . . And though much time has passed, His words and promises always last."[283]

Similarly, with "The Resurrection," Kravitz laid down the basics of Christian doctrine: "The King is near, the resurrection is here to stay, and he's coming back again . . . to reclaim all his souls and set us free. . . . He walked on the righteous path, to keep us from Satan's wrath. . . . We are not alone, and we're going home."[284]

On "In My Life Today," Kravitz personalized his theological pronouncements: "I was bare and I was lost, but You were there and now I'm born, You are the force and strength in my life today. And oh how I thank You, Father, for giving us all over and under . . . . so full of love and sacrifice. . . . And now that the darkness has faded, I'm no longer blinded, I can see. . . . You make me try to do right and throw away my evil ways."[285]

Kravitz was also outspoken in interviews, telling *Rolling Stone*, "If you listen to my records, the main thing I am talking about is the love of God."[286]

In an interview with *Billboard*, Kravitz commented on the transitory nature of fame and the importance of faith. "I guess the more successful I get, the more I pull away and get into my spiritual side," he said. "Fame doesn't mean anything; it's great, but it doesn't mean anything on the inside. Fame without substance has no self-worth. I guess the more I go around and observe, the closer I want to be to God, because that's more real than what's out there."[287]

In 1998, Kravitz released his latest offering, titled *V*, opting for more oblique but no less inspirational references to God and faith, portraying Christ as a cosmic superhero engaged in spiritual warfare with the Devil in "Super Soul Fighter": "The lord of the wasteland he don't want us to be free, but he can't stop our hero or his supersonic V . . . He has come to save the day."[288]

In "I Belong to You," Kravitz gave fans a more personal take on his relationship with the Almighty: "You are the flame of my heart, you light my way in the dark, you are the ultimate star, you lift me from up above," sang Kravitz. "Before you I was blind, but since I have opened my eyes, and with you there's no disguise, so I can open up my mind."[289]

Ashley Cleveland

Born in Knoxville, Tennessee, Ashley Cleveland moved to northern California with her mother after her parents divorced. Growing up in the church gave her multiple opportunities to play music, but it was only after dropping out of college in Knoxville that she decided to pursue her dream of making music.

"Ultimately I just kind of reached a dead end," she remembered. "There is no music industry there. I decided I needed to live in a major industry town. In my mind that meant either Nashville, Los Angeles, or New York. I had just had Rebecca, and I was by myself, and the idea of trying to relocate to New York or LA with an infant, knowing no one and with very little resources, was just too overpowering to me. So I opted to go to Nashville."[290]

It was a move the budding singer quickly regretted. "I realized I was in the wrong town almost immediately," she remembered. "It didn't occur to me that labels had different focuses depending on where they were. Nashville was a country music town, which had nothing to do with what I was doing. It took me a long time to make any headway getting jobs in the industry, working singing background on records, getting a publishing deal where I could draw an income, just anything that would prevent me having to make a living as a waitress."[291]

Cleveland's hard work led to a contract in 1991 with Atlantic and the release of her first record, *Big Town*. Though not a major hit in the pop market, it came to the attention of many in the CCM market who were eager for expressions of faith from the "other side." Soon, Reunion came knocking with a plan to release her records in both markets through its association with RCA, but Cleveland was skeptical. "I had never really entertained an idea of being on a gospel label, because I wasn't sure that had a lot of bearing on what I was doing in terms of what was fitting in that format," she said at the time. "I had some concern that Reunion might [ask] me to alter what I was doing or move a little bit in their direction [musically]. In no way have they done that. In fact, they're hoping the market will be encouraged to move toward me. I couldn't ask for better than that."[292]

Cleveland's first outing with Reunion/RCA, *Bus Named Desire*, was "not what I would think of as a gospel record," she said, "although that brings up a whole other issue of why couldn't it be. I think it's brave of Reunion to take this stance, because it is unusual, and because it doesn't fit the current format. . . . I don't have any expectations. Right now on the front end of it, I am very curious. I would imagine that some people will be really responsive and able to receive what I am doing with a lot of enthusiasm and get it. I imagine it would be difficult for a segment of the Christian population. I would be surprised if the record were not somewhat controversial, because there is controversial content, to my mind, but more because it's not what people expect."[293]

Ultimately, though the record didn't sell well in either market, Cleveland successfully fused her artistic and spiritual sides into one holistic presentation, no small feat.

> My faith, in essence, has permanently altered the way I live my life and my perspective on life. There have been times when I've tried to avoid faith in terms of how it impacted my life, and I can't get away from it. It just is. It is my virtual reality, period. And from that place, I feel I can write with confidence and that's what I feel qualified to talk about. . . . Who knows, the next record may be entirely faith-driven and deal very specifically and only with my faith, because that may be where I am at the time, and that would be valid too. I write what I know and what I know right now is trying to negotiate this enormous change in my life. I spent many years by myself and now I'm married to somebody and that is largely what I am dealing with. And it's wonderful and horrible and exciting and terrifying, and I think the album is very much reflective of that. I think it has everything to do with my faith, but it is certainly not the typical expression.[294]

"My life is lived at a very human level," she said. "So that is where I express it. I don't have any lofty spiritual ideas. At best, I just have a sense of hanging on for dear life, and then I have the most wonderful taste when I know that God is intervening with me directly, and it's sort of beyond expression."[295]

Galactic Cowboys

A band that emerged in the early 1990s on the Geffen label was another group of musical protégés of producer Sam Taylor who called themselves the Galactic Cowboys. Taylor managed and produced both King's X and the Cowboys under the Wilde Silas moniker, and nurtured both bands artistically and spiritually.

Comprised of vocalist Ben Huggins, guitarist Dane Sonnier, bass player Monty Colvin, and drummer Alan Doss, Galactic Cowboys coalesced around Doss and Colvin. Like King's X, several members of the Cowboys did time in CCM popster Morgan Cryar's band.

They were signed to Geffen by A&R man Gary Gersh, whom Taylor had brought in to see the band. Without so much as seeing a show, Gersh and Geffen signed them. Not unlike Stryper, the Galactic Cowboys were apparently signed without the label knowing of their faith.

"I don't know," responded Colvin when asked what the label thought of the band members' faith. "Really, we haven't talked about it. We write the songs and we do what we do and they seem to like that, and hopefully our lives are good examples."[296]

"We never went in and [said], 'Look man we're Christians and you better understand that from the beginning,'" added Huggins.[297]

The band's first record was titled *Space in Your Face* and featured cuts that mixed the group's whimsical outlook on life with more weighty issues, all set to a sound best described by one critic as "the Partridge Family on acid." Typical of their whimsical fare was "Someone for Everyone," of which Colvin commented: "My father would always say, 'Don't worry, there's someone for everyone. The right one will come along.' Then one day, not long ago, I was walking through a mall and saw this couple—not two of the most attractive people I've ever seen in my life, and I thought, 'Yep, there sure is someone for everyone.' Hey, I'm glad they found each other."[298]

While all of the members of the Galactic Cowboys were clearly Christians, they, too, had been carefully steered away from CCM by Taylor, and made records that reflected, but refused to hype, their faith. "We're artists, we're musicians," said bassist Monty Colvin. "We're not preachers. We write about things that are on our minds. We have a responsibility to be creative and be artists, but we're not going to put Jesus in there just so we can please a certain crowd or serve one particular audience. If we do, it's going to be because the songs call for that. We do what we do and we write about things that we're thinking about or doing at that time."[299]

Of the Christian community, which didn't always understand bands like his, Colvin said, "I would hope Christian people would listen to us just because it's good music and it's artistic, and hopefully there's nothing in there that offends 'em. That's why I want people to listen to us: we've got something to say and it's good, or it's something that really excites 'em to listen to—not just because we say we're Christians, which we are."[300]

"We're Christians and we all believe," added Dane Sonnier. "We all follow and attempt to live our lives the way that Christ did. That's where it's at, really. That's where we're coming from. That's what we're trying to attain."[301]

Atomic Opera

Another band to emerge from the Taylor camp was Atomic Opera, whose first record, *For Madmen Only*, received airplay on MTV. Though believers, the members of Atomic Opera were clear about their role and mission. "Atomic Opera is not a gospel band," said singer Frank Hart. "That's not what we're about. We write songs about things that happen in our life. . . . We're about writing songs and issues that we want to see exist—things that should exist. There's music that I want to make, so I do. We record it and we try to do it as a band so that we're happy with it. That's all. If we can have some small part in shaking people's preconceptions and having them ask themselves questions about everything that moves us in our lives to make us write lyrics."[302]

Hart added:

> I'm not very comfortable with being called a Christian or with that particular baggage that comes with what it means to be a Christian in our culture. I find that I have very little in common with Christians that I run into. It has a lot to do with their view of art and their view of culture. It has very little to do with theology. . . . I just know that a lot of people, you know, like King's X, have come off to other Christians like they're trying to sell out—they're trying to deny Christ and trying to backpedal. If there is some way to let Christians know that what I'm talking about here is not being ashamed of Christ. It's not being ashamed of whatever that means to me. It is being ashamed of what the connotations of being a

Christian in our culture are, because I am ashamed of that. If you want to try and lump in what I am with televangelists and the state of the church, and all of the cultural baggage that comes with what most people perceive as Christianity, that's foreign to me. That's foreign to how I live my life and how I understand my role. It has nothing to do with who Jesus was. It's that I am ashamed of what Christianity and the church is in our culture and what that means to most people.[303]

FIVE

Mainstream Attempts

*O*ver the years, many have attempted to introduce recordings by artists who were Christians into the popular music market by forming non-CCM record labels or by associating their label with an established player in the pop market. All of these labels ultimately failed for a variety of reasons.

Songbird

One of the most ambitious crossover attempts, launched in the early 1980s, was MCA's Songbird label. Once an independent black gospel label distributed by ABC Records moniker, Songbird was adopted by MCA in 1979 after ABC closed shop. Headed by artist/producer Chris Christian, Songbird began signing CCM artists who they believed had crossover or mainstream potential.

At the beginning, "Chris had a commitment from B. J. [Thomas]," said music executive Charlie Shaw. The Songbird roster eventually grew to include artists like Dan Peek, Mylon Lefevre, Roby Duke, Barbara Mandrell, and the band Fireworks, "but it was a strained relationship at best," said Shaw. "The mainstream didn't care, and the Christians cared a little. Payola was still in play to have a hit record, and you had to have a lot of money to get one. It was a pioneering effort until Amy Grant broke water and showed that sales could come from that genre."[1]

The contract arrangement allowed MCA to distribute products into the general market while Sparrow was commissioned to take the product into the CCM world. Average sales of between five and ten thousand records in the pop market did not make for a successful venture, however, and by 1982 when MCA's Nashville president, Jim Fogelsong, was put in charge of the operation, he had figured out the difficulties of walking in two worlds.

"We have found that gospel's a totally different record business than the record business MCA is in," he said. "We haven't found a successful way to make it tick."[2]

Spirit

Sparrow Records' attempt at forming a pop market entity took the form of Spirit Records, a label formed in 1979 by producer Greg Nelson.

"We had Benny Hester, Pamela Duell Hart, and others,"[3] said industry veteran Jack Hafer, who moved from Sparrow to Spirit to help Nelson. When Sparrow subsequently sold the Spirit label to a group of Beverly Hills attorneys, Hafer became president of the fledgling company.

"They asked me if I would come and run it," said Hafer. "It was Sparrow's closest attempt at crossover that was their real contemporary label. We took it to Beverly Hills and worked with it for a year,"[4] before problems with the investors forced Spirit to close its doors.

Refuge

In 1980, Hafer, Greg Nelson, and another music veteran, Ray Nenow, moved to Nashville and began a new label called Refuge Records. Refuge succeeded in signing artists who had made a splash in the pop world, but ultimately failed to establish a credible presence in the music market. Eventually, the label settled for being a player in the CCM market.

According to Hafer, who today pastors a church in California, Refuge's original goal was to "provide a place of refuge for secular artists who had become Christians to be able to make a statement about the gospel in musical form without jeopardizing their other careers."[5]

"At the same time we were doing this," said Hafer, "Kerry Livgren had just released *Seeds of Change*, through Columbia. . . . He probably sold a hundred thousand of those albums, which at that time . . . our good albums were selling sixty [to] seventy thousand. Because of his association with Kansas, he was able to get the record into the bins. That just reconfirmed for us the validity of what we were doing. Our goal was to utilize the reputations of our artists to reach our artists' fans."[6]

Refuge's first signing was Joe English, the drummer for Paul McCartney's band, Wings. "Paul was excited that Joe had become a Christian," said Hafer. "[Joe had] already left Wings and the other jazz group he was with, so we took over his management. Joe was the first and Bonnie [Bramlett] was our second. . . . At the time, we broke the two acts kind of together, with a short blurb in *Rolling Stone* by Kurt Loder."[7] Bramlett, who had toured and written extensively with Eric Clapton, among others, was well known in music circles. Her debut with Refuge was titled *Step by Step.*

Refuge's goals were clearly spelled out in its statement of purpose. Many Christian-oriented companies drafted such documents to get their spiritual objectives down on paper. Unfortunately, this strategy often had the unintended consequence of alienating non-Christians, who were not used to such overt religious goal-setting.

"A refuge is a shelter into which you can come to get out of the storm," began Refuge's statement. "Our label provides a place for secular artists to come and be refreshed in order to say who they are to the world. It is, hopefully, a label where listeners can come and gain strength for the storm that exists. Our message is that Jesus is a place of refuge in the middle of the storm, not necessarily that all your storms will stop."[8]

In the mid-1980s, after a series of marginally successful releases from a small contingent of pop and rock stars, the company was sold off. Refuge continued to produce records for several more years before closing its doors. "Bottom line," said Hafer, "we didn't change the world."[9]

What?

In the mid-1980s Word had formed a label distribution agreement with A&M Records that allowed, at least in theory, artists on the Word label to be distributed to the pop world by A&M. Soon Word formed What? Records, a label headed by Word executive Tom Willett that was specifically designed to turn out artists well suited for the pop world. Willett dreamed of a world where artists who were firmly grounded in their Christian faith would make music for the culture at large.

"There's been a growing contingent of artists with the understanding of how to write a commercial song that could be an across-the-board hit," Willett said when the label was launched. "At the same time, [they can] let out real insight into life and what it means to be a human on this earth and tied into the Creator. The idea behind What? was that there needed to be a place where these people could do what they do so well without being forced to fit into either of the two molds."[10]

Some of "these people" included L. A. rocker Tonio K.; veteran CCM artist Mark Heard, who recorded under the name Ideola; and rocker Dave Perkins.

From the start, What? had an image problem. They were seen by many as too hip and edgy for the CCM market. It didn't help matters when an article in *CCM* magazine included a photograph of What? executive Tom Willett, producer T-Bone Burnett, Tonio K, and others, that showed Burnett offering the lens a canister of chewing tobacco. Despite the efforts of brilliant artists like Tonio K, who produced a solid record for What? called *Romeo Unchained*, the label struggled to find its footing.

Tonio K, who had released three critical favorites for labels like Epic and Capitol, had recently come to believe in God and was eager to make a record that would hit both markets but not have the "Christian music" stigma attached to it. Similar to Bob Dylan's experience, a woman whom Tonio had dated opened his mind to faith.

"She explained to me what aspects of the faith had eluded me and how simple it really was—because I'd believed it all along. I mean, I, along with Einstein, knew that this was a creation, and though I couldn't prove it conclusively and exhaustively, I could prove circumstantially and to my own satisfaction that Jesus was who He said He was."[11]

Although the music was good and definitely oriented toward a Christian worldview, Tonio K made the mistake of doing with his words what T-Bone Burnett had done with his tobacco—insulting the Christian subculture by telling a reporter, "I know what we're doing and I know it would be good for some of these people [CCM fans] to actually hear some of what the rest of the world is about, so that maybe they'll know it's OK to be living on the planet without hiding."[12]

In spite of those comments, Tonio K's debut did respectable business in that market, but it was perceived as a "religious" record and was largely ignored on the pop side.

Despite his inarticulate attempts to communicate to the CCM world, Tonio K continued to advance his agenda of making records that would be acceptable to both markets.

"To use the cliché . . . all truth is God's truth," he said, "whether or not it specifically deals with Christianity. Whether it talks about Jesus and the church, or whether it talks about how screwed up relationships are on the streets these days, that's all true and all part of the same incredibly huge truth that goes along with the fact that this is a creation and we have a Creator."[13]

The artist's first single, "True Confessions," went to the top of the CCM rock charts, but questions about What?'s purpose persisted. Marketing director Melissa Helm tried to clarify the issues: "I know we aren't trying to hide the fact that the artists on this label are Christians," she said. "If somebody asks, we tell them right up front. What this label isn't is 'contemporary Christian music.' This label is music done by Christians."[14]

It was debatable whether the hair-splitting made any difference to rock critics, who typically dismissed anything that smacked of CCM. After a few records had been released, Word pulled the plug on What? and ended the experiment. Nevertheless, What? was an important step forward for the idea that musicians who happened to be Christians could make music for both the CCM and the pop world and not have the music labeled "secular" or "sacred."

Exit

In the early 1980s, in Sacramento, California, a label was launched by Christians intent on being taken seriously by the rock marketplace. Exit Records, founded in 1983 by a pastor's wife named Mary Neely as an off-shoot of a church called the Warehouse Christian Fellowship, featured a dazzling array of talented artists, led by Charlie Peacock, the 77's, Vector, Steve Scott, and others. Neely had had experience in the music business producing a program called *Rock Scope*, a radio series carried on more than two hundred rock stations from 1978 to 1983. In response to what she considered the sheer lunacy of the CCM paradigm, she started a record label that had distribution deals with both Island and A&M Records for the pop market and Word for the CCM market. "The CCM field was creating music for Christians and marketing only to Christians," she complained. "They were providing Christians with Christian music. The non-believer wasn't speaking the same language. We had to develop music that reached them using metaphors and parables like Christ did, and develop many styles of music."[15]

Sacramento quickly became a mecca in a burgeoning music scene centered around Neely and Exit. "The only way I can explain it," said Mike Roe, the 77's vocalist at the time, "is that this cow-town excuse for a city is a giant vortex that mysteriously sucks people in—especially musicians."[16]

"We provide a gathering place for the musicians," Neely said. "On any given day, you can see anybody who's anybody in town pass through our doors. We try to see ourselves as an art-minded indie, a family of artists, sort of like IRS or Slash. We have a common vision, both artistically and spiritually. And that's to take the gospel to every nook and cranny we can."[17]

The most interesting of the Sacramento artists was Charlie Peacock, born Charles Ashworth, a slight twenty-something musician, who hailed from nearby Yuba City. He got his start playing small bars, but his music was difficult to categorize.

"The crowds were pretty small when I started" recalled Peacock. "I played mostly the off nights. But, curiously, people started turning out. It was a lot of fun. We were described at one time or another as jazz, new wave, rock and roll, funk, and country. Someone even said we were a cross between the Archies and Manhattan Transfer. Truth is, we are a mixture of all of those. You can hear all those elements in our older stuff."[18]

Bourgeois Tagg, a five-piece band named for former Peacock band members Brent Bourgeois and Larry Tagg, was signed directly to Island but was nonetheless part of the wider Exit musical community. Another band, Vector, was a talented three-piece group with a polished pop sound, and the 77's were an archetype American rock band.

"We've welded elements of everyone from Elvis to the Smiths," said 77's bass player and co-founder, Jan Eric Volz. "We stick to our guns about playing only basic rock 'n' roll—American music."[19]

After building a recording studio, called Sangre, Neely used her years of experience in the music business to get her acts signed to labels that could bring them out of the backwaters and into the mainstream music culture. Neely first approached A&M Records in search of a distribution deal.

"I just went down and played specific acts like The 77's and Charlie Peacock for them, told them this was totally different than Amy Grant, and asked them if they heard radio material—and they did," said Neely.[20]

Initially, at least, the band Vector benefited the most from the A&M relationship when their A&M distributed Exit album spawned a hit, "I Can't Help Falling in Love with You."

Neely shrewdly signed her artists to a management deal with the powerhouse management firm Bill Graham Productions, which helped overcome any stigma that might otherwise have kept these artist Christians from reaching the general marketplace.

"The level of musicianship is incredible," said Arnie Pustilnik of Graham Productions, "and the reason we're so keen on them is because

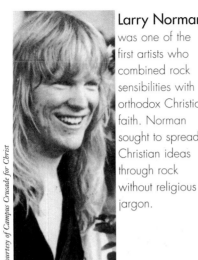

Larry Norman was one of the first artists who combined rock sensibilities with orthodox Christian faith. Norman sought to spread Christian ideas through rock without religious jargon.

One of Larry Norman's protégés, **Randy Stonehill** (right) went on to become one of CCM's biggest stars in the 1980s. (Photo ca. 1973)

Leaving the rock world shortly after his conversion to record hymns, **Al Green** became a pastor but later returned to pop music, learning to integrate songs of faith with songs of love.

Former
Santana
member
**Leon
Patillo**
left the
group to
record for
CCM in
the late
'70s.

Courtesy of Dan Wooding

Photo by Jim Shea

Grand Funk
Railroad singer
Mark Farner
left the group
for a time to
record in CCM
before rejoining
the band
in the '90s.

Photo by Harry Langdon

Once Elvis's chief competitor in the burgeoning rock scene, **Pat Boone** recorded dozens of pop hits in the 1950s and spent decades in CCM before regaining the attention of the culture with heavy metal and R&B records.

Former Outlaws bassist **Rick Cua** left the group to perform as a solo artist in the "Christian music" world.

Courtesy of Rick Cua

Southern California pastor **Chuck Smith** (left) welcomed hippies into his church, creating an artist-friendly environment for rock musicians.

Music legend **Johnny Cash** emerged from years of drug abuse to make records that reflected his faith and often performed at Billy Graham's evangelistic crusades.

Disco diva **Donna Summer** refused to retreat to the religious music subculture after her conversion, instead consistently made records for the pop mainstream that reflected her deep Christian convictions.

Courtesy of Stan Moress Management

Gary Cherone (right, pictured with bandmate Eddie Van Halen) began his career with the Boston-based rock group Extreme, producing the hit songs "More Than Words" and "Hole Hearted." Cherone came to faith through the work of radio pastor Chuck Swindoll and drew lyrical inspiration from the Bible. After Extreme, Cherone became the lead singer of the legendary rock group Van Halen.

Photo by F. Scott Schafer

The founder, guitarist, and chief lyricist of the rock group Kansas, **Kerry Livgren**'s conversion rocked the band, leading to the departure of its lead singer. Livgren later resumed a solo career.

The **Galactic Cowboys** brought a whimsical quality to their songs, which sometimes discussed spiritual issues.

Courtesy of Pamplin

When Kansas picked **John Elefante** to replace their singer, they didn't realize they were getting a devout Christian *and* a great singer. Elefante took the band to new heights on songs like "Fight Fire with Fire" and "Play the Game Tonight," before returning to the Christian subculture.

A pioneering band that mixed heavy metal with strong Jimi Hendrix and Beatles sensibilities, **King's X** mastered the art of mixing serious faith with rock and roll. (l-r) Ty Tabor, Doug Pinnick, Jerry Gaskill

Photo by Catbrine Wesel

Photo by John Scarpati

Courtesy of Victoria Sweet

Taking a jackhammer to the wall of separation between rock and faith, **Stryper** combined loud rock with aggressive Christian-themed lyrics and tossed Bibles into their audiences. Visionary drummer Robert Sweet began his career in music early, forming Roxx Regime, which later changed its name to Stryper. (l-r) Oz Fox, Tim Gaines, Michael Sweet, Robert Sweet

Robert Sweet
(circa 1970)

A pioneering Seattle punk-pop band, **MxPx** built a strong following in CCM before signing with A&M where their single "Chick Magnet" gained notoriety. (l-r) Yuri Riley, Mike Herrera, Steve Wisniewski

Photo by Ken Schles

A visionary pop artist who charted the course for many artists with Christian convictions, **Amy Grant** refused to stay in the Christian subculture and gained a following in pop music.

Courtesy of A&M Universal

A lanky pastor's kid, **Steve Taylor** was a brilliant artist/producer who emerged from the CCM market first as an artist with his band Chagall Guevara and later as a record mogul who guided the career of pop sensation Sixpence None the Richer.

Courtesy of Steve Taylor/Photo by Ben Pearson

Photo by Victoria Pearson

The brother/sister duo **BeBe and CeCe Winans** parlayed a gig with Jim and Tammy Bakker's PTL network into a pop/R&B career as a duo in CCM and later as solo artists in the R&B world.

Led by Michael Been, who questioned the effectiveness of CCM,
The Call recorded deeply spiritual lyrics for the mainstream.

Musical chameleons, the three members of **dc Talk** gained notoriety as rappers, before morphing into grunge pop and eventually solid pop artists who left their CCM deal to record for Virgin Records but remain a strong presence in both the CCM and pop worlds.

Michael W. Smith wrote songs and toured with Amy Grant before launching his solo career. Smith often questioned the effectiveness of CCM and sought to be a part of the pop world—succeeding in 1990 when his song "Place in This World" hit number six.

Photo by Randie St. Nicholas

Austin, Texas-based **Sixpence None the Richer** (led by Leigh Nash, far left, and Matt Slocum, center) toiled for seven years in CCM before two visionary executives, Steve Taylor and Stephen Prendergast, helped relaunch their careers with the success of their single "Kiss Me."

One of the first "defectors," **B. J. Thomas** left pop music after a conversion experience in 1976 and began a career in "Christian" pop music.

Courtesy of Goldwest Management

Photo by Paul Elledge

Flint, Michigan-based **Full on the Mouth** refused invitations
from CCM labels, choosing to record with the Pioneer label
and earning a coveted spot on the Warped tour.
(l-r) Dwight Mohrmon, Andy Barancik, Grant Mohrmon

Photo by Maryanne Bilham

Southern California
pop-rockers,
The Tories, led by
Steve Bertrand (seated,
center), married pop
with clear
references to faith on its
debut CD produced
by Phil Ramone,
representing a new
breed of faith-based
artists who sought to
stay in the primary
culture. Their song
"Time for You" became
the theme song
for the hit television
show "Jesse."

Courtesy of Zomba Music/Photo by Norma Jean Roy

Garnering widespread airplay on pop stations with its debut single "Flood," and opening on the road for artists like Sting and Jewel, **Jars of Clay** represented a new generation of artists with Christian convictions who refused to keep their music in the religious subculture.
(l-r) Matt Odmark, Charlie Lowell, Dan Haseltine, Steve Mason

Part of the Sacramento-based Exit musical community centered around music executive Mary Neely, **Charlie Peacock** recorded for Island Records before moving to Nashville where he records and produces in the CCM world.

Courtesy of Dechant-Hughes and Associates/Photo by Ben Pearson

A visionary hard rock artist and producer, **Ken Tamplin** balanced success in the rock world, including a solo career and songwriting for popular artists with a commitment to playing and producing in church circles without charge.

Photo by Nigel Skeet

these guys are out there writing hits. We're not going to paint their images as Christians first, then musicians. We're going to introduce them to the public on the merit of their music."[21]

Later, Island Records president Chris Blackwell came to Sacramento to hear Neely's artists and seemed undisturbed by the lyrics, telling Neely, "I have U2. Religious music doesn't bother me."[22]

Peacock's album for Exit/Island, which only sold twenty thousand or so units, nonetheless placed the up-and-coming artist in the pop music marketplace—rather than CCM—and gave him the opening slot on tours with bands like General Public and the Fixx. The eponymously titled record was produced by Nigel Gray, who also worked with the Police and the Sex Pistols. Gray said of Peacock, "Charlie's songs are very strong. Very melodic. It takes time to present a new artist to the public, but I think he'll be around a long, long time."[23]

References to faith on *Charlie Peacock* were vague, but nonetheless present throughout the album. On "Dizzy Dean Movie," Peacock remembered his childhood wistfully, then added, "I only prayed on Sundays then."[24] On "I Will Need Your Help," he sang, "Keep me informed as we walk through this passage/I will be calling you constantly, seeking new information and reconfirming the old/I will need your help whatever happens, whatever comes down."[25]

Along with numerous references to his faith, including the brilliant plea for divine mercy on "Down in the Lowlands," Peacock laid out his heart on the opening track "Message Boy," warning the listener that his Christian-themed messages may not always be pleasant. "I am the message boy," sang Peacock, "I might bring you good news—/a message boy does that/I might bring you bad news. . . . There is nothing in this world that can stop me from my task/I'll respect you and your privacy, where and when is all I'll ask/I'm the message boy, only the message boy."[26]

Although Island and A&M released ten or more albums by Exit artists, Neely pointed to restlessness within the various bands as the reason the venture came to an end in 1989. "The bands felt that Island wasn't promoting them," she said, "so I went to LA and, working with my attorney, Fred Davis, the son of Clive Davis, did some showcases hoping to get them signed to secular labels."[27]

Her efforts were unsuccessful, and most Exit acts ended up signing with CCM labels—Peacock, Jimmy A, and Vince Ebo with Sparrow, and the 77's with Myrrh.

"We tried to do everything as a group of artists," lamented Peacock of the Exit experience, "but finally it was decided that it would be a better strategy to divide up and go where we could feel some individual interest. The idea to keep us all together was more of a ministry strategy—that the whole was greater than the sum of its parts. . . . A lot of good things came out of it. I've just got to kind of wait and look to see what the eternal summation is."[28]

In 1997, long since departed from the music business, Neely said she had learned many lessons from the Exit venture. Refusing to subscribe to the persecution complex that seemed to afflict some in the subculture, she offered some candid insights into the realities of the pop music market. Once, when she complained to the president of Island about the lack of attention her artists were getting, she remembered being reminded, "Mary, you have to think of your bands competing with Stevie Winwood and U2." It was a lesson Neely never forgot. "Just because they're Christians, people think they can short circuit the process—that the Lord's gonna help 'em."[29]

Though her own venture ultimately failed, Neely remained hopeful. "This can be done," she said, speaking of the effort to bring artists who are informed by their faith into the pop mainstream. She cited the work of Jars of Clay and others, but was quick to add, "success is ultimately about doing what God wants you to do."[30]

Music business executives like Mary Neely, who combine spiritual passion with a desire to get their artists heard by the culture, are still few and far between. On the bottom line, the numbers tend to rule—and for years those numbers have clearly shown that, for most artist Christians, it makes much more sense to focus on the CCM market—selling 100,000 units and making a respectable living—than to venture into the unknown depths of the pop and rock world, where success and failure are more pronounced.

SIX

Of the World

When devout Christians retreated from their place in the center of the culture into the safe haven of a "spiritual" subculture, they spawned a new theology that changed the word *Christian* from a noun to an adjective. As a noun, *Christian* refers to one who is a follower of Christ. Twisted into an adjective, the word *Christian* came to be used to describe records, books, trinkets, greeting cards, and other *things* instead of people. When this phenomenon arose, few bothered to ask where such a strange, new theology had come from.

One who did question this theology was author and musician John Fischer. "I ran into two young Christian entrepreneurs . . . who were excited about their new business of designing greeting cards," wrote Fischer. "Caught up in the thinking of the day, I asked them if their cards were Christian cards. They replied, 'Well, they aren't all saved, but we pray for them every day.' That was when I first started to wonder about the way we were using the word 'Christian.'"[1]

The term *Christian music* raises all sorts of questions. For example, if a Christian individual sings love songs, would the songs be considered "Christian music"? If a non-Christian sings "Christian" lyrics, does that constitute "Christian" music? If a Christian records a "Christian" song for a "secular" label, is the song a "Christian" song? The lack of a clear definition illustrates the problems that arise when the word *Christian* is applied as an adjective to *things*.

It is becoming increasingly clear to many observers that there is simply no justification for creating an artificial genre of music and calling it "Christian music." It is bad business and, more importantly, bad theology. It would be difficult to find biblical justification for calling one song "Christian" and another "secular," based on such factors as the spiritual status of the employees of the record label or the number of times the name of Jesus is evoked in a song.

In place of the old secular/sacred distinction, many are recognizing the need for a new standard modeled on the writings of the Chinese philosopher Watchman (To-Sheng) Nee, who, through his many writings and speeches, urged believers to stay engaged in the culture and transform it.

"Everything we do," wrote Nee, "be it in field or highway, in shop, factory, kitchen, hospital, or school, has spiritual value in terms of the kingdom of Christ. Satan would much prefer to have no Christians in any of these places, for they are decidedly in his way there. He tries to frighten us out of the world and if he cannot do that, to get us involved in his world system thinking in its terms, regulating our behavior by its standards."[2]

Music, far from being inherently "Christian" or "secular," should instead be viewed by believers as either consistent with the Bible and therefore honoring to God, or inconsistent with the Bible and therefore dishonoring to God—period.

This standard may be uncomfortable for some, because occasionally a non-Christian will write or perform a song that is completely consistent with a Christian worldview. Conversely, it is also possible—though perhaps less likely—that a singer who adheres to the Bible will create or perform a song that is inconsistent with it.

Vanessa Williams's hit song, "Save the Best for Last," was a love song that embodied everything the Bible teaches about human love. Don Henley's "Heart of the Matter" presented the loss of human love in a profoundly biblical way, addressing topics like forgiveness, grace, trust, and pride. Steve Winwood's "Higher Love" challenged the listener to "think about it, there must be higher love. . . . Without it, life is wasted time."[3]

On the other hand, the 1978 smash single "You Light Up My Life" was performed by a committed Christian, but its message that something "can't be wrong when it feels so right"[4] was profoundly troubling to those who sought to line up their beliefs with the Bible. The same could be said about "Pumps and a Bump," a single by MC Hammer, another devout believer.

Is the distinction between "Christian" and "secular" music truly valid? If so, what set of criteria makes the difference? When a child is put to bed by a parent singing "Mary Had a Little Lamb," is that a "secular" activity? Is it possible to give glory to God while enjoying a beautiful piece of music written by an unbeliever or dedicated to a "secular" theme?

The term *Christian music* makes little sense because there are no logical boundaries, nothing to keep it in its box or identify it as Christian or differentiate it from so-called "secular" music. Nevertheless, observers who view the issue in radically differing ways have divided into several camps.

The first camp includes those who believe that music sung by a believer is automatically "Christian" music. In other words, the heart of the artist makes a song Christian or not Christian. That is why until very recently Christian-oriented songs by non-Christians or marginal Christians were never very welcome in the CCM market. Of course, the heart of the artist is a great intangible, for no man can see into another man's heart, but nonetheless some believers have sought to define "Christian" music by who sings it. Christian-themed songs by artists such as Aretha Franklin were traditionally unwelcome in the CCM marketplace because of the artist's perceived lack of fervency in her faith.

Another definition of "Christian music" says that the lyrics must contain references to Jesus to be truly "Christian." This stipulation poses a problem for any artist who might choose to use vague references to the Savior that could also be interpreted as referring to a boyfriend or girlfriend—a style best described by the music-loving philanthropist Howard Ahmanson Jr. as the "God is my girlfriend" song.

Amy Grant used this technique early in her career on such songs as "Walking Away with You" and "Arms of Love." For the Christian listener, both songs can be interpreted as referring to divine love, but because the object of the love is identified only as "you," the casual listener could think that the love is merely earthly.

This technique is a valid form of songwriting that has been used in hymns for centuries, but it doesn't satisfy those who insist that "Christian" music must refer to God or Jesus by name.

Others define "Christian music" even more narrowly, arguing that it has nothing to do with the music itself but with the company that releases it. After CCM became a full-fledged musical genre, for some, only songs that were released within that narrow world would be called "Christian."

Separate but Equal

Most of the confusion within the Christian subculture stems from a fundamental misunderstanding of the admonition to be "*in* the world but not *of* it." In practice, most contemporary "Christian" music is the exact reverse—*of* the world but not *in* it. While rock may be "of the world," hiding music away in "Christian" bookstores or in the inspirational sections of record stores, or playing this music only on "Christian" radio stations and in church concerts does not constitute being "in the world."

Before the practice of cultural isolation became popular in the subculture, it was established as a theological construct by using several Bible verses out of context and twisting them to legitimize a separatist music empire.

The cornerstone of the separatist movement was the biblical admonition to "come ye apart and be ye separate." Never mind that this verse occurs in the context of the apostle Paul's exhortation to believers to remain in the world in body but be separated in spirit. Instead, it has been taken to mean that Christians must occupy a parallel universe where interaction with unbelievers is severely limited if not totally eliminated.

"Nowhere in the New Testament is there any call to believers to form a separate culture from the world," observed John Fischer. "We were called to be separate from the world, but never to leave. Some Christians confuse 2 Corinthians 6:17 as a call to leave the world: 'Therefore come out from them and be separate, says the Lord. Touch no unclean thing.' This section, however, concludes, 'Since we have these promises, dear friends, let us purify ourselves from everything that contaminates body and spirit, perfecting holiness out of reverence for God' (2 Cor. 7:1). Paul is talking about an internal, personal holiness, not a separate culture he wants us to create, as if living in it will make us holy by osmosis."[5]

Another frequently cited passage was Christ's statement that his followers would be hated because they were his. Taking out of context a verse that was clearly not intended by Jesus to be a universal statement to every believer in every situation ever encountered, separatists took Christ's words and deduced that anybody who was appreciated or lauded by the culture must not be truly one of his. Rejection by the culture became a badge of honor—and rejection stories became the substance that confirmed a believer's true faith.

For the musician who was a Christian, such stories—sometimes real, sometimes imagined—became an excuse for their failure to connect with a "secular" audience, and a confirmation that they were indeed deeply spiritual artists, whose faith was more important than popular acceptance.

In a sense, such a persecution complex was the very glue that held CCM together. It was the equivalent of a father insisting that his daughter stay in the basement because the boys outside wouldn't like her because she was ugly. Yet to the girl's shock, when she did surface on occasion, the boys not only thought she was beautiful, they asked her for a date.

Amy Grant's hits "Find a Way," "Baby, Baby," and "Every Heartbeat," Michael W. Smith's "Place in This World," and Kathy Troccoli's "Everything Changes" were tentative steps into the popular music culture, all engineered by the management team of Blanton and Harrell. The CCM community, with its preconceived notion that a song that spoke clearly about God would be rejected by "the world," was hard pressed to explain the success of Grant's "Find a Way," in particular with its clear lyric, "If our God His Son not sparing came to rescue you, is there any circumstance that he can't see you through?"

As these and other songs, albeit few and far between, became successful in popular music, the untruth—used to keep the girl in the basement, or in this case the artists in the Christian world where the owners of CCM had their markets identified—would be exposed.

Sam Cooke

The tragic story of Sam Cooke, the legendary soul musician, showed clearly why believers needed to come to a coherent understanding of the sacred/secular issue. Born in Clarkdale, Mississippi, on January 22, 1931, Cooke was one of eight children born to a Baptist minister named Charles Cooke. The youngster's talents grew at his father's church, but it was under the tutelage of Rebert H. Harris, the leader of a popular quartet known as the Soul Stirrers, that Cooke matured into a full-fledged recording artist whose records would sell millions for RCA.

"Harris started training Cooke when he was ten years old," noted George W. Stewart of the American Quartet Gospel Convention. "When he was in his late teens, Cooke joined the group and became the closest thing gospel had to a matinee idol."[6]

When Harris left the Soul Stirrers, Cooke took his place, and by 1951 he was recording standard gospel fare like "Peace in the Valley" and "I'm Gonna Build on That Shore." In 1956, Cooke was approached by music producer Robert "Bumps" Blackwell, who suggested that Cooke should record "secular" music.

"Bumps told me I ought to switch to the pop field," said Cooke. "Frankly, the pop field hadn't much attraction for me up until then. I was happy enough on the gospel trail and making a nice living for myself. But the more I thought about the pop field, the more interesting it became. Bumps of course had a good deal of influence. He was constantly prodding me to make the change whenever he got the chance."[7]

Eventually, Blackwell got his way when Cooke recorded "Lovable" under the name Dale Cook. He hoped to avoid disappointing his fans by hiding his identity, but the ploy didn't work. Cooke's next single, "You Send Me," went straight to the top of the charts in 1957, spending three weeks at number one. Over the next seven years, he recorded twenty-eight more Top 40 pop hits.

Unfortunately, caught between two false alternatives—recording gospel music only or recording only "secular" pop—Cooke was consumed with guilt over his choice to leave gospel music. "Cooke took his place as the greatest of all black male singers in commercial music," observed Viv Broughton. "Fawned upon by the press, idolized by women for his excessive charm and looks, revered by the rising generation of young gospel singers who would soon themselves dominate the pop market, he was the very first true superstar of soul, but he was forever looking over his shoulder at the church he'd left behind."[8]

The pop world welcomed Cooke's departure from gospel music, but the Christians would have nothing to do with their fallen idol, who had committed the dastardly deed of refusing to limit himself to spiritual topics in his songs. Cooke felt the rejection keenly when he was invited to perform at a Soul Stirrers anniversary concert in Chicago. Mounting the stage, he was met with a stunning silence from the audience, which gave way to shouts of anger.

"Folks were hollering, 'Get that blues singer down,'" remembered Harris. "'Get that no good so-and-so down. This is a Christian program,' and it pierced my heart; it shamed me how he was rejected by the home people. He walked offstage tearin'. He was hurt badly."[9]

Then, shortly afterward, on December 11, 1964, Sam Cooke was shot and killed by a motel clerk in Los Angeles under mysterious circumstances.

"For those who love parables there can be none more ironic than the story of Sam Cooke," wrote critic Steve Turner. "Riding on the crest of pop stardom in 1964, and married to his childhood sweetheart, he checked into a Los Angeles motel with a twenty-two-year-old woman named Elisa Boyer. According to testimony, she wanted to leave and she departed with Cooke's clothes. Cooke pursued her, semi-naked, and when he couldn't find her he battered down the door of the manager's office. The manager, fifty-five-year-old Bertha Franklin, responded by pumping three bullets into him from a .22 caliber pistol. He died instantly."[10]

It was a parable that may have influenced artists with deep religious convictions to remain inside the religious music subculture. The real tragedy, however, was that Cooke shouldn't have had to leave his Christian convictions behind to make records for the larger culture. He should have, instead, been free to make records for both gospel and soul fans and allowed to integrate his earthly feelings of love and concern for social issues with his keen interest in spiritual matters. Unfortunately, Cooke never found that path and chose instead to go down the "secular" road, which left him estranged from his faith, his church, and most importantly, his God.

Aretha Franklin

Aretha Franklin, the daughter of one of America's foremost black Pentecostal ministers, C. L. Franklin, learned to sing in the church choir and later mastered the art of separating her music into the "secular" and "sacred" categories, though she spent most of her career singing "secular" music. Sixteen years after releasing her first "sacred" album, *Amazing Grace*, in 1971, Franklin made another, called *One Faith, One Lord, One Baptism*. In between those two gospel albums, she released R&B songs like "Freeway of Love" and "You Make Me Feel Like a Natural Woman," which hit number eight on the charts in 1967. Though "Natural Woman" paled in comparison to songs that would later populate the charts, it wasn't exactly a song consistent with Franklin's gospel albums.

"A woman sits at her windowsill on a rainy morning," observed rock critic Dave Marsh. "She feels pretty good about herself and that's something new. Her guy is the reason. Why? Well you can only tell between the lines from the metaphors she uses—she'd never say it out loud—but the most sensible guess is that she's finally found someone with whom she can achieve orgasm. So she sings her song of ecstasy. And if that's not it, you better have a . . . plausible alternative explanation for these lines: 'Oh baby, what you done to me/ You make me feel so good inside/ and I just wanna be close to you/ you make me feel so alive.'"[11]

Of course, the song may have been written about a marriage partner, which certainly would not have contradicted Franklin's faith, but the most troubling question raised by Franklin's efforts was her apparent notion that songs of faith belonged on one record, and songs about the rest of her life, including some that seemed to contradict that faith, belonged on another.

"It seemed there was always another special, always another taping, always another commercial, always someone waiting," said Franklin, explaining the many years that elapsed between gospel albums. "I had to just put my foot down and say, 'OK, I am long overdue for a gospel album and we do it now.'"[12]

This type of separation mentality would prove to be harmful both for Franklin's religious and nonreligious fans, for when an artist like Franklin made a "religious" record, the language that tended to be used in such cases was often church lingo—indecipherable for the rest of the population and thus only of interest to true believers in the religious subculture.

The "secular" record, on the other hand, would suffer because Franklin may have felt that she had made her spiritual statement on the "gospel" record and was now free to sing about other topics. The "gospel" record in essence gave license to make a "secular" record, and thus, the "secular" market would get a record free of pesky religion and faith.

In the long run, what would be far more beneficial to both the believer and the unbeliever alike were records made by artists of faith that were simultaneously "Christian" and "worldly" in their content—worldly not in their willingness to take on an extrabiblical worldview, but in their ability to weave the principles of their faith into songs about everyday issues of life.

With the recent song "Between You and Me," for example, (a song that climbed the pop charts) dc Talk sang of a broken friendship, something all human beings could relate to, but managed to skillfully introduce key Christian principles through lines like "I wanna get it straight before the sun goes down" and "As I approach the Son I must consider this, offenses unresolved will keep me from the throne, before I go to him my wrong must be atoned."[13]

The Big Confusion

At heart, the relationship between an artist and his or her listener should be like a marriage, an intimate exchange of ideas. When artist Christians who make music in the pop world leave the relationship to make records that are heard only by the religious subculture, it drains the artist of the spiritual passion that should be part of his or her pop record. "Secular" fans are thus left with records devoid of spiritual and religious content by an artist who has already made such statements in the gospel market.

To critics like Larry Kelley, what was especially disturbing about the separatist rationale that served as the foundation for CCM was the fact that the concept of "secular" vs. "sacred" does not exist in the Scriptures. "Many of us are familiar with thinking in terms of sacred and secular," noted Kelley in a 1991 essay, "and many divide the world into three categories: sacred—that which is holy and belongs to God, although we may function within that area occasionally; secular—an area in which a believer may function on a regular basis, but an area that God does not operate in, since by definition it is secular not sacred; and sin—an area that God does not participate in and neither should a believer."[14]

Such a view, Kelley believed, was not consistent with the Bible and Christian teachings. "The definition of the sacred and the sinful can be easily found in Scripture, but where does the concept of the secular come from?" he asked. "Certainly not the Bible. Just as the phrase 'separation of church and state' cannot be found in the Constitution, so also the concept of the secular cannot be found in Scripture."[15]

In his summation, Kelley identified the philosophy that seemed to unite CCM's cheerleaders with those who sought to keep the pop music market religion-free. "Some people would like Christians to believe there is a secular arena that, upon entering, requires Christians to divest themselves of their spiritual ideals," he wrote. "This limits the reality and relevancy of faith in daily life. It creates a spiritual schizophrenia, a devaluation of what really is sacred and confusion about what is pleasing and displeasing to God."[16]

SEVEN

Advancing CCM As a Genre

The most damaging mistake made by leaders in the CCM industry over the years has been their dogged insistence on advancing contemporary Christian music as a separate genre of music. In their view, success meant CCM joining the ranks of rock, pop, alternative, jazz, classical, R&B, and others as a musical genre of its own rather than advancing artists who were Christians and the ideas embodied in their work into each of the various styles of music. As noted by Kerry Livgren, the determined insistence that the *genre* succeed made critics wonder if the point of CCM was to win converts to Christ or to the genre of music called CCM.

Unfortunately, too often it seemed that the latter was true. The fact remained, however, that many nonbelievers or cultural Christians had been socially conditioned in twentieth-century America to be wary of ideas that came from sources identified as "religious." The idea that such persons would embrace a separate genre of music called "contemporary Christian music" and travel to "Christian" bookstores and "Christian" rock music festivals amounted to little more than wishful thinking.

Author and political activist Franky Schaeffer, son of the late philosopher Francis Schaeffer, turned up the heat on CCM in the early 1980s with the publication of his book *Addicted to Mediocrity*. "Most of the output in Christian media is aimed at maintaining the evangelical establishment, a whole little subculture," wrote Schaeffer. "Success is measured by comparing the sales and popularity of these inbred artists as they are rewarded by those who populate this little ghetto. . . . Many of these people have grown up in the evangelical ghetto and are not even aware of the existence in real terms of the whole world God has made out there, either the world of nature or man."[1]

Yet CCM's supporters marched on, insisting that more shelf space be allocated in "secular" music stores for their product—usually categorized as "inspirational," "contemporary Christian," or "gospel" music—advancing their genre at the expense of artists whose music would consequently never be taken seriously by the culture at large.

What the proponents of CCM failed to realize was that a fundamental shift had taken place in the culture during the years they were building their ghetto. Simply being labeled "religious" now meant automatic disqualification from the great cultural debate for such artists or products, and thereby denied the person a storefront in the marketplace of ideas.

"Classifying a viewpoint or theory as religious may have the effect of marginalizing it," wrote UC Berkeley scholar Phillip Johnson in his work *Reason in the Balance*. "A viewpoint or theory is marginalized when, without being refuted, it is categorized in such a way that it can be excluded from serious consideration. The technique of marginalizing a viewpoint by labeling it 'religion' is particularly effective in late twentieth-century America because there is a general impression, reinforced by Supreme Court decisions, that religion does not belong in public institutions."[2]

Johnson's statement was foreshadowed by T. S. Eliot in a 1935 essay titled "Religion and Literature." "When you qualify poetry as 'religious,' you are indicating very clear limitations," he wrote. "For the great majority of people who love poetry, religious poetry is a variety of minor poetry: The religious poet is not a poet who is treating the whole subject matter of poetry in a religious spirit, but a poet who is dealing with a confined part of this subject matter: who is leaving out what men consider their major passions, and thereby confessing his ignorance of them."[3]

For the most part, however, the leadership of the CCM industry, by their actions, chose to remain in the ghetto, perfectly content to be on the fringes of American pop culture, despite the warnings from Schaeffer and others about the clear dangers of failing to be recognized by the wider culture.

Syndicated columnist Cal Thomas, in his work titled *Book Burning*, astutely identified how the same problem affected the world of publishing. "Of course, our voices have not been officially silenced," he observed. "We can, after all, have our own radio stations and publishing houses, just as we can have our private schools. According to the National Religious Broadcasters, one new Christian radio station signs on each week and one new TV station begins broadcasting each month. . . . Why? It is because Christians believe their views, their values, their concerns have been shut out and are unaddressed, except in simplistic and stereotyped and often scornful ways in public forums."[4]

Thomas was right, but he forgot that part of the problem was that Christians at once sought to be separated from the world and acknowledged by it, clearly an impossible task. Thomas set an example for believers in all fields of endeavor when, soon after the publication of his book, he resigned his position as vice president of the Moral Majority and began to write a column for the *Los Angeles Times* syndicate. He later hosted a talk show on CNBC, proving that it was possible for serious believers, once they had disposed of silly separatism, to be accepted or at least tolerated by the culture.

In myriad ways, the CCM industry invited rejection by the wider music industry. The marketplace of ideas is where people congregate and advance their ideas. In such a setting, nobody has the luxury of insisting on a label and demanding that one's entire category of ideas be accepted uncritically and that those who loathe them must cooperate in the dissemination and distribution of those ideas. In fact, the United States is full of all sorts of people who bring their values and spiritual and religious beliefs to the table without insisting that their entire subgenre be allowed to cross over and then claiming religious persecution when this is resisted.

Richard Gere, though a devout Buddhist, never sought to label his work "Buddhist movies" or insist that his films be shown in "Buddhist theaters," making deals with major studios to allow for his and other "Buddhist movies" to cross over into popular movie theaters. Rather, Gere continued to make movies that in some way reflected his belief system. On his time off, he devoted much of it to serving and promoting the Dalai Lama because Gere seemed to understand the importance of advancing one's beliefs step by step within the construct and framework and scrutiny of the marketplace of ideas.

Tina Turner, another Buddhist devotee, likewise operated within the culture and used interviews to advance her beliefs. One memorable event occurred when Turner took TV talk show host Larry King into his break by chanting "*Namyo horengekkyo,*" to the obvious amusement of the host.

Turner and Gere could easily have created a Buddhist music and film industry and become the heroes of their subculture, but they both apparently realized the importance of staying put in the marketplace of ideas, doing their job and patiently advancing those issues or causes in which they strongly believed.

By contrast, the primary goal of the leaders of the CCM industry was to advance "Christian music" as a genre and raise its profile by getting more Christians to buy records. A 1990 survey by the Barna Research Group highlighted their challenge. Among Christian teenagers surveyed, 91 percent had heard of artists like Tone Loc and LL Cool J, but only 52 percent had heard of artists like Petra, 42 percent Michael W. Smith, and 20 percent DeGarmo and Key. To those who run CCM, the answer was simple: get more Christians to buy more "Christian" music.

For Kerry Livgren, such a mindset was deeply troubling.

> This is the only nation that has secular and Christian record companies and bookstores, which I feel is a thing that hampers ministry. In Europe, you can go into any store and everything's there: radio stations play all kinds of things. They don't have that separation. A lot of Christian artists desire very much to reach an audience of unbelievers, which I think is a very important thing. At a Christian concert, the only unbelievers who are going to hear it are those who are dragged along to the concert by a Christian friend. I don't believe on their own initiative they're likely to go. I know that I wouldn't have before I was a Christian. I would've had no interest, but the person who reached me was a person who was playing in a secular band, and that was Jeff Pollard of LeRoux.[5]

When John Fischer attended a Jars of Clay concert, which also featured performers like Jewel and the Cowboy Junkies, he was stunned at what he learned. "The guy next to me, the one with the facial jewelry, had asked when I first came in, 'Are you with Jars?'" wrote Fischer. "Yes," I said. "If you're going to see them afterwards, would you thank them for me? I became a Christian listening to their CD." Stunned, Fischer wondered to himself, 'You mean he got everything he needed to know to become a Christian off of one CD?'"[6]

"I played it over and over and figured out just about everything," said the young fan. "I went and got a Christian friend of mine—pulled him out of a party—and told him I wanted to get saved right away. He didn't believe me. You wouldn't have either. I hated Christians."[7]

Former CCM executive Charlie Shaw, who today oversees sales in Pat Boone's Beverly Hills office, regrets his role in perpetuating the genre, noting that the goal from the beginning was clear: sell CCM records to more Christians.

In 1977, Shaw joined Word as a West Coast rep to "help bring the mass market into the gospel market. We ran some campaigns and even did a Jimmy Swaggart promotion in K-Mart, and we did some nice numbers. Roland Lundy's vision was that you could capture the Christian buyer who doesn't go to a Christian bookstore, in a K-Mart."[8]

"Billy Ray [Hearn] wanted to make contemporary music for the church—Second Chapter of Acts, Keith Green, Barry McGuire—aimed at the church," said Jack Hafer, once an executive with Refuge Records. "He wanted to go to a younger audience that hadn't bought George Beverly Shea. We wanted to go out of the church and found it difficult. Benson [Music] didn't seem to be interested in getting into the bins that we wanted to in K-Mart [and] Tower Records, and at that point it wasn't being done."[9]

It was an accusation that Hearn seemed proud to accept. "I think it's wonderful that's happening for Amy and Michael W. and Take 6," he said. "I think whenever you get a record out of a Christian artist that's good for the general market, then go for it. *But I'm not one who wants to produce records for that market. I produce records for the Christian market [that] I know will pay for it, and minister to those who I've been commissioned to make records for*"[10] (italics added).

Hearn's commission was not shared by most artist Christians who desired to be a part of American pop culture, and he cited persecution as the reason why it could not be done. "Your mainstream Christian white artist is still going to have a very rough go in the secular market," he maintained. "Black artists have advantages in that marketplace—it is more open to gospel artists and there is no real aversion culturally. The white entertainment industry is still, in many ways, anti-Christian."[11]

In Jimmy Bowen, Hearn found a perfect partner. Like Hearn, Bowen believed that Christian music as a genre could be crossed over into the mainstream. Bowen was a veteran of the music industry, having written and produced songs for artists like Dean Martin and had once served as president of MGM Records before moving to Nashville and heading up labels like Warner Bros., Elektra, MCA, and EMI. As president of Capitol Records Nashville, later called Liberty, Bowen signed his biggest act—Garth Brooks. Bowen first heard of an idea formulated by a record business veteran named Charlie Lico, who had drawn up a plan in 1988 to bring CCM artists out of the ghetto and into pop music unencumbered by marginalizing labels. Yet somewhere along the line Bowen had taken Lico's idea and perhaps through Hearn's influence, changed it to become more of an effort to introduce CCM as a separate *genre* into the "secular" music market.

Bowen had grand designs for the CCM market. "I've been watching Christian music for the last five or six years," he said, "and I always knew that if the time was right, I wanted to get involved with it. It quickly became clear to me that if you can do $100 million worth of business in Christian book-stores, reaching maybe 10 to 12 percent of the total potential customers, what do you think you might do if you got it to the full sixty or seventy million? I'm just amazed at how many calls I'm getting every day from people saying, 'I'm so glad you are doing this . . . I want to help.'"[12]

Bowen was from a bygone era when the "secular" and Christian worlds were not at war, and he never seemed to understand that the culture simply would not embrace a genre known as "contemporary Christian." "If you put it up front, with price and position, it will sell," he enthused. "Once they see it's moving, you can't tell me the outlets will be afraid to sell Contemporary Christian because it says 'I love Jesus.' Look what they sell in the rap lyric. If they will sell rape and murder and incest, which is part of life, and I'm not saying they shouldn't, then why would they care if they sell someone else's opinion of what life is? They won't."[13]

The difference, of course, was that in both cases, separate genres of music like contemporary rape music or contemporary murder music were never advanced. Rather, those artists who enjoyed rapping about rape and murder brought their ideas into the mainstream music culture without creating a separate category of music.

Bowen failed to appreciate the social construct of the struggle and the trap of marginalization that Christians had repeatedly fallen into. He seemed genuinely astonished when newly-signed CCM artist Carman's forceful support of school prayer raised the hackles of music journalists. "I grew up in the '50s—we had prayer in the schools and it didn't hurt me at all," he said. "If Carman's views were 'we should murder one another,' or that the sale of cocaine should be legal, I would have a problem with that. But I think if you poll the 270 million Americans, you'd find a huge percentage that would say, 'I don't think it's harmful.' When I was a kid, sometimes I listened to the prayer and sometimes I didn't."[14]

Although his solutions were garbled, Bowen had clearly identified the problem: "The Bible says take it to the people," he said. "What they have been doing for years in Christian music is preaching to each other. You can't make any headway doing that."[15]

Yet like many others before and after him, he made the critical mistake of trying to advance the genre rather than advancing individual artists who happened to have Christian beliefs and were talented musicians. He said,

"I'm not in this for crossover to pop radio; I believe [CCM] is its own genre. It is different than secular music"[16] (italics added).

Although Bowen's analysis of the problem was correct, his solution only exacerbated the problem because it assured the leaders of the CCM industry that they could continue to make "religious" music neatly tailored for the subculture without bothering to think about whether it would be understood or appreciated by those outside of it. Bowen didn't change the focus, he simply took over ownership of a CCM label and attempted to expand the pie to reach more true believers. His goal was not to bring in more non-Christians to hear the music, but to get more Christians to buy the CCM product.

This strategy was based not on divine revelation but on hard numbers. A study published in the *CCM Update*, in 1992, delivered the news that there were, at minimum, 13 million untapped Christian market consumers.

"It reads like a good news/bad news joke," observed *CCM Update*. "The bad news is, 51 percent of active Christians say they have never purchased any Christian music for themselves. Ever. The good news is: Half of those newly exposed to contemporary Christian music say they like it and would buy it. And that half means a ripe market of almost 13 million consumers. Additionally, the data show that just over half of all first-time contemporary Christian music buyers make another purchase within six months."[17]

The study was commissioned by a number of organizations with a stake in increased sales of CCM products, including the Gospel Music Association, the Christian Booksellers Association, the Southern Baptist Convention's Sunday School Board, and sixteen other companies, and it provided ammunition for men like Bowen and other recording executives who saw a profit to be made by getting more Christians to be aware of the art emerging from their own community.

It was not just at the retail level that CCM executives fretted. They also worried that too few fellow believers were listening to CCM radio stations. "How do we get Christians to listen to Christian radio?" asked one radio programmer at a National Christian Radio Seminar in 1993. The problem, said one participant, was that "Christians listen to secular radio more than they listen to non-secular. Why is that? Maybe it's because we as Christian broadcasting are not as good as we should be. Maybe it's because we should be playing the hits, have air personalities who sound as good as air personalities across the street. Maybe our promotions should be as good or better."[18]

Once again, the focus had less to do with getting music by such artists heard by the pop world, but in systematically crossing over a genre of music.

Many, like Eric Rhoads, the publisher of *Radio Ink*, believed in following the country music model. "What Country is doing today is not a mistake," he told the conference. "It was a plan. They developed a step-by-step plan. You can image yourself to advertisers, to your listeners, to your potential listeners, to national advertisers."[19]

Country music exploded onto the national stage in the early 1990s with the success of artists like Garth Brooks and Reba McIntyre. An analysis of the boom showed that it had much less to do with a sudden increase in popularity of the genre and more to do with the revamping of the system used to track hit records. Prior to the introduction of the SoundScan system in the early '90s, record sales were tabulated by phoned-in reports from record store employees. It was widely speculated that this arrangement led to the overreporting of young, hip bands (the favorites of the specific breed of people who populate many record store counters) and the underreporting of more traditionally oriented fare, including country and gospel. The same was true in the publishing world as well, something Cal Thomas had observed in 1983.

> Like the flawed television rating system, the weekly or monthly "best seller" lists determine sales by polling a few hundred bookstores across the nation—mostly large book chains, where decisions about which books to stock and which not to stock are usually made at a corporate headquarters far away from the community where the store is located. Specialty stores, such as religious bookstores, are not polled. Since the large book chains fail to buy many religious books, it is rare indeed when a religious book shows up on the best seller lists, no matter how many hundreds of copies it has sold. At the end of 1979, the *New York Times Book Review* published a list of the decade's best sellers. Surprise of all surprises, Hal Lindsey's *The Late Great Planet Earth*, published by Zondervan Publishing House, topped the list of non-fiction sellers of the 1970s. That's right, for the entire decade! And yet the book had never appeared on any weekly bestseller list for the *Times* until Bantam, a secular and therefore legitimate house, published a mass market edition. What's more, the *Times* never reviewed the book.[20]

SoundScan offered a more precise measurement by registering each sale at the point of purchase. There was simply no way to fudge the figures—what was sold was counted. When the system was implemented, the entire composition of the charts changed immediately and hordes of country artists made strong showings on the charts, confirming the suspicions about less-than-honest record store reporters.

"Even children's albums like *Barney's Favorites, Volume 1*, now shot up in *Billboard's* Top 20 as a result," noted *CCM Update*. "Unfortunately, sales of gospel products at Christian retail outlets, where the majority are sold, are not included in general market charts, sustaining perceptions shared with country sales before SoundScan."[21]

Many leaders in the CCM market correctly believed that SoundScan would revolutionize their industry, making it a viable genre in the pop market. Others, especially retailers, opposed it, correctly anticipating that it would take the Christian consumer out of their small mom-and-pop Bible bookstores and into large retail chains.

Though many CCM leaders saw SoundScan as a way to simply enlarge the genre and show its muscle, they should nevertheless be credited for helping to introduce it because it went a long way toward showing the power of the Christian consumer and brought national attention to artists with Christian beliefs. Michael W. Smith and dc Talk, for example, entered the Top 20 during the first week of their album releases; dc Talk's *Supernatural* debuted at number four; Amy Grant's *Behind the Eyes*, and Jars of Clay's *Much Afraid* debuted at number eight.

"SoundScan legitimizes the art form and ministry more to the industry," said CCM distributor Spring Arbor's president, Rick Pigott. "We will have a lot more records in the Top 200 of the *Billboard* charts. Gospel music has been losing credit for sales and would finally get within its one or two point share of the market. We have a sufficient size of merchants through SoundScan to get accurate accounts. Contemporary Christian and gospel music does one quarter billion dollars at wholesale, and much of that revenue is from independents."[22]

As anticipated, the introduction of the SoundScan system immediately changed the composition of the charts. Finally, country and CCM artists would get their due by being listed on album sales charts, thereby garnering additional media attention. The voices of Franky Schaeffer, Cal Thomas, and others had finally caused at least one area of the Christian subculture to understand the importance of recognition by the larger culture, but CCM executives by and large still seemed to miss the point that when it came to penetration of that culture, the task needed to be done by individual artists rather than an organized and separate genre of music known as "contemporary Christian music."

EIGHT

The Rebels

As the CCM market began to grow by leaps and bounds, the separation mentality that had served as its reason for existence began to be severely questioned. An increasing number of young artists, record executives, and cultural critics no longer defined success by the size of the CCM display at Tower Records, or how many radio stations were devoted to playing it exclusively. No longer content to ride in the back of the cultural bus, up-and-coming artist Christians began insisting on full integration into the cultural mainstream.

Some of the architects of CCM, though long gone from positions of influence in the music scene, began to express doubts about the value of what they had accomplished in establishing a musical genre based on lyrical content appealing almost exclusively to the faithful. A growing number of artists began to publicly question the wisdom of perpetuating a separate music industry and demanded changes in the way their music was marketed.

Amy Grant

One of the artists most responsible for breaking down the barriers to the pop market was Amy Grant, who made the transition from the CCM market to pop on her own terms in the mid-1980s.

Born November 25, 1960, as the youngest of four daughters, Grant grew up in an affluent and comfortable home. As a teen, her life was turned upside down when she was invited to a Bible study. "Though I had grown up in church, it was very different from anything I had ever experienced," she said. "These were kids from an inner-city church. No one had money for anything. But all of that was superfluous. What mattered was, when they talked to God, they really knew He was listening. This was what I had been searching for. This was the relationship I had been longing for."[1]

Grant explained her encounter with God in unique terms.

> I guess I felt that for my whole life, I had been in a room looking through a window. I thought I could see who God was and who I was in His eyes, but I realized that I was standing on the back wall of the room opposite of the window and all I had was a pinhole view. Through the process of this group, I found myself walking up to the window. The horizon went all the way up from the left and all the way to the right and as far up as I could see. It was the first time I had ever literally fallen down on my knees, prayed with everything in me and felt God's indescribable presence. Not just spirit but Holy Spirit. When you see yourself—by some miraculous divine inter-vention—the way God sees you, it's very heavy.[2]

Though she had been raised in a traditional southern Christian home, the revelation opened her eyes to a new and vibrant faith. "I thought of verses that I had known from the time I was two, but I never really knew what they meant," she mused. "All of a sudden: 'Wait a minute, that's me! He's talking about me! This is a two-way street. This is Holy Wine! It's deeper than anything I've ever drunk, and it makes me giddy with joy.' I felt alive, I felt the fire and I was different. There were fifteen or so of us, and it all happened to us simultaneously, hand in hand."[3]

Though Grant was a believer, her musical persona was shaped not by gospel music, but by the popular music of her time. "I always listened to my older sister's albums," she remembered. "When I was in the eighth grade, . . . the albums I listened to most were Judy Collins, Jethro Tull, Carole King's *Tapestry* and *Rhyme & Reason*, all the James Taylor albums, Bette Midler, Elton John, Loggins and Messina. I mean, those are the peo-ple I really cut my teeth on."[4]

Just into her teens, Grant was already an aspiring musician, who had gotten a job at a recording studio doing such unglamorous chores as sweep-ing floors and de-magnetizing tape heads. "I started writing songs when I was fifteen, and had written a dozen or so songs and decided to put them all on one cassette tape for my mom and dad," remembered Grant. "A friend of mine was working as a part-time engineer at a recording studio called the Gold Mine. Anyway, I just asked him if he would run off some copies of this cassette when nobody was in there and he had some free time."[5]

One day, the studio's owner, singer, and producer, Chris Christian, heard the tape of Grant's songs. "It was not even a very good tape, but Chris had some connections with a record company in Texas called Word Records," Grant remembered. "He called them and played it over the phone, and I guess it sounded good over the phone. It didn't sound that good when you were in the room. I didn't even know my tape was being played for a record company, and when I was called and asked if I would do an album, I thought it was a practical joke. Then I realized it wasn't and I said, 'Well, let me talk to my mom and dad.'"[6]

"Nobody was waiting with bated breath for the new Amy Grant record," she laughed. "I was seventeen, and it came out spring break of my senior year in high school. I basically recorded it in secret, because I didn't want any of my friends to know I was doing such an off-the-wall thing. Also, if it were a total flop, I didn't want them to feel like they had to console me."[7]

The record was anything but a flop, and as Grant graduated from high school and enrolled at Furman University, her music quickly overtook her studies as she began to tour, and her recording career picked up steam with the release of two more hit albums, *Father's Eyes* in 1979 and *Never Alone* in 1980.

Around this time, CCM rocker Eddie DeGarmo received a call from Michael Blanton, then a staffer at Word Records. Blanton told DeGarmo, "'Dan Harrell and I are going to start managing Amy Grant. We really want to try and toughen her image a little bit. Do you guys have a song she could sing with Dana on your album?' So that's how their duet of 'Nobody Loves Me Like You,' came about. Then we went on the road with Amy for about fifty or sixty concerts," remembered DeGarmo."[8]

Grant's CCM-market breakthrough album, *Age to Age*, was released in 1982 and dominated the industry's charts for several years. After another pair of successful albums, *A Christmas Album* in 1983 and 1984's *Straight Ahead*, Grant was poised for pop superstardom with her 1985 smash hit, *Unguarded*, which benefited from a short and otherwise ill-fated joint venture between Grant's label, Word, and A&M Records.

Unguarded, along with its prime single, "Find a Way," brought Grant to the attention of the general public. The album stayed on the Hot 100 chart for thirty weeks and the single cracked the Top 40. With success came increased media scrutiny as well, something Grant wasn't altogether prepared to handle. "Sometimes in conversation you say things that don't translate well into print," she said at the time. "The media attention has been refreshing, but sometimes I screw up."[9]

The offenses Grant had in mind were her surprisingly candid admissions to several publications that she had been skinny dipping in South Africa, and her comment to *Rolling Stone* writer Michael Goldberg that "my hormones are just as on-key as any other twenty-four-year-old's. . . . I feel that a Christian young woman in the eighties is very sexual." She also critiqued a Prince concert she had attended, saying, "I didn't get off watching him create an illusion of masturbating."[10]

Unguarded was a critical and popular success, but Grant's career made an extra leap forward when former Chicago front man Peter Cetera asked her to sing a duet, titled "Next Time I Fall," for his solo record. The song went straight to number one, thanks to the powerful chemistry between Cetera and Grant, yet it fostered some controversy because of Cetera's sexy come-on to Grant: "Tonight, I was thinking that you might be the one who breathes life in this heart of mine."[11]

It was a line that stood in stark contrast to Grant's own sexual ethic. "I made a conscious effort to say, 'I am going to save the most intimate part for the person I spend the rest of my life with," she said. "I was twenty-one when we married, and I said to [husband Gary Chapman], 'Man, that was tough. There were a lot of guys I deeply loved and would have enjoyed knowing fully, man-to-woman, woman-to-man, but I persevered so that I could give myself to you.'"[12]

Then, in trademark fashion, Grant turned the tables on critics who made fun of her for her sexual stance, making *them* seem weird. "People say 'Prude, prude, prude,' but I'm glad I didn't cross certain barriers, because I wouldn't want to compare Gary's moans with some other guy's."[13]

With a number one song under her belt, Grant returned in 1988 with *Lead Me On*. Though the album was a hit, it seemed to disappoint executives at A&M, who may have been hoping for a different kind of record than the contemplative, dark, and spiritual album that reflected the marital troubles Grant and Chapman had endured, as well as the difficult pregnancy that produced her first son, Matthew. Grant affirmed her faith throughout the record, and critics of her jump into the pop mainstream were hard pressed to complain that she had abandoned her beliefs in order to be accepted.

In 1991, Grant again reached the top of the pop charts with the single "Baby, Baby," from the album *Heart in Motion*. A second single, "Every Heartbeat," also cracked the Top 10. Once again, Grant recorded an album that suited her own sense of relevance, and the public snapped it up.

The only game plan, if there was any, was to make an album that my nieces and nephews would listen to. I have eighteen nieces and nephews, and I found it odd that they did not listen to my music, though we listen to a lot of the same things. Why wasn't I making music that spoke to them? That became the challenge of the album. I was playing this one song at my sister Mimi's house—that I felt really strongly about—to all the kids that were in the house at the time, and by the time the song ended, all the kids had left the room! Mimi said, "Hey, I really liked that one," and I shook my head. It's not on the album.[14]

Her next album, *House of Love*, produced a minor hit, "Lucky One," but to some the record lacked heart—it was pop music reduced to formula.

In 1997, however, Grant returned with a bold and powerful album called *Behind the Eyes*, on which she departed from the slick production values of much of her earlier work and returned to a more earthy sound. Grant also took control of the songwriting process to a greater extent than ever before.

"I look back at the songs that had an impact on people—that I've written—and, in fact, very few of them have initiated from me," she said of her previous releases. "I was either asked to write the music or the lyric, but the hook was already established. I still poured my heart into it, but there's a difference between somebody saying, 'Here's a piece of art I'm doing, help me connect the dots,' and somebody saying, 'Here's a blank palette, what do you want to put on there?'"[15]

In early 1999, Grant and husband Gary Chapman were divorced, ending a sixteen-year marriage that had produced three children.[16] In spite of her personal troubles, Grant's contribution to the Christian subculture was her willingness to confront the dominant entertainment culture with her beliefs and mores. Grant firmly rejected separation from the wider culture and refused to be marginalized, a stance adopted later by dc Talk, Jars of Clay, and MxPx, but, she insisted, she hadn't always felt that way.

"There was a time when it was important for me not to cross over," she explained in 1991. "Ten years ago, I said, 'I want to write songs for Christian kids; I want to make an impact on them.' But today, it's important to go into the mainstream. I'm not going to cling to what I was doing back in 1981, because that's not the issue for me now. *If somebody says,*

'You're trying to go secular,' I say, 'Of course I am: That's the whole point'"[17] (italics added).

Although other CCM artists have seemed ashamed for wanting to go mainstream, Grant was completely unapologetic and logical in her relentless determination to break free of the constraints imposed upon her by the subculture. "When Christian artists in the mainstream setting promote godly living," she said, "their songs are going to shine like light out of the darkness. A Christian on pop radio is not the same as a non-believer on pop radio. You almost can't find a song today that doesn't promote the antithesis of a godly lifestyle. Kids are hearing, 'Have sex with your sister, touch me all over,' and cussing—all kinds of nasty, crass, crass stuff."[18]

Grant also went a long way in framing important issues, such as how many songs on a given record should have overt evangelical content and how many should simply speak about life from a Christian worldview. "I've never believed that the *quantity* of information about God is most important," she said. "It's the quality of the information—the impact of a word timely spoken. If Christians make every three-and-a-half-minute song a sermon, always pounding in 'the message,' people are going to quit listening. I'd rather do a record chock full of great songs that make it to hit radio and have one song at the end that says, 'Have I earned the right to say something really important to you?' Some people wait a lifetime to tell a dear friend about the impact that Jesus has made on their lives, for that right moment."[19]

Grant simply viewed a record as one might view a conversation, a revolutionary concept for many CCM artists and generations of Christians, who were trained to believe that because each moment might be the last, the overwhelming burden was on each person to immediately lay out all of their cards and convert the heathen.

Yet to Grant, the issue was not about one standard or another, but about obedience to the silent voice of God. "It's like this time when I'd been talking to a guy next to me on a flight," she remembered. "As we were getting ready to land, I felt God communicating to my heart, 'Don't let him go without saying something about Me.' My first reaction was, 'No, we've landed now and there's not time.' Then I felt myself breaking out into a sweat. So, I started talking to this guy about God. As it ended up, we were stalled on the runway for twenty minutes and had a really interesting talk. In both cases, on the plane and with this record, you do what God tells you, or else you live with the 'sweats.'"[20]

Perhaps Grant had never accepted a key premise of CCM, that its records were to be songs about faith only. If she accepted the party line, it was only for awhile and because, at first, only one record label, Word, had come calling.

"When I was fifteen and started writing songs, I wrote about the whole spectrum of my life experience," said Grant in 1988. "When I signed a record deal with a Christian record company, they were aware that I wrote all kinds of songs, but asked me to record only my gospel songs. That was fine with me, but I think all along I felt that what really gave credibility to my Christian songs was that my relationship with Jesus had had a radical effect on all areas of my life."[21]

"Now I've come full circle and I'm starting to sing on vinyl the things I've written since I was fifteen. The reality and the pulse of my life is rooted in my relationship with Jesus. It doesn't make sense if all I do is sing Christian-type songs. But to say, 'This is the reality of my life. This is how the other fits into it'—suddenly there's a palette there and the paint makes sense."[22]

The cultural withdrawal that had come to characterize much of the subculture was firmly rejected by its leading light, Amy Grant. "Why isolate yourself?" she asked. "Your life isolates you enough. I'm isolated when I walk into a room and somebody says, 'She's a Christian,' and nobody offers me a joint and all the coke disappears. I don't want it anyway, but it doesn't mean that we can't be friends."[23]

Grant's desire to be in the middle of the culture, however, was balanced by her own determination to be there on her own terms.

"For maybe five or ten minutes during concerts I'll say who I am and what Jesus means in my life," said the singer. "I don't want to browbeat a crowd for two hours. . . . That's one reason I started writing songs . . . . This way my audience can sit back and draw their own conclusions, and I feel a certain freedom because I've communicated what I think and the audience's interpretation of it is its own responsibility."[24]

Leslie/Sam Phillips

Another woman who strongly challenged the direction CCM was headed was Leslie Phillips, who broke into the scene with a song called "Bring Me Through," which appeared on a Maranatha! Music sampler album, *Back to the Rock*. With Phillips singing passionately about being "in the basement groping for the light," the song touched a normally taboo topic in CCM—depression—and it didn't offer a tidy ending, concluding simply, "I need your spirit Lord to quicken my soul, to conquer this evil that's taken hold."[25] Having not grown up in a particularly evangelical home, Phillips was used to dealing with real life issues and perhaps hadn't realized yet that such topics were off limits for good Christian singers.

When asked about her upbringing and whether she came from a religious home, Phillips would often say no, then add a caveat. "Every time I say 'no,' my dad goes, 'What?' I'm thankful that I didn't grow up in a Christian home. I basically had to seek it out on my own and I think my relationship with the Lord means a lot more to me because I didn't have it shoved down my throat. I didn't have it all done for me."[26]

Her first exposure to CCM was when she was ten years old and was invited to a local church production of the musical "Come Together," featuring a singer named Jimmy Owens. Later, she saw a band called the Way, at Calvary Chapel in Costa Mesa, and was impressed. Others didn't impress her nearly as much.

"When I was exposed to a lot of the middle-of-the-road music and half-done rock 'n' roll, I kind of went, 'Ugh'," she recalled. "I was a little impudent at that point and said, 'Well, I'm fourteen years old and I could write better songs than that.' So I picked up the guitar."[27]

It was a bold statement by a courageous young woman, and Phillips was quickly snapped up by Myrrh, which had successfully launched Amy Grant several years earlier. Her debut was titled *Beyond Saturday Night*, the title track warning listeners that the pleasures of life were fleeting.

By the time her second album, *Dancing with Danger*, was released, Phillips was the brightest star in the CCM firmament, and her zeal was clearly evident on her records, delighting the subculture. On the title cut, Phillips chronicled the life of a wandering young Christian with screaming vocals: "Raised with a Bible in your hands, you met your parents' strict demands and now that sweet religious child is like a hurricane gone wild . . . you're dancing with danger."[28]

Yet, even as Phillips articulated a strong message, she stood apart because of her willingness to be honest about her own struggles. It was an in-your-face Christianity that made a strong stand for morality while candidly admitting to the struggles and failures that she herself faced. On "Light of Love," for instance, Phillips went beyond a simple proclamation of abstinence, taking the listener on a journey through a close call when she was forced to fend off an eager boyfriend with the gentle but firm words, "I don't want to love you, at least not the way you're thinking, I don't want to climb the stairs up to your room." For the sake of authenticity, Phillips concluded the song with the deeply confessional words, "I have lonely sunsets where my heart sinks into dust, and I want someone to hold me through the night. I know that you are willing, but if it's not forever, I just can't walk away from what is right."[29]

She followed a similar line in "I Won't Let It Come between Us" by admitting something that was often carefully avoided in many Christian circles, that sin is actually fun—at least for awhile. "You know wrong can sure look good sometimes," sang Phillips, "and it caught my eye just like a jewel that shines, driven by desires in the wind, evil's foot is in the door and it's coming in."[30]

It was an honesty that was rare in the Christian world at that time, and Phillips knew it. "I was told in church that evil was terrible and awful, which it is," she said, "but the seductive beauty of evil was never addressed. In youth group, I heard that evil could never be fun or appealing. But the Bible also says that Satan is a beautiful, beautiful angel, who comes to us as an angel of light. He really puts on a good face."[31]

Phillips dealt with less weighty matters on the playful "Powder Room Politics," recounting a visit to the ladies room where she found herself judging the looks of others and being judged herself. After regretting her own attitude, Phillips concluded, "Well, I told that girl that she had nice eyes, and then I stopped worrying about my size. And as I left, I was glad to leave the lies of powder room politics."[32]

No doubt some within CCM circles were offended by a gospel singer discussing bathroom encounters, but her fans loved it, and by the time Phillips's third album, *Black and White in a Grey World*, was recorded, she was the premiere female CCM rock singer. Yet, Phillips quietly and slowly began to succumb to pressures from the CCM world to write the music she thought it wanted to hear—and the subculture liked what it heard.

"Strength of My Life," a song that has worked its way into modern church hymnbooks, was trademark Phillips fare, as she tried to relate her daily, normal existence to the spiritual world. The track opened with the lines, "I open my eyes to the sound of morning rush, and wish for ten more minutes left to sleep. And as I get into the shower, the thoughts of facing one more day overwhelm me, and I begin to weep."[33]

Today, when "Strength" is sung in churches across America, the first verse is conveniently skipped over in favor of the uplifting chorus: "Everyday I look to You to be the strength of my life." The way this song is used today in church circles is a metaphor for what is wrong with CCM, where many prefer music that skips over life's difficulties and focuses on its rewards.

Many of the tracks on *Black and White in a Grey World* were decidedly middle-of-the-road pop, a choice that Phillips defended at the time. "I keep the praise songs and some of the ballads in there because I feel that's part of me. I don't want to be stereotyped as a hard-nosed rock 'n' roller. The praise songs I've written are really reflective of the way God has worked in my life, and I think He can use those little choruses to help people."[34]

Yet, a year later, the mercurial Phillips retracted her earlier comments. "Basically I let the pressure get the better of me and some of the songs were sellouts," she said. "I didn't do what I knew I should do."[35]

What became a scandalous spring for Phillips began with a performance at southern California's Knott's Berry Farm, which shocked the audience and forced Phillips to cancel the rest of her tour. Her golden locks had been dyed black, her form-fitting skirt was cut well above the knees, and she peppered her set with unexpected tunes like Dylan's "It Ain't Me Babe." The audience, which clearly had come to hear a different set, quietly but steadily streamed out. Phillips had obviously decided to go out with a bang by provoking a confrontation, though she feigned surprise afterward.

"I played songs that they didn't know, but it was all about show biz," she remarked years later. "It didn't have anything to do with spirituality. This is the problem, this is the big thing: people in Christian music really confused spiritual issues with show business and musical taste. And that's really frightening, because that's a comment on our culture more than anything else, because it's saying that celebrity and show business are way too important. It's unhealthy, but it's inescapable."[36]

The next thunderbolt came when Phillips was profiled by *CCM* magazine at the time of the release of her album *The Turning*. The article began with this quote from Phillips: "This is my last album for the Christian music market. This is the last."[37]

The album would indeed be her final CCM studio effort, and it is widely regarded among the greatest of all time. An amazing piece of work, in part due to the liberating production of Phillips's future husband, T-Bone Burnett, *The Turning* was clearly an album with a message targeted at the Christian music world.

"On the last record I made," Phillips said of *Black and White in a Grey World*, "I just walked up to the microphone to sing—and I wasn't involved in the making of that record at all; I mean, the producer did all the tracks. I was emotionally so gone at that point, I had some other things go on and at that point it was like a chain reaction."[38]

With the widely respected Burnett at the production helm, Phillips felt liberated. "T-Bone was just encouraging me to be generous as an artist, to let it out—and believe me it just poured out," said Phillips. "I did demos of all the songs, where I sang and played all the voices and instruments, and I took them to T-Bone, who said "OK, great!" All through the project, I would say, 'What do you think?' and he'd say, 'It's your record, what do *you* think?' He really made me take most of the responsibility."[39]

Phillips's comments were clearly intended as a slap to her previous producer, Dan Posthuma, but she was also rejecting something larger—the stifling coat of armor that she and other CCM artists labored under, which was akin to King Saul's bulky armor that David discarded before facing the giant Goliath.

"There's something wrong with modern recording technique," said Phillips. "Producers build this incredible instrumental track, which is like a shell with nothing in the middle. The singer's just sort of thrown on at the end and you end up with a hollow center. What we did was start with a vocal performance and build outward. The vocals were sung to just an acoustic guitar or a drum program, which was later replaced with real drums. I think that a performance and a human being is what music is all about. Touching or communicating to another human being is really important."[40]

The record itself was not shy about "God issues," but from its black-and-white record jacket to its searching song titles like "When Answers Don't Come Easy," it was clear that Phillips was stepping back from all that she knew and believed and was asking questions and questioning assumptions.

After *The Turning*, Phillips released a greatest hits package for Myrrh to fulfill her contract, and was soon picked up by Virgin Records, where she released several records under the name Sam Phillips, which attracted strong, critical acclaim but never broke through to widespread appeal.

Looking back over her career in CCM, Phillips had much to say—not only about the genre, but about the lessons she had learned. "When I was signed I didn't know how to make records, I didn't know how to sing, I barely knew how to write songs . . . ," she remembered. "I was a complete novice. I was so young and I was trying to find my way. I was trying different sounds, I was hearing different things that I liked and I would try it this way, maybe try to sound like different records that I liked. I just didn't have enough experience, and when I did, I was able to look back and know that what I had done was not what I wanted, not what I had intended."[41]

Beyond the music, Phillips looked back on a career that began at the age of eighteen, and questioned whether she was ever qualified to be such a high profile spokesperson for the Christian faith. "I had a very sheltered reality from the time I was fourteen until I was about twenty-three," she remembered. "I really put my head into focusing and studying Christianity and religion and philosophy heavily. So when I woke up at twenty-three and had gone through adolescence—well, really hadn't gone through adolescence I guess is the point. And I started reading books and listening to music and meeting all different kinds of people, and the fundamentalism I experienced in gospel music didn't hold up."[42]

"When she began to express more of her grown-up ideas, she says, they were squelched," observed industry critic Brian Quincy Newcomb. "She was encouraged to produce propaganda that supported the status quo and promised to please the record buying public."[43]

Phillips went a step beyond, questioning the assumption that a teenager onstage with a guitar could be expected to provide answers to the deep questions of life. "Christian audiences expect you to teach and be this incredible example," she said. "I mean I haven't been to seminary. I've been to a year of Bible college and studied the Bible personally, but gosh, there was so much that was expected. The pressure on Christian artists is incredible. We expect them to be our heroes, to exemplify Christianity, and to do what we can't do."[44]

At Virgin, Phillips's first record, *The Indescribable Wow*, was in the vein of her final Word record, and she maintained that her spiritual stance had changed little. "I still have a deep faith," she remarked, "but I've had to start over with my faith and go back to that question, 'What does love require?'"[45]

She didn't leave without getting in some good digs aimed at the broader Christian population. "I think the so-called born again movement in this country has about as little to do with real Christianity as a Xerox of a hundredth generation print of the Mona Lisa has to do with the real thing," she said. "The born again movement is more about obsession and narrow-mindedness and repression, and true Christianity is about mercy and freedom and love."[46]

Unfortunately, such statements showed the same kind of judgmentalism that she claimed to find distasteful among conservative Christians. Nevertheless, her objections to CCM were well founded and her goals were realistic. "I guess the main thing is, I want to grow as an artist and I want to be able to write about whatever I want to write about," she said, "and I really don't want to be restricted—and I feel like I am in gospel music. Also, I don't agree with it; I think a lot of it is selling God."[47]

When Leslie became Sam, a vital part of CCM died. It would have been easy to write off Phillips as a good girl gone bad, but she had not rejected her faith—only the subculture. On subsequent records, her anger at it was tangible, but so was the acknowledgment of her need for God.

Although it would take nearly a decade for other artists to follow in her foot-steps, Leslie, aka Sam, Phillips had fired the opening shot in a war that would precipitate CCM's conceptual collapse.

Michael W. Smith

Another musician who shared an eagerness to speak to the wider culture was a pop singer named Michael W. Smith, a Kenova, West Virginia, native who relocated to Nashville in search of the musical big time. Smith's father toiled with a local oil company and his mother worked at the church, and at first young Michael dreamed of a career in baseball, not music. When he did listen to music, it was the Beatles, Elton John, Billy Joel, and classical composers that caught his ear. Smith was introduced to his faith at a young age and was every bit the devout teenager.

"I wore this big cross around my neck," he remembered. "I was a Jesus freak. It was very real to me. All my friends my age were out drinking beer and being kind of crazy. I was over there with my older church friends with my Bible, singing, praying, studying. I was into it."[48]

It wasn't long, however, before Smith left his faith behind.

> I was deceived, and I know kids don't like to hear, "Well there's a Devil and there's a Lord, and Satan got me," and all that kind of stuff. Well, I'll tell you what, that's exactly what happened. I believe there's good and I believe there's evil, and the good is God and the evil is Satan. That's what the Bible says, and I believe that. There's a constant battle going on for people's lives and people's hearts, and I started listening to these voices that weren't God. And before you know it . . . I started smoking pot . . . on a Sunday afternoon and letting it almost wear off in time to get to church to play piano for the youth choir.[49]

Smith's battle with drugs continued in Nashville. "I was down here trying to write songs and stuff, and I wasn't writing songs very well. I was out partying too much and I knew where my heart belonged. I knew 'surely this is not my destiny, to do this the rest of my life.' I would enjoy it, but then I'd wake up and feel just horrible. . . . So I began to pray, because I knew the Lord heard me, I knew God really loved me. I started praying, 'Lord you gotta get me out, 'cause I'm stuck.' I finally just came to the end of myself. I knew I couldn't live that way anymore."[50, 51]

Smith met a songwriter named Randy Cox, and soon he was touring with Cox's group. Eventually, he joined Amy Grant as her opening act before releasing his own record, *The Michael W. Smith Project*. Smith soon followed

Grant into pop music with the release of a single from his album *Go West Young Man*, titled "Place in This World," which hit number five on the pop charts in 1990.

It was a big year for Smith, who was also selected by *People* magazine as one of its fifty most beautiful people of the year. Yet, for Smith, pop success in 1990 was exactly four years later than when *he* had planned. In 1986, his album *The Big Picture* had been slated for release through A&M Records, hot on the heels of Amy Grant's deal with A&M the previous year. Smith had prepared for the challenge, writing and recording an album that was tailor-made for pop success.

"I think we made a big mistake," he said of himself and the management team of Mike Blanton and Dan Harrell that guided his and Grant's careers. "We got distracted with the *Unguarded* thing. 'Find a Way' was a hit and we all thought, 'Man we're gonna go for it,' and I learned a big lesson from that record. I was chasing it. I think Mike and Dan were chasing it too. We all sit around and talk about it, 'Man were we chasing it or what? Instead of just letting things happen like we need to.' I don't regret making *The Big Picture*. There were some neat things on the record, but I think we just got ahead of God."[52]

When A&M decided, instead, not to release the record, Smith lost hope. "I was crushed," he remembered. "I was really disappointed. But I got up and thought, *Life goes on*, and then the whole next year we all began to reevaluate what our motives were. We did *The Big Picture* tour and it was great, one of the best tours I've ever done. I bounced back. I think probably *The Big Picture* is where I really changed my whole way of thinking, going, 'You know what? I'm just going to make a record, I'm not going to chase this thing anymore.' When I made *Go West*, I didn't try to make songs to get on pop radio; I just made a record."[53]

Smith had traded in his rifle for the musical equivalent of five smooth stones, and like the young shepherd boy, he had conquered the pop market with reckless abandon and a sense of nonchalance. It often happens this way, fervent Christians will tell you, that God often rewards those who have given up seeking success with the very success they so coveted. Smith's case was no exception.

"'Place in This World' was a fluke in some ways," he said. "There was no marketing set up for it. There was this woman at Geffen who believed in it and went in there and it just took off. It was like pulling teeth, going to people, 'Please play it—just play it and see if you get a response.' And once people started playing it, it caught on like wildfire."[54]

When the song hit the Top 10, Smith won the "best new artist" award at the American Music Awards.

"I'm not really sure I was ready for it then," he said of his earlier attempts at pop stardom. "There are a lot of women coming on to you and all that sort of thing, and being in clubs. . . . My wife's a Christian, all our family are Christians—and all of a sudden . . . I've been in the world, which I regret, but boy, I forgot what the world is really like. Believe me, it's a far cry from going and doing a little autograph thing at a Christian bookstore. But it was good, because you know what? These people need Jesus and I really feel God opened up a lot of opportunities to be able to share my faith with people."[55]

As the pop world embraced him, Smith found himself questioning many of CCM's assumptions, especially the notion that artists should make two records—one spiritual and one about the other issues of life.

> I don't want to do that, and I didn't really know why I didn't want to do it back then, but I do now. Because, to me, I just can't separate the two. This is just who I am, and if it sells, "Great!" And if it doesn't sell, I'll have to deal with that. I'm not making a record for Geffen and a record for Reunion. I don't think I'm forgetting my roots and I think there's a balance there. I haven't gone off the deep end. But my whole mindset was "don't get in this frame of mind where oh, we gotta protect the Christian market and we gotta do the pop thing too." I just said I'm not going to do that. I'm really being myself. I really have searched deep down inside and I feel like we've really come up with some great things to say.[56]

Smith's follow up to *Go West Young Man*, *Change Your World*, didn't pack the same punch, though it yielded a small hit with the Diane Warren tune "I Will Be Here for You." Smith soon found himself axed from Geffen when Reunion's deal with Geffen was abruptly canceled.

What Smith had in common with Amy Grant was the driving force behind their success—the management team of Blanton and Harrell, who more than anybody else at the corporate level of CCM had a vision for being a part of pop culture. They had met in the early 1980s when Harrell, Grant's brother-in-law, was a bank officer and Blanton was an executive at Word, who had worked A&R for various early groups.

"They were young and business-wise," said Don Butler, a former Gospel Music Association executive. "Mike Blanton was in charge of Word Records' Nashville office; he took care of recording details for them here. Dan Harrell was a banker. They designed a formula and stuck with it. . . . Of course, they were Christians with high principles, but not so dogmatic as not to see the possibilities of reaching out with music as the message. They have done things differently than the normal gospel agencies and management teams, from the way they promoted . . . to controlling the venues and types of interviews and media exposure."[57]

After forming a management company, which handled Grant, Smith, and Kathy Troccoli, the two created their own label out of necessity. Unable to get record deals for Smith and Troccoli, they formed Reunion Records and began to release records in the CCM market via Word distribution.

"We teach them how to walk, talk, eat, and dress," Harrell said during the mid-'80s of his charges. "And we provide them with accounting and investing services—if they're making money."[58]

It was Blanton and Harrell's brilliant planning that allowed for Grant to cross over in 1985, which in turn paved the way for Smith's big break in 1990.

"The move had been planned . . . for a couple of years," noted one observer. "It would be implemented in high gear once they decided on A&M to distribute Word's Myrrh Records product through secular outlets. Amy was about to do what many others in the gospel music industry probably wished they could do, but were either too closely tied to the fundamentalists and church organizations or too evangelistic to be successful. No one in Amy Grant's camp cared if the traditionalists and old guard castigated her music. They were aiming at a younger, more upscale audience of Christian youth."[59]

Smith clearly benefited from Blanton and Harrell's determined planning as well as Geffen's Claire West's dogged efforts to get "Place in This World" played on pop radio. With his music and his approach to the market, Smith systematically undermined the CCM mentality and culture of separation. Smith spoke for many when he said, "I think Christian music was a mistake a long time ago, where we started our own little thing over here. I think God's used it, it's been a good thing, but obviously, I think it's really separated us from where we need to be."[60]

In 1999, in an interview given just prior to the CCM industry's awards show, the Dove Awards, Smith gave his most candid assessment yet of the industry, which that year gave him several of its highest honors. "I . . . hate that term 'Christian music,' a lot," he said, "because I've never been able to separate the sacred and the secular. . . . I'm not really sure it was smart to really ever start Christian music. . . . We decided, 'Oh, we're not going to be in that world because that's so evil. We're going to start our own thing over here.' And so then we started this subculture, and then we all live in this subculture and we just do our own thing over here and we feed Christians and we have our own little club. And I absolutely hate it. I don't like it at all. I just don't think that's what Jesus would do."[61]

Steve Taylor

Although not nearly as dramatic as Leslie Phillips's exit from CCM, Steve Taylor's departure was felt by fans and industry watchers alike. Taylor had burst onto the scene in 1983 with an EP released on Sparrow Records amusingly titled, *I Want to Be a Clone*, which poked fun at the bland types that tended to populate evangelical churches with which Taylor was obviously familiar.

"Be a clone and kiss conviction good-night, cloneliness is next to godliness, right?"[62] mocked Taylor on the title cut. On "Whatever Happened to Sin?" he attacked modern Christians who wanted to explain away sin and depravity as cultural constructs. "Steeplechase" found Taylor trashing church-hopping Christians. "You like the big ones/Worship incognito/Your problems ain't getting solved/You try a small one/Oops, you must retreat-o/You'd rather not get involved."[63]

Taylor found wide acceptance in the very community he was mocking because he attacked from the social, theological, and cultural right wing. Evangelical Christians have long been open to—and sometimes have even welcomed—attacks upon their style of living from somebody accusing them of not being conservative and Christian enough, as Taylor did.

A closer look at Taylor's work, however, showed that he was difficult to pin down politically, and he himself rejected the notion that he was a right-wing reactionary.

"It strikes me as ironic, since I've always gone out of my way not to align myself with either the right or the left," he noted. "I even got specific about it as early as the song 'Bad Rap': 'To my left-wing band with their head in the sand, to the might-makes-right playing chicken. . . .' I would hope that much of the energy and controversy in my work comes from its defiance of traditional notions of left and right."[64]

Taylor, the son of a minister, grew up in Denver, Colorado, but never saw much in the faith of his parents to rebel against. "My parents were real consistent between what they said and what they did," he said. "So there wasn't really a whole lot to rebel against. They were good examples."[65]

Good Christian examples and a lack of rebellion didn't keep Taylor from listening to punk bands during the '70s.

> I was really influenced by the punk and new wave thing from England right around '77. It got me interested in music again, because it just had a different feeling to it. . . . Their music was motivated by the desire that they had these songs they had to get out to people, and there was . . . a real passion behind the music that I felt

was lacking in most music at the time.[66] . . . The band that had the biggest influence on me was the Clash. I never doubted for a minute that they believed what they were singing about. I didn't agree with a lot of it, but they yelled out the words with such conviction and fire. Also, in their interviews you could tell that they were really trying to live out what they were singing about. I thought, "Well, if I'm a Christian and I know about ultimate truth, I want to write songs with the same kind of conviction and power behind them." And I also knew that new wave music was, essentially, four guys getting together who couldn't play musical instruments, and that appealed to me because I couldn't play anything either.[67]

At Biola University in suburban Los Angeles, Taylor's singing was deemed unworthy for the school's choir. "I thought I wanted to get into music," he said, "[but] I couldn't make the chorale or even the choir, and I was getting all this advice like, 'Maybe you should try chemistry.'"[68]

In college, Taylor also experienced his first doubts about his faith. "At Biola, I had a crisis of faith," he said. "[I began] wondering if all this stuff about Christianity was true or not. A Christian college can be very beneficial, but I felt so isolated from the world that I started wondering if I had been fed a line all of my life. It was at this time I did a lot of checking out of the historical claims of Christianity, reading people like Josh McDowell and Francis Schaeffer, while trying to do my own research as well. At that time, I decided Christianity was credible."[69]

Transferring to the University of Colorado, and beginning to help out at his father's church, Taylor made a profound discovery.

> I really enjoyed youth work, and it was during this time of going to college and serving as the church's youth pastor that I realized two things. First, I saw that music was the language of my culture. That was it. If you wanted to get through to kids, you did it with music. You don't try to hype sports figures anymore, and they don't listen to politicians. They listen to music and musicians. Second, I felt that music at that time was not communicating much of anything to them, and that included most of the so-called contemporary Christian music. So when I started to write, I tried to take some of the things I had been teaching my kids in youth group and put them into a musical format that I liked.[70]

Taylor also discovered in 1984 what Ralph Reed proved a decade later: A powerful coalition could be built among modern evangelical Christians who opposed the racism that had infected American Christianity in the past and who loathed the secularist establishment that seemed to have nothing but contempt for the simple faith practiced quietly by millions.

By the time his second record, *Meltdown*, was released, Taylor had hit his stride. On "We Don't Need No Color Code," he mercilessly pummeled Bob Jones University for its policy at the time of not allowing interracial dating, then bashed the press for its secularism on "Meat the Press." *Meltdown* also staked out Taylor's ground on social issues like abortion and euthanasia with a tender ballad titled "Baby Doe," which delivered the haunting ending, "Behind your disguise, your rhetoric lies, you watched a baby starve . . . I bear the blame. The cradle's below and where is Baby Doe?"[71]

Taylor's satire knew no bounds and nobody was spared from his wicked pen, including Bob Dylan, whom Taylor mocked in the song "Meltdown": "Dylan may be fillin' the puddle they've designed, / is it gonna take a miracle to make up his mind?"[72]

By 1985, Taylor was at the top of the CCM heap and had an album budget big enough to bring in some big guns, including producer Ian McDonald of King Crimson and Foreigner fame. Taylor emerged with a stellar release that shot straight to the top of the CCM charts, called *On the Fritz*, which included a brilliant single titled "This Disco." It used a church recently converted to a disco as a metaphor to describe the Church, which in Taylor's view, had increasingly lost its relevance by trying to be all things to all people at the expense of its soul.

> The main thrust of that song was country-club Christianity, and where a church preaches what people want to hear in order to draw a certain crowd. But it was inspired by an actual disco I investigated in New York City. It really used to be a church, but now it's a disco, with two thousand people bouncing up and down on the sanctuary floor, video screens lowered down over the organ's pipes, and records being played from what used to be the pulpit. So I just imagined that this was a Sunday night and the deacons had just devised a new way of getting new members into the church. It's like the idea of country-club Christianity and trying to gear our services to the beautiful people, [even though] Jesus made it very clear He didn't come for the people who were well but for those who needed a doctor.[73]

The final track, "I Just Wanna Know," perhaps hinted at Taylor's subsequent conclusion that he was really, in the end, only preaching to the choir—an evangelical cheerleader with larger aspirations. "I just wanna know, am I pulling people closer?" he sang. "I just wanna be pulling them to you. I just wanna stay angry at the evil, I just wanna be hungry for the true."[74]

By 1988, Taylor was ready for what became his swan song to the CCM market—at least for awhile—the wacky *I Predict 1990*, which was openly protested by a Texas evangelist who accused Taylor of featuring a tarot card on his cover.

"I think what happened, up until I put out *1990*, the stuff seemed controversial for all the right reasons," said Taylor. "But at that point, it turned into me being accused of using tarot card album covers and new age hand signs," he said. "It was really, really, way out. That kind of stuff, I'd never dealt with before. I felt stupid even responding to that kind of thing, and that sapped a certain amount of energy. . . . When you have to go around saying, 'I'm a nice guy and I go to church,' it's like, suddenly, I was in the position of defending that I really was a Christian. It felt like it was a big step backwards."[75]

Taylor opened the record with an uproarious snipe at abortion clinic violence on a song called "I Blew Up the Clinic Real Good." It was a raucous, saxophone-laden song with Taylor borrowing the voice of an ice cream truck driver blowing up clinics because, "If we run out of youngsters, I'll be out of a job."[76]

It was a song that confused Taylor's fans, and "Clinic" was not a favorite of Taylor's label, Sparrow, either. He was soon forced to find another home for the record. "I was never a big money-maker for them, because even though we'd sell a lot of records, the stuff we were doing cost a lot," he said. "[Also] I think a turn toward more traditional Christian music happened with that company about the same time as this record started getting out of hand—everything else was moving in one direction and I was moving in another—and so that combination of things I think maybe caused them to reconsider whether it was such a good idea for me to be on the label and whether maybe the money could be put to better use."[77]

Still, Taylor remembered the label fondly. "While I doubt Sparrow was crazy about the tone of certain songs and they seemed to me to be getting more conservative in their musical tastes," he said, "they never interfered with my creative choices during our entire relationship, which is pretty rare. The reasons for our reluctant separation were a combination of their financial struggles at the time and my inability to finish the album soon enough for their bottom line. Instead of pressuring me to deliver the album as is, they generously agreed to let me find a new label home."[78]

I Predict eventually ended up on Word's Myrrh label and predictably did not fare as well as his previous efforts. Taylor retired from CCM, but without the bitter words that had characterized Leslie Phillips's parting.

"When I said I retired," remembered Taylor, "that was the best term I could use for it. You don't retire when you're angry, you quit. Retirement felt like the appropriate word, because I wasn't angry. But the future did not look inviting, so that was the best thing to do, just retire. I maintained all my friendships and just moved on to try something else. At that time I did not know what the next thing was going to be."[79]

That "next thing" for Taylor was the formation of a band with several longtime buddies and a deal with MCA Records. Calling the group Chagall Guevara, after the painter Marc Chagall and Marxist revolutionary Che Guevara, Taylor set out to make "revolutionary art" along with bandmates Dave Perkins, CCM executive Lynn Nichols, drummer Mike Mead, and bassist Wade Jaynes. It was Taylor and company's triumphant entry into the mainstream market. Despite its obvious Christian outlook, the record was welcomed with open arms by critics. "Not since the Clash has a group so effectively turned militant discontent into passionate rock and roll,"[80] raved *Rolling Stone*.

"Chagall Guevara's debut is very much a Christian album. Not evangelical, but definitely Christian," wrote critic Brian Mansfield of the *Nashville Scene*. "There's no specifically stated spiritual intent and the members of the band are wary of being favored or feared because of their beliefs. But the group's strong spiritual life remains apparent in the music."[81]

For Taylor, who had never intended to sing only for Christians, Chagall was his big opportunity to fulfill his original mission. "I want to communicate," he had said in his early days. "I want people to question things. I want the non-Christians to open their minds to the idea that maybe a lot of them have been lied to about what Christianity is all about. Maybe the reason they've rejected Christianity is not because they're rejecting Jesus, but a hypocritical church. And for the Christians, I want them to think about what it means to be a Christian in today's society, how that affects everyday life, and what demands that makes on us as believers. I want to communicate the responsibility we have to live out our faith, so communication is the key. If that doesn't happen, I think I'm wasting my time."[82]

For guitarist Lynn Nichols, the departure of the members of Chagall Guevara from the subculture was a result of the conservative turn in that market when executives had begun to realize that the crossover movement of the 1980s, led by Amy Grant and others, was bad for their bottom line.

"I think the windows were open for Christian music to be broader," said Nichols. "That's why I came in. It was almost like there wasn't a ceiling. I think what happened is, for whatever reason, those windows shut. Things changed. When that happened, it was like our jobs were phased out. If we believed in what we wanted to do, we had to go someplace else and do it."[83]

"It flip-flopped a little," added Taylor. "Because at the same time things started shutting down in Christian music, the idea of doing music that was socially and spiritually conscious on a pop label became acceptable. That really wasn't the case in 1982."[84]

In a brief, shining moment of hope, the CCM world paused and wondered whether Taylor and company would make it in "the world." They didn't.

Although precise reasons for the ultimate failure of Chagall Guevara are difficult to pin down, several factors contributed to the band's demise. Alternative music was just breaking in 1990, and nobody seemed to know quite what to do with their album in the pre-Nirvana era when it came out. Another problem was touring.

"If you're gonna do it, you've gotta go whole hog," said Taylor. "One of our members wasn't into touring."[85]

Another factor that stopped the group dead in its tracks with MCA was the philosophical incompatibility between the band and its label. "Discrimination" had been cited so often in CCM circles as an excuse for failure that when it really occurred, albeit in small ways, it tended to be disbelieved. But Taylor remembered the day when the band flew to L.A. to meet with the MCA staff in charge of the artwork and promotion of the record.

"We were waiting at the airport for about an hour and we got hungry," he remembered, "so we called Domino's and ordered a pizza while we were waiting. When we got to MCA, we told one of our A&R directors the story and she asked us why we had bought pizza from 'the Nazis.'"[86]

The 'Nazi' she had in mind was Domino's founder Thomas Monaghan, a fervent supporter of antiabortion causes. Taylor was furious, and an argument with the MCA employee ensued.

"Our other A&R director eventually called a truce, but he later took me aside and asked, 'What's gonna happen if you're interviewed by *Spin* and they ask you your views on abortion?' I replied that I'd tell them what I believed. It was obvious he didn't think that was a good idea.'"[87]

Though the record was a critical success, Taylor returned to the CCM fold after the Chagall Guevara experience for several reasons, including the opinion of his minister. "The critical factor came when I talked with my pastor," he said. "He said two things: Number one, he said 'I liked your band, but I felt that you guys did a better job figuring out what you weren't than what you were,' and that definitely struck a chord of truth. And the second thing he said was, 'I plead with you to do another solo record.' His thinking was that there was something that was going on as a solo artist that wasn't happening in this band, that what I was doing as a solo artist was important."[88]

As Taylor returned to the subculture to record another solo album, this time for the Warner Alliance label, he seemed to have tired of the struggle to break out of the CCM box. "I realize that it may be 'Steve Taylor, Christian artist' for the rest of my life. But if that's how it is, then I'm fine with that," he said.[89]

That was not to be the case, however, for Taylor soon began producing other artists and in 1997 initiated his boldest move ever, forming a new music and film company called Squint Entertainment with a plan to release records in both the CCM and pop markets. His first signing, Sixpence None the Richer, shocked the music world when a single, "Kiss Me," rose to number two on the pop music charts and was used on the TV series *Dawson's Creek* and in the popular teen movie *She's All That*.

To a large extent, Taylor had set the agenda for many up and coming artists in the CCM world, and it was his brand of thought, inspired by the late philosopher Francis Schaeffer, and others, that lived on through younger, aggressive bands like dc Talk and Jars of Clay. It was Taylor who bludgeoned the CCM mentality while he recorded for a CCM label not out of choice but necessity. His social conservatism and antiracism were later adopted powerfully by dc Talk, his introspection by Jars of Clay, his commitment to art by Sixpence None the Richer, and his wicked sense of humor by the Newsboys.

Through these and other bands, Taylor and his ideas lived on in the subculture and powerfully fed a generation who would finally rise up and demand changes in the CCM power structure that Taylor himself had long questioned.

BeBe and CeCe Winans

After a long career of recording primarily for the CCM market, BeBe and CeCe Winans eventually landed separate pop recording deals—CeCe with Pioneer Music Group and BeBe with Atlantic. The siblings were the offspring of Dolores and David Winans, the popularizers of what was known as the "Detroit sound," who raised their children to listen only to gospel music. The senior Winanses had paid their own dues in gospel music as part of the Lemon Gospel Singers and had played with the likes of Sam Cooke and Lou Rawls.

"We couldn't bring any secular albums into the house, so we were raised on gospel," said BeBe. "Our folks loved traditional quartets and choirs, but when Dad would leave the house, man, we'd put on Andrae Crouch, and the Hawkins family, and crank it up. We had to go to church, but we fell in love with that. We had youth choirs and activities all the time. It was not what you'd call a boring church. And like the Bible says, in the end we just didn't want to depart from it."[90]

CeCe remembered:

> It wasn't always easy when I was growing up. As a child, you don't necessarily understand the reasons behind your parents' strictness. Things came up that weren't even particularly sinful—just things that weren't edifying. Instead of going on some outing, for instance, we'd be in church. But because my parents made us go to church, we were able to hear God's Word and were able to begin loving God for ourselves. We learned early what it meant to fast and to pray, and how to stand for God in the hard times. When I look at my background, I think God knew what He was preparing us for. We didn't realize as children that someday we would have to be in dark places holding up the light. I don't think I would have lasted if it weren't for that upbringing. It gave me discipline. It taught me how to stand alone. It taught me to not be afraid to be different—to resist peer pressure. It taught me how to be a leader.[91]

Another lesson that the Winans kids learned was to take their music into the culture because their parents had instilled within them a desire not only to be true to their God but to be relevant to the culture.

The eldest Winans brothers, Marvin, Carvin, Michael, and Ronald, first made a splash in 1986 with their album *Let My People Go*, but the success of their younger siblings soon outshined the rest of the family. Not that the road was easy. BeBe and CeCe took an unusual and unexpected path to fame, one that dragged them through the heart of the greatest religious social scandal of the twentieth century.

In 1980, the siblings traveled to North Carolina to audition for televangelist Jim Bakker's PTL singers. CeCe, then just sixteen, made the cut, but her brother didn't. He was later asked to join anyway.

"I was going to stay and work at a grocery store just to support her," remembered BeBe. "But it so happened I was hired as a singer too. We were just singing in the choirs and the two of us began leading a lot of songs. Audiences started asking for us to sing together, then a lot of churches began requesting concerts. Things just took off from there."[92]

They first stirred PTL viewers with a Christianized rendition of the Joe Cocker/Jennifer Warnes hit, "Up Where We Belong," and though it wasn't exactly the best way to break into the music business, BeBe remained grateful to the Bakkers, even after their fall from grace.

"I thank God for my time there," he said. "I believe we were used to tear down some walls of segregation that existed, and they taught us the artistry of being a gospel artist, how to present yourself to an audience and a camera. I look in my pocket and I can't even find a pebble to throw. We're talking about two wonderful people that had a big dream and big hearts, who made big mistakes—and there but for the grace of God go I."[93]

The PTL experience also taught the Winans siblings how to cross over to the predominately white CCM culture, which for the most part had only been penetrated in a serious and sustained way by Andrae Crouch.

"It was a learning experience to go from a predominantly black surrounding—church, home, school—and be set in an area where, for the first time, we were the minority," said BeBe. "There were differences we learned to cope with . . . that go way beyond skin color."[94]

After one album with PTL in 1984, and the subsequent fall of the PTL empire, BeBe and CeCe moved to Sparrow Records where they released an eponymous album. By the time their second release, *Heaven*, debuted in 1988, thanks to a distribution agreement to the pop market through Capitol, they had established themselves as Christians who would neither leave their faith behind nor succumb to singing "God songs" for one crowd and "crotch songs" for another.

"A lot of young people don't listen to gospel music or go out and buy it because they don't feel it relates to them and don't feel the freedom to be young and express themselves," said BeBe. "We like to have fun in our performances and get the point across that living for Jesus, living a clean life, doesn't mean living a boring life. We condemn each other for everything under the sun in the church. We tell each other we sound too 'secular,' whatever that is. We believe all music comes from God, and that liberates us to express ourselves in a wider range of artistic expression than some others."[95]

Winans had tough words for both the strictly "secular" and strictly "Christian" approaches to music. "Real love is not expressed in today's music," he said. "And the Christians haven't done much better. We've been beating people up with our lyrics, condemning the world harshly. You don't have to tell someone they're locked up in prison—they already know that. They want to know how to get out, where the key is—and that key is God's love, which is more powerful than hatred. This is a pleasant and warm message to the world, one they need and want to hear."[96]

Winans also learned that being real as an artist meant being willing to open up a part of himself to the listener, which he did on a song that emerged from a painful period in his life. "There's a song on *Different*

Lifestyles called 'It's OK,'" he said. "It's about how my marriage just about ended. Recording that song was painful; all of us broke down and cried in the studio, but the tears were tears of joy because God has brought us through it. There are a lot of people who think that, because they're Christians, they shouldn't have marital problems. Not so. That doesn't eliminate heartaches, troubles, ups and downs. But we're human beings. And it's not easy. I'm still learning how to be a good husband. You work at it—relationships, a good family life. You work at balancing it."[97]

As the Winans became increasingly visible in the culture, many R&B artists flocked to them, and before long they found themselves performing with Whitney Houston, Stephanie Mills, Freddie Jackson, Anita Baker, and others. To some Christians, it was unconscionable for performers like the Winans to associate with unbelievers. It was the kind of talk that BeBe simply let roll off of his back.

"A lot of these people have come from gospel backgrounds and seem to appreciate the fact that we've stayed with it," he said of the many artists who sought them out. "At the least they are encouraging us to keep going, and some of them even seem to wish they were doing it. One of the reasons I've become friends with these people is because I've loved them right where they are. Even if some of them don't stand for right, or haven't given any positive values back to the community, I've chosen to love them, and in return they trust me and consider me a friend."[98]

"Not everyone could be in the same position that we're in, being part of both the Christian and the mainstream worlds while maintaining a true relationship with God," said CeCe. "If I'm still standing, it's because of my upbringing. I can't take any credit for that."[99]

By 1997, BeBe and CeCe Winans had moved on to solo careers, a split that seemed amicable and one that for CeCe was both frightening and exciting. As she prepared to reach the pop/R&B market in a more focused and targeted way, this time recording for a pop label that also had CCM market distribution, Winans began to hone the message for her audience.

"Whether you are a believer or not," she said, "spirituality is real. It is something that every human can relate to, because we are all created from the same source. Believer or not, everybody has that God-space in their heart."[100]

BeBe's deal with Atlantic also allowed for separate distribution to the CCM market, and on his self-titled debut album as a solo artist, he was able to bring in big guns like Luther Vandross and Eric Clapton for musical help, and Denzel Washington, who directed the record's first video clip.

Like many other members of the new generation, BeBe rejected a segregated view of culture. "It's not who I am," he said. "God has people everywhere, and I'm honored that my music can be understood and service both Christian and non-Christian markets. . . . My songs can speak to both issues of love toward Him, but also about relationships and sex, because God is concerned about all those things."[101]

Julie Miller

When Leslie Phillips left CCM in 1987, she created a major void that needed to be filled immediately. Julie Miller was picked to fill the gap. A jet-black-haired, quirky, Cyndi Lauper soundalike, Miller had made her inauspicious debut singing a duet with an artist named Benny Hester on a soulful ballad called "Remember Me." It would be a few years before Myrrh discovered Miller and introduced her to the CCM market with a debut record simply titled *Meet Julie Miller*.

"When I first had the opportunity to be in gospel music, I was very hesitant, and actually for a few years rejected the notion," Miller remembered. "I wanted to be true to what Jesus wanted me to do, but I didn't want to alienate the people my heart was going out to. I was always like, 'What should I do God? What should I do?'"[102] She was overjoyed when she found a Bible verse, Isaiah 49:6, that she thought applied to the situation.

"I thought that the verse said, 'Is it too small a thing for you to do to help restore the tribes of Israel?' meaning the church, and I thought, *He wants me to sing to my brothers and sisters!* And I was so excited. The next day, I looked at the verse again and it said, 'It is too small a thing.' So it was like I had this promise that God was going to use my life, not just to my brothers and sisters, but also to the people who were unchurched and didn't know the Lord."[103]

Unfortunately for Miller and her calling, it would be nearly a decade before her music reached the ears of unbelievers as she slogged through three records for Myrrh and one for Street Level. Her career at Myrrh was not helped by Miller's insistence that a song called "S.O.S.—Sick of Sex," encouraging chastity no less, be included on her record. The CCM market didn't understand it, and soon Miller was out of her contract.

By 1997, however, Miller had landed a solo deal with the small, independent label Hightone, and released her first pop album, *Blue Pony*, to rave reviews by *Entertainment Weekly*.

Miller was finally where she swore she would be, in the midst of unbelievers.

My heart when I came to know Jesus was, "I've got to go back to the honky tonks and get my friends." That's our mission. . . . It's a matter of being sensitive to the audience this record is going out to, and finding common ground, finding the human emotions and struggle that everyone can relate to that's still there in myself. One thing that's always made me feel kinda bad is that gospel and Christian music . . . by putting itself under that label, instantly puts these barriers up to the general population that they think they're singing to. They're really singing to each other about getting saved.[104]

Looking back, it was not just the message that Miller felt got lost in her days in the CCM market, but her music as well. "I think that, musically, it's much easier to be myself in this place than it was in the Christian market," she said. "That market is very pop-centered musically, and when I started doing music, it was in bars in Austin, doing hippie-country-funky-blues-rock kinds of things. This is a lot closer to what I started out doing. But when I became a Christian and continued to do that style, nobody liked it. So I tried to find some styles where somebody might want to listen. This was musically and stylistically comfortable for me."[105]

Throughout her struggles in and out of CCM, Miller's faith remained vibrant, but she also had learned lessons that she wouldn't soon forget. "I do think that the more Christians have confidence in God and being who He created them to be, being truthful, real, honest, and vulnerable, I think that music will progress," she said. "We're not quite being real and honest, and we're people pleasing, and we're not God-pleasing in our art."[106]

On *Blue Pony*, Miller sang about life from her firmly entrenched Christian worldview and sought to bring in listeners who would never darken the door of a Christian bookstore. "I'm thinking of a certain audience, and they're not *700 Club* members," she said. "These songs, they're not my story, but they're stories from people in my family and people that I know. They're meant to say, 'I understand you.'"[107]

dc Talk

Another important voice in the rebellion against the status quo came from the members of dc Talk, a band that got its start at Jerry Falwell's Liberty University.

"Toby [McKeehan] and I were best friends back in college before we met Kevin," said Michael Tait. "We grew up in the same high school and in the same area."[108]

At Liberty, they met Kevin Smith and formed dc Talk.

Starting out as a rap band, they released several records for Forefront, the label founded by CCM rocker Ed DeGarmo, before their foray into grunge pop landed them a deal with Virgin Records that also included distribution of the band's records to Christian bookstores by Forefront.

In 1989, their first outing, titled *DC Talk*, showcased some juvenile but nonetheless high-energy rap that was distinguished by the amazing pipes of Michael Tait, who handled the singing when Toby McKeehan wasn't rapping.

By the time their second record, *Nu Thang*, was released in 1990, the group had managed to marry pop and rap in a manner similar to MC Hammer's hit singles "Pray" and "U Can't Touch This." But unlike Hammer, who seemed to stagnate musically, dc Talk had the chameleonlike ability to change with the times, and by the time their third record, *Free at Last* was released in 1992, they had abandoned the softer side of their pop sound in favor of a harder, more aggressive and more musical style that was characterized by their in-your-face rendition of the Doobie Brothers' "Jesus Is Just All Right," and a memorable ode to prison life, called "The Hardway."

In 1995, they completed their musical transformation from rap to hip-hop to grunge pop. It was a stunning turnabout, but dc Talk pulled it off brilliantly with one of the finest albums ever to emerge from the Christian subculture, called *Jesus Freak*. Unlike earlier efforts, where McKeehan seemed to be the dominant player in terms of production, songwriting, and performing, *Jesus Freak* showcased a fairly equal contribution from each of the members.

"More happens from Kevin and me on this album than any other album," said Michael Tait. "That's why we think *Jesus Freak* is that much more interesting. The quiet personalities, if you will, have finally spoken up. I wasn't into rap; I'm still not into rap. I've always sung. Nothing really in our past lent itself to that as much as *Free at Last* did, and now *Jesus Freak*. So it gave me more of a drive to want to write for this album and to want to be more involved."[109]

For those who believed the record was a cynical attempt to follow the trends, Tait offered this reply: "All of our music we describe as dc Talk music. You really can't put a label on it—that it is just rock, or pop, or R&B and soul. You have three individuals working together, and what comes out is what comes out. We all agree on the direction—definitely more on this album than on the other albums. *Jesus Freak*, as far as its direction, wasn't influenced more by anything in particular, other than we just all enjoy this style of music right now."[110]

"I think we have different things we want to say and we try to say them in different ways musically," said McKeehan. "I don't think we felt any type of a confinement as far as the way we chose to say things. I don't think there are any rules. We went into the studio with no formula this time and said musically whatever comes out comes out, keeping our same goal in mind to use our music to point people to God."[111]

"People see many portraits of dc Talk on this record," explained Kevin Smith. "The song 'Jesus Freak' is an aggressive portrait. dc Talk has always been very up-in-your-face about what we believe in and how we position ourselves as people. But I think that, musically, when people hear the rest of the record, they will understand more where we lie right now. We have not gone down the road to alternative grunge as much as they think we have. We are trying to face who we are. We're a strange band, let's just face it. We come from three different backgrounds musically. We've all kind of latched on to the alternative thing in the last two years, but none of us are alternative grunge listeners. That is not what we'd want this band to be."[112]

As their deal with Virgin showed, dc Talk was not content to languish in the subculture, yet their music contained not a hint of compromise with the world that they sought to be a part of. On "Jesus Is Just All Right," they had sung, "If Christ can't be crossed over, I'll keep my beat-up Nova," but, as it turned out, Christ could be crossed over because their album *Jesus Freak* became a hit on the pop charts, spawning the hit single "Between You and Me."[113]

Though they gave Forefront the right to sell records to Christian bookstores as part of their deal with Virgin, much of the band members' rhetoric questioned the existence of CCM. "I think it is unnatural to my spirit to want to segregate what we have," said Kevin Smith. "Why segregate something that is almost like food to the hungry? . . . It is unnatural to want to put faith in a box and make it a club."[114]

"We have a lot to say, but don't want to say it to just the Christian world," said Michael Tait. "That's such a small, small part of the big picture. We've always wanted to take our music to the masses, and Virgin is going to be able to get our music to places that a Christian label sometimes couldn't. We want to be able to affect people. We know music can't change the world, but God through music can."[115]

"We want to make it very, very plain that the Christian market is the base of everything we do," said Tait, assuring the CCM audience that they would not leave their faith behind. "That's our foundation. But we believe in the Great Commission. We take it literally. We're not going to change our message. This just gives us a larger platform."[116]

Tait echoed Smith. "To me, that is the Great Commission: To go into the world, and not be of the world, but in the world, because you physically are. You have no choice. And so when we do music, it is great if Christians enjoy it. It is great if it encourages them along in their walk and it changes their lives. But Jesus didn't hang out in the churches all the time. He hung out in the weird places and He hung out with people who were ostracized by society, and the freaks, because they were the ones that needed to hear. He tried His best to understand their culture, to walk in their culture, but to shed light on all they were missing out on."[117]

The strongest opinion on the subject predictably came from the band's most outspoken member, Toby McKeehan, who seemed genuinely befuddled by the CCM concept. "It doesn't make sense," he said. "It never made sense to us. We have always wanted to go out and tell the world. If you find something good that works in your life, you want to share it with people that don't know about it. Why are you sharing it with people that do know about it?[118] It has always been our goal for our music to be on a level where we're recognized by the world for the simple fact that we believe we have a message to share."[119]

In 1998, dc Talk followed up *Jesus Freak* with a solid effort, *Supernatural*, which though lacking the vision and power of *Jesus Freak* nonetheless won accolades from cultural outposts not typically given to praising the work of serious Christians. *Supernatural* was met with glowing reviews from *Rolling Stone* and *Guitar Magazine*, among others, and the *Los Angeles Times*, in a story titled "At a Crossroads, dc Talk Keeps the Faith," noted that the band "remains true to its spiritual roots as its popularity grows."[120]

In spite of dc Talk's progress at gaining the attention of the popular music culture, nearly all of their tours featured opening acts from the CCM market and seemed to be geared primarily toward and attended by Christian teens. In press materials provided by their new label home, Virgin, they were consistently referred to as "Christian music" stars, something that was completely inconsistent with the band's wishes. "We never wanted to just sing or write songs for people that agree with us," said McKeehan. "We wanted to catch the ears of the whole world and fall on open ears. We don't want to be promoted and marketed any differently."[121]

Nevertheless, dc Talk soldiered on, empowered by a desire to communicate their deep, Christian convictions to a generation that was hungry for transcendent faith.

"Our job is to focus on making great art," said McKeehan. "When I write a song, my faith comes out, and if that moves you in some way, that's great. But we're not trying to stuff it down people's throats by any means. We want to encourage people to think about where they stand, but not be preachy about it. We're not ordained ministers . . . by no means do we have it all together. We struggle with human inadequacy and believe that we can be more responsible as role models if we talk about what we're thinking and how vulnerable we can be."[122]

PFR

When producer Brown Bannister, best known for his work with Amy Grant, launched his own CCM label, Vireo, in the early 1990s, one of the first bands out of his gate was a group of three Minnesotans who called themselves Pray For Rain. In an industry poll taken by the trade magazine *CCM Update* in 1993, Pray For Rain was voted by rival record executives as the band other labels most wished they had signed. The group was led by vocalist and guitarist Joel Hanson, who had been the music leader at a camp where he met up with his two bandmates, Patrick Andrew and Mark Nash.

Their first record sold moderately, but their sophomore release, *Goldie's Last Day*, hit the top of the CCM charts. PFR, as they came to be known when another Pray For Rain threatened to sue, expanded the bounds of what could be sung about on a hit record. In the process, they caused people to question the definition of CCM, which historically had been a haven for people who wanted to sing "religious" music. To this group of artists, no topic was off limits, as they proved with their song about Andrew's favorite canine.

"My dog passed away, we had to put her to sleep," he said. "She had cancer. On her last day, I just wanted a picture of Goldie, and I have this blue Plymouth Volare wagon. We put Goldie at the driver's wheel of my car and took some pictures of her. I told these guys about it and we started writing this song—it just started flowing out of us."[123]

The song was a melancholy look at the life of Goldie the dog, with the catchy refrain, "Wish you coulda been there for Goldie's last day."[124] There were no spiritual allegories made, no references to life after death, it was just a fun/sad song about life in the real world, where dogs usually die long before their human best friends. As the song climbed to the top of the CCM charts, it called into question what was and was not a "Christian" song, and whether the distinctions even mattered anymore.

Then, suddenly, despite their status in the upper echelons of CCM, and though they were poised to cross over to the pop world, PFR's last day followed close on the heels of Goldie's.

"Because of being gone so much on the road, I hadn't been to church in four months," said drummer Mark Nash. "I was kind of starving spiritually. I was trying to sort that out: Was it my fault because I wasn't finding things on the road to keep me up, or was it the band? If I wasn't in the band, would I be in a higher place spiritually getting beat up? I was just sorting that out and asking those questions of myself."[125]

The other members felt similarly, and to the horror of their record company, the band quit after the release of their next album, *Them*, which rose to the top of the charts. Of course, the decision was not made without trepidation. "The paychecks stop when we stop playing," said Patrick. "That is a scary thing, but I don't think that we can let that direct our lives or rule us. God has always provided, even before this band. I've always had food in my mouth even when I was living in my car, even if it was a can of tuna. He's always been there. I don't think He'd fail me now."[126]

For Hanson, the move was about living life to its fullest: "What I'm becoming the most afraid of is that I don't want to look back and go, 'I didn't live. I didn't experience this abundant life that God has offered me.'"[127]

"I'm sure you haven't heard the last of us," said Andrew. "Maybe not all together, but there is more to come."[128]

Though some of the members later regrouped in other bands, PFR's greatest contribution to the ongoing debate was their magical song about Goldie the pooch, which showed a generation of young CCM fans that rock bands comprised of Christians could sing about anything, and that this was entirely proper in the eyes of God.

Dakoda Motor Company

In 1993, a band emerged on the Myrrh label, which was not exactly known for signing daring acts, that would question much of the CCM establishment and raise some important questions. Led by Peter King, San Diego-based Dakoda Motor Company was quickly formed when King's older brother, David, of the band Mary's Danish, told Peter that if he assembled a band, they could open for his.

After gaining valuable experience opening for Mary's Danish, Dakoda inked a deal with Myrrh and released two records, *Into the Son* and *Welcome Race Fans*, which showcased their brand of high-energy alternative surf rock and landed them a spot opening for the aging rockers Petra, playing Christian venues in addition to nightclubs.

In 1996, King switched labels to his brother's Holiday label, which was owned by Atlantic. "We always from the get-go were trying to get a major record deal," said King. "We just got so busy working within the Christian market that we never really pursued many showcases outside of that."[129]

King later took a giant stride out of the subculture by himself, becoming an MTV personality and hosting various programs for the channel. Once he was on the inside, he discovered that much of CCM's rhetoric, which often was used to explain why their videos were never played on the channel, was not true.

"There were some artists in the Christian industry a couple of years ago saying, 'Oh MTV isn't playing our videos because we're Christians,'" said King, "but that was a lie. Yeah, I'll say these things and I'll take the heat, but everyone knows that it's true. I know these people; they are playing whatever is a hit. . . . Jars of Clay is on MTV because they've got a gold record and their song is an absolute hit. That's the only reason. Nobody cares if they're Christian or not. MTV will take a chance on a band they like."[130]

Larger questions centered around King's involvement with the channel, something not a few fans from the CCM world were unhappy about. "I go and play a Christian show and get asked, 'How can you work at evil MTV?'" said King. "I just think, 'You don't know who I work with. You're making a judgment about somebody you know nothing about.' Is there anyone more arrogant and annoying than Christians? . . . I don't think MTV is evil. I think it is a radio showing pictures. MTV does not have an agenda like people think they do. They definitely have some liberal hosts, and I would say MTV News is very liberal. But you would be surprised—(MTV veejay) Kennedy goes out and speaks against abortion all the time. The people I work with are the nicest, most respectable kinds of people I have ever met. They are totally supportive of everything I am into."[131]

As King entered the rock market, appearing on MTV and recording for Atlantic with gusto, his vision began to expand. "We are just trying our hardest to be a really good rock band; that's our goal . . . to have a lot of musical integrity—I mean, obviously, no tracks or any of that crud," he said of the tendency of some CCM artists to perform with prerecorded music. "It shouldn't even be an issue, but it is, because in this Christian industry we see a lot of that, which just grosses us out. A lack of integrity. What I call *queso*, which is Spanish for cheese."[132]

King also admitted to what was sometimes denied in CCM circles where people were quick to say that what they were doing was ministry and not business and that the two were somehow mutually exclusive: "We are trying to make money," he declared. "We make no bones about it. I don't think that's a bad thing. 'The worker is worth his wages.' We want to be worth that fifteen bucks that someone spends on our CD. We don't want to rip people off. We want to be for sale everywhere and allow everyone the opportunity to dislike Dakoda."[133]

Though King had no qualms about selling music, the selling of Jesus troubled him. "We don't go in as our marketing standpoint and say that we're gonna preach about Jesus, and we're using the music as a weapon to trick the kids," he said. "We are not the Jesus cheerleading squad that comes into town jumping up and down saying, 'We love Jesus, how about you? Which side of the crowd loves Jesus more, let's hear you roar!' and then realize that that sells about $2,000 more worth of T-shirts a night. I can't do that, I can't sell Jesus out like that. It is too easy and it is gross."[134]

King's dislike of the "Jesus Cheer" also applied to the pressure he felt from some audiences to talk about his faith from the stage. "Jesus is not a light subject matter and shouldn't be dealt with as such," he said. "So not only should we not be expected on stage to callously talk about Jesus, but audience members shouldn't be yelling out, 'Talk about Jesus more!' like it's a bubble gum thing. A relationship with Christ is such an emotional and deep thing; how ironic that people would cheapen it to the point where they put a formula to it and expect you to sing in a trite way a couple of Jesus slangs. What kind of box do they have Jesus in? I have got to be true and I can't treat God so lightly and with so much disrespect, personally."[135]

The bottom line, according to King, was that it was money, not hatred of Christians, that moved popular music. "A lot of people think, 'Oh, you're on a secular label, you can't talk about Jesus,'" said King, "but nobody at the label cares about that. That is a myth. They just want you to sell records. Atlantic is jazzed for us. They let us do what we want to do and say what we want to say."[136]

Dakota's lead singer, Melissa Brewer, agreed. "It's not like secular labels have this huge agenda, that they want to make everybody evil or corrupt people. They want to take your money," she said. "They don't care what you say, [or] if you say 'Jesus' in your songs."[137]

"I don't think there should be Christian record companies any more than there should be Christian doctors associations that only cater to Christians," added bassist Derek Toy.[138]

Summing up Dakota's philosophy, King asked, "Why are there 'Christian bands' then? Because it is a marketing ploy, that's why. Because a lot of the Christian industry exists to market and sell Jesus, and that is disgusting. I think so, and you think so, and everybody thinks so, but we don't say it and we're always trying to pretend like we're not really doing that. I don't care if you're Jewish, Buddhist, black, white, green, Mormon, Christian or not, I want to play Dakoda's music for you and I want this music to impact your life. Not because I'm selfish, but because I want you to dig my music. I mean, that's why we do this."[139]

Though King and his bandmates seemed to have a keen understanding of the CCM industry, in their zeal to be considered "just another band," they may have underestimated the power of music—which generations of black gospel singers understood—to move the soul in the direction of the God they believed in.

"I just don't see rock music as a powerful Christian ministry," said King. "I really don't. Rock 'n' roll, as far as I'm concerned, is just rock 'n' roll, and I love it for what it is. I don't think there's anything wrong with that."[140]

True to that philosophy, by the time of Dakoda's third release, *Railroad*, any mention of faith—oblique or otherwise—was completely stripped away from the music. The resulting album, while not in any way offensive to a person of faith, seemed nonetheless powerless to move and inspire, because it lacked the undergirding pillar of faith. The songs were about life, but by failing to note the dimension of the spiritual, even in passing, *Railroad* was just another alternative surf record by just another band.

Kirk Franklin

In 1993, a young singer named Kirk Franklin signed a recording contract with an obscure independent label called Gospocentric. After releasing his debut album, *Kirk Franklin and the Family*, he watched the record hit the gospel charts and cross over to the R&B charts. Franklin was another in a growing group of artist Christians who refused to stay in the Christian subculture, but his assault on the pop music world was just beginning.

Raised in Dallas by an aunt, Franklin never knew his father and was abandoned at a young age by his mother. By the age of four, he was playing the piano, and seven years later was leading the adult choir at Mt. Rose Baptist Church. When he tired of being the goody-goody church kid, Franklin began to run with a fast and wild crowd, until one of his fifteen-year-old buddies was shot and killed. Returning to the church, Franklin eventually began a recording career.

In Franklin, some observers saw fulfilled the unfulfilled promises of
stars like Sam Cooke, Andrae Crouch, BeBe Winans, Marvin Gaye, and Al
Green. Unlike Cooke and Gaye, Franklin would not bow to those who
wanted him to either separate his gospel music from his "secular" work or
shut down the "gospel" side altogether. Instead, Franklin developed a worldview and a philosophy that integrated art and ministry, and the pop music
culture ultimately benefited.

"An entertainer is someone who moves the crowd," said Franklin. "A
minister is someone who moves the soul, but at the same time he moves the
crowd. . . . Some Christians are so deep they think, 'Oh, he's an entertainer,
he's going to hell,' but when people are paying ten or fifteen dollars to come
see you, you have to minister *and* entertain. When you're ministering to
them, you have to make them laugh, smile, to touch their hearts. That's also
entertainment. But there are different levels of entertainment. I'm trying to
entertain them, but have them leave saying, 'Man, I never knew the church
could be like that. I never knew that God could be that loving.'"[141]

For Franklin, entertainment was one way to the heart of an unbeliever.
"You entertain them to move them into the ministry," he said. "They work
hand in hand. . . . People of different faiths walk up to me and tell me that
the music just moves them and inspires them. That's a step. If they're listening to the music, in God's time they may even listen to the message of the
Word. You have to plant the seed. Apollos watered the seed, but it was God
who gave the increase."[142]

Unlike Al Green and Andrae Crouch, Franklin refused to be relegated
to the religious music ghetto. In a controversial move, he recorded an album
with his group, God's Property, on the B-Rite label, in partnership with
Interscope Records, which was known for its association with Gangster rap
labels. Franklin was unmoved by criticism.

"All Christian labels have affiliations with secular labels," he said. "The
people at Interscope are trying to get away from their association with Death
Row, and they wanna get into some good stuff. The Bible says that God uses
the foolish to confound the wise, and that's what I'm gonna be doing.
Interscope has more money, so I can take my message further."[143]

Franklin's album, titled *God's Property featuring Kirk Franklin*, hit the
number three position on the pop charts and produced a chart-busting single, "Stomp," that was featured prominently on MTV. The album was marketed by Interscope whiz Jimmy Iovine as an R&B record, thus avoiding the
damaging gospel or CCM label that had spiked so many records before.

Franklin clearly had a long road ahead of him, and if history was any indication, the odds against him maintaining his faith in the midst of all the pop music culture had to offer were not good. Perhaps mindful of this, Franklin surrounded himself with people who knew him inside and out, and who would keep him accountable, he insisted.

"It helps being around people you started with," he said. "They know you from back when. Everybody in my crew, they're the same people I had when I had nothing. The guy that manages me is the guy that, when I was seventeen and eighteen, I used to sleep in his church when I didn't have a place to live. I keep it all close to home. I have a pastor that reminds me that, 'Brother, you ain't all that,' said Franklin. "I'm thankful that on Sunday morning he treats me just like everybody else. It's no special thing. I need that."[144]

Most of all, Franklin knew Franklin. "I know the Kirk that y'all don't know," he maintained. "I know the Kirk with all his screw-ups and mistakes, and all the things he's done in his past that should've stopped him from having all that God has given him. When you know yourself like that, you are so humbled, worthy only of praising Him. I let Him know, 'You didn't have to do all this for me, and I'm gonna do my best not to let you down.'"[145]

Jars of Clay

In 1995, when a group of college students calling itself Jars of Clay released its self-titled album on the tiny Essential Records label, nobody had any idea the record would produce a Top 40 song, with airplay across the country on both pop and alternative radio.

The four members of Jars—Matt Odmark, Dan Haseltine, Steve Mason, and Charlie Lowell—met at Greenville College, an evangelical institution that numbered nine hundred students. Taken from a Bible verse that used the analogy of treasures hidden in jars of clay to illustrate God's Spirit being infused through salvation into the frail bodies of men, Lowell thought it a good name to keep the band members humble—and humility would be needed in generous amounts very shortly.

Responding to an ad for a talent contest in a magazine, the group submitted a demo and eventually won the grand prize, playing before a crowd of executives and fans in Nashville in early 1994. CCM labels were soon swarming over the band looking to make deals.

Returning to Greenville, Jars members began to field phone calls on their dorm pay phone from executives eager to sign this talented band.

"Initially, what I saw in Jars of Clay was four guys, with extremely innocent spirits, [who] didn't fully realize the magnitude of their talent and the gifts that God had given them," remembered Robert Beeson, who signed them to his label, Essential. "They approached music from the heart, as opposed to formulas. They cut through the clutter, in that there was nothing else like them."[146]

Jars biggest break came when an intern at Essential delivered a copy of the group's demo to her uncle—who happened to be Adrian Belew, a prolific songwriter and guitarist, famous for his work with David Bowie, Nine Inch Nails, and King Crimson, among others.

Most of the songs on the group's debut record like "Love Song for a Savior" and "He" were self-produced, and while pleasant, they lacked the pure magic of the two Belew produced songs—"Liquid," and the song that would capture American pop and alternative radio, "Flood."

Belew created a lush, ethereal music bed for both tracks, "Liquid" detailing the crucifixion story and "Flood" subtly using the story of the biblical character Noah, with references to rain, floods, and forty days, to describe a slide into and up out of crippling depression. The song culminated in the chorus, "Lift me up, when I'm falling."

"Flood's" success propelled the album onto the pop charts where it remained in the Billboard Top 200 for fifty-two consecutive weeks, eventually selling two million copies.

Although they couldn't have orchestrated that success, which was partly due to the pop label Zomba's purchase of Essential, Jars of Clay was a band that clearly did not buy into the CCM paradigm. "I think God has really shown us and taught us a lot about how, for Jars of Clay, it's really a platform that doesn't necessarily find its entire life within the Christian marketplace," said lead singer Dan Haseltine. "We've tried really hard to break that separation of Christian band and mainstream band, because as far as we're concerned, there really shouldn't be that separation. We don't want our music to be just for the Christian marketplace."[147]

Jars of Clay set out to do nothing less than "reshape Christian music." "Is it proper to sacrifice art for ministry?" asked Haseltine. "I think the conclusion is pretty simple—it's not. I think God calls us to do the best with our abilities and to be relevant with style. It seems the Christian industry has been somewhat stagnant in developing creative artists. I think God gives you the gifts; you just have to use them."[148]

To Haseltine, as the culture reached a point of near total secularism, the doors to a band like his flew wide open. "I think a lot of people really see where society is going," he said. "For awhile there hasn't been much to base anything on as far as making decisions and having people to follow. It is like we have gotten to this bare bones society, where everybody has to start making decisions on their own again, and they are looking for ways to make educated decisions. Spirituality can definitely provide a backbone for a moral standard and reasons for having a certain lifestyle."[149]

The bottom line, according to Jars, was that the gospel was all about getting out of the subculture. Staying true to that vision, they ventured outside of the tried and true CCM formula of bands playing large, youth-group-type functions and ventured out into the club scene where real, live, non-Christians tended to go to hear music. Beginning at the House of Blues and the Roxy in L.A., Jars ventured out on the road with opening acts like the Samples, the Gufs, Duncan Sheik, and Matchbox 20. Touring with bands that didn't share the faith was a taboo for most in the CCM world, but Jars was unlike most other bands, and they later used their hard won success to gain the coveted slot on Sting's world tour.

For their second album, *Much Afraid*, the band recruited Steve Lipson, producer to artists like Annie Lenox, Prefab Sprout, and Simple Minds, and recorded a solid record that debuted at number eight on the Billboard pop album chart.

"It is good to see music getting spiritual and getting people to be aware of it, because that is going to open doors," said Haseltine. "It has for us, and I think it will continue to open doors for other Christians to get in there and to give them a chance to share their faith. People are coming to our shows in bars and clubs and getting a glimpse of Christianity, and seeds are being planted. That is real important."[150]

MxPx

Another band that emerged in the pop market out of the CCM field was a group named Magnified Plaid, which eventually shortened its name to MxPx. Mike Herrera, Tom Wisniewski, and Yuri Riley, teenage punkers from Seattle, garnered attention when they opened a show in their hometown for the Sex Pistols and made albums with songs like "Chick Magnet," "My Mom Still Cleans My Room," and "Today Is in My Way."

In addition to their unique brand of punk music, MxPx showcased a certain whimsical attitude, unlike many of their CCM forefathers, that showed they didn't take themselves too seriously. The band's name was a case in point. While many artists prided themselves on choosing group names with deep theological meaning, like Second Chapter of Acts, Point of Grace, or 4Him, MxPx had no such pretentiousness.

"The name is kind of a joke," explained band leader Herrera. "It was a T-shirt (friend) Andy had. It was, like, a big plaid design, and one of our friends called it 'Andy's magnification plaid shirt.' We liked the name and give it to the band. . . . Then the name got shortened to Magnified Plaid when we officially named the band. Finally we abbreviated it to MxPx."[151]

Although the three members are definitely Christians, the term "Christian music" was not one they chose for themselves. "It's kind of weird," explained Herrera, "because we're Christians and everybody knows we're Christians, but a lot of times because of where Christian music has been, saying that we're a 'Christian band' makes people prejudge what they think of us."[152]

Unlike many of their musical forefathers, Herrera and MxPx didn't feel comfortable playing in churches. "I'm just not into playing sanctuaries," he maintained. "I don't really think that's the place to have a show. . . . We don't wanna spit on the floor or mess anything up."[153]

Herrera also made an important distinction on the issue of music as ministry, a point of confusion in many CCM circles. "I guess we're ministers in the fact that God uses us and that every Christian is called to minister in some way, but I don't consider myself a preacher or anything," he said. "We just don't feel called to be like that. There are so many bands that do that. . . . I don't think there's anything wrong with having diversity. Not everything should be the same."[154]

Herrera unequivocally rejected the mantle of spiritual teacher or minister that artist Christians often found placed on their shoulders. "MxPx is just a band which plays music," he said, "and music really isn't all that important in life when it comes down to it. What is important is the decisions you make. . . . We're not here to do it for you, just because we play music."[155]

In 1997, following the lead of dc Talk, which had engineered a similar deal with Virgin and Forefront, MxPx signed a deal that made them A&M artists for the pop market and Tooth and Nail artists for the CCM market. The first album to emerge from this arrangement was *Slowly Going the Way of the Buffalo*, which the band supported by joining an all-star cast of rock bands, like Bad Religion, Rancid, and Less Than Jake, on tour. Herrera's response to tour mates like Bad Religion was far different from the typical responses that had come from early CCM artists like DeGarmo and Key:

> Bad Religion influences thousands of kids to hate God. I went to its show in Seattle. It felt so evil. And it's not that the guys in the band

are evil or anything—they're nice guys who just don't know God. And if we're asked to be on a tour like that, God is using us. . . . None of the guys in the band believe in God, but Greg Graffin, the lead singer, really doesn't believe. He thought it was funny that we were Christians. He's thirty-five, a college biology professor, and we're these little kids in a punk rock band! So he'd made little jokes. Somebody would come into the dressing room and he'd say, "The boys were just leading us in a word of prayer." Then on a flight from Switzerland to New York he'd say, "I guess we're not gonna go down—we've got you guys on board!" Most of the time it was funny, but other times it kinda stung.[156]

Later, conversations with the band turned serious. "They'd be asking us what we believe, if we really prayed and read the Bible," remembered Herrera. "One time Greg Hetson asked Yuri to pray for his wife and kids because they were sick. So they seemed to have an open mind. Our faith was interesting to them. . . . That whole experience made us focus more on God. We want to do what's right. I mean, we care about those guys as people and they don't know God. So it made us more conscious about what we did and what we said."[157]

Slowly Going the Way of the Buffalo continued MxPx's tradition of mixing songs about everyday life with expressions of faith.

"Tunes like 'The Final Slowdance' (a love song that suggests 'no one wants to spend eternity alone') and 'Party, My House, Be There' (which opposes substance abuse by its noticeable absence in a party anthem) focus on a desire for community and divine-human contact," noted critic Brian Quincy Newcomb. "The positive values expressed in these songs and the rest of the record should not be undervalued. Mike Herrera sings in 'Tomorrow's Another Day,' 'God is faithful even if you don't have faith in yourself.'"[158]

Nearly a decade younger than dc Talk or Jars of Clay, MxPx represented the next step in the rebellion of modern-day American Christian kids who refused to be relegated to the corner of the culture, and Herrera was their spokesman. "We'd like Christians to be the standard, not the minority," he said, "more accepted and less weird. And so we get to go out in these larger circles and throw in our ideas, and that's what'll influence and change people's minds. As a band, we want to contribute to everyone—not just Christians. . . . We love playing, we love being on tour, and we love talking to kids. From the very beginning, we didn't really play 'Christian' or 'secular' shows. We didn't realize there was a difference, kind of like when you go to high school and there are all different kinds of students, but they all go to the same school."[159]

Sixpence None the Richer

Long before its song "Kiss Me" climbed to the top of the American pop charts, in the early 1990s, an Austin, Texas-based group that called itself Sixpence None the Richer was signed to the tiny Nashville-based independent CCM label REX. Formed in New York by a young heavy metal fan named Doug Mann, REX had been purchased by a South African expat named Gavin Morkel, who quickly signed dozens of artists to the label.

"Leigh and I met in high school," recalled Matt Slocum, who together with singer Leigh Nash formed the nucleus of the group. "We went to the same school and church. I really liked her voice and asked her to do this vocal on a song I wrote. She agreed and we put it down on this little four track I had. I printed up 200 copies and sent them out to friends. It ended up getting passed through the hands of this guy who had a small independent label. We had a deal before we even had an actual band."[160]

Like King's X before them, Sixpence was another band that was strongly influenced by British writer C. S. Lewis. Slocum had taken the band name from a Lewis book that compared man's feeble attempts to give back to God to a child's request of six pennies from a father in order to buy the father a gift.

Young kids active in church, it was only natural for Slocum and Nash to take their music to the CCM world. Like most young Christians with musical aspirations, it was the only road they knew of. "When I was 14 . . . I felt like Christian music was what I should be doing to best express my faith," said Slocum. "I got into it and quickly realized that it wasn't. Once the band got into it, we realized it was a confining thing."[161]

For REX, the band produced two solid albums, *The Fatherless and the Widow* and the mesmerizing *This Beautiful Mess*. Before long, Morkel and REX were in financial distress, and after unloading another promising band, Fleming and John, to Universal, the entire catalog, including Sixpence, was sold to the Platinum label, a move that was not appreciated by Slocum and the band.

"In February of '97 we were being prevented legally from making any music," recalled Slocum. "We were making this record underground and the band was just totally unhappy. . . . The morale was extremely low. The record deal we had sucked, so we recorded this record in defiance of that whole thing."[162]

"This record" referred to the group's groundbreaking self-titled record that was released on Steve Taylor's newly formed Squint record label. "He's a producer, songwriter and filmmaker," said Slocum of Taylor. "I went to him for help because I didn't know what to do. The band was on the verge of a breakup and that would've been the end of it. . . .We had such a close relationship with him and knew that he was an artist and would understand our point of view. He was really good at putting together a good record deal for us."[163]

With Squint positioned in the pop marketplace as a "regular" record label and Sixpence as unhyphenated artists, reviewers soon filled pages with superlatives. "It's not very often that you discover an album that captivates you the way the self-titled release from the modern pop band Sixpence None The Richer does," raved *CDNOW* reviewer Greg Carpenter. "It's refreshing to hear one that is able to add so many distinctive earmarks to its music without sounding overblown or self-absorbed," noted the respected alternative music journal *CMJ*.[164]

Even before their chart success, Sixpence had caused controversy in the Christian subculture by accepting a slot on the Lilith Fair tour that included artists like Bonnie Raitt, Paula Cole, Shawn Colvin, and the Indigo Girls, but was sometimes criticized because of its celebration of the mythical Lilith figure.

Singer Leigh Nash welcomed the chance to play her music for non-CCM audiences. "Non-Christians tend to find our music hopeful," said Nash, "and people who don't know we are Christians respond to the lyrics and ask, 'So what's going on?' and we can talk about it. It's sad," added Nash of criticism from fellow believers critical of the Lilith involvement. "Really, because people in the mainstream music community, they've been the kindest people. They know our music and where we are coming from. There is not this taboo for being Christians. The taboo is with the Christian audience."[165]

For Matt Slocum, Sixpence's mission was clear: to position the band as a band—period—and make music that would keep their old fans in the Christian world and bring in new ones who may not agree with the band members' faith.

"There are a lot of stereotypes attached to doing Christian music and it exists in its own little world a lot of the time," he said. "I realized early on that I am a Christian and it's my faith, but I really don't want to play music to a certain group of people. I would really like to embrace the world at large. We got into that situation and made a lot of fans. We don't want to deny that was such a huge help in shaping us. On the other hand, we'd like to move beyond that into other areas."[166]

Dave Palmer, a Squint executive, articulated what has come to be the collective vision of a new generation of Christians who no longer accept the status quo. "What this means to us is fulfilling what we set out to do as a company," he said, "and what the band set out to do personally and professionally: to impact our culture by being a part of it."[167]

"We're really thankful of the place we've come to and the place we're going and I hope people can realize that we're not just a one song band," added Slocum. "There is a lot more to this band and I hope that is a relationship we can develop over the next three to five years. I want to let people know who we are as a band and that we go a lot deeper than just 'Kiss Me.' Hopefully, we can really meet people through this song and develop a deeper relationship through our music."[168]

NINE

Second Thoughts

*I*t wasn't just young artists like Jars of Clay and MxPx who were questioning the CCM arrangement. To their credit, many industry veterans,
including some executives, were also raising objections. One who publicly
questioned what the great Christian retreat accomplished had himself been
a pioneering CCM artist. For nearly thirty years, John Fischer recorded for
the market and authored numerous books and columns for *CCM* magazine.
Over the years, Fischer consistently questioned the legitimacy of CCM. As
he began increasingly to question many of his own earlier assumptions, no
one captured the plight of the artist caught between two worlds as succinctly
as he did when he wrote in 1996:

> We started trying to save the world and ended up trying to get a
> record contract, find out what Christians wanted, justify ourselves to
> the First Baptist Church. Somewhere along the line, we compro-
> mised and took the easier safe road. We listened, even though we
> knew better, to those who said that, if we were Christians, our music
> was going to have to be Christian music, and what we came up with
> was restrained, contained, and stifled. We listened to those who said
> our music must be sacrificed on an altar. It must take second place.
> And thinking we only had one heart to give, we gave half of it to the
> Lord and half of it to music, and both came out halfhearted. We
> knew better. When the Lord is in your heart, you can give all of it
> to everything you do. We listened even when we knew better when

they said that a Christian could never be popular with the world. We'd have to sacrifice too much and compromise too much to get there. So we settled back into second best where it was safe, where we didn't have to deal with our egos, while we pampered them and gave glory to God. As soon as we all realized we were playing only for Christians, we no longer had to compete with the Knopflers, the Claptons and the Dylans. In fact, when we played our best licks, we got criticized for not ministering. It seemed pointless to extend ourselves, and so, even though we knew better, we gave up being the best.[1]

Stan Moser was another top executive who added his voice to the growing chorus of second thoughts. Moser began his career at Word in 1970 and before the decade was over had become the president of the company and a leader of the emerging industry. He was also the executive responsible for signing Amy Grant. By the time he retired in 1996, he had spent twenty-six years shaping CCM at its highest levels.

"In the '70s, we were on a mission from God," Moser told *Christianity Today*. "We had no choice but to communicate the gospel. Now we've built our careers, we've built our ministries, we've built our houses, we've built our companies and we've sold them at great profit. We've made money and now we're accountable to make more money for the new owners. In many cases, we are creating music because it's time to create more music. But to be candid, I look at the majority of the music I hear today and think it's virtually meaningless."[2]

Moser and Fischer were not the only ones who had been questioning the very premise of CCM. Others had been writing and speaking on the issue far earlier. Billy Sprague, once part of the mighty Reunion Records roster and a popular artist, began to express doubts about what he was doing early on. "Why is it that our society and even a majority of Christians are not familiar with the growing number of Christian musicians churning out hundreds of albums a year?" Sprague wondered in a 1988 guest editorial in *CCM* magazine. "I rejoice at the growth of Christian music as an artistic expression over the last fifteen years. There is much to be applauded. But I lament the fact that Christian music does not penetrate our society like it could."[3]

One of CCM's earliest and most important writers was Pat Terry, who made waves as an artist with his band, the Pat Terry Group, and as a songwriter, writing hits for artists like B. J. Thomas. After many years in CCM, Terry retired to his native Georgia and left active recording and touring, but continued to lament what he saw in the subculture.

When I first started writing, I didn't want to be in the gospel music business. In fact most of the artists that got started during the Jesus Music movement in the '70s would say the same thing. I don't think any of our concepts were that we wanted to be the new gospel music. If anything, we were reacting against gospel in the '70s and saying, "Hey, we want to communicate our faith in a way that kind of crosses those religious borders and can address truthful things in truthful ways, and especially regarding our faith." Now that is what gospel music is. . . . In its formative years, there was a lot of honesty and a kind of commitment that's different from what I see today—there wasn't all the trappings of an industry. It was really about communication in the most bare, even crude, sort of way sometimes, but it really connected with people; and unlike any other genre of music, contemporary gospel has forgotten its roots.[4]

Reed Arvin, another veteran of the scene who wrote and produced for a number of artists, including Amy Grant and Michael W. Smith, observed in a 1990 essay that those who were serious about reaching the culture needed to rethink their assumptions. "The musical and lyrical elements in obtaining airplay on Christian format radio stations are narrow and well understood," he wrote. "These stations rightfully cater to their established audiences. For the music minister attempting to make good his promise to reach out to the unsaved world, however, conventional music ministry approaches become less and less relevant to an audience that no longer even understands the vocabulary of faith. The truth is that we have been singing lovely songs to ourselves, and the world not only hasn't been listening, it hasn't even known we've been singing."[5]

Amazingly, according to Arvin, CCM musicians rarely listened to fellow artists. "Most consumers of this music would be surprised to learn that the people who make that music tend not to listen to it themselves; the awful truth is we find it musically and lyrically unsatisfying, with certain exceptions. In my eight years of involvement in the Christian music business, I have seen my peers really excited about a new Christian record at the most five or six times."[6]

To Emmy award-winning television executive Bob Briner, who took a strong interest in the subculture after his retirement from the TV world, the issue was simply a failure of Christians to show up. "Shameful," he noted. "We have failed and are failing America. I am sorry. In failing to show up in the places that really count, where the moral, ethical and spiritual health of our country is concerned, we have left our country exposed and vulnerable to all the ills we now see besetting it. We have not provided a way of escape, even though we profess to know the way."[7]

Looking back on thirty years of cultural segregation, one can only wonder how different popular culture would be today had the Christians who comprised the group Love Song accepted Ahmet Ertegun's offer to record for Atlantic Records instead of signing with the CCM label Good News; or if Keith Green had signed with Clive Davis instead of with Billy Ray Hearn and Sparrow.

These, to be sure, are the exceptions that prove the rule, because the rock culture was sometimes intolerant of songs with Christian themes, as artists like Bob Dylan and Kerry Livgren of Kansas found out after their conversions. Nevertheless, the example set by Dylan, Livgren, Donna Summer, and others—of artists experiencing religious conversions and sticking around to tell the world about it—is increasingly carrying the day. The wall separating serious faith and popular music is crumbling as more and more rock stars who experience such conversions refuse to quit their bands and jump into CCM, as in the recent cases of Lou Gramm of Foreigner and Alice Cooper.

Not only are well-known artists refusing to be lost in the CCM world, so are new artists who want to avoid cultural marginalization at all costs.

Records by recent artists like Hanson, Collective Soul, Creed, Judson Spence, the Tories, Full on the Mouth, Burlap to Cashmere, and many others are emerging from artists that would, in the not too distant past, have been ushered into the CCM market.

A clear indication of the power of this surge in Christian involvement in pop music came when Eric Clapton's "Change the World" received a Grammy for record of the year. Clapton's track was written by three veterans of the CCM world: Wayne Kirkpatrick (a producer and writer for Amy Grant, Michael W. Smith, and others), along with Gordon Kennedy and Tommy Simms, two alumni of the band Whiteheart.

Clearer still was the amazing success of CCM veteran Bob Carlisle's *Butterfly Kisses* record, which rose to number one on *Billboard's* album chart while the single reached the top of the adult contemporary singles chart thanks to listener requests and the purchase of Carlisle's label by the Zomba label.

Carlisle's song was especially significant because it put a dagger through the heart of a widespread untruth spread by CCM supporters—that a song that speaks clearly of God or Jesus would not be accepted by pop radio and must stay inside the Christian world. Carlisle obviously wasn't listening, because "Kisses" wove references to his daughter's "bedtime prayers" and "talking to Jesus" and Carlisle's "thanking God for the joy in my life" into an irresistible song about the difficulty of letting go of a grownup daughter—an experience common to believers and unbelievers.

As these and other artists of faith entered the mainstream music culture, they quickly learned that it was possible to be tolerated—and sometimes even embraced—so long as they wrote songs where faith informed but didn't overpower their music in a way that made it difficult for non-Christian listeners to understand. Orthodox Christians in twentieth-century America had become accustomed to and comfortable in their cultural ghetto—their spiritual Negro baseball league. While ghettos may be good places to protect members who have no desire to have their ideas or abilities recognized by the wider mainstream culture, they are by definition places where most people do not live and only visit in extraordinary circumstances. Why then would believers retreat to a spiritual ghetto where few nonbelievers ever found themselves?

As the wall that separated CCM from mainstream pop continued to crumble and new alliances were formed, hope grew that artists of faith would once again be allowed to navigate in the marketplace of ideas. In fact, they already are. And just as Roy Campanella, Jackie Robinson, Lou Brock, and thousands of others crossed the color barrier and competed with the best that America's pastime had to offer, so a new generation of artists are insisting that they be heard by the wider pop music culture.

The notion of separate-but-equal has been relegated to the trash bin of history; so will the modern Christian subcultural notion of being *of* the world but not *in* it—the belief that Christians should attach their beliefs to rock music and then refuse or fail to market it to the non-Christian music-buying public. In its place will emerge a vigorous, fighting faith that not only insists on the right to be heard by the culture but continually strives to be in a position to be heard by avoiding marginalization through labeling and being a participant in the popular music culture of the day.

For all the triumphalism that may emerge from people of faith actively engaged in the culture, however, there should also be a tinge of sadness for the great men and women of music who were never afforded the opportunity to take their craft and ideas into the mainstream of popular culture. The militant secularists intent on silencing voices of faith and the shortsighted Christians intent on building a separatist religious music empire owe a generation of silenced artists and the culture that never heard their music an explanation and an apology.

Two questions linger in the meantime. First, those who have profited by channeling music inspired by faith in God into the subculture and away from the masses must consider Kerry Livgren's query: "Are we making converts to Christ, or to Christian music?"

Second, for an entire generation who were deprived of the voices and instruments of men and women who loved and served their God, the question that will continue to haunt them and their culture was posed by rock star and guitar hero Ted Nugent. When asked who was the world's greatest guitar player, Nugent was reported to have asked, "What happened to that Phil Keaggy? He could have saved the world with his guitar."[8]

TEN

Making Music

In a post-CCM world, what kinds of songs should be written by musician Christians who seek to impact the wider culture without alienating listeners who share their faith? How will they be accepted by the pop music world? These and other questions have yet to be answered by a music world in transition.

Fortunately for the faith community, the pop music culture is becoming more, not less, open to songs with spiritual messages—sometimes even relatively explicit Christian ones.

"We've come to the end of our rope as to what secular society can offer in terms of inner peace and happiness," observed ABC's religion reporter Peggy Weyhmeyer. "Our culture neglects the spiritual. If you do that for long, people will get hungry and go search for it."[1]

Songs of Faith

While songs like Joan Osborne's "One of Us" and Jewel's "Who Will Save Your Soul" have recently found acceptance on pop radio, this was not always the case.

Michael W. Smith's 1990 smash single "Place in This World" was a pop radio programmer's dream. Engineered by Humberto Gatica, known for his work with the group Chicago, the track had all the sound and feel of a Chicago ballad, but its lyrics set it apart from just another love song. Capturing the restlessness and angst common to Generation X, songwriter Wayne Kirkpatrick crafted lyrics that acknowledged the experiences common to Christians and non-Christians alike, and from there led the listener to his assumption that God was in heaven and willing to guide the lost: "If there are millions down on their knees / among the many can You still hear me / hear me asking where do I belong / is there a vision that I can call my own / show me / I'm looking for a reason, roaming through the night to find my place in this world."[2]

It was soft sell to be sure, but one can make the case that that is exactly what singles released to pop radio should be—allowing the listener to comfortably be introduced to an album that may be laden with deeper spiritual truths on other songs.

By the mid-'90s, the strong opposition that had made the effort to get "Place in This World" played on pop radio such a battle had changed, and radio stations no longer had to be cajoled into playing songs like Osborne's "One of Us," just the type of song that should be encouraged as Christians spread out into the culture and make music for the culture. Osborne picked up the song written by Eric Bazilian, of the '80s band the Hooters, who had made a name for himself by writing some intriguing songs that raised important spiritual questions.

"I just take credit for being the scribe," said Bazilian. "I thought, 'This song knows what it's saying even though I don't.' Whoever dictated this piece knew where it was going . . . [the song] just appeared in my head. It came out full-blown. I never thought about any of it."[3]

Although Osborne's album was by no means the work of an orthodox Christian, "One of Us" was nonetheless an interesting take on the incarnation of Christ. Osborne used the song to ask profound theological questions without the slightest trace of embarrassment, but she did it in a way that gave the listener (and radio programmers) room to think that she may actually have been making fun of the Almighty. With her smooth vocal delivery and her devil-may-care inflections, Osborne cooed, "If God had a face, what would it look like and would you want to see, if seeing meant that you would have to believe in things like heaven and in Jesus and the saints and all the prophets?" then added, "What if God was one of us / just a slob like one of us?"[4]

"What if God was one of us?" asked Bazilian. "A guy you walked by asking for dimes on a cold street corner? What if that really is God, slumming for a few days, checking out His creations, how they're taking care of their own?"[5]

The song was reverent enough to make the faithful think the incarnation was being honored and irreverent enough to allow the cultural gatekeepers to think that perhaps she was making fun of the whole thing. "The ambivalence is part of its appeal," noted the *Washington Post*'s Richard Leiby in a feature on the song. "Any song that includes a reference to the pope calling God on the phone can't be completely serious. Yet it's also wide-eyed in its reverence, like Linus's reading from the Gospel of Saint Luke in the "Peanuts" Christmas special. Anything but preachy, "One of Us" offers a haven to both agnostics and pew packers."[6]

Osborne's triumph, whatever her own spiritual beliefs, pointed out the problem with much music made by deeply religious people. Because the text of such music was often very literal, there was often little room for the listener's imagination. Clearly, if one valued the intentions of the author, "One of Us" wasn't a song making fun of God at all. The fact that some listeners may have taken the slob reference to mean something unintended was part of the nature of art. People interpret different words in different ways. For the most part, Christians welcomed the Osborne song.

"I am one of those NARAS members that voted for 'One of Us' for song of the year," said artist Ashley Cleveland. "I think that she captures that fellowship of suffering that our Lord shares with us. I don't know what her perspective is. . . . To me the song is more reflective of a person trying to make sense of their world."[7]

Others also welcomed the changing climate and the growing acceptance of messages with spiritual content on the part of the pop music culture.

"We may be in a time of knowing one's lostness and getting in touch with that," said Bill Mallonee of the band Vigilantes of Love, "even if it is only a feeling Christians have, a vocabulary to describe, that [others] don't. But they have the same feelings, and those feelings tend to come out as songs. We are coming up to the very end of basically four decades of pop music in which a lot of these themes have been explored through almost every possible genre of music you can listen to and the world is coming up empty-handed. As the world careens toward the year 2000, people are realizing there is not really a whole lot out there to give anybody hope, short of some kind of faith relationship in a 'god' they hope is there. I think the church has an incredible chance to be Christ to the world."[8]

"One side of me would say that is a very heavy mantle to put on an artist to encapsulate profound spiritual truth in a three-and-a-half-minute pop song," he added. "The other side of me would say that music, because it is such a gift from God, is almost beyond words. Occasionally there will be moods and feelings expressed in music that are above and beyond words, not antithetical to words but almost supralinguistic. I think that when it is done well, music can help us get at something that is raw and underneath."[9]

"People say we should write about this or that," said Mike Herrera of MxPx, "which is what they consider spiritual and righteous; and you should only write about things like that. I feel like everything is equal as far as subject matter. As Christians, we are supposed to write about Christian things, but what's a 'Christian thing'? God created this world and everything in it."[10]

Bob Carlisle's "Butterfly Kisses" was another example of this method. Carlisle was a veteran who had knocked around in several CCM bands for years before going solo in the early '90s. He released several mediocre records and was dropped by his label, Sparrow, only to be saved by the up-and-coming Diadem label. At Diadem, Carlisle released an album that was not particularly noteworthy, except for one sleeper hit song called "Butterfly Kisses."

Carlisle's manager, Ray Ware, had been talking up the song for nearly a year to anybody who would listen, and though it did garner a Dove award (the CCM world's equivalent of a Grammy) for song of the year, it wasn't until Diadem's parent company, Zomba, and its president, Clive Calder, got involved that the song was shipped to pop radio.

In an interview with the *Los Angeles Times*, Carlisle amazingly, and no doubt unwittingly, gave away the formula that is imposed on artists by the CCM hierarchy when he said of his hit song: "It was the best way I knew how to express intimately how I felt about her. *It wasn't written to be on my record, or anything like that*"[11] (italics added).

Of course, that's exactly what music is supposed to be about—the listener hearing the intimate words of the songwriter—but Carlisle, after years of conditioning, had come to a place where he apparently separated his intimate feelings from what was supposed to be on a record. "My wife strong-armed me into playing it," he said. "I was shy about it, frankly, because it was such a personal song, but I played it for them and they just insisted that I put it on the record."[12]

"Kisses" became a hit in the CCM world and would have ended there—as thousands of other potential hit songs have over the past thirty years—had it not been for a Florida disc jockey who heard about the song from his daughter and played it.

"After that, it spread like a brush fire," said Carlisle. "I mean we just couldn't keep up with it."[13]

"'Butterfly Kisses' is one of the most powerful 'reaction records' we have ever had," said Frank Bell, vice president of Sinclair Communications, which owns radio stations across the country. "On one AC station in Buffalo, we received fifty-four phone calls after playing it. With that many requests, we knew we had a hit. At that point, I started talking to our Top 40 stations and they also reported an incredible response. It has been an involuntary chemical reaction."[14]

"Kisses" touched Bell like it did millions of Americans, on a personal level. "I have a daughter and so I reacted to the song right away," he said. "The reason I believe it has been so successful is because everyone can relate to it, because it talks about parenthood and fatherhood. Women relate to it, because it talks about feelings and family. And everyone is either a parent or a child; so, really, it's for everyone."[15]

When Diadem's owner, Zomba, realized it had a hit on its hands, they wisely retitled Carlisle's album, from the churchy-sounding *Shades of Grace* to *Butterfly Kisses*, and threw away the oh-so-sincere close-up shot of Carlisle on the cover and replaced it with a large butterfly. Before long, it was the number one record in the country, thanks to promotional plugs from Oprah Winfrey and Rush Limbaugh.

With "Kisses," Carlisle proved that a song that talked about faith, and even explicitly mentioned the name of Jesus, could become a hit song if it connected with listeners on an emotional level.

For Gary Cherone of Van Halen, who aggressively and at every opportunity injected his music with Christian messages, it was only natural for artists to look at the condition of their own souls and sing about their faith. "You can go back to the Beatles going on a trip and taking it one step further from 'Love Me Do,' and getting into the spiritual," he remarked during his tenure with Extreme, "and whether it's drug induced or not, I think there'll always be an audience for it. It's tough, because we dip into that and we would hope to think that the people who buy the record swallow the whole thing, but it's really up to them."[16]

Songs of Love

Writing love songs had long been considered taboo by some in the CCM community. In 1981 Sweet Comfort Band released its album *Hearts of Fire*, which included the song "Just Like Me," an unabashed love song that left no room to be interpreted as a "God is my girlfriend" song. The lyrics contained the plain words of a man in love, who wondered if somebody "just like me" could be loved by somebody as magnificent as the woman he was singing the song to.

The song left some wondering what the purpose of CCM was. After all, love songs were what "secular" music was for. Why clutter CCM with such songs when Olivia Newton John, Hall and Oates, and Toto were doing those songs and doing them well?

At the heart of this notion was the misunderstanding that certain parts of a believer's life were fleshly and not deserving of integration with Christian principles. Whereas the Author of the holy Scriptures felt comfortable enough with human sexuality to include the Song of Songs and recorded human sexuality in the stories of King David and others, the modern Christian world seemed uncomfortable with not only sex, but love as well, even when addressed by artists of faith in the context of a moral relationship.

Tom Willett, a former Word Records liaison to the Epic label, who faced the Herculean task of getting Epic excited about Word's product, believed that the inability of many Christians to address the physical realities of life reflected an immature faith. "We cannot keep Christ in a box," he said. "We cannot keep him isolated from all of our experiences. The age-old question is, 'What's the purpose of Christian music? What's Christian, what's gospel? Is it or is it not?' It's the wrong question. The question is, 'What is the Christian life?' I think the Christian life has to do with letting Christ integrate and infiltrate all areas of our lives, so our music should reflect that."[17]

Willett anticipated songs like Carlisle's "Kisses" in 1992:

> There's a current trend going on with a lot of artists who have been in contemporary Christian or gospel for a long time. They've also been believers for a long time, and they've come to the place in their walk with Christ where their frontier, spiritually, is to move on and to try to integrate their faith with a broader range of issues. Whereas in the mid-'80s there were a lot of people purposely trying to cloud the message, purposely trying to write these double-entendre songs, "Is it God, is it my girlfriend?" Now there is a healthy, and in fact, belated phenomenon going on; finally Christian artists are actually integrating their faith with things that matter in real day-to-day life. We have relationship songs that deal with our marriages, with our lives, with our businesses, with all aspects of our humanness. Certainly that's our model in Christ. I mean, He wasn't just a Spirit. He was God in flesh.[18]

Charlie Shaw, an industry veteran, believes today's artists are also crafting better songs. "The songs are more authentic," he said, "much more honest. There's a little less joy, more reality. In the '70s, there was way too much joy and prosperity. The struggles of life were denied. Now it's much more real."[19]

For Richie Furay, onetime leader of two major rock bands, Poco and Buffalo Springfield, there is a liberation that comes from integrating every-day life and faith into a cohesive package that allows true expression. "As a Christian, I can write a love song about my wife, or I can write a praise song that praises and exalts Jesus Christ. Who I am as a person is what is reflected in the music and in the songs I write. It doesn't necessarily have to mean everything I write is a worship song or a praise song. It can talk about my life experiences, and 'Dance a Little Light,' 'I Still Have Dreams,' and 'I've Got a Reason' all did that. . . . I feel there is a good message that secular rock 'n' roll can have. There's not really a song on any of the Poco records, or for that matter, on the Springfield record that I participated in that I would have any problems singing."[20]

But there are songs, Furay contended, that he simply will not sing. "I did have a lot of problems with the Poco reunion project we did, because there were outside writers brought in—and, for some reason, the people that took over the management really believed there had to be some cruder mate-rial. It caused a big strain between me and the management and even some of the members in the band at one point in time. The original lyrics to 'Call It Love' were 'Call It Lust,' and there were other lyrics in a couple of the other songs that were just blatant 'anti-what I felt I could really sing and feel good about,' particularly and specifically the songs Rusty, Jimmy, or I didn't write."[21]

Songs of Life

For Charlie Peacock, who once recorded for the pop market on Exit and Island Records, and who now records and produces for Sparrow, cre-ativity is the key to great songwriting, and knowing the Creator of the Universe is the key to creativity. "Imagination grows in an environment of freedom, and true freedom doesn't exist except in an environment of love," said Peacock. "That's why the Scripture says 'perfect love casts out all fear.' When you know that there's nothing you can do to make God love you less, and you can truly own that idea, and in a sense preach the gospel to yourself day in and day out, then you've got a starting point for that freedom, for what it means to be a son or daughter of the living God, and the freedom to imagine and to chase after those things you imagine."[22]

Peacock disagreed, however, with a notion common in Christian cir-cles that the Almighty bequeaths songs to artists, whose job is to take the "divine dictation." "The Christian music life is not one of, day after day, God dropping songs into your lap," he said. "I don't see anywhere in Scripture that says that's indicative of anyone's everyday life. I see a lot of struggle, I see a lot of commitment, I see Scripture calling for preparedness, for skill and ability—and when Christians miss that, I think they miss part of what it means to be human. Because when you're human and you're a Christian, that's just the beginning. There's a lot of work to be done to be considered excellent."[23]

Using the example of a pilot, Peacock urged artists not to use God as an excuse to quit striving. "You wouldn't want your airplane pilot to fly you from here to Florida if they didn't have a certain number of hours put in," he said. "You wouldn't want a surgeon to open you up if they didn't have their eight, ten, twelve years of medical school. I feel the same way about the arts. It's foolish to assume that Christian musicians, Christian artists, can have an impact without preparedness."[24]

Peacock also advanced a word of caution to those who believed that the gospel message couldn't be communicated without music. "Does the gospel really need music?" he asked. "I don't think so. I think it's great when music can hold the gospel, that's one thing music can do. But you know what? The gospel doesn't need music. The gospel is so powerful, all you need to do is speak the gospel. That's my only challenge to that notion that music is a tool to preach the gospel. It's a nice thought, but you know what? The gospel doesn't need any help."[25]

Michael Been, the driving force behind the group the Call, though himself a strong believer, was often a critic of "Christian" pop songs. "I don't know why Christian rock music sounds . . . like they all use Richard Marx's band or something," he said. "It's hard for me to figure out. Without knowing why they sound the way they do and why they tend to put [out] these little Sunday-school-type of feelings, which put Bible verses to melodies. To me it shows an astounding lack of their identity. They haven't found themselves, they haven't found their own voice; they're not telling their own story, they're repeating another story and not doing it very well."[26]

For Been, the job of such artists should be to articulate faith in God in the artist's own words. "They're not bringing it in a new language," he said. "It's an inability to speak from their own heart. They're mimicking, and it becomes parrot-like; you're just regurgitating stuff people have heard forever. To me the whole point of this is to say it in a new way and apply it to your own time and tell your own story."[27]

The worst part of the whole dilemma of CCM songs, according to Been, was that the world recognized that the art was bad, though the topics, namely God's relationship with his creation, should have led to the creation of interesting music. Been cited an editorial by nationally syndicated "drive-in movie critic" Joe Bob Briggs. "Unlike his normal editorial, . . . he wanted to clear up and define all the different types of radio formats," remembered Been. "CHR radio, Top 40, ACR, new age, classic rock—he made little definitions of all of them. Then he gets to Christian rock music and it said, 'Bad songs about God written by white people.' And then under gospel music, he said, 'Good songs about God sung by black people.'"[28]

"As Christians, we're called to tell the truth—interpret what is going on in a real perspective," said Been. "I write really honest, truthful songs. I tell the truth—whether it is in a spiritual context or not. It is imperative for Christian music to talk about the places where people are hurting—that's the reality of the world. Stop being afraid of the fact that Christians go through hard things. It is self-evident. You have to connect with people. The more disconnected and unreal artists become, the less people are going to relate. With Christian music, it seems so ironic that the ultimate reality is filtered."[29]

For Frank Hart, leader of the band Atomic Opera, the challenge for believers was to move beyond propaganda to art. "Most Christians' view of evangelism are along the same lines of the propaganda campaigns of Nazi Germany," he said. "They have this 'us against them' concept, and they destroy art. They want to make films and music that make their philosophical position look good, which is not the same thing as art. That's part of the problem. The art has to have its own integrity. It's gotta be a good song, but a lot of times people sacrifice the art being good in favor of making all of its good aspects serve the propaganda end. It's just a platform."[30]

Author and poet Steve Turner, for one, believes propaganda has a role in music. "Propaganda has its place, but it has to be said that propaganda is usually adored by those who already accept its message," he observed. "The people who sang 'All You Need Is Love' and 'We Shall Overcome' were already convinced by the arguments of the peace movement or the civil rights movement. They weren't changed by the songs. Propaganda songs can't allow for subtlety or twinges of doubt. They're there to boost the morale of supporters, not to struggle with the issues."[31]

It is satire, Turner believes, that will be far more effective at waking unbelievers from their spiritual slumber. "Satire can be a more effective form of propaganda. Instead of explicitly stating your own view, you cleverly expose the inconsistencies of the view you oppose. You make fools of the enemy. Throughout the Old Testament, the prophets repeatedly attacked the beliefs of idol worshipers by letting them know that their idols were cut from the same blocks of wood that were also used for firewood. The prophets of Baal were asked if their gods had gone to the toilet when they failed to set the sodden bonfire alight. . . . From the point of view of faith, it is secularism and new ageism that are absurd. Maybe instead of shouting, 'This is it!' we should spend a little time saying, 'This is not it!'"[32]

Bill Mallonee of Vigilantes of Love said,

> Christian music doesn't challenge me. There are some great players in it and there are some great writers, but as far as the way they approach some of the themes, I can't stand most of it. I am not saying that it is not nurturing to somebody, somewhere, mind you—it may be. I am simply saying that I don't find it engaging, for the most part, because it doesn't seem to deal with the reality that most people have to live—the nitty gritty of the day to day. I think Christians need to throw out the buzzwords and get in touch with what is going on inside them and even admit, "Hey, I am disappointed in myself; there are such things as feeling broken and fragile even when God is in my life." That is not denying God; that is simply saying this world isn't heaven yet. Christians need to figure out how to relate to the world around them with a better vocabulary that everybody uses. I am not down on Christian music, but I do think there is sort of a stranglehold from the past that the industry has called for a particular kind of music, and therefore it has left a whole lot of other bands and artists trying to figure out, "How do I write honestly about myself and still glorify God?"[33]

"You have to be attuned to things," noted Pat Terry. "You have to hear songs and see songs wherever you are . . . things that sort of pop out of life that seem more real than others, things that crystallize ideas. . . . There's always something to write about "[34]

For Amy Grant, no topic was considered off limits so long as songs were written from a clear philosophical starting point.

> There are a lot of songs that I just write, and the only differentiation between them and secular pop music . . . is that they are an observation of everyday life from a Christian perspective. Like, I wrote a great song about my great-grandmother one time, and somebody who was really serious about what the lyrics should say might say, "You say you're a Christian singer, but I've played this song about your great-grandmother for my friend and they were not saved. You're a failure." A hard-lined gospel songwriter might say that. But my point of view would be that, instead of just writing songs about this one little piece of the spectrum, I'm just, as a songwriter, approaching life.[35]

For artists like Grant, the new approach was a liberating one that allowed artists to address the full spectrum of issues that believers and unbelievers alike faced in daily life. "In the past, . . . we as Christian artists have felt like every song, every album had to encompass everything that it means to be Christian," said Grant. "A lot of us now feel like 'let's approach all aspects of life from a Christian perspective.' Now it doesn't mean that suddenly every song doesn't have to be 'Blood on the Cross.' That's never not included. But it's just saying there's so many areas of life to be discussed, and it's important to have somebody discuss it from a Christian perspective. How great to have a song that says, 'You know, it's really bad between me and my husband, but I know that love perseveres.'"[36]

Turner echoed Grant's assessment.

> A Christian worldview may not be obvious if we write a song about a fish or paint a picture of a warm bath, . . . but a worldview is precisely that—a view of the world. Someone would need to look at, read or listen to a whole body of your work before they could see where you were coming from. The great thing about this is that those who might be indifferent or opposed to Christianity have the opportunity to see the world through Christian eyes. Maybe they will come to see how much of that view they already share and it will make them more concerned to see why they differ with you on the deeper issues. Art about the whole of our lives invites people in and asks them to share.[37]

Speaking the Language

An important point that must be understood by a new generation of devout artists if they are to connect with and make music for unbelievers is that the culture has changed so drastically that it no longer shares a common Judeo-Christian heritage in the language itself.

"Expressions Christians have used for decades, like 'God loves you and has a wonderful plan for your life,' no longer necessarily connect," wrote author and philosopher Chuck Colson in his work *The Body.* "Christians understand them, but few others can relate. For example, proclaiming that 'the Bible says . . .' commanded respect in the 1930s and 1940s, even into the 1960s—when 65 percent of all Americans believed the Bible to be literally true. Today only 32 percent believe the Bible is true. The majority find it an interesting collection of ancient legends and stories, but they don't believe it. So if you say, 'the Bible says,' only one out of three Americans is even ready to listen."[38]

Colson learned this lesson the hard way when trying to discuss his faith with a colleague.

> He had told me he was intrigued by my commitment to Jesus Christ, and we met for dinner to discuss it further. I was armed with all sorts of arguments, ready to tell him about my own experiences. But when I started talking about what Christ had done in my own life, he cut me off. "It's wonderful that you've found peace and fulfillment through Jesus," he said in effect, "but I don't believe in Jesus." He told me he had friends in the New Age movement, who had found spirituality too; it had worked for them as well as Christ had "worked" for me. So I shifted gears and began to talk about eternal life. This man had had some health problems in the past; surely he had done some thinking about his own mortality. Again he cut me off. Death was simply the end, he said. When we die we are just like a tree or an animal: we return to the dust. No such thing as an afterlife. I talked about the Bible. He put his hand up, palm outward. "All legends," he said firmly. What could I say? He didn't care about God's plan for his life, getting into heaven, or what the Bible said. Perhaps it's when we are caught short—when our canned answers don't work—that God uses us most effectively. For even as I was fumbling with my fork and my facts, an idea popped into my head. "Have you seen Woody Allen's *Crimes and Misdemeanors*?" I asked. He had, and we talked about it for a few minutes. Then catching him off guard, I asked, "Are you Judah Rosenthal?" He laughed, but it was a nervous laugh. "You may think this life is all there is," I said, "but if so, then there is still an issue at hand—how do you live with yourself while you're here? I know you have a conscience. So how do you deal with that when you know you do wrong?"[39]

Using Woody Allen, Colson turned the conversation to Tolstoy, C. S. Lewis, and—eventually—the Book of Romans.

"It is no different than if you or I were talking with a Hindu about issues of life and religion," concluded Colson. "We wouldn't assume that he or she was coming from a Judeo-Christian perspective. We would start from the Hindi presuppositions about the world, probe their worldview, find the points of contact and concern and then begin to challenge or question those presuppositions. Only then could we begin to present our case effectively. . . . On a purely rational level, apart from the benediction of the Holy Spirit, the secular person's existential mind-set precludes his or her understanding us. . . . So we must be familiar with the prevailing worldview to look for points of contact and discern points of disagreement."[40]

Steve Turner echoed Colson's assessment. "In the seventeenth century, when John Bunyan wrote *The Pilgrim's Progress*, most English people were 'churched,' and so issues such as 'are you really sure that you're saved?' and 'do you understand the Bible correctly?' were high on the agenda. It would be foolish today to address these questions as if they were the normal concerns of ordinary people. Part of our duty is to keep the issues that God considers to be important on the agenda. We must prevent relevancy appearing to be irrelevant."[41]

Turner likened the situation to one he had encountered at a journalists' roundtable.

> We were on an arts weekend and had spent some time discussing issues of importance to us. Then on the Sunday afternoon, an evangelist who had produced a magazine—and who therefore saw himself as a journalist—turned up midway through a session and threw a bundle of his magazines in the middle of the circle we were sitting in. He sat down and waited for us to start talking about his work. What he did was inappropriate. He hadn't heard what we had already discussed. He didn't know what conclusions we had already reached, what mood we were in, or what our needs were. He didn't sit and wait to pick up the drift of the conversation and see where his experience might be of help. He just tossed in his contribution, uninvited, and sat back to see what the reaction would be. I often think of that Sunday afternoon, because it's a picture of how Christians often react to the culture at large. They don't bother to listen in to the debate that is taking place. They don't take note of the issues that are causing concern. They just hurl their conclusions in the direction of the debaters. If they're ignored, it's interpreted as hardness of heart. If they're rejected, it's interpreted as demonic opposition.[42]

If artists of faith are to make great art, they must also reject the tenets of modernism that have found a home in the world of modern art. "The same addiction that has degenerated modern art has also infected theology," noted Drew University philosophy professor Thomas Oden. "The marvelous tradition of Cezanne, Braque, Picasso, and Chagall has withered into a speedway race of faddists, who have placed such a high value on 'doing something different' no matter what, that artistic excellence has been lost in the frantic search for novelty. An inversion of value has occurred in which the highest value is placed not on aesthetic imagination, craft, meaning, or beauty, but on novelty, Dadaism, and compulsive uniqueness. The more outrageous it is, the more 'creative' it is viewed by connoisseurs and the more boring it is to most of us."[43]

One artist who firmly rejected such an approach, in favor of excellence, was the late Mark Heard, whose work profoundly influenced a number of artists like T-Bone Burnett, Bruce Cockburn, and Sam Phillips. Heard first came to the public's attention by way of Larry Norman's Solid Rock label in 1979, with his album *Appalachian Melody*, and later released several more albums on the Home Sweet Home label, including *Stop the Dominoes*, *Victims of the Age*, *Eye of the Storm*, and *Ashes and Light* before moving to Myrrh.

Although a part of the CCM scene, Heard was keenly aware of its limitations and disagreed with much of its construct. "Someone might classify the songs, as they are apt to do, and say that this one is a theological song or this one is a song about human needs or a love song, but I see it differently," he said. "The Christian music industry seems to generally encourage artists to be a bucket with a hole poked in the bottom, so that the water runs right straight through. My approach has been to not poke a hole in it and just let the water fill up and spill over as it might. A lot of those things are inseparable, it's not like it's ever just a love song."[44]

The bottom line for many was summarized by King's X vocalist Doug Pinnick, who once noted, "A friend of mine asked me one time: 'When you go to the laundry, do you go because they're Christians or because they do a good job?' If I go to a laundry because they do a good job, and then I find out that they're Christians, that makes it more special. But if you go to a laundry because you know they're Christians, and they're not good at what they do, then what purpose is that?"[45]

Being good at what one does is something artists who are Christians must focus on if they are to make an impact out of their subculture, not an easy task for believers who must translate absolute truth into art. "It is important to write from your heart," noted Turner. "Write like a person and not an instruction booklet. Make people feel what you feel. Create art that convinces people that this is about real life because it has all the shading and complexity of real life—light and darkness, certainty and uncertainty, joy and sorrow, humor and seriousness."[46]

The mission must also be about excellence, added Kerry Livgren.

> When I play and when I write, I have a pyramid of priorities. At the top of it is to give glory to God and to proclaim His name, and in doing that, a priority or goal that I have in mind is to do music that is of a very high quality. I look at arts in the light of the Bible. For instance, in the Old Testament, where the Jews were given the directions to build the tabernacle and the ark of the Covenant, the standards were so high in craftsmanship that there was not a man alive who was able to fulfill it. God actually had to anoint craftsmen to build this thing for his glory. Now, to me, that's a fascinating principle. And if I have a goal in mind, it's craftsmanship in relation to

music. There's a statement that Oswald Chambers made which I use as my motto, and that's "my utmost for his highest."[47]

For writer Flannery O'Connor, the job of the writer who is a Christian is to get the culture's attention at all costs, in order to get his or her ideas across. "The novelist with Christian concerns will find in modern life distortions which are repugnant to him, and his problem will be to make these appear as distortions to an audience which is used to seeing them as natural; and he may well be forced to take ever more violent means to get his vision across to his hostile audience. When you can assume that your audience holds the same beliefs you do, you can relax a little and use more normal means of talking to it; when you have to assume that it does not, then you have to make your vision apparent by shock—to the hard-of-hearing you shout, and for the almost-blind you draw large and startling pictures."[48]

Finally, artists who are informed by their Christian faith and seek to write songs that reflect it must come to an understanding of how music does and doesn't affect people. Media critic Terry Mattingly described what media theorists call the "magic bullet" theory, a popular school of thought among many conservative Christians, whether they realize it or not. "Too many Christians want to believe that one media signal can get one person to commit one act," he said. "This allows us to bash secular signals claiming that they cause specific actions by people. But it also gets rid of that nasty free-will stuff and lets us dream that we could create the perfect evangelistic song, or movie, or whatever. This is at the heart of millions of Christian messages."[49]

Mattingly rejects the notion that a magic bullet, or a single, magic spiritual message, transforms lives. Instead, he subscribes to the "stalagmite" theory, which holds that many smaller messages can cumulatively, over time, have a profound effect on listeners. "Magic bullet theory doesn't work," he contends. "Media works in layers over time, and in a society as a whole. Individuals remain awesomely free—like it or not. The only magic bullet that works is human flesh and the Spirit of God."[50]

ELEVEN

The Road Ahead

*W*hy must the present setup—with devout Christians in their own world making music for each other, and everybody else in the general marketplace making music for the entire culture—be changed? How will this be worked out practically? How will these changes affect the church? How will pop music culture be affected? What new roles will emerge?

The Case for Engagement

Before these questions can be answered, the faith community must acknowledge that the present system simply hasn't worked very well for taking their message out of the church and into the mainstream of American popular culture. It's time for that community to make music for the wider culture, as surely their leader would have done had he lived in the year 2000 and played a guitar. By doing this, they will not only lift the CCM culture out of inbred musical stagnation, they will also bring life to a pop music world sorely in need of spiritual passion and creativity, something people who are in touch with the Creator of the universe presumably possess.

For the general market, this will also be good for the bottom line, which will be greatly enhanced because any record company, film studio, publishing company, or television network that ignores the fact that Americans are deeply interested in issues having to do with spirituality does so at its own economic peril.

"That's one of the things that society is very slow in coming to a recognition of, at least the elites, if you will," said pollster George Gallup Jr., "that the faith factor is probably the most powerful dynamic in American life. It has more to do with who we are and what we say in society than does politics or education or where we live. The intensity of our religious faith really is a very decisive factor in so much in our life."[1]

In addition to the impact of the SoundScan system of counting CD sales, the sudden surge in popularity of country music appeared to have more to do with the lyrical content and less with the style of music itself. Did Americans suddenly develop a taste for country in the early 1990s, or were they embracing what rock and pop music weren't providing them—a discussion of moral values and an affirmation of faith?

In short, while it's bad business for the music business to ignore issues that are important to millions of Americans, it's even worse to encourage those artists who are primarily interested in the subjects of faith, morality, heaven, hell, death, life after death—the big issues of life—to play their music in a subculture where the general record-buying public can't easily and comfortably access their ideas.

Author, film critic, and radio talk show host Michael Medved's observations about movies apply equally to music. "Hollywood's persistent hostility to religious values is not just peculiar, it is positively pathological," he observed. "Rather than readjusting their view of a reality in order to come to terms with the religious revival in America—and the widely reported resurgence in church attendance and affiliation—most people in the movie capital simply choose to ignore what the surveys tell them. They retreat ever deeper into their precious and hermetically sealed little world of Malibu 'enlightenment' and continue to write off all religious believers as so many slope-browed bumpkins who get their clothes from K-mart and their ideas from the *National Enquirer*."[2]

As recording companies discover what they have been ignorant of all along, that the American record-buying public seeks spiritual values in its music, they will greatly enhance their profits and open up new markets and find new buyers for their products.

As for the Christians, reentering the mainstream of American musical life will do more than allow them to get their message out to nonbelievers. It will also serve to make them better artists and go a long way in reintroducing the concept of art into the daily lives of Christians who make music, and help them to avoid the pitfalls some such artists fall into when they communicate the faith at the expense of—instead of in harmony with—the art.

C. S. Lewis—Oxford don, British writer, and no slouch of a Christian himself—recognized the inherent dangers when a community of artists makes music for others who believe exactly as they do, when he lamented that the crucifixion of Christ was often detailed in songs that failed to connect with him. "As for many hymns and sermons on the subject—endlessly harping on blood as if that were all that mattered—they must be the work either of people so far above me that they can't reach me or else of people with no imaginations at all."[3]

Tension often has the unintended effect of producing great art, and the inevitable tension that results from the struggle between people of faith and unbelievers can often be positive, because it introduces passion, which cannot always be produced by people of faith grouped together, agreeing with one another and attempting to create art.

So, what's next? What will happen, if anything, to CCM once many of its stars jump back into popular music? Will it just disappear? Will some remain behind to make music for "true" believers? Will such artists record for pop record labels? Will their work be censored?

Calling

The first question that must be considered by artists who are believers and desire to play music should be, "What is your calling?"—that intangible asset that is bestowed by the Creator, generally defined as one's life work. Most artists tend to reply that they are called to sing for the entire culture—the churched and unchurched.

Rarely does such an artist say they are called to only sing for other believers. This is as it should be. A military campaign involves thousands of troops on the front lines as well as a small group in the mess hall, in administration, and in the medical unit (that is, those troops assigned to meet the needs of the troops). In the battle for the hearts, minds, and ears of the popular culture, the percentage of those catering to the Christian subculture and those who perform music for the entire culture should roughly parallel that of a military enterprise that operates under the 80/20 principle—that is 80 percent on the battlefield and 20 percent in various forms of service to that 80 percent.

When a band that has declared that they want to sing for the entire culture signs with a "Christian" music label, it is no different than an eighteen-year-old recruit who says he wants to be on the front lines signing up for kitchen duty in the mess hall. To be sure, kitchen duty and working in a medical unit are no less important duties, but they are clearly not the place for a person with a calling to be on the front line, nor should they be more heavily staffed than the battlefield.

The Christian As Rock Star

For the 80 percent who are called to be in the popular music culture, the mission will be simple: a rejection of what author Franky Schaeffer identified in his book *Sham Pearls for Real Swine* as "pietistic Christianity."

"There are people who would urge a Christian musician to abandon his music in favor of 'doing the Lord's work' or at least to 'use his music for God,'" wrote Schaeffer. "This attitude misunderstands the fact that Christianity is truth and all reality comes from God, and because of that a musician is using his talents for God just as much as a missionary, even if he is playing 'secular music.' For Christians, adopting a worldview based on the concept of Truth brings freedom from false guilt and other dreadful burdens."[4]

Holy Work

Artists who intend to have their music heard by the entire culture, along with the industry support organizations (including management, record labels, magazines, and radio stations) must firmly embrace one of the major tenets of the Reformation—that all work is holy—and reject the popular notion that work carried on for profit is immoral.

"Luther's view of God's sovereignty altered established concepts of work and vocation," noted Chuck Colson. "For one thing, it rent the veil between the sacred and the secular. 'In God's sight,' Luther wrote, 'the work of monks or priests was in no way whatever superior to the works of a farmer laboring in the field, or of a woman looking after her home.' All work was noble and worthy if it was done to the glory of God."[5]

The notion that most work carried on for profit is immoral is continued today in the Christian world among those who contend that their work is really a "ministry," affiliated with a tax exempt parachurch organization, and that somehow it is wrong to earn a living at their craft in the music business. Such people must grow comfortable with the idea that they are in the world of commerce, not ministry, but that ministry opportunities are always a part of life in the world of commerce for the believer.

Dropping Labels

A most important part of the new paradigm will be the need for CCM industry leaders to finally come to terms with the fact that music, record labels, radio stations, magazines, and other support organizations that are explicitly called "Christian" will never be a serious part of the entertainment industry because one of the unwritten codes of life in the marketplace of ideas is that anything that has been labeled "Christian" will not be given a place at the table of ideas.

Perhaps the best and most telling example of this was highlighted by the success of Jars of Clay, a band that, though signed to the CCM label Essential, slid right through the cracks and became a hit in the pop music world. "Had I known it was a Christian record when I started hearing about it, I hate to admit it, but I probably wouldn't have been as amenable to the idea," acknowledged Mike Morrison, director of radio station KSCA in Los Angeles, of the band's single, "Flood." But I started liking it before I realized it had those roots."[6]

In 1990, when Geffen struck a deal with Reunion, it was expected to be a simple agreement giving Reunion access to Geffen's distribution network and nothing else, but somebody apparently forgot to tell a young Geffen employee named Claire West, who asked for permission to work to garner radio airplay for the song "Place in This World" by Michael W. Smith.

West was told that that was not part of the agreement. When she threatened to quit her job, she was allowed to work the single, but only on her own time. What she soon discovered astonished her.

> We went through the most horrible prejudices from people who just did not want to accept the fact that this man had . . . a very, very visibly Christian message. And some people who had an idea of who he was felt that he should have stayed in the market he was in. And those who didn't know him said, "What? Are you kidding?" The purpose in our promotional efforts was to get the record to a point where the people who listened to the radio could decide whether or not they felt that this record belonged on radio, and "Place in This World" is very obviously a Christian message. We were lucky to find some key programmers, some of them Christians and some of them not, who just dug the idea that we were gonna do this thing. Those people really helped us to take the music out there, and we were able to create enough buzz so that the CHR department was forced to release the record into the Top 40 area. Then we kind of married our efforts and walked the record into the top five.[7]

For West, the key to success was personal interaction:

> If you're going to get around anybody's prejudices, the only way to do it is to confront them and to deal with them one-to-one on it. And at times you've got to go, "Hey, I don't care whether you dig the fact that this guy is Christian or not. Let your listeners make a decision about the music. Let's talk about him as he stacks up to Michael Bolton or Gloria Estefan or anyone else you play. Why is it that you can play 'From a Distance' by Bette Midler, yet you can't play my artist singing about what he's singing about?" They say, "Well, you're right, that's Bette Midler. She's huge, she's a big artist," and I say, "Well, OK, let's go to a concert. Let's see what kind of people go listen to this kind of music."[8]

West's tenacity paid off as Smith's single cracked the Top 10 on *Billboard*'s pop singles chart and the album, *Go West Young Man*, broke into the Hot 100 album sales chart.

Understanding the Times

The artist who has made the decision to impact the wider world with his or her faith must resist the temptation to sit in the subculture and lose touch with the larger world, and must resist the easy road of getting signed to a "Christian" label. Instead, they will do well to model themselves after the sons of Issachar of Old Testament days, who, it was said, "understood the times and knew what Israel would do."[9]

Author Jim Peterson, in his book *Church without Walls*, wrote, "A primary reason for His coming and for our remaining in this world is to bear witness to the world. . . . God's people are in the world for the sake of the lost. . . . It's not the sole reason for our being here, but it is certainly a primary one."[10]

Peterson used one of Christ's parables to show how Christ intended his followers to live in the world. "Jesus repeatedly addressed the importance of the sending or scattering of his people into the world. . . . He gives us the parable of the good seed and the weeds. He said, 'The Kingdom of Heaven is like a man who sowed good seed in the field, but his enemy came and sowed weeds among the wheat. The owner's servants came to him and asked, 'Do you want us to go and pull the weeds up?' 'No,' he answered, 'let both grow together.' The good seed belongs in the ground, right there alongside the sons of the evil one. 'Isn't that a dangerous place to be,' we ask? Jesus replies, 'Yes it is, but I have prayed for them that they will be protected from the Evil One.'"[11]

Writer, musician, and thinker Kemper A. Crabb outlines the importance of the Isaccharian model. "They knew both Scripture and their culture's history intimately and they knew how to apply the Scriptures effectively to their situation," he wrote. "The knowledge of both the Bible and our cultural situation are necessary if we are to know how to proceed. . . . This is especially true in a culture that worships art and entertainment as our culture does."[12]

Crabb believed that ignorance produced a generation of artists who were fundamentally out of touch with their own culture. "Many artists today . . . assume that art is ahistorical, that it has no reference to culture as a historical process. Consequently, they don't put much effort into understanding how their art fits into their cultural situation."[13]

To those who argued for separation, Crabb countered that engagement would impact a culture with faith. "We must remember that art is not done in a vacuum," he wrote. "It is directed to an audience of real people. Artists must understand the state of their audiences, in light of these factors that shape those audiences where they are now and are shaping them towards where they are moving, so that the artists can serve their audiences by helping them see where they should be moving towards in light of God's Word. It is necessary to understand what influenced an audience to become what they are before we can either engage them artistically or speak authentically to their situation."[14]

For Crabb, the apostle Paul should be the model for such artists.

> When Paul spoke to [the Athenians], his whole address was arranged according to an extremely structured rhetorical form, developed by Quintilianus and used by all the educated pagans of the day, which Paul could only have learned by studying pagan classical speech forms. And, if that wasn't enough, Paul quotes the pagan poets Epimenedes, Cleanthos, and Aratus, and alludes to Homer and Plato. Once again, he could only have learned these poets by studying them. Paul used these fruits of a classical education to establish cultural points of contact with his educated pagan audience on the Areopagus, and these points provided the platform to present the gospel's truth to the salvation of Dionysius, Demacis, and others.[15]

Rejoining the Culture

The future of CCM will depend largely on the willingness of its leaders to join the culture at large and bring their worldview to bear on that culture. What could that future look like?

It could consist of radio stations that play not "Christian" or "secular" music, but music that is consistent with its owners' biblical worldview. That could mean, for example, a rock radio playlist featuring Guns 'n' Roses' "Sweet Child of Mine," dc Talk's "Jesus Freak," Verve Pipe's "Freshman," Extreme's "Hole Hearted," and King's X's "Legal Kill." Or a pop playlist featuring Sandi Patty's "Another Time, Another Place," Vanessa Williams' "Save the Best for Last," The Newsboys' "Shine," and Janet Jackson's "Let's Wait Awhile."

Such a move on the part of Christian-owned radio stations might even have the effect of causing artists who are not believers to strive to record music that will be played at such stations, creating a financial incentive to do the right thing.

It could also feature record labels, TV networks, music video channels, magazines, and so forth that though owned by Christian individuals aren't explicitly labeled "Christian" but whose offerings, or criticisms of other works, are consistent with their owners' worldview.

A new generation of artists must emerge from the faith community, ones who sing and play at a level superior to their counterparts; whose excellent art points to the inspiration of the Creator; who are not afraid to concisely articulate their faith in God, avoid moral compromises that would mock their stand of faith, and generally participate in projects that advance their ideas.

Admittedly, this new standard would be difficult to implement because it would require the evaluation of music rather than the blind acceptance of what has been approved by a musical-religious establishment. For the believer, all songs must be held up for scrutiny, using the Bible as the standard. In the new paradigm, artists formerly marginalized as "Christian artists" must be allowed to be heard by the wider culture while "secular" artists shouldn't be banned from Christian audiences when they produce appropriate work.

Artist-Ministers and Church Music

At the outset, much of CCM was not church oriented, but was, from its earliest incarnation as Jesus Music, fundamentally evangelistic—an attempt by artists like Larry Norman and Randy Stonehill to be understood by the wider popular culture. However, a portion of it has always been geared toward the faithful for the purpose of exhorting fellow believers.

Artists like Steve Camp, Keith Green, John Michael Talbot, Sandi Patty, and others primarily sang for churchgoers.

While an entire subcategory or genre of "Christian music" does not make sense, a category of music set aside for the sole purpose of worship and solely aimed at the church-going community might. There is precedent for such a distinction. Traditionally, various church traditions have had special vestments that were used for the sole purpose of worship during a church service. Thus a small fragment of all the clothing manufactured in any given town was set apart for purely religious purposes. There were, however, no "secular" or "Christian" distinctions with regard to articles of clothing. A tunic was a tunic, regardless of who produced it or wore it.

In a similar way, some music could be set aside for exclusive use by the believer in worship—both personal and corporate—and be performed by artists who are also ordained ministers.

In the coming post-CCM era, there will be room for the medics and the cooks—the Steve Camps, Michael Cards, and John Michael Talbots, but there should be a clear delineation between those who are called to sing for members of the church and those who are supposed to be singing for the wider culture, including fellow believers.

Steve Turner noted,

> Preaching the gospel is the job of the preacher. The tasks of the artist and the preacher are complementary, but not identical. The preacher can easily quote the artist, but the artist can't easily quote the preacher, and this is possibly because the artist approaches the gospel in a different way. A preacher will depend on facts, whereas an artist will trust the imagination. A preacher will deal in certainties, whereas an artist will toy with doubts and test out unresolved images. The preacher will say, "This is so," whereas the artist may want to ask, "What if this were so?" The artist can use metaphor rather than slogan, allegory rather than commentary. This is not a cop-out. This is art and art works in a different way to preaching.[16]

Before his untimely death in 1982, Keith Green was the uncontested leader of the category of artists whose work seemed to be directed toward fellow believers who needed to be challenged to live more vigorous lives of faith. Critics called Green's music an attempt to induce guilt, and supporters considered it a call to repentance inspired by the Holy Spirit. Green's work included songs like "Asleep in the Light," with its strong exhortation to church members: "The world is sleeping in the dark and the church just can't fight, 'cause we're asleep in the light / How can you be so dead when you've been so well-fed / Jesus rose from the grave, but you—you can't even get out of bed."[17]

Like the Hebrew prophets of old, popularity should not be what these artists seek, which points up the inherent problem when ministry and artistry are intertwined in a world where popularity and marketability determine market access for an artist.

"There are some people who are called into ministry and I believe that's possible if they're supported by the church body and don't charge admission for what they do," observed Kerry Livgren. "But when you do charge admission, then what you're doing is Christian entertainment business."[18]

What should remain of CCM when all of the artists who belong in pop music have left will be the likes of Camp, Talbot, Card, and others who feel exclusively called to sing for believers for the purposes of rebuking, exhorting, uplifting, and encouraging. Such artists should be considered modern-day musical prophets and be allowed to flourish without regard for market conditions since their message is one that may not always please fellow believers.

For years, some artists have insisted that they were "ministers" and not mere artists, though they were seldom ordained by nor accountable to a body vested with the authority to strip them of their platform should it be abused, and they didn't hesitate to earn money from royalties, concerts and merchandise sales. Keith Green, alone, walked the walk by giving away albums for whatever fans could afford.

In the new world of church music, as CCM might be renamed, this should change. Artists who decide that their calling is to be ministers of music and to remain in Christian circles will have greater demands placed upon them, consistent not with the lives of rock stars, but with those of ministers.

Such artists should be under the authority of a local or national church or denomination, perhaps linked together with other churches and denominations to form a national coalition, which could market, distribute, and oversee the production of music for the church-going public.

These artist-ministers, being more than simply rock stars, should be expected to be ordained as ministers by these church bodies and accountable to whatever leadership is placed upon them. They should be treated no differently than their local pastors—held strictly accountable for their behavior and doctrines and held to the standards laid out in the Scriptures for ministers.

They should forego all record royalties or concert earnings, and instead receive a set yearly salary comparable to the one paid to a national pastor or evangelist like Billy Graham. (Some artists like Talbot appear to be doing this already.) This will accomplish two important things: First and foremost, it will free them to speak and sing their minds without regard for public favor. They will have no need to sing to please the audience since their salaries would be received regardless of what they sang about. Second, it will keep in check the natural desires of the flesh, which inevitably creep into the world of gold albums, sold-out concerts, and worldly popularity.

In short, this will restore, though at a national level, what has been the traditional distinction between the lay Christian and the minister. While both stand for their faith, something extra is required of the latter that, while not as draconian as the Catholic requirement of lifelong celibacy for priests, for example, nonetheless means that such ministers crucify their fleshly desires by taking a meager salary.

Singer Barry McGuire observed,

> I know that record companies are married to the business world. I know they have warehouse workers and office workers, computer programmers, bookkeepers, salespeople, and distributors. So they need to make x amount of dollars a month to keep the doors open and that means they have to sell x amount of records. They have to produce records that people will buy, so they have to come up with a sound that they think people are listening to. People usually don't want to hear what they need to hear. They want to hear something that they like. So record companies sometimes must choose between people who minister and people who sell records. The person who really sells records is gonna win every time, because the company has to keep the cash flow going or they are out of business. That is the reality of business. But that has very little to do with ministry—it's business. It's dollars and cents.[19]

Hence the importance of minister-artists who should be paid a salary and encouraged to give up rock star ambitions and salaries in exchange for a contemplative life, creating music for believers, and keeping in mind their prophetic roles.

How will artists know whether they are called to be an artist-minister or a part of the popular music culture? CCM pioneer Ed DeGarmo at one time seemed to clearly understand his role, not as a rock star or record mogul, but as an artist-minister.

> Many people have come up to me and said, "Tell me what's different from what you do than what U2 does." And I say, "Well, the difference for me is that I feel like God has called me into a ministry, and even though I'm an entertainer, I know I'm an entertainer and I love

to play music. I have a blast when I get up there on stage, and I thank God for that. But the difference for me is that if I could not reach kids for Christ, or could not exhort Christians to a better walk with Christ, I'd find another way to do it. Now, what U2 does: U2 is a rock and roll band with a couple Christians in it. And their faith is reflected in their songs sometimes. But where the rubber meets the road for me is when you give your audiences a chance to respond. Last year we saw five-thousand kids come forward in our concerts to make decisions to follow Jesus. U2 doesn't do that. I'm not trying to say one is better than the other. I'm not trying to say that. I'm trying to say what we do is different."[20]

It remains to be seen whether such individuals will be willing to accept the limitations and responsibilities that have traditionally been imposed upon ministers, including the willingness to forsake royalties, executive salaries, expensive cars and homes—in short, giving up the material rewards of being a rock star/record mogul.

"Some artists unashamedly want to create for the Christian community," noted critic Steve Turner. "They are not interested in any form of crossover success. I think that this, too, is a worthy calling. . . . There is nothing wrong with addressing a subculture, unless God requested that you speak to the wider world."[21]

For those called to minister to the subculture, this new paradigm will allow their work to flourish—and they would do well to model themselves after Green, who made records as monies were available and then gave them away.

The Artist and the Church

The new paradigm should also result in a realignment of the roles of the church and the artist who is in the pop music culture and the way they intersect. The model that existed in the early days of rock, which often saw artists shunned by the church, was improved in the 1970s primarily due to the efforts of Pastor Chuck Smith of Calvary Chapel in southern California. Currently, many artists charge to play in churches, with fees ranging from $50 to $5,000. Some such artists are criticized by the churches for expecting payment, with some pastors contending that artists should be willing to play for a "love offering," or for a very small fee that hardly enables an artist to make a living. At the same time, the church tends to frown on artists who work in "secular music," which may include singing background vocals for "secular" artists or playing at a local club or hotel bar, discouraging them from making a living at their craft.

Of course, the church cannot have it both ways, and thus the need for a new arrangement that will benefit both sides is clearly called for. It is imperative that the church allow artists who are Christians to make a living at their craft, as some—like Abraham Laboriel, Tommy Funderburk, and Paul Jackson Jr.—have been doing quietly for years. Except in extraordinary circumstances where the work is exceptionally vile, musicians should not be kept from plying their trade because the artists or company executives they happen to be working with are unbelievers.

Once musicians are allowed to make a living at their craft, they may be far more willing to give back to the church without charge, on occasion providing music at a Sunday service, playing a few songs at an evangelistic rally, or perhaps bringing their skills to help the church produce a CD.

The church in turn must respect the artist's work and not abuse the privilege of hearing the artist's work for free, which in other settings would cost money. Care should be taken to make sure, for instance, that a church-sponsored event doesn't threaten the economic vitality of the artist's own concerts. A good way to ensure this would be to limit the performance to two or three songs by the artist. Rather than keeping people away from the artist's own concerts, this would serve to attract concertgoers to see the artist's full show at a local club or arena. In much the same way that a plumber who fixes the church's plumbing gratis, isn't then expected to provide free service for each church member, the musician will give to the church with no expectation of remuneration.

Such artists would do well to remember that just as a wise president refuses to hoard high approval ratings, but instead expends political capital by forcefully pushing his program during times of peak popularity, so an artist's popularity gives a clear opportunity to advance his or her beliefs. Johnny Cash has been doing this for years, singing in the popular music world and performing at Billy Graham crusades when asked. It was an arrangement inspired by Graham.

"He and I spent a lot of time talking the issues over and we determined that I wasn't called to be an evangelist," remembered Cash. "That was work for people other than me. He advised me to keep singing 'Folsom Prison Blues,' and 'A Boy Named Sue,' and all those other outlaw songs if that's what people wanted to hear—and then, when it came time to do a gospel song, give it everything I had. Put my heart and soul into all my music, in fact; never compromise; take no prisoners. . . . It was I who told him that if he ever wanted me to sing at one of his crusades, I'd be there. He took me up on that and after June and I worked a few of his crusades, we decided that we'd appear whenever he asked."[22]

Like Queen Esther who used her position to forcefully defend her Jewish brothers and sisters from extermination, so artists should be willing to use their position to advance their beliefs. When Esther hesitated to bring the plight of her people to the attention of the King, she was reminded by her uncle, Mordecai, that she had been placed in her position "for such a time as this." The same may be said of such artists.

In short, the new arrangement will be a win/win arrangement for both the artist and the church, as both work in harmony to advance the music and its central message.

Robee Nero, who leads music at Calvary Chapel in southern California, has provided a clear example of how this model can work. Instead of being hired by the church full time to provide music, Nero has maintained his career as a professional musician—singing jingles for radio commercials, performing at weddings, and singing background on various recording projects. Nero composes and performs music for his church without charge, as his tithe of time to the church. As a result, both Nero's music career and the church's music have flourished and benefited from the structure of the relationship. As a musician, Nero is free to grow and develop and make a living at his craft while maintaining his work for the church on a manageable time schedule.

Ken Tamplin is another who has learned to balance his responsibilities as an artist and a person of deep spiritual conviction, without compromising his responsibilities to either part of his life. Tamplin spends most of his time composing songs for other artists, television programs, motion pictures, commercials, and recording his own records. He has written songs that are consistent with his worldview for artists like KISS, composed music for "Baywatch" episodes, Ford commercials, and films like *Major League II*. He has also given back to his church by composing and producing music and occasionally traveling with missions groups to perform overseas at no cost, as his tithe of time and talent.

Both Tamplin and Nero are useful models of how the artist of faith can in the future allow faith and art to flourish without compromising either.

The Boycott

Author and entertainment executive Bob Briner believed that the modern Christian model of protest, the boycott, must be set aside in favor of engagement.

Real Christian penetration is not easy. For example, it is infinitely easier to boycott objectionable television programs than it is to create, produce, sell, and distribute a quality television program or series that would extol virtue, family values, Christian courage, and eternal truths. Participating in a boycott of the products of companies sponsoring trashy television programs might make us feel good and righteous, but it has very little to do with being salt in the world. It certainly does not call for the kind of commitment Christ asks for. Compare sending a few dollars to the boycott headquarters and refraining from buying a certain brand of soap for a few weeks to committing oneself, one's resources, and one's career to providing, for the homes of the national television audience, programming that would glorify Christ.[23]

Briner believed that such engagement is the only hope of producing lasting change. "Salt must penetrate the meat to preserve it. Christians must penetrate key areas of culture to have a preserving effect, and penetration does not mean standing outside and lobbing hand grenades of criticism over the wall. It is not about being reactionary and negative. It is about being inside through competence and talent and, with God's help and the Holy Spirit's leading, offering scripturally-based alternatives to those things that are corrupting and evil."[24]

Michael Medved, once a strong advocate of the boycott strategy, agreed with Briner's assessment.

As recently as five years ago, I viewed such efforts as promising and appropriate and wrote approvingly of "the boycott weapon" in *Hollywood vs. America*. Subsequent developments, however, have persuaded me that a confrontational response to the popular culture is even more doomed and impractical than an emphasis on isolation and separatism. . . . In the same spirit that suggests that politics is actually too important to leave to the politicians, so, too, it should be obvious that pop culture is too important to leave to Hollywood hacks. . . . The engagement alternative has never seriously been tried, so there are no guarantees of success—but doing nothing is a virtual guarantee of failure. If those committed to a Judeo-Christian worldview continue to turn away from this challenge, we can surely anticipate a further degeneration of our mass media culture toward the demonic and the destructive.[25]

The Exiting Executives

Although many industry leaders in CCM continue to have a tin ear when it comes to hearing the demands of Generation X, a few are more visionary and are heeding the Great Commission by allowing the artists—ideas in tow—to penetrate the culture.

"I think what people are buying or tapping into isn't so much the concept of Christian music, but a Christian doing music," observed producer Michael Omartian. "I think that's a distinction that has to be made. I know, for me personally, I've done a lot of work in both the mainstream and Christian sides, but I'm still a Christian doing both things. I think there's a way to reach more people, a more encompassing way of doing it . . . being a Christian out there in the world like we're called to be."[26]

One executive who seemed to fully grasp the difference was Interscope Records executive Jimmy Iovine, himself no stranger to Christians making music, having worked with the likes of Judson Spence, U2, and Maria McKee. Iovine's brilliant positioning of Kirk Franklin's *God's Property* record as an R&B record allowed the single "Stomp" to garner widespread airplay on radio and at MTV, while the record itself went all the way to number three on the pop charts.

As others in positions of influence within the CCM industry begin to leave for pop music labels, or form new labels that are not pegged as "religious," they will also open up channels and opportunities for artists of faith in the mainstream music world.

In 1996, Charlie Lico, the man responsible for setting into motion the plan for EMI to purchase Sparrow, who resigned when he saw the mistaken direction it was taking, started his own label with the backing of Tokyo-based Pioneer Electronics, forming Pioneer Music Group in Nashville. Lico immediately recruited a talented A&R staff, including ex-Eagle Bernie Leadon and an A&R whiz named Tyler Bacon, who had successfully nurtured several important bands like Sixpence None the Richer, and Fleming and John.

Lico's goal was to create a single entity that would be active in both markets but not labeled "Christian." His first release by CeCe Winans hit the top of the charts in the CCM market and, marketed as an R&B record, did solid numbers in the pop market where a single, "Well, Allright," landed on the R&B charts. Other artists like Full on the Mouth, Judson Spence, and Vigilantes of Love were also on Pioneer, and though the economic recession in Japan forced its premature closure, Pioneer and Lico made an important contribution by creating a label that would nurture artists of faith and give them the opportunity to make records that reflected that faith without making them irrelevant to the wider culture.

Similarly, Claire West, nee Parr, in her new position as vice president of the Curb record label, has helped to relaunch the careers of various former

CCM artists, including Whiteheart and Michael English, while shepherding teen sensation LeeAnn Rimes to success in both the pop and CCM markets.

Brandon Ebel was another. A young media mogul who got his start at the CCM label Frontline, then moved on to start his own label, Tooth and Nail, Ebel was not happy with the status quo. "I want to be a normal record label," he said. "I'll never sign anything that goes against what I believe—stuff that's vulgar."[27]

The other matter that Ebel received scrutiny over was his decision to be a record executive and not a pastor to his artists. Whereas many CCM labels were part church, part record company to their artists, Ebel believed that mixing the two led to a confusion of responsibility and roles.

"I'm a record company, not a baby sitter," he said. "At the same time, they need to be held accountable by somebody. All my bands go to church; I know they're all saved and have personal relationships with Christ, but as far as watching over them, there's only so much I can do. Personally, for the office, we have prayer time every morning at eight o'clock, and I'm having a college pastor come in and teach a small thirty-minute Bible study every Monday to hold all of us accountable in our business practices. As far as the whole label goes, I don't have any set requirements of what the bands can or can't do—I just trust the Holy Spirit will be their guide."[28]

In 1999, a young executive named Barry Landis, who formerly headed up Warner Brothers' "Christian" division, headed to Atlantic Records, where, working closely with Atlantic chairman Val Azzoli, he began the hard work of bringing artists of faith into the Atlantic family without being stigmatized.

Azzoli seemed a bit confused about the arrangement, first correctly noting, "By categorizing it we wind up ghettoizing it. I think that basically music is music and when you don't categorize it, you're not limited in how you sell and market it," while later adding, "This isn't a crossover label as much as it's a Christian label with crossover potential."[29]

Would Atlantic allow artists of faith to be fully integrated into the company and be marketed to the pop world like the other acts on the label, or would the company start a "Christian music" division, producing "Christian artists" thereby marginalized and unable to make a serious bid for the culture's attention? Only time would tell.

For his part, Landis seemed to clearly understand where he wanted to take the company. "I think we have set up a company that has at its core the essential imperative in the Great Commission: to go into all the world."[30]

Still, nobody was able to match the astounding success of Squint Entertainment led by its president, Steve Taylor, and vice president, former

BMG executive Stephen Prendergast, who worked hard to position Squint as a regular record label, distributed by ADA in the pop marketplace and Word in the CCM world. Its flagship artist, Sixpence None the Richer, saw its first single, "Kiss Me," rocket to the top of the pop charts thanks to its inclusion in the soundtrack of the film *She's All That*. "Kiss Me" eventually landed at the number two position on *Billboard*'s Hot 100 Singles chart.

Prendergast in particular had never understood or accepted the CCM paradigm and consistently refused to let his label or his artists be marginalized, at times battling record stores to make sure his artists weren't placed in the religious section of popular record chains. Though successful in most cases, when one national chain refused to move his group out of the "inspirational" section of their stores, Prendergast soon learned the real reason: the buyer in charge of purchasing CCM product for that chain was refusing to move it to the "normal" section because it would mean a loss of commission that the agent earned on sales that generated from the "religious" section.

"Once we were successful in getting our artists played on pop radio, we knew that those listeners would not go into the Christian or inspirational section looking for that record," observed Prendergast. "Those records needed to be racked outside of those sections. That's something that most CCM people don't recognize. Even if you are successful in 'crossing over,' those crossover people would be lost in looking for that record in any of the sections they normally would look for it."[31]

Prendergast was also instrumental in getting the song placed in key films like *She's All That* and in television shows like *Dawson's Creek*, outlets that CCM leaders would have traditionally shunned because of their content.

Squint's success had been made possible by the backing of Gaylord Entertainment, which, with the help of industry veterans Michael Blanton and Dan Harrell, had purchased Word and funded Squint's assault on the pop charts. The involvement of Gaylord and Blanton, in particular, held out the promise that Word might evolve into a label where Christians made music for the entire culture, instead of a CCM label geared exclusively toward fellow believers.

The Road Pastor

An important role that will emerge in the new paradigm is that of the road pastor. One of the first to occupy this previously unrecognized position was a young minister named Michael Guido, who traveled with bands like

Stryper, dc Talk, Michael W. Smith, Jars of Clay, and others. The role of road pastor will be important for three key reasons.

First and foremost, the road pastor plays the role of reality checker. In ancient Rome, when a hero would return from battle and ride through the streets of the city to the cheers of the people, there was placed next to him an officer, whose job was to remind the hero every once in awhile of his own mortality. "Remember you are human," he would whisper. Similarly, the role of the road pastor must be to remind the artists—in the midst of thousands of adoring fans—that they are not to be worshipped, that they are messengers of God and not gods.

Secondly, if artists of faith are to be in the center of popular music culture, they will need such a pastor to draw spiritual strength from on the road—if they are to remain creative, inspired artists drawing upon the endless creativity of the Creator of the universe.

Finally, a pastoral figure will take on new importance in the lives of these artists, because once they are no longer signed to CCM labels, there won't be record label people around to ensure that the messages communicated by the artists are intelligently reflective of their faith. It will certainly be appropriate for artists to check with such a person to make sure that their songs are not biblically illiterate.

Certainly taking a pastor on the road will be an added expense for the artist and the label, but in the long run it will be money saved by avoiding things that have traditionally plagued rock stars on the road: affairs, paternity suits, family breakups, trashed hotel rooms, drug problems, and so on.

Seminaries and churches must adjust as well, training pastors who can live on the road with bands, following the example that has been set by the pioneering work of Michael Guido.

The Interpreter

Finally, the collapse of CCM as we know it will create the need for another key player—one who can analyze lyrics and the general philosophical overtones of records. For the past thirty years, CCM-label executives have pulled double duty—as theologians and music industry executives. They alone have had to decide whether a particular artist's ideas were "Christian." In the future, as artists of faith spread out into the culture, it will be imperative that biblically informed cultural voices rise up to analyze records and help the listener to understand if a particular record is within the broad realm of a biblical worldview or not. Several such voices have already emerged and must be ready to take on a broader role.

Al Menconi, a popular speaker, along with his assistant, Dave Hart, provide capable analyses of various records. Menconi and Hart measure the lyrics against the Bible and help give readers an idea of what worldview is being articulated through the music. Bob Smithouser does similar work for a Focus on the Family publication, *Plugged In*.

Some are fearful of this breakdown in leadership because they fear that good, Christian kids will be bombarded with anti-Christian or pseudo-Christian messages disguised as true faith. For Dan Haseltine of Jars of Clay, these are the necessary risks that must be taken if artists of faith are to venture into mainstream culture. "With anything, you've got to have your checks and balances as a Christian listening to artists and the things they say," he said. "It is the same when you go into a church and you listen to what a pastor has to say. There should always be a part of you that is on your guard checking things with Scripture. You really need to pray about things like that and definitely have a filtering system."[32]

For CeCe Winans, it's important in the case of children for parents to guide them, not only in musical selection but in making them aware of competing worldviews. "You have to teach what is right and what is wrong," she said. "You have to let them know the difference between Christianity and non-Christianity. Music is very powerful and it can influence people to do right or wrong, it can uplift you or depress you. You strive to do all you can do in your home, and you try to instill that in your kids, and the rest is in God's hands."[33]

For Kenny Greenberg, a producer and songwriter with kids of his own, it's something he has been forced to begin to do himself. "It's tricky and real subjective," he said. "I have a thirteen-year-old who is really up on the pop scene. When a child is a preteen, I don't think you are going to be wanting them to listen to Nine Inch Nails. While, sonically, NIN may be amazing, the message is not so good. You don't want to let an impressionable pre-teenager think it's OK to be having sex or to be drinking or to be doing violent things just because the hip record on MTV says it's okay to do that. It's my job as a parent to say, 'Here is this record and this is what I think is wrong with it and why."[34]

Fully in the World

As artists of faith reject the subculture approach and rejoin the mainstream artistic community, they must simultaneously be vigilant to maintain

their faith and be open to new experiences and new people who may not necessarily agree with them. In fact, they must prepare to deal intimately with
people who completely disagree with everything they stand for. Such are the
rigors of a full life of faith in the middle of the culture for those who wish to
follow their Master's decree that they be in the world but not of it.

A good place to start for such artists would be with the writings of the
Chinese philosopher Watchman (To-Sheng) Nee. Nee argued for the emergence of vigorous men and women of faith who do not shrink back from culture, but rather embrace it physically while rejecting it spiritually.

> Suppose I put to you the question, what work are you engaged in?
> You answer, "medical work." But if I tell you that medical science is
> one more unit of a system that is Satan-controlled, what then?
> Assuming that as a Christian you take me seriously, then you are at
> once alarmed and your reaction may even be to wonder if you had
> not better quit your profession. No, do not cease being a doctor! But
> walk softly, for you are upon territory that is governed by God's
> enemy, and unless you are on the watch you are as liable as anyone
> else to fall prey to his devices. . . . Many think that to escape the
> world is a matter of . . . dedicating themselves more wholeheartedly
> to the things of God. No, it is a matter of salvation. By nature, we
> are all entrapped in that satanic system and we have no escape apart
> from the mercy of the Lord. All our consecration is powerless to
> deliver us; we are dependent upon His compassion and upon His
> redemptive work alone to save us out of it. He is well able to do so.
> God can set us upon a rock and keep our feet from slipping. Helped
> by Him, we may turn our trade or profession to the service of His
> will for as long as He desires it.[35]

Another philosopher widely read in Christian circles echoed Nee's
observations. "The key to missionary devotion means being attached to
nothing and no one, saving our Lord Himself," observed Oswald Chambers,
"not being detached from things externally. Our Lord was amazingly in and
out among ordinary things; His detachment was on the inside towards God.
External detachment is often an indication of a secret vital attachment to the
things we keep away from externally."[36]

In his book, *Love Not the World*, Nee continues the discussion.

> Physical separation does little in making men holy. Man seeks to
> solve the problem of the world by removing himself physically from
> what he regards as the danger zone. But physical separation does not
> bring about spiritual separation; and the reverse is also true that
> physical contact with the world does not necessitate spiritual capture
> by the world. . . . However close our touch with the world may be

outwardly, we are released from its power when we truly see its nature. . . . Let me ask you: what is your occupation? A merchant? A doctor? Do not run away from these callings. . . . Religious people . . . attempt to overcome the world by getting out of it. As Christians, that is not our attitude at all. Right here is the place where we are called to overcome. . . . To separate ourselves from the world today, and thus deprive it of its only light, in no way glorifies God. It merely thwarts His purpose in us and in mankind. "Go ye into all the world and preach the gospel." This is the Christian's privilege. It is also his duty. Those who try to opt out of the world only demonstrate that they are still in some degree in bondage to its ways of thinking. We who are not of it have no reason at all to try to leave it, for it is where we should be. So there is no need for us to give up our secular employments. Far from it, for they are our mission field. In this matter there are no secular considerations, only spiritual ones. We do not live our lives in separate compartments as Christians in the Church and as secular beings the rest of the time. There is not a thing in our profession or in our employment that God intends should be dissociated from our life as His children.[37]

C. S. Lewis offered advice to writers that echoed Nee and Chambers' words.

I believe that any Christian who is qualified to write a good popular book on any science may do much more by that than by any directly apologetic work. The difficulty we are up against is this: We can make people attend to the Christian point of view for half an hour or so; but the moment they have gone away from our lecture or laid down our article, they are plunged back into a world where the opposite position is taken for granted. As long as that situation exists, widespread success is simply impossible. . . . What we want is not more little books about Christianity, but more little books by Christians on other subjects—with their Christianity latent. You can see this most easily if you look at it the other way around. Our Faith is not very likely to be shaken by any book on Hinduism. But if whenever we read an elementary book on Geology, Botany, Politics or Astronomy, we found that its implications were Hindu, that would shake us. It is not the books written in direct defense of materialism that makes the modern man a materialist. It is the materialistic assumptions in all the other books. In the same way, it is not books on Christianity that will really trouble him. But he would be troubled if, whenever he wanted a cheap popular introduction to some science, the best work on the market was always by a Christian.[38]

Coming Up

Until people of faith are fully integrated into the popular music culture, there will be a time of transition that may take ten or twenty years before the proper divisions are achieved—that is, a large pop and rock universe where artists, including Christians, make music for the wider culture, and a far smaller group of artist-ministers who make music exclusively for the clear purposes of corporate and personal religious devotion and worship.

Until then, it is encumbent on new artists to refuse any and all labels, including "CCM artist," "Christian artist," "gospel artist," or any other description that has the effect of marginalizing the artist and keeping him away from unbelievers. Each artist and group must insist on being called musicians—period—and refuse to allow their enemies to silence them through labeling. For as Bob Dylan once observed, "Make something religious and people don't have to deal with it."[39]

Artists who are currently signed in the CCM market should follow the example of dc Talk, which fulfilled its contract with Forefront, signed a recording contract with Virgin Records, then gave Forefront the rights to distribute future records to the Christian bookstore market only. With the help of like-minded entertainment attorneys and managers, artists should renegotiate their contracts so that they are signed directly to pop labels, while giving CCM market rights to CCM labels. Other artists who once were trapped in the CCM market have already followed dc Talk's example, including BeBe Winans, CeCe Winans, MxPx, Jon Gibson, and others.

Artists like dc Talk would do well to take their stand a step further by politely declining Grammy nominations in the gospel category, respectfully reminding the Grammy nominating committees that they should be nominated in the category that best describes their music be it pop, rock, classical, jazz, or whatever.

As for new artists who are being wooed by CCM labels, if their goal is truly to sing for the wider culture, they must steadfastly refuse to sign recording agreements that will silence them. Instead, they should follow the example of bands like the Tories, Full on the Mouth, Judson Spence, Fleming and John, and others who have refused consistent invitations to sign with the CCM market and held out successfully for pop recording agreements instead. They might also consider signing primary recording agreements with pop labels and secondary distribution deals with CCM labels.

In the new dynamic, a role must be carved out for the CCM, or Church labels, and they will have much to do if, in addition to their role in signing the minister-artists, they will accept the secondary role of distributing to Christian bookstores the music of artists from pop record labels who share the Christian worldview. This arrangement will assure the Church Music labels an income as the industry makes the transition to the new paradigm.

A prime opportunity to implement this approach was the recent Johnny Cash record, *Unchained*, produced by and released on Rick Rubin's label, American Recordings. A deeply spiritual and specifically Christian record, *Unchained* was Cash's swan song of faith, with many references to Jesus, the afterlife, godly living, and life in a fallen world. Yet, amazingly, no CCM label picked up the record for the Christian bookstore circuit.

The same is true of many other popular artists. An artist like Johnny Cash deserves to be heard by the subculture, and as many young artists of faith refuse to be locked into the ghetto, the CCM world must come to terms with the fact that they are losing talented artists. Such labels must be willing to settle for being the release point for albums already released into the pop market by artists who are fundamentally in agreement with their values.

As terms like "gospel music" and "Christian music" disappear, groups like the Gospel Music Association (GMA) will be forced to rethink their reason for existing and adapt accordingly. Perhaps they might rename themselves the Gospel in Music Association (GIMA) and give out their Dove awards each year to the artists who have most effectively presented the gospel in their music in the various genres like jazz, rock, pop, R & B, alternative, and so forth, perhaps giving awards to groups like Van Halen, Lenny Kravitz, Creed, and Collective Soul in addition to artists like Michael W. Smith, Jars of Clay, Kirk Franklin, and dc Talk. Perhaps they might also give out separate "character in music" awards for artists who, in addition to making quality music, have exhibited high moral character—Steven Curtis Chapman, Charlie Peacock, or Twila Paris, for instance—so that excellent art and character and godliness are recognized separately.

As these and other artists reenter the mainstream culture of American life, modern delivery systems, including the Internet, will allow their art to circle the globe and influence the world with their songs of faith and hope.

In so doing, they will finally set aside faulty doctrines of separation and misappropriated Scriptures and once again return to the original command given to them to "go and make disciples of all nations."

In Memory

Sometime during the summer of 1997, as I worked on this book, I received a fax from a man named Bob Briner. He asked me to send him information about myself. Having read a column or two of his, I had been vaguely aware of Bob. When I sent him the bio he had requested, he wrote back to thank me.

When he learned that I was writing this book, he offered to help by introducing me to his agent, who subsequently asked for a copy of the manuscript but didn't return my call. Several months later when I mentioned this to Bob, he clicked his tongue and, in a tone that mixed anger and disappointment, said, "Those guys!" He then invited me to Dallas to meet with his publisher and others he thought would be interested. He continued to mentor and advise me, guiding all of my negotiations with the publisher and helping me each step of the way. Communicating via cyberspace several times a week, I also relied on his wisdom for several television shows I was producing and hosting.

Bob was a constant source of encouragement, and though he was a multimillionaire with far more important things and people to attend to, he nearly always ended our conversations with, "How can I serve you?" The first few times I heard this I was silent. I had never been asked a question like that before.

In late 1998 Bob was diagnosed with cancer, and through months of chemotherapy he continued to keep in touch with me. The cancer spread and was unresponsive to the treatments. Three months before his death, he wrote me these words in longhand: "I can hardly wait for your book to come out. I have already learned a lot from it and look forward to reading it again when I can hold the actual book in my hands."

I wanted more than anything to be the one to put it in his hands but fell three months short, and will have to settle instead for putting a copy in his wife Marty's hands.

Bob and I last talked exactly a month before his death. I was leaving for a two-week trip and called to let him know he was in my thoughts. I decided to turn the tables on him and ask, "How can I serve you?" "Just pray," he said. And I did.

My last words to Bob were, "I'll talk to you soon." And that's a promise I intend to keep.

—Mark Joseph

About the Author

*M*ark Joseph is president of MJM Entertainment Group, a television and music production and distribution company and has had a varied career in the entertainment business as a TV and radio reporter, columnist, and music and television executive. His portfolio includes articles for *Billboard* magazine, *World*, *Regeneration Quarterly*, and the *Yomiuri* and reporting for CNN, Group W., FM Tokyo, and NHK. He lives in the Los Angeles area with his wife, Kara.

Endnotes

Chapter 1

1. Steve Rabey, "A Noebel Cause: The Constant Crusader Shares His Rhetoric on Rock," *CCM* magazine (May 1986): 23–25.

2. Ibid.

3. Ibid.

4. Ibid.

5. Ibid.

6. Steve Rabey, "Parents Music Resource Center Socks Rock," *CCM* magazine (January 1986): 22–23.

7. Ibid.

8. Ibid.

9. Ibid.

10. Ibid.

11. Chris Christian, "Too Heavenly Minded," *Love Them While We Can*, Home Sweet Home Records, 1982.

12. Simon Broughton, Mark Ellingham, David Muddyman, and Richard Trillo, *The Rough Guide to World Music* (London: Penguin Books, 1994), 632–33.

13. Ann Douglas, *Terrible Honesty, Mongrell Manhattan in the 1920s* (New York: The Noonday Press. Farrar, Straus, and Giroux, 1995), 95.

14. Phil Petrie, "The History of Gospel Music," *CCM* magazine (February 1996): 47.

15. Ibid.

16. Broughton, et al., *Rough Guide to World Music*, 636.

17. Ibid.

18. Laura Lee Arant and Lynn McCain, "Benson Music Group: The First Ninety Years of a Mission," *CCM* magazine (July 1992): 27.

19. Ibid., 28.

20. Paul Baker, *Why Should the Devil Have All the Good Music?* (Waco, Tex: Word Books, 1979), 173.

21. Devlin Donaldson, "Billy Ray Hearn," *CCM* magazine (June 1988): 46.

22. Ibid., 47.

23. Thom Granger, "Sparrow Soaring at Fifteen," *CCM Update* (June 3, 1991): 1.

24. Ibid., 2.

25. Steve Rabey, "Maranatha! Music Turns Twenty," *CCM* magazine (April 1991): 12.

26. Steve Rabey, "Silver Anniversary: Maranatha! Music Celebrates Twenty-five Years of Ministry and Business," *CCM* magazine (November 1996): 49.

27. Rabey, "Maranatha! Music Turns Twenty," 12.

28. Rabey, "Silver Anniversary," 50.

29. *CCM Update* (February 11, 1991): 1.

30. Steve Rabey, "Frontline at Five," *CCM Update* (April 8, 1991): 1.

31. Thom Granger, "A Little History of Our Own," *CCM* magazine (July 1993): 46.

32. John W. Styll, "Enlarging the Vision," *CCM* magazine (April 1992): 52.

33. John W. Styll, "What Makes Music Christian?", *CCM* magazine (June 1991): 22–23.

34. George Marsden, *Reforming Fundamentalism* (Grand Rapids, Mich.: Eerdmans), 1987, 4.

35. "Spurring On Secularism," *Christian History* 55 (1997).

36. Marsden, *Reforming Fundamentalism*, 13.

37. Ibid., 14.

Chapter 2

1. Paul Baker, *Why Should the Devil Have All the Good Music?* (Waco, Tex.: Word Books, 1979), 43.

2. Steve Turner, interview by the author, April 1999.

3. Ibid.

4. Ibid.

5. Dave Hart, "Pop Music's Unholy Trinity," *Media Update* 8, no. 3, 2.

6. Martha Bayles, *Hole in our Soul—The Loss of Beauty and Meaning in American Popular Music* (New York: The Free Press, 1994), 254.

7. Dave Hart, "Drugs and Their Whirlwind Comeback," *Media Update* 12, no. 3, 2.

8. Ibid., 3.

9. Tori Amos, "God," Sword and Stone Publishing, Inc. (ASCAP).

10. Lars Ulrich and James Hetfield, "The God That Failed," Creeping Death Music (ASCAP), 1991.

11. Trent Michael Reznor, "Heresy," TVT Music, Inc., Leaving Hope (ASCAP).

12. Baker, *Why Should the Devil?*, foreword.

13. Ibid.

14. Ibid.

15. Ibid., 62.

16. Ibid., foreword.

17. Ibid., 62.

18. Larry Norman, "Why Should the Devil Have All the Good Music?", Glenwood Music, Straw Bed Music (ASCAP), 1973.

19. Brian Quincy Newcomb, "Long Journey Home," *CCM* magazine (June 1989): 23.

20. Ibid.

21. Ibid.

22. Andrae Crouch, *Just Andrae*, Light Records, 1972, liner notes.

23. Andrae Crouch, *Take the Message Everywhere*, Light Records, undated, liner notes.

24. Renee Tatum, "Andrae Crouch," *CCM* magazine (June 1988): 43.

25. Dave Urbanski, "The Preacher's Life," *CCM* magazine (February 1997): 27.

26. Crouch, *Take the Message Everywhere*, liner notes.

27. Davin Seay, "What Really Happened," *CCM* magazine (March 1983): 35.

28. Bill Carpenter, "A Mission of Mercy," *CCM* magazine (May 1994): 65.

29. Urbanski, "The Preacher's Life," 28.

30. Crouch, *Just Andrae*, liner notes.

31. Brian Mansfield, "One Man's Ambition," *Syndicate* magazine (March/April 1993): 18.

32. Brian Quincy Newcomb, "Sunday's Child Is Full of Grace," *CCM* magazine (January 1989): 20.

33. Ibid.

34. Ibid.

35. Mansfield, "One Man's Ambition," 18.

36. Newcomb, "Sunday's Child," 20.

37. Ibid.

38. Steve Rabey, *The Heart of Rock and Roll* (Old Tappan, N.J.: Fleming H. Revell, 1986), 93.

39. Baker, *Why Should the Devil?*, foreword.

40. Randy Stonehill, interview by the author, 1987.

41. Ibid.

42. Ibid.

43. Rabey, *The Heart of Rock and Roll*, 94.

44. Stonehill, 1987 interview.

45. Ibid.

46. Ibid.

47. Randy Stonehill, interview by the author, 1990.

48. Stonehill, 1987 interview.

49. Chris Willman, "Turning Twenty," *CCM* magazine (August 1990): 26.

50. Thom Granger, *CCM* magazine (August 1990): 22.

51. Ibid., 25.

52. Stonehill, 1987 interview.

53. Stonehill, 1990 interview.

54. Ibid.

55. Ibid.

56. Ibid.

57. Willman, "Turning Twenty," 31.

58. Stonehill, 1990 interview.

59. Melody Green and David Hazard, *No Compromise* (Nashville, Tenn.: Sparrow Press, 1989), 17.

60. Ibid., 19.

61. Ibid., 20.

62. Ibid., 37.

63. Ibid., 36.

64. Ibid., 134–35.

65. Ibid.

66. Ibid., 138.

67. Keith Green, Randy Stonehill, and Todd Fischkind, "Your Love Broke Through," April Music, King of Hearts Music, 1977.

68. Green and Hazard, *No Compromise*, 156.

69. Ibid., 220.

70. Ibid.

71. Melody Green, "There Is a Redeemer," Birdwing Music, 1982.

72. Green and Hazard, *No Compromise*, 248.

73. James Long, "Elvis Has Left the Building," *CCM* magazine (February 1996): 30.

74. Ibid., 31.

75. Ibid., 30.

76. Ibid.

77. Ibid.

78. Ibid., 31.

79. Eddie DeGarmo, interview by the author, 1989.

80. Bruce A. Brown, "DeGarmo and Key—Still Hot," *CCM* magazine (July 1993): 33.

81. Dana Key, interview by the author, 1998.

82. Brown, "DeGarmo and Key," 33.

83. DeGarmo, 1989 interview.

84. Steve Rabey, "DeGarmo and Key's Saving Grace," *CCM* magazine (November 1987): 19.

85. Ibid.

86. Davin Seay, "Dynamic Duo," *CCM* magazine (September 1985): 22.

87. Ibid.

88. Ibid.

89. Rabey, "DeGarmo and Key's Saving Grace," 20.

90. Dana Key, "Dear Mr. Clapton," DKB Music (ASCAP), 1995.
91. T. L. Faris, "On the Road Again," *Syndicate* magazine (September/October 1993): 15.
92. Ibid.
93. Brown, "DeGarmo and Key," 34.
94. Key, 1998 interview.
95. Ibid.
96. Ibid.
97. Ibid.

Chapter 3

1. Davin Seay and Mary Neely, *Stairway to Heaven* (New York: Ballantine, 1985).
2. Pat Boone, interview by the author, 1996.
3. Seay and Neely, *Stairway to Heaven*.
4. Ibid.
5. Ibid.
6. Boone, 1996 interview.
7. Charlie Shaw, interview by the author, 1998.
8. Boone, 1996 interview.
9. Ibid.
10. Ibid.
11. Cal Thomas, editorial, *Los Angeles Times* Syndicate (February 25, 1997).
12. Ibid.
13. Ibid.
14. Dion Dimucci with Davin Seay, *The Wanderer* (New York: Quill, 1988), 29.
15. Ibid., 18.
16. Ibid.
17. David McGee, *Rolling Stone Album Guide* (New York: Random House, 1992), 199.
18. Dimucci and Seay, *The Wanderer*, 84.
19. Ibid., 85.
20. Ibid., 94.
21. Ibid., 95.
22. McGee, *Rolling Stone Album Guide*, 199.
23. Dimucci and Seay, *The Wanderer*, 154.
24. Ibid., 160–61.
25. Ibid., 161.
26. McGee, *Rolling Stone Album Guide*, 200.
27. Dimucci and Seay, *The Wanderer*, 216.
28. Ibid.
29. McGee, *Rolling Stone Album Guide*, 200.
30. Pat Curry, "Dion: New Directions," *CCM* magazine (August 1990): 13.
31. Ibid.
32. Baker, *Why Should the Devil?*, 211.
33. Ibid., 111.
34. Ibid., 211.
35. Ibid., 67.
36. Ibid.
37. Ibid., 68.
38. Ibid., 67.
39. Paul Evans, *Rolling Stone Album Guide* (New York: Random House, 1992), 541.
40. Baker, *Why Should the Devil?*, 170.
41. Ibid., 170–71.
42. Davin Seay, "Faith and (Body)Works," *CCM* magazine (December 1985): 28.
43. Ibid., 29–30.
44. Baker, *Why Should the Devil?*, 211.

45. Ibid., 132.
46. Ibid.
47. Ibid.
48. Ibid., 133.
49. Ibid.
50. Barry McGuire, *C'Mon Along*, Sparrow Records, liner notes.
51. Devlin Donaldson, "Barry McGuire," *CCM* magazine (April 1996): 56.
52. Devlin Donaldson, "Barry McGuire," *CCM* magazine (June 1998): 35.
53. Ibid., 35.
54. Donaldson, "Barry McGuire" (1996): 56.
55. Sandy Stert Benjamin, "On the Road of Life," *CCM* magazine (April 1993): 18.
56. Ibid.
57. Ibid.
58. Ibid.
59. Ibid.
60. Ibid.
61. B. J. Thomas and Gloria Thomas, *In Tune* (Old Tappan, N. J.: Fleming H. Revell Company), 1983, 131.
62. Ibid., 137.
63. Ibid.
64. Ibid., 141.
65. Ibid., 136.
66. Ibid., 47.
67. Ibid., 48.
68. Baker, *Why Should the Devil?*, 172.
69. Thomas and Thomas, *In Tune*, 52.
70. Ibid.
71. Ibid., 52–53.
72. Baker, *Why Should the Devil?*, 173.
73. John W. Styll, "Cool Crowd Fuels Hot Tempers," *CCM* magazine (October 1982): 38.
74. Ibid., 37.
75. Ibid.
76. Steve Rabey, "B. J. Thomas: Just Can't Help Believin'," *CCM* magazine (June 1997): 46.
77. John W. Styll, "Mylon Lefevere: The Solid Rocker," *CCM* magazine (March 1986): 16.
78. Bruce Brown, "A Child of the Father," *CCM* magazine (October 1988): 19.
79. Steve Rabey, *The Heart of Rock and Roll* (Old Tappan, N. J.: Fleming H. Revell, 1986), 14.
80. Brown, "A Child of the Father," 19.
81. Ibid.
82. Rabey, *The Heart of Rock and Roll*, 16.
83. Styll, "Mylon Lefevere," 17.
84. Rabey, *The Heart of Rock and Roll*, 17.
85. Styll, "Mylon Lefevere," 17.
86. Ibid., 18.
87. Rabey, *The Heart of Rock and Roll*, 18.
88. Brown, "A Child of the Father," 20.
89. Ibid.
90. Styll, "Mylon Lefevere," 18.
91. Rabey, *The Heart of Rock and Roll*, 18.
92. Ibid.
93. Ibid.
94. Brown, "A Child of the Father," 20.
95. Mylon Lefevre, "Stranger to Danger," Angel Band Music (BMI).
96. Styll, "Mylon Lefevere: The Solid Rocker," 19.
97. Ibid.
98. Ibid.

99. Ibid.

100. Brown, "A Child of the Father," 21.

101. Scott Cooper, "Buffalo Springfield's Unsung Singer," *Rock Village*, undated.

102. Paul Evans, *Rolling Stone Album Guide* (New York: Random House, 1992), 95.

103. Cooper, "Buffalo Springfield."

104. Ibid.

105. Ibid.

106. Ibid.

107. Ibid.

108. Devlin Donaldson, "Richie Furay: A Long Trip from Buffalo to Cleveland," *CCM* magazine (January 1997): 50.

109. Page Larson, "A Peek into the Eternal," *CCM* magazine (June 1986): 9.

110. Ibid.

111. Charles Gentry, "The Lord Has Made a Way," *CCM* magazine (February 1981): 20.

112. Bob Darden, "Al Green's Transcendent Reality," *CCM* magazine (May 1992): 19.

113. Steve Turner, *Hungry for Heaven* (Downers Grove, Ill.: Intervarsity Press, 1995), 50.

114. Ibid.

115. Ibid.

116. Reuben Fairfax Jr., Al Green, and Fred. M. Jordan III, "Belle," Al Green Music, Inc., JEC Publishing (BMI), 1977.

117. Greil Marcus, quoted in Turner, *Hungry for Heaven*, 50.

118. Mark Coleman, *Rolling Stone Album Guide* (New York: Random House, 1992), 291.

119. Turner, *Hungry for Heaven*, 50.

120. Charles Gentry, "The Lord Has Made a Way," 20.

121. Ibid.

122. Ibid.

123. Eban Kelly and Jimi Randolph, "Everything's Gonna Be All Right," Pop Spiritual Music/Al Green Music Co. (BMI).

124. Ibid.

125. Leon Patillo, interview by the author, 1988.

126. Ibid.

127. Ibid.

128. Ibid.

129. Ibid.

130. Chris Willman, "Counting the High Cost of Music Ministry," *CCM* magazine (October 1985): 27.

131. Ibid.

132. Ibid.

133. Patillo, 1988 interview.

134. Karen Marie Platt, "Joe English Finds Refuge Under His Wings," *CCM* magazine (February 1981): 8.

135. Allan Sugarman, "Joe English on Wings," *The Beatles Are Back* (Cousins Publications, 1976), 20.

136. Platt, "Joe English Finds Refuge," 8.

137. Ibid.

138. George Melling, "Looking Back on *Venus and Mars*," *The Beatles Are Back* (Cousins Publications, 1976), 62.

139. Platt, "Joe English Finds Refuge," 8.

140. Ibid.

141. Ibid.

142. Ibid.

143. Ibid.

144. Ibid., 9.

145. Ibid.

146. "The Best Records of 1980," *CCM* magazine (February 1981): 23.

147. Platt, "Joe English Finds Refuge," 9.

148. Brian Quincy Newcomb, "No More Mr. Nice Guy," *CCM* magazine (December 1986): 20.
149. Rick Cua, interview by the author, 1988.
150. Ibid.
151. Sandy Smith, "Cua Mellows Out," *CCM* magazine (April 1988): 31.
152. Cua, 1988 interview.
153. Newcomb, "No More Mr. Nice Guy," 20.
154. Cua, 1988 interview.
155. Ibid.
156. Smith, "Cua Mellows Out," 31.
157. Ibid.
158. Willman, "Counting the High Cost of Music Ministry," 26.
159. Ibid., 28.
160. Ibid.
161. Ibid.
162. Ibid.
163. Ibid.
164. Ibid.
165. Ibid., 27.
166. Ibid.
167. Mark Farner, interview by the author, 1988.
168. Ibid.
169. Ibid.
170. Ibid.
171. Ibid.
172. Ibid.
173. Ibid.
174. Ibid.
175. Ibid.
176. Ibid.
177. Doug Van Pelt, "Some Kind of Preacher," *CCM* magazine (October 1991): 36.
178. Brian Quincy Newcomb, "Closer to Home," *CCM* magazine (August 1988): 6.
179. Ibid.
180. Van Pelt, "Some Kind of Preacher," 37–38.
181. Chris Well, "On the Grand Faith Railroad," *Harvest Rock Syndicate* 6, no. 4, 8.
182. Van Pelt, "Some Kind of Preacher," 38.
183. Ibid., 39.
184. Ibid.

Chapter 4

1. Johnny Cash, *Unchained*, American Recordings, liner notes.
2. Ibid.
3. Ibid.
4. Ibid.
5. Ibid.
6. Ibid.
7. Johnny Cash, "The Fire Is Back," *The Unchained Bio*, American Recordings.
8. Cash, *Unchained*, liner notes.
9. Bill Miller, "Johnny Cash: An American Legend," *Autograph Collector* magazine (October 1993).
10. Ibid.
11. Cash, *Unchained*, liner notes.
12. Ibid.
13. Johnny Cash with Patrick Carr, *Cash* (New York: Harper/San Francisco, 1997), 170–71.
14. Ibid.
15. Ibid.

16. Ibid., 174.

17. Cash, "The Fire Is Back."

18. Ibid.

19. Ibid.

20. Ibid.

21. Johnny Cash, "Meet Me in Heaven," Songs of Cash, Inc. (ASCAP), 1996.

22. Steve Turner, *Hungry for Heaven* (Downers Grove, Ill.: Intervarsity Press, 1995), 174.

23. Ibid., 177.

24. Paul Baker, *Why Should the Devil Have All the Good Music?* (Dallas: Word Books, 1979), 169.

25. Cliff Richard, *Questions* (London: Hodder & Stroughton, 1970), 21.

26. Ibid., 22.

27. Ibid., 23.

28. Thom Granger, "Cliff Richard: Fearless," *CCM* magazine (November 1985): 18.

29. Ibid., 18–19.

30. Turner, *Hungry for Heaven*, 177.

31. Billy Graham, *Just As I Am* (New York: Harper/Collins, 1997), 688.

32. Bob Dylan, "Gotta Serve Somebody," Special Rider Music (SESAC), 1979.

33. Catherine Kanner, interview with the author.

34. Robert Shelton, *No Direction Home* (New York: Beech Tree/Morrow, 1986), 484.

35. Ibid., 489.

36. *Saved! The Gospel Speeches* (Madras and New York: Hanuman Books, 1990).

37. "Dylan Tells Story of Christian Conversion," *CCM* magazine (February 1981): 11.

38. Alan Jacobs, "The Songs Are My Lexicon," posted at Bob Dylan.com (April 9, 1999).

39. Ibid.

40. "Dylan Tells Story."

41. Shelton, *No Direction Home*, 485.

42. Jonathan Cott, *Dylan* (New York: Doubleday, 1984), 211.

43. "Dylan Tells Story."

44. Ibid.

45. Dan Wooding, "'Please Pray for Bob Dylan,' Asks His Former Pastor" (April 25, 1999).

46. "Dylan Tells Story."

47. *Saved! The Gospel Speeches.*

48. "Dylan Tells Story."

49. Ibid.

50. *Saved! The Gospel Speeches.*

51. Shelton, *No Direction Home*, 483.

52. Davin Seay and Mary Neely, *Stairway to Heaven* (New York: Ballantine, 1986).

53. "Dylan Tells Story."

54. Ibid.

55. Melody Green and David Hazard, *No Compromise* (Chatsworth, Calif.: Sparrow Press, 1989), 222.

56. Ibid.

57. Ibid.

58. Ibid.

59. "Dylan Tells Story."

60. *The Bob Dylan Companion*, Carl Benson, ed. (Schirmer Books, 1998), 165, 167.

61. Shelton, *No Direction Home*, 488.

62. Al Kasha, interview with the author, February 1999.

63. Shelton, *No Direction Home*, 487–88.

64. Larry Yudelson, "Dylan: Tangled Up in Jesus," *Washington Jewish Week*, 1991.

65. Bill Parr, interview by the author, 1998.

66. Derek Wesley Selby, "The X-men," *CCM* magazine (December 1996): 48.

67. Kasha, 1999 interview.

68. Shelton, *No Direction Home*, 497.

69. Ibid., 489.

70. Yudelson, "Dylan: Tangled Up."

71. Turner, *Hungry for Heaven*, 169–70.

72. Jon Parales, "A Wiser Voice Blowin' in the Autumn Wind," Internet posting (September 28, 1997).

73. "Standing in the Doorway," Special Rider Music (SESAC), 1997.

74. "Till I Fell in Love with You," Special Rider Music (SESAC), 1997.

75. "Standing in the Doorway," Special Rider Music (SESAC), 1997.

76. Sharon Gallagher, "Faith and Hope and Rock and Roll," *Radix* magazine 21, no. 3.

77. Jacobs, "The Songs Are My Lexicon."

78. Parales, "A Wiser Voice Blowin'."

79. Hank Williams, "I Saw the Light," Acuff Rose Music, Inc., Hiriam Music, 1948.

80. A. P. Carter, "Keep on the Sunny Side," Peer International, 1928.

81. Ralph Stanley and Windy Smith, "Let Me Rest on a Peaceful Mountain," Trio Music Company, Inc., Fort Knox Music, 1969.

82. "Rock of Ages," public domain.

83. "Hallelujah, I'm Ready to Go," public domain.

84. Alice Cooper, Stephen Emil Dudas, Mark Jeffrey Hudson, Robert Pfeiffer, "Cleansed by Fire," Do Dis Music (BMI), Ezra Music Corp., Music Corporation of America I, Sony/ATV Songs LLC.

85. Jack Blades, Alice Cooper, Tommy R. Shaw, "It's Me," Ezra Music Corp. with Sony/ATV Songs, 1993.

86. Alice Cooper, Robert Pfeiffer, and Dan Wexler, "Nothing's Free," Ezra Music Corp./Music Corporation of America/Sony/ATV Songs.

87. Brian McCollum, *Kansas City Star*, Knight Ridder Newspapers (August 22, 1997).

88. Julia Duin, "Spirituality Finds Favor Again in Pop Music World," *The Washington Times* (May 12, 1997).

89. McCollum, 1997 article.

90. Ibid.

91. Ibid.

92. Cooper, "Cleansed by Fire."

93. Alice Cooper and J. Vallance, "Lullaby," Sony Music Entertainment, Inc., 1994.

94. McCollum, 1997 article.

95. Steve Rabey, *The Heart of Rock and Roll* (Old Tappan, N.J.: Fleming H. Revell, 1986), 54.

96. Ibid.

97. Ibid.

98. Ibid., 55.

99. Ibid.

100. Ibid., 56.

101. Ibid., 60.

102. Ibid.

103. Ibid.

104. Ibid., 61.

105. Ibid.

106. Ibid., 60.

107. Ibid.

108. Ibid.

109. Ibid., 61

110. Ibid., 60.

111. Ibid., 61.

112. Elliot Mintz, "Penthouse Interview," *Penthouse* magazine (1980).

113. Ibid.

114. Ibid.

115. Craig Rosen, "On Nashville, Christmas, Barbara and Image Breaking," *Billboard* magazine (September 3, 1994).

116. Ibid.

117. Ibid.

118. Mintz, "Penthouse Interview."

119. Dave Marsh, "The Wanderer: A Rock and Roll Road Map of Donna Summer's Soul," *Rolling Stone* (February 9, 1981).

120. "Donna Summer—A Retrospective," *Blue & Soul* magazine 656 (undated).

121. David A. Keeps, "Disco's Born-Again Bad Girl," *Pop View*, undated.

122. "Donna Summer—A Retrospective."

123. Kerry Livgren with Kenneth Boa, *Seeds of Change* (Wheaton, Ill.: Crossway Books, 1983), 129.

124. Ibid., 133.

125. Ibid., 134.

126. Ibid., 136–37.

127. Ibid., 137.

128. Ibid.

129. Ibid., 155.

130. Doug Van Pelt, "What Dio Sez," *HM* magazine (May/June 1987): 50.

131. Ibid.

132. Livgren and Boa, *Seeds of Change*, 161.

133. Kerry Livgren, "Relentless," Don Kirshner Music/Blackwood Music (ASCAP), 1980.

134. Kerry Livgren, "Crossfire," Kirshner CBS Music Publishing.

135. Stert Benjamin, "Kerry Livgren's Vinyl Confessions," *CCM* magazine (October 1982): 34.

136. Ibid.

137. James Long, "John Elefante, A Quarter-Hour of Fame," *CCM* magazine (April 1996): 28.

138. Ibid.

139. Ibid.

140. Chuck King, interview by the author, 1998.

141. Livgren and Boa, *Seeds of Change*, 169.

142. Ibid.

143. Benjamin, "Kerry Livgren," 35.

144. Long, "John Elefante," 28.

145. Ibid., 28–29.

146. Ibid.

147. John Elefante and Dino Elefante, "Chasing Shadows," Full Grown Man Music, Mastodon Music (BMI), 1982.

148. John Elefante and Dino Elefante, "Face It," Full Grown Man Music, Mastodon Music (BMI), 1982 (all rights administered by Full Grown Man Music).

149. Benjamin, "Kerry Livgren," 35.

150. Ibid., 36.

151. Long, "John Elefante," 28.

152. Benjamin, "Kerry Livgren," 36.

153. Ibid.

154. Ibid.

155. Long, "John Elefante," 29.

156. Ibid.

157. Ibid., 28.

158. "Mastedon: The Rock Stomps Here," *Harvest Rock* Syndicate, 5, no. 3, 10.

159. John Elefante, *Corridors*, Pamplin Records, artist biography, 1997.

160. Thomas Mann, "Capitalizing On New Found Freedom," *CCM* magazine (February 1989): 6.

161. Ibid.

162. Eamon Dunphy, *The Unforgettable Fire* (New York: Warner Books, 1987), 71.

163. Turner, *Hungry for Heaven*, 178.

164. Terry Mattingly, "Rockers Finally Speak Out about Their Rumored Faith," *CCM* magazine (August 1982): 24.

165. Ibid., 26.

166. Dunphy, *The Unforgettable Fire*, 58.

167. Ibid., 59.

168. Ibid., 152.

169. Turner, *Hungry for Heaven*, 180.
170. Quoted in Chris Willman, "Shaping the Sound of U2," *CCM* magazine (December 1988): 11.
171. Ibid.
172. Turner, *Hungry for Heaven*, 186.
173. Dunphy, *The Unforgettable Fire*, 167.
174. Ibid., 170.
175. Paul David Hewson, Laurence Muller, Adam Clayton, and David Evans, "I Still Haven't Found What I'm Looking For," Polygram: International (ASCAP).
176. Paul David Hewson, Laurence Muller, Adam Clayton, and David Evans, "Wake Up Dead Man," Polygram: International (ASCAP).
177. Chris Willman, interview with the author.
178. Turner, *Hungry for Heaven*, 170.
179. Ibid., 171.
180. Ibid.
181. Ibid., 172.
182. Chris Willman, "The Call: Singing the Struggle," *CCM* magazine (November 1990): 16.
183. Chris Willman, "Mr. Mister, Have They Found What They're Looking For?" *CCM* magazine (December 1987): 14.
184. Ibid.
185. Ibid.
186. Ibid.
187. Ibid.
188. Robert Sweet, interview by the author, 1996.
189. Ibid.
190. "No Hype, Stripes or Stereotypes," *Heaven's Metal*, no. 32, 14.
191. Ibid.
192. Robert Sweet, 1996 interview.
193. "No Hype, Stripes or Stereotypes."
194. Robert Sweet, 1996 interview.
195. Ibid.
196. Steve Rabey, *The Heart of Rock and Roll* (Old Tappan, N. J.: Fleming H. Revell, 1986), 65.
197. Randy Rocker, "Hollywood and Hein," *CCM* magazine (November 1991): 42.
198. Ibid.
199. Craig Johnson, "Stryper Gives the Devil Hell," *CCM* magazine (December 1986): 17.
200. Ibid.
201. Ibid.
202. Ibid.
203. Dave Hart, "Stryper Denies Rolling Stone Report, Defends New Album," *CCM* magazine (August 1990): 10.
204. Ibid.
205. Ibid.
206. Ibid.
207. Ibid.
208. Ibid.
209. *Heaven's Metal* magazine (May/June 1995): 26.
210. Ibid., 27.
211. Todd Chatman, "Sweet Release," *CCM* magazine (November 1995): 64.
212. Thom Granger, "Taking Stryper Seriously," *CCM* magazine (August 1988): 20.
213. David A. Jenison, "The King and Run-DMC," *Syndicate* magazine (September/October 1993): 33.
214. Ibid.
215. Ibid.
216. Ibid.
217. Ibid.
218. Ibid.

219. Ibid., 35.
220. Debra Akins, "Brotherly Love," *CCM* magazine (March 1997).
221. Ibid.
222. Ibid.
223. Thom Granger, "Take 6: A Distinctive Debut," *CCM* magazine (July 1988): 11.
224. David McGee, *Rolling Stone Album Guide* (New York: Random House, 1992), 690.
225. Akins, "Brotherly Love," 37.
226. Ibid., 36.
227. Ibid., 37.
228. Ibid., 38.
229. Ibid.
230. Selby, "The X-men."
231. Brian Quincy Newcomb, "Telling the Story in a Strange Land," *CCM* magazine (November 1989): 13.
232. Ty Tabor, interview by the author, 1998.
233. "What's a King's X?," *Heaven's Metal*, no. 43, 68.
234. Mike MacLane, interview by the author, 1998.
235. Doug Van Pelt, "Displaying the Mark of the King," *Heaven's Metal*, no. 22, 6.
236. Ibid.
237. Ibid.
238. Newcomb, "Telling the Story," 12.
239. *CCM* magazine (December 1996).
240. Newcomb, "Telling the Story," 12.
241. Doug Pinnick, interview by the author, 1998.
242. Dave Plemmons, "King's X," *Pure Rock Report*, no. 39, 1.
243. King's X, "Goldilox," Jetydosa Music (ASCAP), 1987.
244. John Hotten, "Silent Is Golden," *Kerrang!* magazine, no. 214, 30.
245. King's X, "Over My Head," Jetydosa Music (ASCAP), 1989.
246. Doug Van Pelt, "King's X—You Can't Help But Love 'Em," *Heaven's Metal*, no. 28, 9.
247. Ibid.
248. King's X, "Everywhere I Go," Jetydosa Music/Akee Music (ASCAP), 1990.
249. King's X, "Legal Kill," Jetydosa Music/Akee Music (ASCAP), 1990.
250. Tabor, 1998 interview.
251. Selby, "The X-men," 49.
252. "History of the Band Up to Dogman," *Illinois Entertainer*, Internet posting (February 24, 1994).
253. Ibid.
254. Plemmons, "King's X."
255. Ibid.
256. Pinnick, 1998 interview.
257. Tabor, 1998 interview.
258. Ibid.
259. Doug Van Pelt, "Getting Extreme," *Heaven's Metal*, no. 28, 16.
260. Ibid., 17.
261. Ibid., 18.
262. Ibid., 16.
263. Doug Van Pelt, "What Extreme Says," *Heaven's Metal*, no. 52, 34.
264. Ibid.
265. Ibid.
266. Ibid.
267. Ibid.
268. Ibid., 33.
269. Van Pelt, "What Extreme Says."
270. Gary Cherone, interview by the author, 1993.
271. Van Halen, "Dirty Water Dog," Van Halen Publishing, LLC (ASCAP), 1998.
272. Van Halen, "Once," Van Halen Publishing, LLC (ASCAP), 1998.

273. *The Living Bible* (Wheaton, Ill.: Tyndale House Publishers), 1971.

274. Van Halen, "Fire in the Hole," Van Halen Publishing, LLC (ASCAP), 1998.

275. Gary Cherone, interview posted at Cherone.com (April 4 ,1999).

276. Ibid.

277. Ibid.

278. William Shaw, "Are You There, God?," *Details* magazine, November 1995, 158.

279. Lenny Kravitz and Henry Hirsch, "Believe," Miss Bessie Music/Henry Hirsch Music (ASCAP), 1993.

280. Shaw, "Are You There, God?"

281. Lenny Kravitz, "Rock and Roll Is Dead," Miss Bessie Music (ASCAP), 1995.

282. Craig Ross, music, Lenny Kravitz, lyrics, "Beyond the Seventh Sky," Miss Bessie Music (ASCAP), Wigged Music (BMI), 1995.

283 Lenny Kravitz and Henry Hirsch, "God Is Love," Miss Bessie Music/Henry Hirsch Music (ASCAP), 1995.

284. Lenny Kravitz and Craig Ross, "The Resurrection," Miss Bessie Music (ASCAP), Wigged Music (BMI), 1995.

285. Craig Ross, music, Lenny Kravitz, lyrics, "In My Life Today," Miss Bessie Music (ASCAP), Wigged Music (BMI), 1995.

286. *Rolling Stone* magazine (November 17, 1994).

287. *Billboard* magazine (August 12, 1995).

288. Lenny Kravitz, "Super Soulfighter," Miss Bessie Music (ASCAP), 1998.

289. Lenny Kravitz, "I Belong to You," Miss Bessie Music (ASCAP), 1998.

290. T. L. Faris, "Ashley Cleveland, It's a Feel Thing," *Syndicate* magazine (September/October 1993): 29.

291. Ibid., 30.

292. Ibid.

293. Ibid.

294. Ibid.

295. Ibid.

296. Doug Van Pelt, "Galactic Cowboys—The Men, The Madness, The Moon," *Heaven's Metal*, no. 29, 13.

297. Ibid., 14.

298. "Metal Tracks," *Heaven's Metal*, no. 31, 29.

299. Doug Van Pelt, "Galactic Cowboys in Your Face," *Heaven's Metal*, no. 42, 19.

300. Ibid.

301. Van Pelt, "The Men, The Madness," 14.

302. Doug Van Pelt, "The Mad Men Behind Atomic Opera," *Heaven's Metal*, no. 49, 26–28, 76.

303. Ibid.

Chapter 5

1. Charlie Shaw, interview by the author, 1998.

2. "MCA Gears Down Songbird Division," *CCM* magazine (November 1982): 58.

3. Jack Hafer, interview by the author, 1997.

4. Ibid.

5. Ibid.

6. Ibid.

7. Ibid.

8. Refuge Records press release.

9. Hafer, 1997 interview.

10. Chris Willman, "What's New?: This Label Has a Real Point of View," *CCM* magazine (June 1986): 10.

11. Chris Willman, "Tonio K Unchained," *CCM* magazine (October 1986): 20.

12. Ibid.

13. Willman, "What's New?," 10.

14. Ibid.

15. Mary Neely, interview by the author, 1997.

16. Dean Capone, "See What Sacramento Hath Spawned," *CCM* magazine (May 1986): 20.

17. Neely, 1997 interview.

18. Ibid., 22.

19. Debra Akins, "Brotherly Love," *CCM* magazine (March 1997): 36.

20. Neely, 1997 interview.

21. Capone, "Sacramento," 22.

22. Neely, 1997 interview.

23. Capone, "Sacramento," 22.

24. Charlie Peacock, "Dizzy Dean Movie," Blackwood Music, Inc., Western Sierra Music, Andi Beat Goes On Music (BMI), 1986.

25. Charlie Peacock, "I Will Need Your Help," EMI Blackwood Music.

26. Charlie Peacock, "Message Boy," Blackwood Music, Inc., Western Sierra Music, Andi Beat Goes On Music, (BMI), 1986.

27. Neely, 1997 interview.

28. Brian Q. Newcomb, "Charlie Peacock: One Hep Cat," *Harvest Rock Syndicate* 5, no. 1, 9.

29. Neely, 1997 interview.

30. Ibid.

Chapter 6

1. John Fischer, *What On Earth Are We Doing?* (Grand Rapids, Mich.: Servant Publications, 1996), 27.

2. Watchman Nee, *Love Not the World* (Great Britain: CLC, 1968), 27.

3. Steve Winwood and Will Jennings, "Higher Love," Blue Rider Songs, Irving Music, Inc., Warner-Tamerlane Publishing (BMI).

4. Joe Brooks, "You Light Up My Life," Big Hill Music Corp. (ASCAP).

5. Fischer, *What On Earth?*, 26.

6. Phil Petrie, "The History of Gospel Music," *CCM* magazine (February 1996): 48.

7. Davin Seay with Mary Neely, *Stairway to Heaven* (New York: Ballantine Books, 1986), 80.

8. Ibid., 81.

9. Ibid.

10. Steve Turner, *Hungry for Heaven* (Downers Grove, Ill.: Intervarsity Press, 1995), 44–45.

11. Dave Marsh, *The Heart of Rock and Soul* (New York: Plume, 1989), 20.

12. Robyn Frazer, "Aretha Franklin: Ridin' on a Labor of Love," *CCM* magazine (January 1988): 8.

13. Kevin Smith, Michael Tait, Toby Mckeehan, and Mark James, "Between You and Me," Fun Attic Music (BMI).

14. Larry D. Kelly, "Christians in 'Secular' Music: Is Nothing Sacred Anymore?" *CCM* magazine (November 1991): 34.

15. Ibid.

16. Ibid., 35.

Chapter 7

1. April Hefner, "Don't Know Much about History," *CCM* magazine (April 1996): 42.

2. Phillip E. Johnson, *Reason in the Balance* (Downers Grove, Ill.: Intervarsity Press, 1995), 21.

3. Steve Turner, "Being There: A Vision for Christianity and the Arts" (1998): 15–16.

4. Cal Thomas, *Book Burning* (Wheaton, Ill.: Crossway, 1983), 98.

5. Sandy Stert Benjamin, "Kerry Livgren's Vinyl Confessions," *CCM* magazine (October 1982): 36.

6. John Fischer, "Only a World to Reach," *CCM* magazine (August 1996): 94.

7. Ibid.

8. Charlie Shaw, interview by the author, 1998.

9. Jack Hafer, interview by the author, 1997.

10. Thom Granger, "Sparrow Soaring at Fifteen," *CCM Update* (June 3, 1991): 2.

11. Ibid.

12. David M. Ross, "Jimmy Bowen: Why He's a Believer in Christian Music," *CCM Update* (November 2, 1992): 1–2.

13. Ibid., 2.

14. Ibid., 7.

15. Ibid.

16. Ibid.

17. Stephen Speer, "New Study Claims Potential 13 Million Untapped Christian Music Consumers," *CCM Update* (June 29, 1992): 1.

18. Sandy Smith, "How Do We Get Christians to Listen to Christian Radio?", *CCM Update* (May 10, 1993): 1–2.

19. Ibid., 2

20. Thomas, *Book Burning*, 103–104.

21. "Industry Looks at SoundScan," *CCM Update* (January 17, 1994): 1.

22. Ibid.

Chapter 8

1. Amy Grant, *Lead Me On*, artist's biography, Word Records, 1988.

2. Ibid.

3. Ibid.

4. Grant, 1988 interview.

5. Ibid.

6. Ibid.

7. Ibid.

8. Bruce A. Brown, "DeGarmo & Key: Still Hot," *CCM* magazine (July 1993): 33.

9. Bob Millard, *Amy Grant* (New York: Dolphin/Doubleday, 1986), 163.

10. Steve Rabey, *The Heart of Rock and Roll* (Old Tappan, N. J.: Fleming H. Revell, 1986), 106.

11. Robert Hunter Caldwell and Paul Howard Gordon, "Next Time I Fall," EMI Blackwood Music, Sin Drome Music (BMI).

12. Millard, *Amy Grant*, 128.

13. Ibid.

14. Thom Granger, "Amy Grant: Relatively Speaking," *CCM* magazine (March 1991): 22.

15. Deborah Evans Price, *Billboard* magazine (August 9, 1997).

16. Quote deleted at press time.

17. Todd Hafer, "Amy Grant, A Heart in Motion," *Bookstore Journal* (February 1991).

18. Ibid.

19. Ibid.

20. Ibid.

21. Amy Grant, *Lead Me On*, artist's biography.

22. Ibid.

23. Millard, *Amy Grant*, 169.

24. Ibid., 168–69.

25. Leslie Phillips, "Bring Me Through," Maranatha! Music, 1981.

26. Chris Willman, "Leslie Phillips: A Thinking Girl's Rock," *CCM* magazine (January 1986): 26.

27. Ibid.

28. Leslie Phillips, "Dancing with Danger," Word Music (a div. of Word Inc.), 1984.

29. Leslie Phillips, "Light of Love," Word Music (a div. of Word Inc., ASCAP), 1984.

30. Leslie Phillips, "I Won't Let It Come between Us," Word Music (a div. of Word Inc.), 1984.

31. Rabey, *The Heart of Rock and Roll*, 46–47.

32. Leslie Phillips, "Powder Room Politics," Word Music (a div. of Word Inc., ASCAP), 1984.

33. Leslie Phillips, "Strength of My Life," Word Music (a div. of Word Inc.), 1984.

34. Willman, "Leslie Phillips," 27.

35. Thom Granger, "Leslie Phillips Saves Her Best for Last," *CCM* magazine (May 1987): 24.

36. Brian Q. Newcomb, "Sam Phillips: Telling the Truth," *Harvest Rock Syndicate* 6, no. 5, 14.

37. Granger, "Leslie Phillips Saves Her Best," 23.

38. Newcomb, "Sam Phillips," 32.

39. Granger, "Leslie Phillips Saves Her Best," 24.

40. Ibid.

41. Newcomb, "Sam Phillips," 32.

42. Ibid., 32–33.

43. Ibid., 32.

44. Granger, "Leslie Phillips Saves Her Best," 25.

45. Chris Willman, "Sam Phillips: Has She Turned Away?", *CCM* magazine (November 1988): 8.

46. Ibid.

47. Ibid.

48. James Long, "Michael W. Smith: I'll Lead You Home," *CCM* magazine (July 1996): 32.

49. Chris Well, "Picture Perfect in Progress," *Harvest Rock Syndicate* 7, no. 4, 21.

50. Ibid.

51. Long, "Michael W. Smith," 32.

52. Well, "Picture Perfect," 13.

53. Ibid.

54. Ibid.

55. Ibid.

56. Ibid.

57. Millard, *Amy Grant*, 98–99.

58. Ibid., 141.

59. Ibid., 153.

60. Well, "Picture Perfect," 13.

61. Jim Patterson, "Michael W. Smith: Hit 'Love Me Good' Not Gospel?", Associated Press (April 20, 1999).

62. Steve Taylor, "I Want to Be a Clone," C. A. Music/Birdwing, 1982.

63. Steve Taylor, "Steeplechase," C. A. Music/Birdwing/Cherry Lane Music Publication, Inc., 1982.

64. Steve Taylor, interview by the author, 1998.

65. Steve Taylor, interview by the author, 1987.

66. Ibid.

67. Rabey, *The Heart of Rock and Roll*, 75.

68. Taylor, 1987 interview.

69. Rabey, *The Heart of Rock and Roll*, 75.

70. Ibid., 74.

71. Steve Taylor, "Baby Doe," C. A. Music/Birdwing Music, Cherry Lane Music Publishing Company, 1984.

72. Steve Taylor, "Meltdown (at Madame Tussaud's)," C. A. Music / Birdwing Music, Cherry Lane Music Publishing Company, 1983.

73. Ibid., 73.

74. Steve Taylor, "I Just Wanna Know," C. A. Music/Birdwing Music (ASCAP), 1985.

75. Brian Quincy Newcomb, "Steve Taylor: Living Life in the Open," *CCM* magazine (February 1994): 40.

76. Steve Taylor, "I Blew Up the Clinic Real Good," Soylent Tunes (ASCAP), 1987.

77. Chris Willman, "Steve Taylor: Rock'n Role Model," *CCM* magazine (January 1988): 16.

78. Taylor, 1998 interview.

79. Newcomb, "Steve Taylor," 39.

80. Parke Puterbaugh, review, *Rolling Stone* magazine (1991).

81. Brian Mansfield, "What's in a Name? Chagall Guevara," *CCM* magazine (March 1991): 30.

82. Rabey, *The Heart of Rock and Roll*, 72.

83. Mansfield, "What's in a Name?", 30.

84. Ibid.

85. Taylor, 1998 interview.

86. Ibid.
87. Ibid.
88. Newcomb, "Steve Taylor," 39.
89. Ibid., 40.
90. Thom Granger, "BeBe and CeCe Winans: Heavenly Love," *CCM* magazine (February 1989): 16.
91. James Long, "Relaxed in His Presence," *CCM* magazine (January 1996): 53.
92. Bruce A. Brown, "BeBe and CeCe Winans: Addicted to His Love," *CCM* magazine (July 1991): 34.
93. Granger, "BeBe & CeCe Winans," 17.
94. Brown, "BeBe & CeCe Winans," 35.
95. Granger, "BeBe & CeCe Winans," 17.
96. Ibid.
97. Brown, "BeBe & CeCe Winans," 36.
98. Granger, "BeBe & CeCe Winans," 17.
99. Ibid.
100. Gregory Rumburg, "The Other Side of the Tracks," *CCM* magazine (July 1996): 40–41.
101. Ana Gascon Ivey, "Easy Does It," *CCM* magazine (January 1988): 27.
102. Lucas Hendrickson, "Return of the Invisible Girl," *CCM* magazine (July 1997): 51.
103. Ibid.
104. Ibid.
105. Ibid.
106. Ibid.
107. Ibid.
108. Gregory Rumburg, "The Rockford Files," *CCM* magazine (December 1995): 36.
109. Ibid., 35.
110. Ibid., 36.
111. Ibid., 37.
112. Ibid.
113. dc Talk, "Jesus Is Just All Right," A Reynolds, Alexis Music, BMG Songs (ASCAP).
114. Ibid., 38.
115. Debra Akins, "dc Talk Inks General Market Deal," *CCM* magazine (January 1997): 10.
116. Ibid.
117. Rumburg, "The Rockford Files."
118. Ibid., 39.
119. Akins, "dc Talk," 10.
120. Marc Weingarten, "At a Crossroad, DC Talk Keeps the Faith," *Los Angeles Times* (1999).
121. Ibid.
122. Ibid.
123 April Hefner, "Off the Leash," *CCM* magazine (January 1994): 34.
124. Joel Hanson and Patrick Andrew, "Goldie's Last Day," Careers-BMG Music Publishing, Inc., and Sparrow Song (a div. of the Sparrow Corp.)/Line Drive Music (BMI), 1993.
125. Hefner, "PFR's Last Day," *CCM* magazine (August 1996): 43.
126. Ibid., 44.
127. Ibid.
128. Ibid.
129. Michael Ciani, "All Aboard!" *CCM* magazine (July 1996): 35.
130. Ibid.
131. Ibid.
132. Ibid.
133. Ibid.
134. Ibid.
135. Ibid.
136. Ibid.
137. Ibid.

138. Ibid.
139. Ibid.
140. Ibid.
141. Melissa Riddle, "The Reign of a New Franklin," *CCM* magazine (August 1996): 35.
142. Ibid.
143. Ibid.
144. Ibid.
145. Ibid.
146. Rumburg, "The Other Side of the Tracks," 42.
147. Debra Akins, "Jars of Clay Faces the Critics," *CCM* magazine (November 1996): 24.
148. Ibid.
149. Rumburg, "The Other Side of the Tracks," 42.
150. Akins, "Jars of Clay," 24.
151. Devlin Donaldson, "Punks with a Point," *CCM* magazine (August 1995): 68.
152. Michael Ciani, "MxPx Takes Issue with Matters of Cheese, Age, and the Selling of God," *CCM* magazine (March 1997): 35.
153. Ibid.
154. Ibid.
155. Ginny McCabe, "MxPx: Plain ol' Ordinary Guys," *HM* magazine (December 1977): 17. (*HM* is published monthly and can be subscribed to by calling 1-800-777-0955 or writing to HM magazine, P. O. Box 141007, Austin, TX 78714-1007, http://christianmusic.org/cmp/hmmag/)
156. Dave Urbanski, "Where the Buffalo Roam," *CCM* magazine (August 1998): 37.
157. Ibid.
158. Ibid.
159. Ibid.
160. Jay Cooper, "Sixpence None the Richer," *Network* 40, issue 461 (April 30, 1999).
161. Ibid.
162. Ibid.
163. Ibid.
164. Greg Carpenter, posted at CD Now, 1994-99, College Media, Inc.
165. Gregory Rumburg, "Sisterhood?", *CCM* magazine (September 1999), 10.
166. Cooper, "Sixpence."
167. Rumburg, "Sisterhood?"
168. Cooper, "Sixpence."

Chapter 9

1. Quoted in Mark Joseph, "The New Musical Negro Leagues," *Re:generation Quarterly*, issue 3.2.
2. "We Have . . . ," *Christianity Today*, Internet posting (June 4, 1997).
3. Billy Sprague, "Rekindle the Creative Torch," *CCM* magazine (August 1988): 17.
4. Pat Terry, "Pat Terry: Thoughts for Christian Songwriters," *CCM* magazine (July 1992): 64.
5. Reed Arvin, "Christian Music Ministry in a Post-Christian Culture," *CCM* magazine: (August 1990), 14.
6. Ibid.
7. Terry Mattingly, "Beyond Becky Goes to Bible Camp," Scripps Howard News Service (May 5, 1999).
8. Brian Quincy Newcomb, "Sunday's Child Is Full of Grace," *CCM* magazine (January 1989), 20.

Chapter 10

1. Gregory Rumburg, "The Other Side of the Tracks," *CCM* magazine (July 1996): 40.
2. "Place in This World," Amy Grant, Michael W. Smith, and Wayne Kirkpatrick, O'Ryan Music (ASCAP), Emily Booth (BMI), Age to Age Music (ASCAP), 1990.
3. Richard Leiby, "The Pop Hymn That Everyone's Humming," *The Washington Post* (December 19, 1995).
4. Eric Bazilian, "One of Us," WB Music Corp. (ASCAP), 1995.

5. Leiby, "The Pop Hymn."
6. Ibid.
7. Rumburg, "The Other Side," 40.
8. Ibid., 41.
9. Ibid.
10. Ginny McCabe, "MxPx: Plain Ol' Ordinary Guys," *HM* magazine (December 1997): 15.
11. Jerry Crowe, "Dad's 'Butterfly Kisses,' Zooms Up the Charts," *Los Angeles Times* (1997).
12. Joan Brasher, "The Kiss of Success," *CCM* magazine (July 1997): 8.
13. Ibid.
14. Ibid.
15. Ibid.
16. Gary Cherone, interview by the author, 1993.
17. "Moving into Mainstream," *CCM Update* (September 7, 1992): 10.
18. Ibid.
19. Charlie Shaw, interview by the author, 1997.
20. "For Christ's Sake," *Rock Village*, Internet posting (August 6, 1997).
21. Ibid.
22. Lucas Hendrickson, "Mr. Cerebral and Lady Soul," *CCM* magazine (August 1996): 56.
23. Ibid., 58.
24. Ibid.
25. Ibid.
26. Chris Willman, "The Call: Singing the Struggle," *CCM* magazine (November 1990): 16.
27. Ibid.
28. Ibid.
29. Ibid.
30. Doug Van Pelt, "The Mad Men Behind Atomic Opera," *Heaven's Metal* (September/October 1994): 27.
31. Steve Turner, "Being There: A Vision for Christianity and the Arts" (Steve Turner, 1998), 17–18.
32. Ibid., 22.
33. Rumburg, "The Other Side," 43.
34. Pat Terry, "Thoughts for Christian Songwriters," *CCM* magazine (July 1992): 64.
35. Bob Millard, *Amy Grant* (New York: Dolphin/Doubleday, 1986), 155.
36. Ibid., 167.
37. Turner, "Being There," 17–18.
38. Charles Colson with Ellen Santilli Vaughn, *The Body* (Dallas: Word, 1992), 336.
39. Ibid., 336–337.
40. Ibid., 339.
41. Turner, "Being There," 8.
42. Ibid., 9.
43. Thomas Oden, *After Modernity . . . What?* (Grand Rapids, Mich.: Zondervan, 1992), 32.
44. Brian Q. Newcomb, "Mark Heard: Looking for the Strong Hand of Love," *CCM* magazine (November 1990): 14.
45. Doug Van Pelt, "King's X: You Can't Help But Love 'Em," *Heaven's Metal*, 28, 9.
46. Turner, "Being There," 21.
47. Sandy Stert Benjamin, "Kerry Livgren's Vinyl Confessions," *CCM* magazine (October 1982): 36.
48. Turner, "Being There," 22–23.
49. Terry Mattingly, interview by the author, 1996.
50. Ibid.

Chapter 11

1. George Gallup Jr., interview by the author, 1996.
2. Michael Medved, *Hollywood vs. America* (New York: Harper Collins, 1992).
3. C. S. Lewis, *The Business of Heaven*, Walter Hooper, ed. (New York: Harvest/HBJ, 1984).

4. Franky Schaeffer, "Sham Pearls for Real Swine," *CCM* magazine (July 1990): 26, adapted from *Sham Pearls for Real Swine* (Nashville, Tenn.: Wolgemuth and Hyatt, 1990).

5. Charles Colson with Ellen Santilli Vaughn, *The Body* (Dallas: Word, 1992), 266.

6. Gregory Rumburg, "The Other Side of the Tracks," *CCM* magazine (July 1996): 40.

7. "Moving into Mainstream," *CCM Update* (September 7, 1992): 10.

8. Ibid., 1, 10.

9. Kemper B. Crabb II, "The Christian and Art," *Heaven's Metal* 43, 67.

10. Jim Peterson, *Church without Walls* (Colorado Springs, Colo.: Navpress, 1992), 54.

11. Ibid., 54–55.

12. Crabb, "The Christian and Art," 67.

13. Ibid.

14. Ibid.

15. Ibid.

16. Steve Turner, "Being There: a Vision for Christianity and the Arts" (Steve Turner, 1998): 18.

17. Keith Green, "Asleep in the Light," Ears to Hear Music (ASCAP).

18. Chris Well, "Kerry Livgren: Prime Farmer," *HRS* 4, no. 1, 5.

19. "Barry McGuire," *CCM* magazine (June 1988): 35.

20. Ed DeGarmo, interview by the author, 1989.

21. Turner, "Being There," 24.

22. Johnny Cash with Patrick Carr, *Cash* (New York: Harper/SanFrancisco, 1997), 208-209.

23. Bob Briner, *Roaring Lambs* (Grand Rapids, Mich.: Zondervan, 1993), 38–39.

24. Ibid., 38.

25. Michael Medved, "Religious Responses to Media and Pop Culture" (1998).

26. Steve Rabey, *The Heart of Rock and Roll* (Old Tappan, N. J.: Fleming H. Revell, 1986).

27. Dave Urbanski: "Independent's Day," *CCM* magazine (May 1997): 58.

28. *Heaven's Metal* 49, 30.

29. *CCM Update.*

30. Ibid.

31. Stephen Prendergast, interview with the author (May 29, 1999).

32. Rumburg, "The Other Side," 40.

33. Ibid.

34. Ibid.

35. Watchman Nee, *Love Not the World* (Great Britain: CLC, 1968), 24.

36. Oswald Chambers, *My Utmost for His Highest* (Uhrichsville, Ohio: Barbour, 1935), 292.

37. Nee, *Love Not the World*, 40–41, 47, 48, 52.

38. C. S. Lewis, *God in the Dock*, "Christian Apologetics," Walter Hooper, ed. (Grand Rapids: Eerdmans, 1970), 93.

39. Steve Turner, *Hungry for Heaven* (Downers Grove, Ill.: Intervarsity Press, 1995), 170.

Index

Bennett, William, 1, 20
Benson Company, 5, 10-11, 12, 13,
  14, 42, 50, 140, 142, 144, 190
Benson, Bob, 11
Benson, John T., 10
Benson, John T., Jr., 11
Benson, Robert, 11
Berry, Chuck, 2, 19
Bettencourt, Nuno, 158, 160
Bill Gaither Trio, 11
Bill Graham Productions, 174
Billboard magazine, 75, 163, 194,
  233, 234, 243, 266, 278
Black Crowes, 21
Blackmore, Ritchie, 51
Black Sabbath, 123, 138
Blackwell, Chris, 175
Blackwell, Robert Bumps, 181, 182
Blank, 144
Blanton, Michael, 34, 181, 197, 208,
  209, 210, 278
Blessed Hope, 14
Bloom, Allan, 1
Bloomfield, Michael, 28
BMG (label), 78, 278
Bodeans, the, 135
Bodyworks, 58
Bogart, Neil, 119
Bon Jovi, 142
Bono, 131, 132, 133, 134
Boone, Debby, 11, 49
Boone, Pat, 32, 33, 42, 48-52, 112,
  116, 189
Bossmen, the, 89
Bourgeois, Brent, 174
Bourgeois Tagg, 174
Bowen, Jimmy, 190-92
Bowie, David, 233
Bramlett, Bonnie, 80, 171
Brentwood (label), 12
Brewer, Don, 89
Brewer, Melissa, 229
Briner, Bob, 242, 274, 275, 285
Brooks, Garth, 190, 193
Brown, James, 25
Bruce, Lenny, 102, 284
Buffalo Springfield, 47, 72, 73, 252
Bunnell, Dewey, 74
Burlap to Cashmere, 243
Burnett, T-Bone, 109, 135, 136, 172,
  204, 205, 259

Butler, Don, 209
Byrds, the, 19

C

Cadence (label), 136
Calder, Clive, 249
Call, the, 136, 253
Calvary Chapel, 15, 57, 74, 79, 202,
  272, 274
Camelot Music, 4
Camp, Steve, 13, 269, 270
Campbell, Glen, 112
Canned Heat, 71
Capitol Records, 22, 23, 125, 139,
  172, 219
Card, Michael, 269, 270
Carlisle, Bob, 243, 249, 250
Carman, 191
Carmichael, Ralph, 25, 26
Carpenter, Greg, 238
Carroll, Rex, 7
Carter, June, 95-96
Casablanca Records, 119
Cash, Johnny, 93-98, 273, 284
Castells, the, 57
Castro, Lenny, 51
CBS, 71, 87
Cetera, Peter, 117, 198
Chagall Guevara, 215, 216
Chapman, Gary, 50, 198, 199
Chapman, Steven Curtis, 284
Chea, Alvin, 147, 148
Cherone, Gary, 157-61, 250
Chicago, 117, 198, 246, 247
Children of the Day, 14
Christian, Chris, 8, 12, 169, 197
Clapton, Eric, 28, 44, 69, 89, 171,
  220, 241, 243
Clark, Paul, 7
Clash, the, 212, 215
Cleveland, Ashley, 164-66, 248
Cockburn, Bruce, 135, 259
Cole, Paula, 238
Collective Soul, 243, 284
Collins, Judy, 196
Collins, Phil, 86
Colson, Chuck, 256-57, 264
Columbia Records, 107, 170
Colvin, Monty, 166, 167
Colvin, Shawn, 238

If you enjoyed *The Rock and Roll Rebellion*, the book, be sure to check out the accompanying cd soundtrack featuring songs from many of the artists appearing in the book.

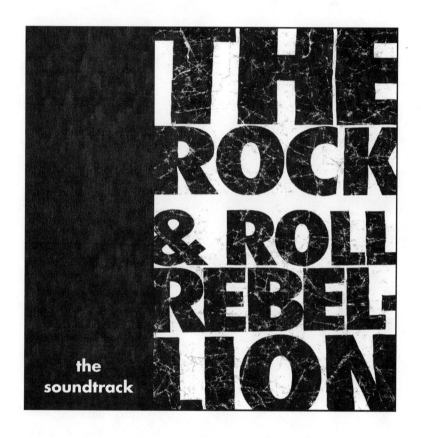

For more information, check out our website at www.rockrebel.com

Available at your favorite music retailer.